David Blunkett

Also by Stephen Pollard

A Class Act – The Myth of Britain's Classless Society
(with Andrew Adonis)

Stephen Pollard

David Blunkett

**HODDER &
STOUGHTON**

First published in Great Britain in 2005 by Hodder and Stoughton
A division of Hodder Headline

The right of Stephen Pollard to be identified as the Author of the Work
has been asserted by him in accordance with the
Copyright, Designs and Patents Act 1988

A Hodder & Stoughton book

3 5 7 9 10 8 6 4 2

A CIP catalogue record for this title is available from the British Library

ISBN 0 340 82534 0   9334 ME

Typeset in Monotype Sabon by
Rowland Phototypesetting Ltd,
Bury St Edmunds, Suffolk

Printed and bound by
Clays Ltd, St Ives plc

Hodder Headline's policy is to use papers that are natural,
renewable and recyclable products and made from wood
grown in sustainable forests. The logging and manufacturing
processes are expected to conform to the environmental
regulations of the country of origin.

Hodder and Stoughton Ltd
A division of Hodder Headline
338 Euston Road
London NW1 3BH

To my parents

Contents

Preface   ix

Prologue   xv

1 An extraordinary ordinary man   1

2 "May your God go with you, whoever he or she
    might be"   34

3 "A strong, well-built boy"   56

4 The fight to be educated   74

5 A leap into the unknown: college and the real world   84

6 Not the typical student: The Socialist Republic
    of South Yorkshire   101

7 A national figure: Labour in the 1980s   138

8 Westminster: "a good fight with a worthy opponent"   177

9 The Shadow Cabinet: the making of a player   194

10 Shaking the trees: Education Secretary   227

11 Criminals, terrorists and louts   264

12 A normal family?   308

13 Postscript   320

Notes on sources   328

Picture Acknowledgements   339

Index   341

Preface

My first encounter with David Blunkett was hardly propitious. I was speaking at a Fabian seminar on education policy in January 1995, arguing that the Labour Party should embrace selection and school vouchers. Blunkett, then the Shadow Education Secretary, was in the audience with his assistant, Conor Ryan. My performance was pretty ropy. I had never before admitted to a Labour audience my belief in such taboos and my nerves revealed themselves in a faltering delivery. What finally destroyed my confidence was a superbly timed heckle as I paused to take a sip of water. Turning to Ryan, Blunkett asked in a loud stage whisper: "Who is this idiot?" The effect was devastating. I galloped through the rest of my notes and shut up as soon as I could.

As a policy wonk, I drew very different conclusions about what was wrong with state education – and what should be done to put it right – from Blunkett. When I became a political columnist on the *Express*, I then used many – too many, perhaps, for the readers' sanity – column inches to write about why he was wrong.

But for all that, I was fascinated by the man. In a government peopled by talking I-speak-your-weight machines, bludgeoning you with their single line, Blunkett was obviously a real human being. When asked a question, he would reply not just with 'the line' but with a proper answer. A Blunkett interview was never dull; unlike many of his colleagues, he seemed to regard questions not as elephant traps to be dodged but as opportunities to say what he thought, answering the questions because he said what he genuinely thought, not what he had been forced by party orthodoxy to think. While some of his Cabinet colleagues happily spout whatever gets them promoted, Blunkett has only ever been on his own intellectual journey, a journey that sometimes leads him to a difference of approach compared to the fashionable Labour types, but which is nonetheless down the same road as that travelled by the Labour Party as a whole.

I could not, however, work him out. On one level he appeared to be a traditionalist, who was thoroughly admirable in his contempt for the left-liberal education establishment, whose ideologically driven policy agenda was responsible for so much of what was – is – wrong with schools. At the Home Office, too, he seemed to be similarly clear in his recognition that criminal justice policy should be aimed at bringing criminals to justice and not at making excuses for their behaviour.

And yet this was the same man who had, as leader of Sheffield City Council, been labelled as a member of the 'loony left' and whose policies had led to the council being nicknamed the Socialist Republic of South Yorkshire. As Education Secretary, too, his actions had caused Chris Woodhead, the Chief Inspector of Schools and the most high-profile of the 'sensible school' of educationists, to resign in despair.

This book is an attempt to unravel these apparent paradoxes, expressed most starkly by David Heslop, a Conservative Sheffield councillor in Blunkett's period as leader: "His whole attitude, body language, speeches, policies, everything he said and did, made me think he was genuinely left-wing. He is totally different now. I have never worked out which is the real one."[1]

Blunkett's career is in many ways a metaphor for Labour itself. He has moved from being seen as a dangerous left-winger with disastrous policy prescriptions, to learning from his mistakes, realising the importance of both means and ends and then grasping the way the majority of Britons think and behave, and ended up being regarded in some quarters as more right-wing than many Conservatives.

Talking to his colleagues, friends and opponents, and reading his speeches and writings, I have found it impossible, nevertheless, to avoid the conclusion that David Blunkett the Home Secretary of 2005 is in large measure the same man as David Blunkett the Sheffield City Council leader of 1980. My starting point has therefore been to answer a deceptively simple question: what is it that makes Blunkett tick?

I have been unable to find another example, either contemporary or historical, of a blind man or woman who has risen to such political heights anywhere on the planet. There have been some who have lost their sight in office, but none who has been blind from the start of his or her career. Blunkett is simply remarkable. This prompts, of course, a further question – a basic, practical question. How on earth does he manage to do his job as Home Secretary (and those that have come before), notoriously one of the most demanding, stressful and paper-dominated jobs in the Cabinet?

I have not attempted a day-by-day, or even a year-by-year, account of his life, especially in government. Nor have I attempted to deal with every issue that has crossed his path in office. To do so would require a multi-volume work, not a book that – hopefully – is accessible to everyone. It seems more instructive to pursue certain themes, for, unlike many home secretaries who have simply responded to events, Blunkett has pursued a consistent and interesting agenda – despite, in the wake of 9/11, having to respond to an event that dwarfs almost any faced by his predecessors. Had it not been far too pretentious, I would have called this a portrait rather than a biography, since it is intended to be more of a painting than a photograph – an impression of the essence of the man rather than a straightforward description of events.

There is a further factor. As I wrote the book, I was continually asked one thing: "Are you a fan?". Blunkett provokes intense feelings either way. Normally calm, measured people will go red at the mention of his name and tell you that he is a dangerous threat to liberty. Others who are usually contemptuous of politicians will praise him to the stars. I hope I am objective. But it is striking, when standing back and looking at the broad sweep of his career, how often he has been judged not on his actions but on perceptions – more often than not false – of his intentions.

The book is not authorised. Blunkett has not read or heard a word of the text prior to publication and will doubtless disagree with much of it. But he has been extremely forthcoming and helpful and has given me hours of candid interviews. Given that I had access to the horse's mouth, it seemed self-defeating and simply stupid not to use, directly, what came out of them. If Norman Gash, Peel's wonderful biographer, had had access to interviews with the former Home Secretary he would surely have leapt at the chance of quoting them verbatim. I have therefore, where appropriate, used Blunkett's own words, but have always tried to put them in context (any quote which is not otherwise attributed is from Blunkett).

On a stylistic point, I have not sourced any of these interviews. I have also kept the names of all other interviewees anonymous in the text. Since so many agreed to be interviewed on condition of anonymity, it made more sense not to reveal any identities. So where there is a direct quote without a quoted source, it is the result of an interview or private conversation with me. Everything else is sourced. One day, when the dust has long since settled, the material will be deposited in an archive.

Blunkett has already written a fascinating autobiography, *On a Clear Day*, which deals mainly with his early years and his dogs. I have quoted extensively from it. Some of his descriptions of events and his feelings are self-evidently worth reading and so I make no apologies for using them.

I have many to thank, above all the hundred-plus people who gave me their time so generously in interview. But since a large number did so on the understanding that they remain anonymous, I think it best not to name any. They know who they are; without their help, the book would not have been remotely possible. It would not even have been started had Katharine Raymond not backed my idea at the outset.

I cannot thank Tricia Jones enough for making sure that I managed to spend time with David Blunkett even as he was enveloped in the recurring crises that are the lot of any home secretary. And Marilyn Casey made my life immeasurably easier thanks to her speedy and accurate transcriptions.

I am deeply grateful to Mike Shaw, my former agent, and Jonny Pegg, my current agent, for their advice and support. And it was a welcome surprise to learn from Rupert Lancaster what a pleasure – and how important – it can be to have feedback from an editor.

Finally I would like especially to thank Simon Crine, Alice Miles, Katherine Sand and Sarah Schaefer for their insightful and helpful comments on early drafts. It goes without saying that the mistakes are all mine; but I will say it, nonetheless.

Prologue

David Blunkett had been Home Secretary for ninety six days when he arrived in Warwick just before lunch on Tuesday 11 September 2001 for his first big, set piece speech in the job. The speech to the Police Superintendents Association on 11/9, as the day had been labelled in the preceding months by Blunkett's Home Office staff, was intended to launch his plans for police reform.

The timing was important. 11 September had been earmarked by Alastair Campbell, Blair's Director of Communications and Strategy, as a pivotal day. The Prime Minister was scheduled to speak to the TUC and that speech, coupled with Blunkett's, was intended to show that the government was focused on domestic issues after a summer of dissent and drift.

Tony Blair had appointed Blunkett primarily to deal with police reform. As Education Secretary, Blunkett had taken on the teaching unions and shown himself to be more than willing to take on a large public sector vested interest. In an article in *The Sunday Times* published two days after his appointment, he had stressed police reform as one of his priorities. Although the police had been left alone in Labour's first term, Blair was determined that the service should be tackled and reformed.

Within the Home Office, Blunkett's advisers had worked on little else since arriving in the Queen Anne's Gate office. Throughout the summer they had drafted and redrafted the speech and worked on a pamphlet to be issued at the conference which would detail the specifics of the changes which Blunkett was to implement. 11 September was circled on calendars in Blunkett's private office as D-Day – when Blunkett would announce himself to the electorate as a bold, reforming Home Secretary.

Blunkett's speech went well. He was received with courtesy and interest by the superintendents, a moderate and progressive group within the police force. His press conference had been trouble free and as he boarded the train back to London, Blunkett felt pleased with a job well done.

He was accompanied by his special adviser, Sophie Linden. Within minutes of the train pulling out of the station, Linden received a pager message from Huw Evans, Blunkett's press adviser, who was monitoring coverage of the speech in his Westminster office.

According to Evans, there had been some sort of plane crash in New York City.

As Linden was receiving the pager message, every phone in the carriage started ringing – Blunkett's protection officers, Linden's and Blunkett's own. His son, Hugh, had called his father immediately after passing a TV shop in Weston-super-Mare and seeing the crash through the shop window. As soon as Blunkett had stopped talking to his son, the Home Secretary's phone rang again – this time with a call from Jonathan Powell, the Prime Minister's Chief of Staff.

Like everyone else, Blunkett assumed the plane crash was a terrible accident – until the second plane hit the second tower. Within seconds, Downing Street was on the phone again. There would be a Cobra meeting at five o'clock that afternoon. (Cobra – an acronym for Cabinet Office briefing room A – is the government committee which deals with emergencies.)

Blunkett recalls the journey: "When the second tower went down, it turned from what appeared to be a disaster into something much greater; clearly a world-shattering event. By the time we got off the train, we'd started to come to terms with the implications. My greatest fear of all was that they would immediately cascade this event across other countries in Europe. I'm still astonished that they didn't have an event in London, in

Paris, in Madrid, in Rome, throughout the following twelve hours, which would have caused panic with the population – and bewilderment and a real problem for an elected democratic government.

Arriving at Euston at 4.15, Blunkett was driven to his office for a short briefing, before leaving for Downing Street and the Cobra meeting. Around the table were Blair, John Prescott, Gordon Brown, Jack Straw, Sir John Stevens, the Commissioner of the Metropolitan Police, Sir John Gieve (the Permanent Secretary at the Home Office), John Warne (the Director of Counterterrorism, Intelligence and Organised Crime at the Home Office), David Veness (the Met's anti-terror chief) and Sir Stephen Lander (the Director of MI5).

No one knew what was happening in New York. "We didn't know the numbers, we didn't know precisely who'd done it, we didn't know what it was all about, we didn't know whether to believe what was being said", according to Blunkett. Was this the beginning of a mass terror attack? Was it to be confined to the US? Was Britain to be hit? Blunkett's first question at the meeting was "whether we had sufficient knowledge of the likely sources of this new form of terror, as compared with what we knew in relation to Ireland. We were fortunate that, after the Good Friday Agreement, we'd started to be able to redeploy some of the security services. Not much, but enough to have at least got some handle on this from the East Africa attacks."

As an immediate precaution, the evacuation of Canary Wharf was ordered and all security alerts put on the highest level. Since there was almost no information or intelligence to work with, the meeting was adjourned, to reconvene the next day.

By now it was early evening. Blunkett returned to the Home Office with Gieve and called all his advisers and senior officials together. The meeting, which lasted an hour, began considering a response. As the group gathered, a rumour swept the building that a plane was mid-Atlantic with hostages on board, destination London. Ten minutes into the meeting, word arrived that the report was baseless. As one of those present puts it: "It was just a rumour. There was nothing more substantial than that. But the atmosphere was so jumpy that we all thought it might be true."

There was no intelligence suggesting that Britain was about to experience anything similar. But neither had the Americans been aware, on the morning of 11 September, of what was about to happen to them. Osama bin Laden, who was already the prime suspect, had not made specific threats against Britain; his threats were directed against America, and her allies only more generally.

Blunkett took the decision that he should not give interviews. The last thing he wanted was further to panic people and there was a risk that an interview might backfire and do just that. As an official puts it: "People would ask him, 'Where does this lead? What do we need to do to protect ourselves?'. The Home Secretary was clear that we needed to have a couple of days to sort the issues out." The media's focus was, in any case, on the situation in the US and so the only government interviews were given by Jack Straw, who was responsible for helping those Britons stranded in the US.

Cobra had taken all the decisions which, in its ignorance, it could take, leaving little for the Home Office to do immediately. Blunkett's mind turned to what would happen next. As an aide puts it: "David's main concern was that the Americans didn't retaliate overnight or go mad, which he thought was a real danger. He made clear how glad he was that Tony was getting stuck in to try and stop that happening." He also made clear to officials that night that he believed the world – and certainly his agenda as Home Secretary – had changed overnight.

Stories emerged over the next few hours of the behaviour and heroism displayed by many of the victims. There was one image which Blunkett could not get out of his mind: "I have a very vivid imagination, so I could imagine the plane entering the tower about two thirds up. I could envisage a pause before the impact and the towers crumbling, and the people desperately trying to get down the stairs – some jumping from the windows. But I've had to shut-off from my mind that jumping from the windows, because I just can't cope with it as an image." There was another which haunted him over the next few days: "The other image that I found really frightening was of people ringing from their mobiles, both those in the tower and those on the plane that was brought down before it could be crashed into the Whitehouse. I found that really moving – the vision of people on their phones trying to say 'I love you' to someone, leaving a message on an answer phone. That will rest with me for a very long time."

The following day, Wednesday 12, Cobra met again. Ministers were told that there was no immediate specific threat. Cobra was focused on the logistics of flying home the bodies of the British victims, and getting the stranded visitors to the US home.

Blunkett decided that he should try to stick to his schedule as much as possible. That night he was due to fly to Paris for a pre-arranged dinner with the French Interior Minister, Daniel Vaillant. The French had been threatening to build a second Sangatte refugee camp, which had been the big news story prior to 9/11, with pictures throughout the summer of hordes coming through the Channel tunnel. Normal politics might be in abeyance but asylum was not going to disappear as an issue and so Blunkett went ahead with the engagement, travelling to Paris at six o'clock.

The journey to RAF Northolt, from whence he was to fly to Paris, was edgy. An official who travelled with Blunkett recalls that "normally, when you get a police escort, people are a bit grumpy – you can see how much they object to being shoved aside in their cars for a car with a police escort. That evening, it felt as if everyone was moving out of the way very quickly. People were so jumpy. Usually, if people hear a siren they don't even turn around. This time it seemed that everyone was looking around." Blunkett returned to Northolt, and thence to his official Pimlico house, later that night.

Before leaving for Paris, Blunkett set in motion a review of anti-terror legislation. That afternoon, Blair and Blunkett had begun to discuss the need for new anti-terror legislation. Parliament was being recalled for the Friday and Blunkett needed to be able to inform the House what the domestic impact of the events in America would be. He had also decided to make his first public response on the Friday morning Today programme, an interview which he would use to stress the need to stay calm or let the terrorists win. It was a line to which he has stuck throughout his time as Home Secretary.

The Terrorism Act had been passed only a year before, put through by Blunkett's predecessor, Straw. The Act proscribed terror groups by name. Presciently, the first such named group had been Al Quaeda. Blunkett ordered his team to prepare for a meeting on the Friday at which all the legislative options would be examined. They spent the next 36 hours working non-stop. The Thursday morning Cabinet had discussed not only 9/11 but also the aftermath of Blunkett's Paris meeting on asylum and Blunkett's staff had to deal with both issues simultaneously and immediately. Neither could wait. A further Cobra meeting on Thursday afternoon considered the immediate situation, now that information had started to flow in properly.

On the Friday morning, Blunkett returned from making his Commons statement to chair the meeting in his office. It was small, with Sir John Gieve and Sir Stephen Lander joined by half a dozen other colleagues. Over the next few hours, they worked through what would be needed in a new stand-alone anti-terror act and how asylum and immigration could be incorporated.

At the meeting, Blunkett raised the idea of ID cards for the first time. An adviser says: "He'd always been well-disposed towards them but he got clearer and clearer after 9/11. The more he was exposed to the issues – the linkages between organised crime and illegal immigration, for instance, and the role of identity fraud in supporting terrorists, (al Qaeda, in particular, is a network which uses multiple identities) – the more all that came together, the more committed he became to ID cards."

The key issue was what to do with those people who, under existing legislation, could not be deported but who were viewed as a security threat. At the meeting, Sir Stephen Lander revealed that there was a core group of fifteen potential terrorists. The question was how to deal with them. MI5 could keep an eye on them but that would not be failsafe. There were two options: the first, detention under immigration powers and allowing them to leave the country if they could find a country which was willing to take them; the second, certification that they were not at risk of death or torture and then forcible deportation to their country of origin. The latter option was eventually ruled out after legal advice that it might be in conflict with the Human Rights Act.

Beverley Hughes, a junior Home Office minister, was brought in to work with Blunkett on the new anti-terror measures and to steer the bill through committee, having already successfully taken a bill through committee when a transport minister in Labour's first term.

Over the next weeks, Home Office officials worked on a new bill, designed to close the gaps which had not been covered in the Terrorism Act 2000. In addition, work focused on 'resilience' – the practical measures against terror, such as security tightening of key terrorist targets and protection. Under Blunkett's chairmanship, two Cabinet committees – DOP (IT) T (for terrorism), which deals with protective security, and DOP (IT) R, which deals with resilience – undertook a thoroughgoing review of homeland security. These committees were, before 9/11, rarely viewed as a priority – a pedestrian, albeit necessary, task. Their work was mainly concerned with natural disasters such as floods. As a member of the resilience committee puts it: "There had been far more floods in mainland Britain in the previous ten years than there had been terrorist incidents."

The reorganisation of Whitehall which had occurred after

Labour's 2001 election victory had hived resilience planning and civil contingencies off to the Cabinet Office, away from the Home Office. But in the new post-9/11 world, with the Cabinet committees under Blunkett's chairmanship, the de facto responsibility returned to the Home Secretary, if not the Home Office itself. Immediately, Blunkett ordered a run-through of how the emergency services would respond to a World Trade Centre-style incident. The result was shocking, revealing that arrangements had stood still since the 1970s' Protect and Survive arrangements, designed to deal with a nuclear attack. As a Home Office official describes it: "They were great if you were flooded but not in response to much else. If you had a nuclear attack you'd either be dead or in a bunker. But a terrorist incident on the scale of 9/11? It didn't bear thinking about. There was nothing in place. Nothing."

Blunkett's workload immediately after 9/11 was immense. Asylum was still raging as an issue and the French Socialist government was offering almost no cooperation. The police reform white paper was in preparation. The impact of the summer race riots was still being digested. All this in addition to shaping a response to a terror threat which almost everyone acknowledged had changed the world. Blunkett would have to take a new, inevitably controversial, bill through Parliament and had to secure bipartisan support.

Politically, Blunkett had been flavour of the month in his last year as Education Secretary, widely expected to secure the promotion which took him to the Home Office. He had yet to face serious criticism as a minister. He knew, however, that unless his mastery of the issues was complete, and far better than that of anyone else in the Commons, he could destroy his entire career in the course of the passage of that one bill. As an aide puts it: "His Home Secretaryship would be over before it had begun."

As the bill was being drawn up, Blunkett pressed his officials with detailed questions on every clause. He sought constant clarification, knowing that he could not afford to let a single comma appear in the legislation without his full understanding.

An aide recalls that "when we were preparing the legislation he was always probing, asking 'Why this? Why now?'". The Home Office historically just puts legalisation in the statute book for the sake of it and nobody ever tries to use it. David was particularly keen with this Bill that it wasn't just used to put things on the statute book that would make people feel better temporarily. He made that clear at the time and gave the officials a very hard time. He was livid at the end of the process when the Treasury said, about one of the financial clauses, "Oh you can drop that, it's not that important".

The measures were presented in a statement to the House of Commons on 15 October and the bill was published barely two months after 9/11, on 14 November becoming law on 14 December. Blunkett had to sacrifice a large degree of political capital to get it through.

An official describes the reaction amongst Blunkett's colleagues: "There was a real feeling of relief when the Act finally got through. We managed to pick up almost everyone we needed. Abu Qatada did a runner, but we picked him up later. I think they'd been expecting the round-up to come a bit longer after the Act came into force, and we surprised them by picking them up within three days. And what the police and security services were finding when they got them . . . let me just say that we knew we'd got the right people."

As the full realisation of the danger posed by those rounded up began to be clear, the atmosphere amongst Blunkett's advisers over the next few weeks changed dramatically. "The Home Office was a very different place from what we had been used to. Few of us came from a security background. We almost looked at the protection officers and security arrangements as being a bit of a novelty. But when you saw the nature of what you were dealing with and the fact these people were here, plotting and planning to do to us what they had done to the US – when you saw all the warrants to be signed piling-up on David's desk in their orange jackets – it brought home the centrality of what we were dealing with. This was about the survival of our way of life."

I

An extraordinary ordinary man

The most frequent questions asked about David Blunkett all begin with the same word: how? How does he do it? How did he get where he has? How does his blindness affect him?

One of the most consistent observations concerns his capacity for work. A former ministerial colleague says that, "although it's probably impossible to work as hard as David, one thing I have learned from him is that you have to be one hundred per cent committed to the job. You have to be on top of everything". Blunkett is helped by an amazing memory. As one junior minister recalls: "We were talking about something and he said, 'Will you look into that?' He didn't take a note and nor did I. About three weeks later he asked me, 'What did you find out about what they're doing in Holland?' I'd forgotten all about it, but he remembered."

That memory is aided by sheer hard work. In opposition, while others would be enjoying the House of Commons bar, Blunkett would be poring over Braille or listening to tapes. He was methodical and conscientious and would often surprise colleagues by quoting from the day's newspapers or in detail from documents. This was partly the result of the huge amount of information that he would process and partly his astounding memory. His capacity for work and for absorbing material is regarded with awe by colleagues. A predecessor as Home Secretary says that he found it difficult to get through the volume of material with which he was confronted and yet Blunkett seems to manage even more. "It is", he says, "a mystery to me. I cannot begin to understand how he does it." And a minister who served under Blunkett says that the main lesson he learned from his boss was "not even to try to read as much material as he does. It's impossible. He outdoes ordinary human beings". An opposition adviser recalls that "Sometimes I'd be with David at nine thirty at night in his room. I'd suggest that maybe I should go home. He'd say, 'That's fine, but I'll hang on here.'"

The details of his routine may have changed since his first years as a councillor but the generalities have been constant. Every letter and document he reads has been dictated on to tape, other than a small number of the critically important which are transcribed into Braille. It is a Whitehall cliché that special advisers act as the 'eyes and ears' of their ministers. Blunkett's really do act as his eyes, reading the newspapers, books and other documents that he cannot make time for and making sure that he gets to hear a tape of those which matter. He dislikes summaries – he would rather listen to three key paragraphs than a similar-length summary of a ten-page document. His civil servants and advisers make tapes for him of important documents and general points which they might otherwise have put in a memo. Every day he will start listening to the tapes which greet him, and each night he will listen to those that have been made during the day. He has developed, through sheer will-power, the ability to listen to a tape recording at double the normal playback speed. To the untutored ear, it sounds as if he is listening to Pinky and Perky gibberish. To Blunkett, the meaning is crystal clear. (His ability to listen to such recordings was pushed to the limit in 2003 by the 300-hour recording he was given of the Treasury's one-and-a-half-million-word report into Britain's membership of the euro.) He will then dictate his own responses to be typed up. Blunkett's letters are legendary among regular recipients; when the mood takes him, he will sometimes meander off on a tangent and a short, brief point can turn into a discursive treatise.

The workload may be immense (one former Conservative Home Office minister was taken aback when, on his first day in office, officials wheeled a trolley full of documents past his desk so that the minister would be able to claim that he had seen them, since there are too many to read individually) but Blunkett hates to slack. One former adviser says that "If there's nothing in the diary or on a tape for a couple of hours in the morning, he won't just sit back and relax; he'll fill it. Any vacuum, he fills it. I used to find myself taping books for him – interesting chapters and suchlike – because he'd want to listen to something if he didn't have work tapes to hear. His mind is always searching for more information." The downside of this is that he can obsess over trivial issues. "I'd go into work in the morning and there'd be a little red light flashing on the telephone with David's messages for the morning. They'd be about what someone had said on 'Thought for the Day' or some obscure piece in a newspaper."

Blunkett is surprisingly sensitive to press criticism. "I don't understand some people [who make a living by criticising others]. I don't understand what motivates them. I'd be interested some time, when I'm not in this job, to sit down with some of them and ask, 'What exactly was it that drove you?'" As a colleague puts it: "It's kind of 'I'm so lovable and I'm doing my best to make life better. How can you possibly be so horrible to me?'"

A close friend says that he is too sensitive and has too thin a skin. "He never forgets these things and he allows them to distract him far too much. He gets drawn into things which sap his energy." His grudges can last decades. One of his closest friends, Keith Jackson – with whom he co-wrote his first substantial book, *Democracy in Crisis* – referred to him in an interview as 'anal'; he has barely spoken to Jackson since. As a former aide puts it:

The Home Office makes this worse – it's a job where everyone thinks they have to have a pop at you. And much as he relishes a fight, it gets to him. He wants everyone to understand what he's doing. He can't relegate the most trivial criticism to the low importance it merits. I do worry that, certainly in the Home Office, there are so many ample opportunities to get involved in public spats about things with judges, opposition politicians or press commentators that he gets deflected from the kind of communication he should be having, where he concentrates on his own themes and his own message.

Blunkett seems unable to resist the lure of saying precisely what he thinks, however injudicious the circumstances. In June 2004 he remarked of a football hooligan who had been convicted in Portugal, flown back to the UK and then released on a technicality that he wanted to 'nail' him, a remark that was characteristic: it expressed a sentiment that was, no doubt, shared by most of the population but which was hardly nuanced or finely judged. It prompted an attack from a retired Law Lord, Lord Ackner, in the House of Lords, in the form of a question to a junior Home Office minister, Baroness Scotland: "Does she take the view that perhaps a senior judge might be prepared to explain to the Home Secretary the fallacy of the proposition that any publicity is better than none? He might also be prepared to continue by pointing out to the Home Secretary that his intemperate outburst seriously undermines the integrity of that great department of state, the Home Office?"[1]

As Shadow Home Secretary, Oliver Letwin similarly attacked Blunkett for not sounding like a home secretary, a theme that is adopted by many mainstream commentators who argue that his language and bearing are too 'populist'. Sir Simon Jenkins, for instance, high priest of chattering-class convention, referred to him as "the judicial equivalent of a football hooligan".[2]

This is, however, quite deliberate. "I've tried to avoid becoming the pompous prat that *The Daily Telegraph* expect Home Secretaries to be – only using certain language, never ever saying anything about the judiciary or their judgments, always coming out with the standard line when court cases are heard, which is that 'the Home Secretary is disappointed'. The Home Secretary might think that something is entirely wrong but he only ever says he is 'disappointed'". It is all too easy to become 'the job', and leave 'the man' behind. "Robin Cook *became* Foreign Secretary. He was much more personable again when he was Leader of the House. He had started to speak as he thought foreign secretaries should speak. He wouldn't have social contact: I'd asked him, when he was having his marriage difficulties, if he and Gaynor would like to have dinner. No. But as soon as he lost the Foreign Secretary's job he wanted to know me again."

Blunkett has certainly avoided sounding like a home secretary. He remarked of a man arrested in Gloucester in March 2004, Sajid Badat, that he "posed a very real threat to the country" – before the man had even been charged. "I was trying to speak in straight terms," Blunkett argued. "As far as the situation over the Terrorism Act and the arrest in Gloucester was concerned, I was reflecting a very simple truth. He had been arrested under the Terrorism Act. We don't arrest people under the Terrorism Act unless we believe that they have committed an act of terrorism."[3]

Blunkett was attacked by *bien pensant* commentators when he said that when he heard the news that Harold Shipman, the mass murderer, had "topped himself" (as Blunkett put it) he was going to "open a bottle". "I regret", he told *The Observer*, "that a conversation over lunch was reported. I don't regret having instinctive feelings. People may not like the instinctive feelings which I have but often they have them as well. But the question is should I, in any form, express them or should I be circumspect?"[4]

As he later put it:

What a terrible thing – actually speaking in the way that the people who elect you feel. We are killing politics by not talking to people properly. Friends have always said to me, when I've done an interview that was full of jargon or full of statistics, 'Well, there was nothing wrong with your interview, you just didn't engage the audience.' That's worth thinking about. The point, surely, is to do it from an intelligent, thoughtful point of view where you have the right information and the background, and you try to shape these factors together into something which can work. So, for instance, my commitment to having fewer people in prison would not be mirrored by my constituents, but my commitment to tougher, harder sentences for deeply dangerous criminals would be. And people will put up with me suggesting that we give community sentences to people if they know that we're tough where appropriate – and they know that I know what I'm talking about and that I'm on their side about life [sentences] meaning life, for instance. It's the same with sex offences.

The flipside of being an open, engaging, thoughtful politician who speaks his mind is that it opens up plenty of fruitful terrain for attacks. Take the storm in June 2002 over forced marriage. Blunkett had spoken in an interview on the BBC about the Dutch politician, Pim Fortuyn. Asked about the incompatibility of Islam with Western society, he replied: "It was a point Pim Fortuyn in his more rational moments was making in the lead-up to his assassination. I believe in diversity through integration. I believe that, as with all other cultures and societies, people adapt and change . . . We had a culture in medieval England of the aristocracy being engaged in forced, not agreed, parental marriages. We changed as the Renaissance, and change around us, including economic change, affected perceptions." Muslims should, and would, leave forced marriages behind them.[5] Blunkett was clear and specific; he was talking, in the course of a thoughtful interview, about forced marriages. And yet he was pilloried for attacking arranged marriages.

Blunkett sees his main handicap as being the inability to flick through documents: "I wonder about how much I could get through in addition to what I do now. There is a frustration in not being able to browse through a library and in not being able to flick through papers. On the other hand I am spared e-mails, which has to be a blessing." And the price of having to go the extra mile in mastering his brief is having far less leisure time than other ministers. There is, however, one time over the week-

6

end when his officials know not to contact him unless there is a dire emergency: five o'clock on a Sunday afternoon. Stephen Byers found out why early on in his time as schools minister. After one call just after five, when Blunkett was unusually short and curt, Byers rang his colleague, Estelle Morris. He was concerned that there was a problem. "Have you spoken to David this weekend?" he asked.

"Yes," she replied. "Why do you ask?"

"Well," Byers replied, "I've just spoken to him and he was incredibly terse with me."

"When did you speak to him – just now?"

"Yes."

"Don't you know? No one calls him between five and five thirty on Sunday. It's when he listens to *Poetry Please* on Radio Four."

The image of the hard man of the Home Office does not fit easily with Blunkett's interest in poetry. His favourite poet is Christina Rossetti. "I'm a sentimentalist at heart . . . She's a bit depressing at times, but it's lovely poetry. It's incredibly expressive. She combines the ability to communicate with great emotion, and I think you can do that through poetry in a way you can't with prose." He also likes Larkin and other poets of "a sort of miserable bent. I've said to friends, 'I'm not moody' – and they've said, 'Oh yes you are. You have downs, man.'" Part of the attraction for Blunkett is the visual imagery: "The best poetry is so vivid that it brings alive the visual." But he does not have an affinity with Milton, who wrote in *Samson Agonistes* of his blindness: "I don't share his perspective on blindness. He had a view of being cut off from the world. But I don't share that view at all. It's understandable, really, because he lost his sight, and I think it's very different for people who feel bereft of that particular faculty. I don't feel bereft."[6]

He not only reads poetry but writes it, such as this description of the Wimbledon tennis championships:

> The ancient grounds
> Green and spacious
> The scent of strawberries and hay
> Grass roasting in the midday sun.

The image took still more of a knock when news emerged in August 2004 of his affair with Kimberly Fortier. Blunkett had first met Fortier, the vivacious, flirtatious American publisher of the *Spectator*, when she had interviewed him. The two hit it off immediately and began to see each other regularly. Their friendship was well known, but almost no one knew that it had soon developed into a sexual relationship until the story was revealed in the *News of the World*. Commentators expressed surprise that so dour a man could be so gripped by love that he would risk the collapse of his career. But Blunkett is a passionate man. He is passionate in his politics and passionate in his defence of and loyalty to those whom he considers his friends. It is hardly surprising that he should also be romantically passionate. Having endured a loveless marriage and a long period alone since his divorce in 1990, when he did finally meet someone with whom he connected, he was not going to let go.

The support network that Blunkett now has was not always there. When he first entered the Commons in 1987 he was treated like any other MP and handed a table in a corridor and a phone. It took six months for him to be given a room, and then only after a special resolution of the House granted him an extra 50 per cent office allowance to cover the costs of Braille and dictation.

Hand in hand with the unusual degree of trust and rapport which he requires of his advisers is his style as a minister. As a former employee in opposition puts it,

He was always very good at team meetings, and he's the same now as a Secretary of State. He likes to build a cohesive team, even if there are personality differences within it. He involves everyone in the discussion and gives them specific tasks to do. In opposition he would give policy research projects to people and send them off to go and look at new things. He made sure all the junior ministers would have some sort of role. It's partly a matter of personality and the ability to chair a meeting well, but also that he is very inclusive in his style.

In part, also, the non-visual skills that he has learned naturally lend themselves to such a style. He can usually tell from a tone of voice whether somebody feels strongly about an idea, or is upset about something. But, he says, "Sometimes you get things wrong because you don't see the way that people are reacting. Because they react visually rather than verbally, or by tactile means, they expect that the normal visual symbols will be picked up. So if somebody says something to me and then smiles, or their eyes twinkle, I miss that; I might hear what they say entirely differently and misinterpret what they are meaning."

The problem is more personal than political: "It's usually when you've fallen out with somebody and they're trying to reconnect, but you're still on the old feeling. Politically, I can normally pick up the signals of body language. You can hear a shuffle, a cough or a scribble. The way people move, the way they engage or disengage from what's going on, the way that they sigh or lean back. I sit between Gordon Brown and John Reid in Cabinet – both very strong characters; I can tell easily how they're reacting to the discussion." It works both ways: the fact that Blunkett cannot see others' facial expressions means he has never learned to exaggerate his own for effect and relies on expressing himself verbally. This can mean, since he is unable to read the silent signals of impatience which others give out when they are tired of listening to him, that he can come across as more overbearing than he intends.

One of his most common habits is to sigh loudly in Cabinet when disagreeing with something being said. Where other minis-ters can see when Blair acknowledges them with a nod, that their interest in speaking has registered with him, Blunkett initially found it frustrating that he had no idea whether the Prime Minister had noticed his eagerness to speak, and would wave frantically. Now Blair will simply say, "I'll call you next, David."

A colleague on Sheffield council says that Blunkett learned these skills as leader: "He became acutely sensitive to people's mood. It was quite uncanny how he could feel the atmosphere in a room. He could feel people's silence and their inner tension."

He can also tell from inflections in people's voices on the telephone what they are really thinking. "I can tell whether somebody's happy or unhappy, whether they're off beam or not, whether they're telling me the truth or not." As a close friend confirms: "If he rings up and says, 'I thought I might come over on Saturday,' and I hesitate for a second, he'll say, 'Oh, it's inconvenient isn't it?' 'No, no, no, it's fine, I just had to pause for thought.' 'I can tell in your voice that you've got something on, haven't you? Truthfully, you know, please say it to me.' He knows what you are thinking." On one occasion he was dining with Trevor Kavanagh, *The Sun*'s political editor, and David Yelland, then the paper's editor, when he overheard people at another table bad-mouthing him as 'a fascist' and questioning his ability to do his job as a blind man. He asked his dining companions whether they would promise not to write up what he was about to do, and they agreed. So he got up, walked across the restaurant and told the diners that while they were at liberty to dislike him and his policies, there was no reason for them to be personally offensive. They went, report observers, bright red with embarrassment.

It is not just his hearing which is sharp. He has an acute sense of smell – sometimes too acute. A fellow Cabinet minister recounts a meeting with Prince Charles at Highgrove. The Prince took the two ministers around his garden. "It was a lovely summer's evening. And there were gorgeous smells from the garden, which of course David was especially appreciating. David said to the Prince: 'That's a wonderful smell. You must have a lot of lavender here.' 'No,' Prince Charles replied. 'That's my aftershave.'"

One former aide recalls a conference in York when he and Blunkett slipped out for a break to visit a local church.

There was a moment when David was very still and quiet. He started talking about the atmosphere and the feeling of the stone and the light that he felt was coming from the windows. It was to do with the general feeling of serenity and calmness in the church environment, the building itself and how he 'felt' the building. I remember thinking at that moment that that's a part of David that doesn't often come through – and also that you should never underestimate what he knows about what's going on around him. There are a lot of people who underestimate him because of his blindness. I'm not talking about 'sixth senses' and all that. I'm talking about his intelligence and his awareness of moods and feelings.

Although he has carefully avoided being seen as a 'blind politician', his blindness raises a fundamental point: the extent to which Blunkett is driven to his extraordinary capacity because, not in spite of, his blindness. The question is how much this is what really drives him. "I sometimes think that I've been trying to over-prove myself. Sometimes I think to myself, Are you doing this to prove a point to yourself? I don't think so any more, however. I don't need to. At the beginning, certainly. I had to break through barriers. I set milestones. But a lot now is simply about confidence." As leader of Sheffield City Council, his blindness was referred to by some of his colleagues as 'The Equaliser'; his abilities were so far ahead of those of his peers that they joked that it was only his blindness which put them on anything like a level playing field.

One close friend, also brought up a Methodist, points to Blunkett's early religious upbringing as being critical in instilling both a drive to succeed and a belief that he need defer to no one. "Methodism gave us both not so much a supreme internal confidence about always winning or achieving, but a sense that we wouldn't be beaten. No matter how difficult things might seem, it instils in you the idea that you just won't let yourself be done down. I think he feels that very strongly. He won't be beaten. That's what drives him."

Confidence is a constant theme; not merely in his own actions, but in how he deals with his junior ministers. Almost everyone who has worked under him says the same thing: that he allows his ministers far more leeway to express themselves and take decisions than other secretaries of state. In part, this is because he has the confidence to choose high-calibre ministers who have the capacity to operate on their own rather than worrying lest they disturb their own shadows. But it is also because he likes to instil them with confidence. "My method is to say, 'Have confidence in yourself. If you feel you've got to say something, say it, and we'll all pick the pieces up afterwards if it goes wrong.' But not saying things because they might upset the apple cart is just not right."

The confidence that he likes to imbue in his colleagues is the other side of the drive to succeed – and to push others to succeed. A former ministerial colleague remarks that "He was always – and rightly so – a hard taskmaster. Those who didn't live up to his standards could feel the cut of his tongue. But that was fine because they deserved it. Yes, you've got to prove yourself."

He has a notable temper. A Sheffield councillor recalls that, as leader, "He didn't like being disagreed with. He would storm out, make for the door, the chair flying, the dog being pulled along. He wasn't afraid to use his temper." Others suspect that he would use it as a means of getting his way. In the early days he was sometimes treated with kid gloves, and colleagues did not like to upset him. Cue temper, cue victory.

Colleagues today all have their own experiences of his temper, but it is a much rarer sight – certainly no longer politically useful – and one that embarrasses him greatly; he will go out of his way to make amends afterwards. One of his advisers relates that "He and I fell out on Sangatte; we had a real disagreement. He thought I'd offered too much in terms of our negotiating position and he quite publicly and angrily aired this disagreement at a ministerial dinner. Then later he gave me a big hug and a bottle of wine. He wanted to clear the air. That's important to him."

Blunkett gives the appearance of relishing a fight, such as when he talked, in an interview on the BBC *Today* programme, about asylum seekers swamping local schools and doctors' surgeries. Sincere as his views are, there sometimes seems to be an element of '*pour épater le bourgeois*' in his expression of them. As an adviser to Blunkett in the 1980s puts it: "He quite enjoyed upsetting the Islington middle classes. He saw the party as too dominated by them. He still loves it when they splutter with rage, and he knows he has the overwhelming majority of the population on his side." This is borne out by the experience of an ally from Sheffield. "When I go canvassing, there's only ever one thing people say: 'I was listening to him the other day, isn't he brilliant?' These are ordinary working-class people. They get him. They see him as their man in the government." Blunkett is an assiduous constituency MP, with regular surgeries which he refuses to hand over to assistants, unlike many Cabinet ministers. That is in part because he believes it is the duty of every MP, no matter how exalted, to make themselves available to their electorate (a trait he shares with his predecessor as Home Secretary, Jack Straw). But it is also because he sees his constituency as his personal focus group. Almost everything he does is thought of in the context of how his constituents would regard it; he makes constant reference to Sheffield and how its people regard the issues in his in-tray.

For all that, his greatest political strength in government has been his bond with the ultimate Islingtonian, Tony Blair. Despite their very different backgrounds, "they think and react in a similar fashion on many of the key issues such as crime and asylum. But where David scores is in credibility. He's experienced it for himself", as a Cabinet colleague remarks.

The appearance of relishing a fight can be deceptive, however.

Blunkett is an emotional man who, as he puts it, gets "screwed up inside just like anybody else when you're in the middle of a major fight". Take the battle over ID cards, which he describes as "incredibly difficult. I wouldn't have gone through that without having a real sense of purpose, because it knocks you for six. You are human and you get punched and punched and punched. And then you think, I've just got to keep going. It's tenacity. What I do relish is not being defeated." Colleagues who have known him for a long time notice that he has changed. In the past, he was obsessive and would fight to the bitter end over even small issues. As one puts it: "Whether something should be delayed for a month or whether we had a slight change in wording – he'd refuse to give an inch and obsess over such relatively unimportant issues." He has learned since becoming Home Secretary 'just to let it go' over small issues and to focus instead on the bigger picture.

Some fights that might seem unnecessary, however, and which appear to be examples of his drive to be controversial for the sake of it, are usually part of a bigger plan. In a speech in Birmingham he argued that immigrants should be able to speak English (a theme he had written about in a pamphlet published on the day of the speech) so as to avoid 'schizophrenic rifts' between generations. They should, he said, talk "in English as well as their historic mother tongue".[7] "I felt the need to say it as part of a jigsaw – changing the culture and attitude that makes other things possible." There was a terrific storm surrounding the speech, after a *Sunday Telegraph* front-page article flagged up the remarks in advance. He had not proscribed or directed anything; and he was simply making the point that in a country in which English is the first language, it makes sense to be able to speak English. But he was attacked for ordaining what language immigrants should use and for racism. Given that he has never seen the difference between black and white skin colour, it is a remarkably odd accusation to make. Blunkett arrived at the hall in Boswell Heath to be greeted by demonstrations.

You could feel the atmosphere. It was a multi-ethnic group, and you could have cut the atmosphere with a knife. I won them over when they heard everything I had to say. But I don't enjoy that sort of thing. You just have to do something about it; you have to make a go of it . . . Now there's no storm at all over it – it's just accepted. But at the time, I was called a colonial imperialist. There was a lot of breath-holding by other people, to see whether I was going to be cut to pieces. When I wasn't, others joined in. I can't afford to be a coward, though, if people are going to trust me. They have to know that I say what I mean.

He faced a similar storm over his use of the word 'swamp' in April 2002, when he said on the *Today* programme that some schools and GPs' surgeries were being 'swamped' by asylum seekers. Blunkett responded that he had used the word deliberately to explain why the children of 3,000 asylum seekers who were to be put up in new Home Office accommodation centres would be educated separately from local schoolchildren (a plan that was later changed): "I don't apologise. I didn't say that Britain was being swamped. I was talking about a school or a GP practice. The idea that a word becomes unusable even though the dictionary definition is straightforward because an ex-prime minister used it twenty-four years ago in an entirely different context and in an emotive way is ridiculous."[8] Blunkett has a favourite anecdote about the incident: "At a lunch we had with the *Guardian*'s editor and senior journalists at Labour Party conference later that year, Polly Toynbee used the word swamp. And I said, 'I'm sorry, Polly, you've just been ruled out of being on the *Guardian* any more.'"

Those who know Blunkett well are united in recognising that, much as his stomach might turn in difficult situations, he nonetheless requires stress to function at full pelt. Officials say they know when the holidays are near because Blunkett will get more and more pressured. He lives off his nerves and stress and holidays are therefore even more essential than usual. One aide remarks that the worst aspect of the news of his affair with Fortier was that it came when Blunkett was on holiday, and thus ruined what was an indispensable break. Instead of returning to work refreshed, he was even more stressed than on his departure.

Blunkett recognises that he lives on his wits: "I'm at my best when things are most difficult. The adrenalin runs. Your senses are sharpened and you haven't the time to waffle." It is not merely that stress drives him to do the various jobs he has been given in his three decades in politics but that he seems somehow to require ever increasing, ever greater challenges in order fully to function. It is something he realises himself: "I couldn't function without the job. I don't know what I will do in years to come. I know that when I'm not in this job I'm going to have to find something really meaningful to do. I won't be retired at sixty-five. I understand why people want to retire – they can stay in bed, they can paint, they can do whatever they want. But it's not for me. I don't know whether I'd ever be able to stop working in one form or another." In part that is because of the buzz that comes from the job.

You go into schools and there's a tremendous buzz. Kids give you something back. They energise you. You come out of a school and you think, these kids are wonderful; they've got a life in front of them and I can help with that. The Home Office is very different. You don't feel that when you go into a prison, a probation unit or the Police Federation Conference. But you learn to adapt to moving the world on, to reforming, to shifting things. And you get a different buzz. When I got to the Prison Officers Association conference in Southport [in May 2003] I was in a foul mood. I spoke to them and got a standing ovation. And you come out of that thinking, blimey, we're getting there. These people are actually prepared to listen. It's a different sort of buzz. It's not as nice but it's interesting.

It is obvious that, to some extent, Blunkett's determination to succeed lies in his need to prove himself to doubters. "It manifests itself with me in terms of trying to do the job too well – spending too much time preparing, so that nobody can actually say, 'Poor old soul, he wasn't really on top of that.' But you've got to be careful that you know when to stop fighting. Because otherwise you're in a permanent state of either sharpened awareness or irritation."

At every stage of his life he has been told that he has done marvellously to achieve what he has but that anything further would be unrealistic. He has then gone on to prove the doubters wrong, to such an extent that those who work with him often forget that he is blind (until, of course, the mechanics of his blindness come into play). He has, however, never doubted his ability: "I have apprehensions [rather than doubts]. When I walked into Sanctuary Buildings [the DfEE headquarters] in 1997 I felt apprehensive, for good reason. I've never actually had doubt about something that I've decided I can do, because having made the intellectual leap that you can do it, you've then got to be absolutely firm in your own mind."

Others, however, do have their doubts, and react in different ways to his blindness. Some are awkward around him; some are patronising; some appear not to notice. But, as he puts it, "It is under the surface, there's no question about that. When I first got into the Commons, Alan Roberts [former MP for Bootle, a close friend who died of AIDS] was very helpful. He used to tell me what people were saying: 'This guy's not going to be able to do the job, how the hell can he?' That sort of thing. His take on it was that it was quite a challenge to them; if they could see and I couldn't, and I was going to do well, that was a bit of a knocker for some people who didn't have their own self-esteem and self-confidence." He will not, as a matter of character, make an issue of it. Early on in his period on the front bench he could not find the despatch box without help. Some Conservatives started to jeer. While others made clear how much they dis-approved of their colleagues' boorish behaviour, Blunkett simply ignored it. He did not want to be treated as 'the blind MP'; if they wanted to barrack him, let them. He would see them off.

Blunkett learned early on to cope with patronising behaviour. As a friend who sees him off duty puts it, "If you go into a restaurant or somewhere public, sometimes people try and help too much, and of course he doesn't want that. David wants to be challenged and he wants to be independent. So you have to get the judgement right about how far you do help him, and I think people who don't know him probably rush in and do too much, which does irritate him." Much of it is unintentional – saying hello to the dog and wanting to talk to him about the dog rather than about himself and his politics. He long ago grew accustomed to sitting in meetings and hearing people talk across him or pass notes in front of him, as if he would be unaware of their behaviour. There was a further prejudice, which a former aide recalls: "He suffered a double prejudice: against his blindness; and against his being 'the boy out of local government'. Don't forget that few local council leaders have gone on to become significant national figures."

The obstacles he faced in making his name went beyond other people's reactions. There were practical difficulties of the sort that most sighted people would not even notice. As one aide puts it:

So many people are not really aware of David's blindness because of the way that he conducts himself. But there are real problems. Take walking into a reception. That's a very different experience for David to that of a sighted person. Sighted people look around the room, notice their friends, spot people they haven't seen for a while, see people milling around and think, so-and-so would be good to talk to; oh, look, there's what's-his-name. David can't do that. I would have to look around the room for him and tell him who is standing where, then guide him over. Otherwise he ends up standing in one place and receiving people like royalty. And that means he's on the back foot – they determine when they come and when they leave. So he'd always try to work the room with someone.

He was not, as a young delegate to party conference, above using his blindness to his advantage; he would regularly ignore the fact that a red light had come on (of which he had been made well aware) to signal to him that he should stop speaking.

Watching Blunkett at a reception is a fascinating sight. No one, of course, stands still at a party. They move around. So although he is told initially who is standing where, the situation will soon change. Often, however, he can tell from the sounds and smells who has moved where and can then make a beeline for them, another example of how his behaviour can put people at ease and help them to forget that he cannot see. This is helped also by his social skills. As a former ministerial colleague remarks, "He's got a human and common touch, particularly when he's in gatherings of people. He's great with people on a personal level. They find him incredibly warm." People usually become nervous in the presence of so powerful a figure as a home secretary. In May 2004 he visited The Haven, a sexual assault referral centre in Camberwell. The visit was deeply distressing. But instead of awkwardness or the false bonhomie that is the stock-in-trade of politicians, Blunkett held a series of private meetings with staff and a former rape victim and gave each of them the feeling that he was no more special than they and was genuinely interested in learning what he could do to help.

This warmth manifests itself in the loyalty that Blunkett inspires. A close friend observes that "he's astonishingly courteous and considerate. He never imposes himself in any way on you. Sometimes you want him to lean on you for support – that's what friends are for – but he hates that". In researching this book, I spoke to many people who had not been in contact with him for a number of years. Not one would speak to me without ensuring first that Blunkett was happy. This works both ways: Blunkett is himself a very loyal friend, and will go out of his way to defend and protect those who form part of the extended family. His behaviour over the Beverley Hughes affair in 2004 was typical. Politically, it was clear that he needed to extricate himself from the trouble her remaining as immigration minister posed. But not only did he go out of his way to defend her, he made clear that any attacks on her position were an attack on his own, with consequences that linger to this day. And when Stephen Byers, his former schools minister, was in dire political trouble as Transport Secretary, Blunkett rang him every Friday night to check he was in good spirits and to offer advice. A political friend says that "David is one of the few politicians I have come across who is totally trustworthy. You can trust him with anything. He is incapable of betrayal."

This loyalty has a practical purpose: he needs it to be able to function, since he needs to trust his colleagues in carrying out some of the most basic tasks, such as the preparation of his tapes and extracts from papers. Blunkett describes this as a variation on the 'community' and 'mutuality' politics that he favours: "We are interdependent. To accept that isn't to be dependent; it's very different to being dependent because it is mutual."

One of the main factors behind the loyalty he inspires is described by a former junior minister: "He's genuinely interested in you and the idea that you are doing things together – you're not just writing the script or doing something for him. He makes you feel as if you're in a collective endeavour. And you know that you're working with somebody whom you can admire, both because he really does want to change the world and because of his personal background. And he so clearly repays your loyalty; once you get into a relationship with him you get it back."

He is especially supportive of women in politics, going out of his way to push them forward. His loyalty to Beverley Hughes was long-standing. As a councillor in Trafford, she had met him only two or three times when, one night in 1990, she picked up the phone to be greeted by the sound of Blunkett's voice, suggesting to her that she put her name forward for nomination in the Bootle by-election. The thought had not previously crossed her mind. Although she got nowhere in Bootle, the idea of becoming an MP took hold; in 1997 she entered the Commons as MP for Stretford and Urmston. She is far from the only female MP who has been mentored by Blunkett.

There are, though, no 'Blunkettites' in the Commons – no army of supporters – and he is sometimes criticised by MP colleagues for not being 'clubbable'. Blunkett has another take on this: he tries as far as possible to lead a normal life, away from the usual political haunts. Not just to keep his 'feet on the ground' and to 'listen to my constituents', as politicians are fond of saying, but for his own benefit. When he arrived at the Department for Education and Employment, for instance, he found cupboards full of alcohol, used by predecessors for after-hours entertaining. He has become more disciplined in his work; where, in the past, he would stay in his office until late at night, he has realised that he needs to pace himself. His Home Office staff expressed surprise early on that he would leave the office after finishing his work; his predecessors, Michael Howard and Jack Straw, would spend long evenings in their office agonising over their decisions and the attacks made on them. Blunkett, on the other hand, will leave whenever possible by 7.30. When he arrives home – he has an official flat in Pimlico – he tries to limit his work to an hour. "People say that they work until one or two in the morning. I have done very occasionally when I've had to, but it's not true! People do not do that. And if they do, they're mental."

For all the characteristic Blunkett intensity, colleagues soon learn to appreciate his irreverence. As one puts it: "He believes that humour and levity help in an argument. He's not at all stuffy." A friend observes that "he will come over to stay with us, we'll go out and walk around and he's always 'hail fellow well met' when strangers approach. He talks easily to people".

In February 2000 Blunkett appeared on *Parkinson* with the actor Martin Kemp and the comedian Alexei Sayle. The interview was striking. Whenever one sees a politician on such a show, they are usually either ridiculous, exuding fake chumminess, or they do not relax at all and are inappropriately stuffy. Blunkett was noticeably normal. The start of the interview was not propitious, however. Descending the stairs, his dog, Lucy, took him to the first chair, and Blunkett sat on Martin Kemp's lap.

The *Parkinson* interview was unusual for another reason. Although Blunkett is usually confident and relaxed on the radio, TV is another matter. He is far less comfortable with the medium, conscious of how people look at him. He worries whether his eyes are looking in the right direction and whether people will be distracted by them and his appearance. (As a young councillor he appeared on the BBC current affairs pro-gramme *Nationwide*, and it was suggested to him that he wear dark glasses. Like many blind people, he finds the very notion of dark glasses offensive – as if the blind somehow need to be hidden from view.)

He learned his skills as a councillor when local radio had only just begun. It was easy for a young, opinionated politician to make his name as a worthwhile interviewee who gave the radio equivalent of 'good copy'. What is especially noticeable about his appearances is that he answers the question he is asked. Unlike many of his colleagues, who stick to a line relentlessly and refuse to vary it no matter what the question, Blunkett is sufficiently confident in himself and his views to relish such encounters. Indeed, he goes out of his way to avoid taking a line: "I'll never forget polling night in the 1992 election. Our spokespeople on TV spent the whole night uttering the same mantra that they started with at ten o'clock when the polls shut, even after it became clear that we'd lost. It was so obviously absurd. I've always thought that I'll just say what I think and if people don't like it, they can lump it. But you need to have the confidence not to worry what will happen if you say something out of line." He repeated the trick after the elections to the European Parliament in June 2004 when, after Labour had been given a drubbing, he did not do the rounds of the studios pro-claiming the usual nonsense – "it was a night of triumph" – but said that he was "mortified" by the results.

There is, of course, a balance to be struck, especially in his current role as Home Secretary: "You can't be the man in the street because you know a lot more about the situation and you have to think about public policy and not how you'd like to react personally. But I try and blend the two. I try and think, speak and respond as people would expect me to because that's what we're here for." Blunkett advised one former colleague to treat radio interviews as like having a conversation in the kitchen and always to remember that the interview was being transmitted into someone's house – and who would want someone in their house who wasn't relaxed?

The directness that is so clear in his radio and TV interviews reflects a typical Yorkshire bluntness. It is also present in his personal life: "You either like me or you don't. And if someone messes me about, I'm sharp with them. I'm not good at diplomacy." This directness clearly plays well professionally: the Jeremy Vine programme on Radio 2 regularly receives more letters and comments in response to interviews with Blunkett than with any other politician.

His relations with the press are extensive. Some go beyond the professional and have developed into friendship. He is close to Paul Dacre, editor of the *Mail*; they count each other as friends. When, in the Commons, he described the *Mail* as "the well-known and reliable newspaper", he was not making a jibe: ". . . [W]hen it gets off its propaganda, its articles are quite informative and extremely well written."[9] Blunkett made a point of attending a reception to mark Dacre's contribution to journalism held in March 2003 (unlike another friend of Dacre's, Gordon Brown, who appeared only by video link) and proposed a toast. Dacre was, he said, "a man who loves to hate, but actually reflects the best of journalism", and that he needed "to read the *Daily Mail* to find out what is going on in my department, then seek immediate medical attention". He wanted "to honour the *Daily Mail*" because it "provides the best of journalism" and acts as an "irritant . . . Paul cannot resist poking the stick even if he agrees with you . . . I owe you one, even if it's just a left hook".[10] While the *Daily Mail* rarely attacks Blunkett personally (it treated his affair with Kimberly Fortier with kid gloves, a favour which would not have been granted to other Labour ministers in the same position), it is nonetheless strident in its attacks on some of his policies, especially immigration and asylum.

Closer still is Les Hinton, chief executive of News International, whom he met through one of his best friends, Paul Potts, chief executive of the Press Association. Potts and Blunkett are regular holiday companions. Potts, a radical Thatcherite, was at one point deputy editor of the *Daily Express* in its most Conservative phase; the two men maintained their friendship, forged in Sheffield in the 1970s, despite their political differences.

Professionally he has good relations, too, with Rebekah Wade, editor of *The Sun* and Andy Coulson of the *News of the World*, despite a serious row over *The Sun*'s coverage of asylum at the beginning of 2003. Although it was the *News of the World* which revealed his affair, both News International tabloids treated him with a respect which they would be unlikely to have given to others in his position. The *News of the World* argued that, "[W]e have no doubt he still has much to offer the nation. The Home Secretary's love affair with a married woman cannot be condoned. But neither is it a matter for resignation . . . And today this politician who holds one of the great offices of state (and is even spoken of as a future Prime Minister) emerges as a very human and vulnerable figure." When Coulson rang Blunkett on the Friday before the paper revealed the affair, the two were able to reach an accommodation over the coverage. For example part of a photograph of Fortier leaving Blunkett's house was masked, for security purposes.

Blunkett has followed classic New Labour tactics in befriending the tabloids. As he puts it, "Great tranches of Labour voters – or potential Labour voters – read these papers. We need to know where they're coming from and how to get in there. And although it doesn't stop them having a go at the government over crime or asylum, it certainly modifies the personal nature of what they do to me." The kid-glove treatment he received over his relationship with Fortier is a case in point. There is only one proprietor he has not yet met, and will do his damnedest to avoid: the owner of the *Daily Express*: "Richard Desmond is the only proprietor I've never spoken to. Never wanted to." Blunkett regards pornographers with contempt and the *Express* as no longer a serious newspaper.

One of Blunkett's main strengths is his ability to *do* politics – a surprisingly rare skill within the government. A ministerial colleague points to his style of trying to take "giant steps forward in order to make what might only be small progress. He knows you've got to overreach where you want to be, because the system and the potential for radical change are so diluted in government. He's prepared to take big political risks in terms of his own reputation and relationships with colleagues – closing Sangatte and ID cards, for example – because he thinks you need to take really big steps forward to get anywhere". As Blunkett puts it, his reputation for slaying a host of dragons at any one time is wrong: "You have to choose which battle to fight. I was prepared to take the NUT on [as Education Secretary]. I've been prepared to take people on all my life. But I don't take them on for its own sake. I wasn't going to go to the Police Federation or the Prison Officers Association, douse myself in petrol and then set myself alight. I'm not a masochist."

A fellow minister compares Blunkett's political skills with those of his successor at Education, Estelle Morris: "One of Blunkett's main strengths was that he would take decisions all the time. Contrast that with Estelle Morris, who would worry constantly about decisions and never take them." Couple this with his attention to detail and the high standards he demands of his staff and it becomes clear why he is both feared and respected as a minister. One of the most senior civil servants to have worked with him explains that "Blunkett was intolerant of anything less than perfection. He would not tolerate sloppy wording or sloppy briefings. Other ministers would be bossed by us. If an official said they couldn't do something, they'd let the civil servant not do it. Estelle Morris, for instance, would let her officials get away with murder. Blunkett would simply reject things that were not satisfactory and demand that they were redone." Former ministers who have worked under Blunkett are remarkably consistent in their view that he allowed them far more leeway and freedom than other secretaries of state but coupled this with a strong sense of support. Stephen Byers, Charles Clarke, Charles Falconer, Tessa Jowell, Estelle Morris, Paul Boateng and Hilary Benn have all gone on to the Cabinet – a far greater number than under any other secretary of state.

The other side of that coin is that, as civil servants who have worked with him almost all say, he is one of the most demanding ministers of both staff and ministerial colleagues: "very challenging", as one puts it in mandarin-speak. He is, the civil servant continues, "insistent and quite single minded. He knows what he wants and there's not a lot of compromise there". A former aide says that "You either shape up or you ship out" – which is confirmed by his track record of reorganising personnel. The aide continues: "His make-up doesn't allow for cock-ups or mistakes. David is incredibly well-planned in all situations."

In Cabinet, Blunkett's style is to ration his contributions – to speak "only when I think it's powerful and necessary". In part that is because his workload is so great that he does not have time to range over other departments' policy agendas. As he puts it: "How many issues do you see from other departments hitting the headlines on a daily basis?" Ministers from other departments, however, tend to regard Blunkett warily – John Prescott, for instance, holds his colleague in a mixture of contempt and suspicion. Blunkett puts this down to the fact that

I just never take no for an answer. I fly ahead and get on with it. He doesn't really understand what I'm about; he's never quite cottoned on. He's right to believe that I am arrogant because I am. I am arrogant enough to believe that I know what I'm doing. However, he's wrong in believing that I will do anything to get my way, which

I won't. He doesn't like that I do what he is good at himself: saying it as it is. If I don't like something, I'll say so. So will he – but he doesn't seem to like it when somebody else is doing it. And he dislikes the fact that I get on well with the right-wing press because he gets on with them so badly.

A particular *bête noire* of Prescott is his 'Two Jags' nickname. Coming out of a Cabinet meeting, he asked Blunkett, "How is it that I get slagged off for having a Jag and you don't?" Prescott has said this, according to Blunkett, "numerous times. I don't really care but it obviously really gets to him".

Having been at the centre of the government since the first day, Blunkett has had the chance to observe all the key figures close up. Some have impressed him, others less so.

I thought Alan Milburn had very substantially grown in competence and ability . . . You could trust him. If he said he was going to say something to Tony, he would do it rather than let you down. John Reid is good. He can talk the hind legs off a donkey but he is very astute. He's already started to change things quite substantially. I think Tessa [Jowell]'s grown [in stature] but it's very difficult because if you're in a junior department you don't have the weight. You do as you're told. I thought she was weak over the Licensing Bill but overall I think she's grown into the job. And then there are people who don't say a lot but actually are quite decent ministers like Paul Murphy. I think there are people who are quite brave and think radically like Peter Hain, but if there's anyone who upsets colleagues more than I do it's Peter. And there are people who are just doing their job like Margaret Beckett, who are really just holding the ring; they're solid but they're not going to come up with anything radical or new.

His view of others is less complimentary. Blunkett has told colleagues that he is disappointed with Charles Clarke, who he has said to believe "has not developed as he expected." And he does not hold Patricia Hewitt in high regard. "I don't think she thinks strategically. She nearly let the Competition Commission demolish local chemists. That's only a simple example but [the job of being a Cabinet minister is] about understanding what's going on in the community."

Ministers judge their colleagues not simply on competence but on more political grounds – how willing they are, for instance, to put their head above the parapet or to disturb shadows.

Alan [Milburn] used to; Steve Byers did. Steve was the best Chief Secretary to the Treasury we've had, because he was the only one who didn't just sign off official letters. He actually read them, changed them and made his own decisions; in other words, he really took on the officials. Gordon [Brown] doesn't have to. He floats above it. It's human nature, isn't it? People don't put their heads on the block unless they have to.

Blunkett has consistently refused to sit back, keep quiet and opt for the quiet life when he disagrees with something. "People are quite happy for somebody else to fire the bullets. There is also sometimes the feeling that 'He's put his neck out on the block, let him have his head chopped off – it won't do us any harm to see him taken down a peg'. I had to take Gordon on quite strongly in the early days in the last parliament because he was throwing his weight around and he pretty well quietened everybody else. I was the one who was prepared to take him on." Although this clearly exacerbated their antipathy, Blunkett argues that it was not an early stage of the much-vaunted leadership battle between the two men. "It was about the real issues – what we did with the New Deal, spending for schools, not being pushed about. And Gordon only respects people who stand up to him." This contrasts him with Blair, who doesn't like being stood up to:

I've said to him on two or three occasions, 'Your best friends are the ones who tell you what you don't want to hear' – as long as they do it in an acceptable way. Ann Taylor used to do it in a very unacceptable way. She bit the dust, not least because of the unpopularity of those she gathered around her in the Whip's Office. Tony had had enough of her. She'd been, in a sort of robust but slightly inept way, telling him what to do and what to say. It's difficult as Prime Minister; you've got to keep the cart on the rails, you've got to keep colleagues talking to each other and working with each other – which is why he's tolerated more from Gordon than he ought to.

The tensions between front-rank colleagues were brought out in Blunkett's reaction to a *Times* leader that called on Blair to begin the hand-over to Brown by promoting to the Cabinet a regiment of ministers nominated by the Chancellor.[11] A minister recalls Blunkett's anger. He ranted: "I've a good mind to ring Robert Thomson (editor of *The Times*) and say, which one of your underlings wrote this? Which of the people who have any seniority at minister of state level and is a Gordon supporter do you believe should be promoted to Cabinet? Like bloody who? Which little bits of slime from under stones would you promote to the Cabinet from his side?"

The job of Home Secretary may be more onerous than almost any other but Blunkett is determined to maintain a semblance of normal life. He will, on his return home from work, always make time to call his friends for a chat. Once his work is done, he goes to bed, listening for twenty minutes or so to a non-political audiobook, more often than not light fiction such as John Grisham.

Given his limited time for relaxation, it is perhaps little wonder that one of his closest friends says that he is most annoyed by slow and indifferent service. "David likes his food; he gets very frustrated by restaurants which can't do the basics right." As Blunkett puts it:

If people care about their job and they care about the service they're delivering to you, their job becomes much more interesting. If they care about how they present the food and what they deliver and they're helpful to you, not only do you get something out of it but they do too. They feel better about it as well, and you're much nicer to them, and the world is a better place. We suffer too much in Britain. We apologise when we are confronted by total inadequacy. If somebody presents us with something that is stone cold, we say, 'I'm terribly sorry to bother you, I really don't want to grumble.' Or we struggle through a steak that saw better times ten years ago.

He is a deeply courteous man; he makes a point of always writing a thank-you letter after a lunch or dinner. In Westminster, where prodigious lunching is endemic, Blunkett restricts his own. But when he does lunch, he makes sure to be properly appreciative and polite. As a friend puts it: "Because he has such good manners himself, he expects the same of everybody else; if he doesn't get it he gets irritated."

The life of a Cabinet minister can be very lonely; their families are often far away from London. When Blunkett returns home after work to his Pimlico flat, he is usually alone (other than when one of his sons is down to stay). That loneliness was exacerbated by his relationship with Kimberley Fortier. When their friendship developed into a full-blown affair in early 2002, Blunkett was keen that they live together as a family. That Fortier chose not to, heightened his sense of loneliness.

He has a housekeeper, but she does not live in. As a friend puts it: "There's no one to cook him a warm meal." Blunkett is partly his own housekeeper, and a frugal one. He makes sure that nothing is left over; every morning, he brings with him into the office a small box of groceries that might otherwise be wasted and hands them over to Dennis (a Home Office institution who has 'looked after' the past three home secretaries) to be used for his lunch. Staff joke that he will ask, days later, "Where's that tomato I left last week?"

His sons – Alastair, Hugh and Andrew – are immensely supportive. Alastair, the eldest, lives in Sheffield but plays what one family friend calls "a huge part in his life". Blunkett and the boys will often holiday together, sometimes with Paul Potts and his wife. The boys will make their views clear – when Blunkett was Education Secretary, they told him repeatedly of their opposition to student loans. In 2003, Blunkett dropped plans to allow much greater interception of e-mails and telephone calls. Admitting that he had not taken into account the widespread concern over the proposals, and that "if you are in a hole you should stop digging and start listening", he confirmed that his son, Hugh, in the IT business, had persuaded him of his mistake: "Look, Dad," Hugh told him, "people are simply seeing this in exactly the opposite direction to what you intended and if you don't get off it, you are going to end up with people not just misinterpreting but believing that their own communications are going to be interfered with."[12]

More even than on his sons, he depends for support, of course, on his guide dogs. As one of his oldest friends puts it: "He's always been blessed with wonderful guide dogs, from Ruby, the first, right the way through to Sadie now. It's only when you get close that you realise how remarkable these animals are – what they can do and the bond between them and their owner."

The dogs that Blunkett has had of late are specially bred by a friend, Val Woolridge, on a farm in Lancashire. Sadie, his current dog, is her predecessor Lucy's half-sister – they have the same father, from frozen sperm. By Lucy's tenth birthday, in September 2002, she was starting to show her age. But she still seemed keen to carry on working. And Blunkett was loath to have to train a new dog, his first since becoming a minister. But it was clear that her joints were not up to the daily grind. Her age was, after all, the equivalent of seventy human years. After coming home from a family holiday in Majorca, Val Woolridge suggested that the time had come to find a replacement and offered Blunkett the choice of two. She also offered to take Lucy for her retirement. Sadie, the dog eventually chosen, started work on 24 January 2003.

Now that he is a minister, his staff have to help look after his dog, just as they do their master. The dog is an extension of him. But he tries whenever possible to take his dog for a run himself.

Just as they are trained to guide him, so they are trained to eat at specified times and to have a run.

On one occasion a pool of rancid water appeared in the Members' Lobby in the Commons. Some wag said that the culprit was Lucy, his dog at the time. The story ended up in a diary column. Blunkett was not merely livid; he was offended. To suggest that his dog had fouled the lobby was to suggest that he had, since he was responsible – and proud to be – for her. He insisted that the Commons authorities investigate the real cause (a leaking flower box from a room above) and that the newspaper print a full and prominent apology.

Blunkett may have been born and brought up, during the school holidays, in inner-city Sheffield, but he prefers the countryside to city life. This is clearly an extension of his blindness. He feels, he says, "trapped" in the city; the country is built on sounds and atmosphere, in contrast to the predominantly visual aesthetic of cities. The textures and surfaces of the country make a different sound to those of the city. "When it rains you can hear entirely different surfaces. You can plot where grass is, where tarmac is, where foliage growth is, all from sound. You get none of that in the city." So he now makes every effort to visit his rented cottage in an affluent area of Derbyshire from Saturday teatime till Sunday teatime. "I don't do it every weekend but a part of that time I spend walking. And even working outside, as I always do whenever I can, is nicer when you're in a decent environment." The cottage also had the benefit of providing a secluded venue for his assignations with Fortier.

In the summer, he tries to work outdoors rather than remain in his Queen Anne's Gate office and will take Sadie for a walk wherever possible. He loves to walk (as do the dogs), and likes nothing better when he is staying at his cottage than walking in the Peak District and around the Chatsworth estate. A frequent companion says that "he fetches a fair old pace". Sheffield's unique closeness to the countryside has given the city a tradition of people who work in the metropolis in the week and then at the weekend get a knapsack, put on their hiking boots, get on a bus and, fifteen minutes later, start walking in some of the most beautiful countryside in the land. As a family member puts it: "David's a Sheffield lad. He doesn't wear coats when he walks; Sheffield boys don't wear coats. He is a Sheffield lad to his boot straps and always will be."

Since the point of walking in the countryside is to feel free, it is hardly surprising that Blunkett tries to limit the inevitable security that has to accompany him. He spent New Year 2002 staying at his friend Paul Potts's holiday home. His bodyguards dropped him off at the remote house and then departed for Sheffield. Potts and his wife, Blunkett and the two dogs retired at one in the morning after seeing in the new year. They woke the next day to a power failure – no phones, no mobile coverage, no fax. The Home Secretary was cut off from the rest of the world. Although the power returned later that morning and there were no ill effects, Potts suggested that in future he should make sure he was always protected. It could not be sensible for the Home Secretary to be so cut off and vulnerable. Blunkett refused even to countenance the idea. He still needed his freedom, no matter what was 'sensible'. As a friend puts it: "With David, once you say, 'You're not the Home Secretary this week, you're on holiday with your friends',' he's a completely changed person."

He takes a direct risk with his personal safety sometimes. One journalist was stunned to see the then Education Secretary arrive at a school on the back of a Harley-Davidson. The bike belonged to a friend he had been staying with, and Blunkett couldn't resist the experience. "We're all such stuffed shirts most of the time."[13] Sometimes he goes further than riding pillion: Blunkett can, and does, drive. He gets a thrill from it, and has been known to go to an open, private piece of land to sit behind the wheel and put his foot down to experience the impact and rush of speed. A metaphor, perhaps, for his political style – and, perhaps, his relationship with Fortier.

2

"May your God go with you, whoever he or she might be"

There are two especially striking aspects of Blunkett's political career. First, that despite the many obvious differences between Blunkett the leader of Sheffield City Council and Blunkett the Home Secretary – one a self-identified Bennite, the other a model New Labour minister – there has been a clear and consistent thread to his views, which means that he is still recognisably the same man. Second, that, whatever the political labels that might be attached to him, he has a rare instinct for speaking in language that sounds normal to the average voter, for acting in ways that seem sensible to them, and for reacting to events in a manner that makes clear that he is a human being and not just a politician.

As Home Secretary, he has introduced anti-terror and law and order legislation that has made him deeply unpopular among the chattering classes. The language he uses – his talk of asylum seekers 'swamping' some schools and GP surgeries, for instance – leads many to recoil in horror. As Shadow Education Secretary, he faced howls of derision from many in the Labour Party for his 'old-fashioned' views on the importance of the 3Rs. Many in the judiciary regard him with contempt. A large number of his parliamentary colleagues find him, at best, an object of fascination, and at worst an aberration as a Labour Home Secretary. He knows that his chances of winning a leadership election from his current position are minimal.

And yet he is almost unique in his instinctive understanding of ordinary voters – only Tony Blair has anything like a similar instinct. As a Cabinet colleague puts it: "His instincts go to the heart of what a lot of ordinary Labour Party members feel. They suffer from anti-social behaviour and they have worries about asylum and immigration. They want their children to be able to read and write properly. David articulates that in a responsible and reasonable way. Whatever the PLP might think of him and his policies, his instincts are clearly in tune with the instincts of most Labour Party members, let alone voters. The party at large still likes him, precisely because of the things he's done at Education and the Home Office which might annoy the party in Westminster."

A close friend – a Conservative who has known Blunkett since his early twenties – says that his fundamental beliefs have remained unchanged: "Decency, communities, self-respect and self-reliance." So, for instance, his argument as Education and Employment Secretary in 2000 that it should be "unacceptable that you lie in bed, that you presume that somebody else is going to fund you if you are able bodied and able to work" was not, as was said at the time, anything out of the ordinary. It was classic Blunkett.[1] On the bread-and-butter Labour issues, the core of his beliefs has always been far more subtle than the traditional left response to poverty. As leader of Sheffield, he made some woefully misguided mistakes and defended some pretty indefensible policies, but even then he was trying to give practical effect to, as the soundbite has it, 'a hand up not a hand-out'. Nothing better illustrates his approach, then and now, than this description from *On a Clear Day* of his own poverty: "I do not use the term lightly. Those who have never experienced real poverty are all too often very sentimental about it and about poor people in general. I have to smile at this and think: if only you knew what it was like, you would know all about aspirations and expectations and why it was that, in the community in which I grew up, escaping the poverty trap and achieving success were the key aims."[2]

For all his belief in self-reliance and a form of workfare, when politics intervenes it can take precedence. In 1995, for instance, Blunkett hit the roof when Brown floated the idea in an interview in the *Daily Telegraph* that benefits might be removed from

work-shy under-twenty-fives. The Shadow Chancellor's favourable remarks about US workfare seemed to presage a move to a
British version, requiring the unemployed to work for their
benefits. Blunkett had little objection to the policy but Brown's
soon-to-be-familiar habit of trampling over departmental bound-
ary lines was almost calculated to offend. Along with Prescott
and Chris Smith (the Shadow Social Security Secretary), Blunkett
complained to Blair. Brown replied somewhat disingenuously at
the next meeting of the Shadow Cabinet that he was merely
reiterating a long-standing policy that those who refused work
should lose their unemployment benefit entitlement.

Some of the roots of the hostility between Brown and Blunkett
lie in the then Shadow Chancellor's mightier-than-thou behaviour in opposition, which was to be stepped up considerably
in government. Within the Shadow Cabinet, Blunkett was part of
an informal anti-Brown group with Robin Cook, Frank Dobson,
Michael Meacher and John Prescott. "It does sometimes get up
my nose to hear myself presented in a way which ignores entirely
the fact that there would be no New Labour if it weren't for the
old lags who had to see the party through the most difficult times
in Labour's (and the country's) recent political history . . . The
only amazing thing for me is not that I have recognised that the
world has changed but rather that, having lived through such
times, I am still surviving."

Take his attitude to the two wars in Iraq. Although, as a
frontbencher, he could not vote against the Gulf War, he was one
of thirty-one MPs who abstained when the Commons voted on
15 January 1991 (along with five other frontbenchers, Tony
Banks, John Fraser, Joan Lestor, Joan Ruddock and Clare Short).
By 2003, however, he was fully supportive of military action.
Blunkett has argued that the circumstances were very different;
by 2003 it was clear that Saddam was in fundamental breach of
the UN. But there are more convincing explanations for his
different stance in 2003 (Saddam had, after all, invaded another
country in 1991, a clear breach of the UN Charter). In 1991,

abstaining cost him nothing and helped him with the Left; he was still trying to get elected to the Shadow Cabinet and needed the support of the left. But there is also a more honourable and straightforward reason: his attitude changed. Indeed, in April 2003 he was caustic in his criticism of the media coverage of the fighting, attacking reporters in Baghdad for giving "moral equivalence" to the Iraqi regime. Journalists in the Iraqi capital encouraged, he said, a "progressive and liberal" public to believe their perspective on the news. The media were quite wrong to give as much weight to reports from behind Iraqi lines as to those from the Coalition side of the front line. "For the first time ever in our history we not only have thousands – literally thousands – of journalists travelling with the troops, but we have broadcast media behind what I would describe as enemy lines, reporting blow by blow what is happening. We have it reported certainly in our own media in the United Kingdom on occasions as though they were moral equivalents. Those of a progressive or liberal bent, in my view, are egged on into believing that this is the right way to get to the true facts."[3]

Another of these differences of approach is his social conservatism. When asked, for instance, about a British Council tour of Mark Ravenhill's play *Shopping and Fucking*, Blunkett replied that "I don't know how much they are spending. But if they are spending a penny on it, it's a penny too much." The play was "full of foul language. Shakespeare didn't need that, did he?"[4] He made his first TV appearance as a twenty-year-old in 1967 as a result of a similar reaction. Sitting at home with his mother, he listened as she described to him the sight on the TV of naked bodies in a morgue. He rang in to complain and was invited to take part in a discussion. He duly arrived at TV Centre in London. The oddity of a blind man complaining about an image on TV did not cross his mind. It did, however, horrify the producer, who had no idea that his guest could not see until he greeted him – and his white stick – at reception. As leader of Sheffield council in 1983, he walked out of a performance of

Howard Barker's *A Passion in Six Days* when he realised that one of the scenes involved nudity.[5]

Often his political behaviour pays scant regard to its cost. In the 1980s, when Labour was still dominated by 'rainbow coalition' ideas and the culture wars within the party appeared to have been won decisively by the Bennites, Blunkett became so agitated by the activities of some London councillors that he risked throwing away precious votes in the annual NEC elections by polemicising in his column in *Tribune* (the left-wing weekly newspaper and his line of communication with the very Labour activists he was to attack) against the 'trendy' left, remarking that: "I am not prejudiced against gays and lesbians but there is no point in trying to delude myself that I feel anything but revulsion at the idea of touching another male." He went on:

Probably one of the most annoying and patronising aspects of trendy Left politics today is the way some people simply trot out the groups which they believe deserve their benevolent positive action. People are lumped together rather than understood as individuals, who at one moment fall into one category, and at another fall into none. So we checklist our own sincerity by talking about women (of course not a minority), gays, lesbians, blacks and, if we remember, the disabled . . . Perhaps the daftest of all are those politicians or pressure group activists who irritate the bulk of the population beyond measure by suggesting or inferring that, instead of reflecting the variety of lifestyles, cultures and interests in our community, we should go so far as to repress the norm in order to avoid the pro-motion of one lifestyle above that of another. As someone with a handicap . . . I would no more expect phrases such as 'blind as a bat' to be eliminated from usage than 'blackboard'. I also expect the bulk of our entertainment and cultural expression to reflect the fact that the majority of the population is heterosexual.[6]

Almost a decade later, Blunkett wrote in the *Daily Mail* about Islington councillors who had allowed "paedophiles, pimps and drug dealers" to victimise children through misguided opposition to homophobia and racism.[7] In 1994, he was one of only thirty-nine Labour MPs to vote against lowering the age of consent for gay men to sixteen and was subjected to vitriolic attacks by social liberals. On a visit to Southampton University at the time he was almost set on. But his argument was not that gay sex was wrong. His objections were based on protecting the young and vulnerable. In 1990, he spelt out why he thought the Human Fertilisation and Embryology Bill was wrong to turn child-bearing into a 'right'. Embryos could legitimately be used for research within the first fourteen days, but:

There is nothing wrong with not having children. No stain or ignominy is involved. They are a product of love, not of science. When we are considering the issue, we have to be clear about the situation in which children are brought into the world. It is clear that, when the egg is fertilised by the husband's sperm, either by IVF or directly in the woman – that would apply also to the partner of the woman concerned – and, despite my difficulties in coming to terms with it, it is also true when there is a properly regulated and controlled fertilisation through a donor in a loving relationship, where it is the wish of both partners . . . Child bearing is not a right. It is part of the unfathomable life force.[8]

'Life force' is a phrase he has often used to describe his religious beliefs, which are inchoate. Although trained as a Methodist lay preacher, he no longer calls himself a Christian. It is in the countryside that he feels this 'life force' to be clearest. "People call it refreshing the soul. I think other people feel it, too, but because they use their visual sense so profoundly, they miss out on it. Sighted people have to look for stimulation elsewhere. And if you get bored, you can gaze out of the window. I can't switch off – I have nothing else to 'look' at but my thoughts." His fundamental religious credo is 'each to their own'. As he put it in the Commons: "I think that (the comedian) Dave Allen's famous phrase, 'May your God go with you, whoever he or she might be', is the way forward."[9]

His religious views may have changed from the days when he thought seriously about becoming a priest, but his core political beliefs have remained pretty constant. Blunkett emerged as a political figure at a time – the 1970s and 1980s – when Labour politics were unrecognisable from those of today. So there are, of course, clear differences between the Blunkett of then and the Blunkett of today. Look at any politician over a thirty-year period and you will see differences. What is most striking about Blunkett, however, is that the similarities between then and now are so clear.

One former Cabinet minister has known Blunkett professionally and personally for almost two decades. "I don't think he has changed much. And he's got a core set of inner beliefs; I don't think they've altered at all. He's a very strong personality with strong views that he will never change. He has found a series of different avenues to achieve his objectives but the inner core has remained constant. That's why he's such an excellent politician; he's remained true to them and hasn't shifted." A friend remarks that the only aspect of his personality which has changed is that he prefers a slightly better glass of wine than he used to.

As leader of Sheffield council, Blunkett did not often speak about concepts such as security and order because the Left then was not interested in hearing about them. But they were there, implicit in his actions and writings. As both Education and Home Secretary he has broadened out the meaning in his own fashion. At Education, he saw his role as making sure "that I actually changed the things that affected people's lives. That kids got a real chance of using their talent. That we would make them self-reliant and give them the assets for them to be participative citizens as opposed to passive recipients of benefit". Similarly, at the Home Office, his aim has been to "create a secure, safe environment which not only restores order and security to people but also changes the political climate. Within that security – whether it's about crime or a fear of immigrants, worries about the criminal justice system not working and the system breaking down, or drugs – the aim is that people actually feel safe enough to be more progressive".

Blunkett's actions at the Home Office are dismissed as 'authoritarian' or 'right-wing' or caricatured as those of a 'hang 'em and flog 'em' moralist by most liberals. Dame Helena Kennedy has written an entire book, *Just Law*, attacking him. Another member of the liberal establishment, Anthony Howard, attacks him for combining "the dangerous qualities of being a natural bully and an instinctive populist. We have not seen a more repressive Home Secretary since the glory days of Sir William Joynson-Hicks in the 1920s".[10] Certainly, Blunkett's background and upbringing instilled in him a clear sense of right and wrong. But as a politician, Blunkett has always been aware of the context of his words and the importance of signals in allowing other policies to take root:

In order to establish a framework in which you are heard and taken seriously, you do have to exaggerate things which establish some signals. We have to establish credentials. If people believe that a Labour government is somehow soft on law and order, soft on criminals, soft on disruption and the destabilisation of communities – that we do not hear the fear, the insecurity and instability of the people who live next door to dysfunctional families, who can't safely walk down the street and are frightened of other things because of that – then they won't hear us on other fronts.

Blunkett's actions have a central thread:

With fear and insecurity in all its guises comes a climate in which the reactionary right flourish. For progressive politics to succeed, people have got to feel not only that they've got a good life but that they've got a safe, secure life, and that the fears that normally worry them are lessened and that they can contribute. That's why I get so upset [with the attacks on what I'm doing from liberals]. They've not read any history here or across Europe. They've no idea that in circumstances of the greatest fear and destabilisation, people turn to the right, not to the progressives.

He was especially taken with a book published in the summer of 2002, *The Shield of Achilles* by Philip Bobbitt, which talks about the remaining role of government being opportunity and security. That is the Blunkett agenda: opportunity at Education and Employment and security at the Home Office.

Blunkett links this to the more general role he sees for the Home Office and for law-and-order policy: "Our job is to create an environment in which regeneration can take place and people can contribute themselves, so they can be persuaded to be active citizens rather than passive citizens. That is the way in which you lift people out of generational poverty. That's the way that you build families that function and give inspiration to young- sters. It's when that's not happening, and there is a vacuum, that the right and authoritarianism prosper."

Such an approach to the job defines the role of Home Secretary far more broadly than ever before. In some ways it parallels the extension of the Chancellorship by Blunkett's great rival, Gordon Brown (and fuels the same resentment felt by Brown over what he saw as Blunkett's creation of an alternative economic and social approach at DfEE). A Cabinet colleague contrasts them with others: "In a not dissimilar way, he and Gordon [Brown] are the two Cabinet ministers who from day one have most engaged with the concept of change. I think Blair's interested in change, but he has just an intellectual interest in it. David and Gordon have a much more visceral interest. It's what brought them into politics. He doesn't want the world to be the same world that he was born to." This, in part, explains Blunkett's attitude to lawyers and judges, described by one adviser as "hatred"! "He thinks that the system is corrupt and wrong and actively works against the interests of normal working-class people – not least in the way liberal judges seem almost to conspire to frustrate him over immigration and asylum".

The Blunkett style and attitude to change is far deeper, how- ever, than the public caricature. His reforms at the Department for Education and Employment have been copied across Whitehall, especially by Alan Milburn at Health and then by Blunkett himself at the Home Office, with the introduction of standards units, performance tables and new forms of accountability. The tools that Blunkett favours are designed to provide an objective test of performance and, as such, to push organisations themselves to change. A civil servant close to Blunkett feels that "he's realised that politicians don't have the answers – he knows now that politicians can't, from the centre, direct change".

Yet there is a contradiction here. Both at Education and the Home Office, he has gathered power to the centre at the expense of local decision-making. This was most starkly illustrated in June 2004 in his response to the Bichard Inquiry into the police's handling of the murder of two young girls in Soham. The report was clear in its condemnation of the Chief Constable of Humberside, David Woodward. On the day of the report's publication, Blunkett called for Woodward's suspension. But Woodward refused to go. Two days later, the Humberside Police Authority refused to make him go. Stalemate. But under legislation that Blunkett had brought in, it was clear that the last word lay with the Home Secretary (although, to avoid a lengthy court battle, Blunkett acquiesced in a fudge which allowed Woodward to remain in post and then take early retirement). The push to reform the police may have been long overdue, but Blunkett's machinery for achieving that reform was situated in the Home Office itself. For all the talk of local decision-making and power drifting from the centre, Blunkett is a centraliser. In this and other cases, he believes that the gentleman in Whitehall really does know best.

There is another form of power which has, he argues, changed for good: "When I entered Parliament [in 1987], government and Whitehall had much greater clout. The European Union was merely an economic market. We didn't have devolution. We didn't have a global economy on anything like the scale we have now. There were major power blocs which simplified the world. People's aspirations weren't as high. Their deference was greater.

And their reliance on government for the day-to-day things was greater than it is now – people couldn't buy their way out if they couldn't get a service." In the same year, he published *Democracy in Crisis*, an apologia for his time as leader of Sheffield and personal manifesto. Today he seems sanguine; then he was angry: "Along with economic power, political control over Britain is being lost to overseas centres of power and regulation such as in the international boardrooms of industry and finance and the EEC. The City of London, as a major financial centre, may be located in Britain, but the interests it serves are not those of the British people."[11] The impact of globalisation feeds into this. In his most recent book, *Policy and Progress*, he writes that it means that "Regions are becoming more important, one reason why Britain needs a proactive, long term approach to Europe".[12]

Blunkett has had little departmental need to involve himself in battles over the direction of Labour's European policy, but he has not strayed too far from his views in *Democracy in Crisis*. In 1990 he made clear his opposition to joining the exchange-rate mechanism of the European Monetary System. The following November – the month before the Maastricht summit – he wrote to *The Times* that he had "long been a sceptic about the enthusiasm for greater economic integration". As Bryan Gould's campaign manager in the 1992 Labour leadership election he stressed, with Gould, the need for devaluation during the sterling crisis in the summer of 1992. At a Shadow Cabinet meeting on 10 September, Blunkett, Cook, Gould and Meacher demanded that Brown, the new Shadow Chancellor, acknowledge the obvious – that sterling was overvalued. But Brown was even more rigid in his refusal to contemplate devaluation than his predecessor, the new leader, Smith: "Our policy", he wrote, "is not one of devaluation, nor is it one of revaluation or realignment." Blunkett responded in November with an attack on the Maastricht "bankers' Europe". And in 1994, before Labour's European conference, he came out with a statement attacking the '*Tafelwein* culture' promoted by Eurofederalists.

(Blunkett might not want the UK to sign up to the euro, but he has found a unique use for the currency. A fellow guest at a dinner party at his friend Les Hinton's house was Rupert Murdoch. At one point in the evening Blunkett ostentatiously drew, very slowly, a euro note out of his breast pocket and waved it gently in front of the euro-sceptical Murdoch.)

As a former adviser to Blunkett in his time as leader of Sheffield council puts it: "In the 1970s and 1980s, 'left' politicians thought the state could do everything – solve everybody's problems and resolve all of society's ills. That was what lay behind much of his policies – the Employment Department, for instance – at Sheffield. I'm sure he doesn't think that for a second any more. Today it's about putting structures in place which allow people to help themselves. He's always talking about the problems that arise when you lead the public to believe that you're going to 'solve' something – removing voters themselves, in other words, from any involvement or responsibility in the outcome."

Blunkett sees this as a general change in politics today: "We have to deal with the fears that exist. We don't control people's emotions, we don't control the media, we don't control the environment; but we have to deal with them. The new politics is about working out how to influence that tide and those influences around us. There are still people who think in old-fashioned terms – 'we can determine the culture and environment in which people will respond'. Well, we can't. We're an influence on it but we can't determine it."

Staff speak often about his intuitive sense of social and economic trends. A civil servant who worked under Blunkett at the Department for Education and Employment remarks that "you always felt he was two or three months ahead of you. It was quite spooky. He'd say something to you in passing and it wouldn't be for two or three months that you realised its import. He was way, way ahead of the game on top-up fees, for example". Given the impact of his handicap – he cannot simply pull an interesting book off the shelves and dip in – it is all the more remarkable that he should be so in tune with current trends in political and societal thinking.

There is some truth in the alternative way of looking at this: Blunkett has rarely moved beyond the confines of the dominant strand of thinking on the Left, albeit with his own preoccupations. In his early years on Sheffield council he was a Bennite. In the mid-1980s, he became a leader of the 'soft left' and on the NEC he was a reluctant Kinnockite. He then became a full-on Blairite. He has been masterful at adapting to the flow of Labour power. If one looks at the policies he pursued at Sheffield, it seems something of a puzzle that he should be so comfortable in a New Labour government. But there is a link, which comes in the word he is most comfortable using when describing his politics: community. An adviser puts it this way: "With David, everything's about responsibility, the solidarity of community and people working together. It's about the dignity of work and not giving people a soft ride. You can't understand David's politics without understanding his commitment to community self-improvement and active citizenship." They stem from his upbringing, as a Methodist on a working-class council estate. His neighbours did not suffer fools gladly. They had jobs of which they were proud, and although they were not well paid they were proud of their status. Many were skilled craftsmen. But they were also caring and supportive to those who needed help, whether the elderly or youngsters. What they would not put up with were scroungers. "The difference between my philosophy and some who have come in from middle-class backgrounds is that they have been very patronising towards working-class people. They've been keen to salve their own consciences – a kind of regret that they didn't have to go through it. There was none of that sentimentality where I was brought up. People who were idle received a great deal of peer pressure to work."

As Blunkett wrote in the *Independent* in 1987, "Although it may be misinterpreted to say so quite so starkly, democratic socialists should be appealing to the very instincts which

Thatcherite Conservatism has attempted to take to its soul. Not the instincts of selfishness and greed, of materialism and self-assertion, but those instincts which are deep-rooted in the communities which made Labour great – beliefs in self-reliance and self-determination; a desire to have the dignity of looking after yourself and not having the state or local government bureaucracy telling you what to do or how to do it."[13] He has continually returned to this theme. In January 1993, for example, he submitted a paper as Shadow Health Secretary to the party's Social Justice Commission arguing that Labour should be "the party of self-reliance . . . We have to take a very hard look at ourselves. The Tories have doubled the number of people on benefits, yet it is the Labour Party that is seen as in favour of mollycoddling people. We have to be tough with ourselves and ask why that has happened. We have to convince people that we are not a tax and spend party".[14] This is part of a more rounded vision of the purpose of economic policy:

If we can create an environment in which people have work to go to and the work pays them, rather than having to pay them benefits, we do everybody a favour. We also create a return to self-reliance, to the dignity which goes with it – which was very evident in the community in which I was brought up. We must try to restore the dignity of work, and people being able to fend for themselves. That way we can start talking about opportunity and democracy because then people can genuinely participate. Patronising paternalism, whether from the state or a charity, doesn't free people by giving them dignity.

Blunkett wants to be remembered for the introduction of citizenship education in schools. The stress on voluntary activity, civil society and community is a powerful strand in his thinking and dates back to his Sheffield days. As he put it at the time in *Democracy in Crisis*: "South Yorkshire's transport policy reflected a different view of human nature [to that of the market]. Social living – from the tribe to the modern city – has always depended on cooperative behaviour."[15]

Blunkett sees tax as being part of that cooperative behaviour. Although he understands the political advantages of New Labour's reluctance to increase the top rate, he is unhappy with the political sleight of hand it involves; since tax has risen, better to argue the case for it than be accused of taxing by stealth. His reluctance to keep quiet about issues on which he feels strongly applies to tax, too. At the party conference in 1989, for instance, when the party was quiescent in its acceptance of the policy review – there was not one amendment tabled to the tax policy review – Blunkett refused to be silenced and objected at a fringe meeting to the proposed 50 per cent upper tax limit, arguing that it was too low – a senior figure in the party essentially saying 'our economic policy's wrong and we should be taxing more'. "It was better to have the debate then than to mess the whole thing up, as we did, by not sorting it out. I didn't believe that going to the electorate saying, 'We will give you more benefits,' which we did, would win a single vote, which it didn't." Blunkett realised after the 1992 election that the issue of 'Labour's Tax Bombshell' was a gold mine for the Conservatives, and would continue to be one. "That's why many of us shut up and decided that we had to find other ways of getting into this, such as through assets accumulation and avoiding poverty and dependence in the first place, rather than ameliorating it through taxes. The party's still to catch up with that – we're still into ameliorating poverty."

By 1993, when it was clear that the usual direct tax battle was over, he was already trying to find a way of shifting the climate. Speaking in Oldham on 3 September, he floated the idea of a hypothecated NHS tax: "We need to win people over to a willingness to pay more. One way of approaching this is to look at earmarking any additional direct taxation, specifically for investment in areas which would command universal public support and would directly increase the wellbeing of the individual and the wider community. This 'hypothecated' tax would be in addition to existing spending and would indicate very clearly to the electorate where additional resources would be directed. Such proposals should aim to win people over, not only to improved services, but investment in economic recovery and increased growth."[16] It was not merely a speech about tax; it was an indirect challenge to the cautious Brownite New Labour vision that Labour's selling point should be 'Trust us – we won't hurt you'.

Tax represents one side of the community equation. The other, for politicians, is re-engaging with civil society. In a Commons debate in 2000, Blunkett spelt out where politicians were failing, and how they could succeed:

In the *Times* this morning, Simon Jenkins accuses me of coming out with too many facts. However, last night I was at Garforth community college, just outside Leeds, where I was accused of not giving enough facts about what the Government are doing. Facts alone do not add up to a political programme; re-engaging with civil society does. It is extremely important that we, as a Parliament and a Government, regard the programme in the Queen's Speech and the run-up to the next Parliament as an opportunity to spell out that we are an enabling Government. We are on the side of men and women in their communities, offering the opportunity, resources and support for them to succeed in getting and keeping jobs, earning a living and building a family, while living comfortably and safely in communities that have a decent environment and the quality of life that we should expect for ourselves, with the safety on the streets that the Government have been endeavouring to restore. In other words, the big picture is of a Government who are on people's side, backing up what they do. Instead of cutting, disinvesting and disengaging from the support that is necessary – the Opposition policy – we are endeavouring to provide investment for the future, to reverse the cuts of the past and to engage with people in their lives where and when it matters. That is doing it with people, rather than doing it to them, and that will enable people to succeed. I understand that the Leader of the Opposition will take part in "Songs of Praise" on Sunday, from Bradford. Last night, the gospel choir at Garforth, who are also taking part in that programme, sang their hearts out about community – about people working and caring together.[17]

Blunkett has always favoured the cooperative socialist approach (in which, the Left of the 1970s and 1980s seemed to forget, lie the Labour Party's own roots) above the dirigiste machinery that post-war Labour thinking promoted. In his 1987 book, he sought to contrast his own views with those of " 'Statist' Labour politicians":

In recent years voluntary organisations without formal political affiliation have played a more significant part in local politics than at any time since 1945. In the post-1945 era, people, having cooperated in the war effort, were ready to join together in building peace. But they were never given a proper active role in building their own welfare state. 'Statist' Labour politicians regarded voluntary organisations, the 'voluntary sector', as a relic of private philanthropy from rich to poor. They forgot the working-class voluntary movement which has provided local support and help to people in difficulty, and brought them together for recreation and celebration, ever since the days of the Goose and Burial Clubs and Friendly Societies in the early nineteenth century. The vitality of working-class traditions of community support was seen again in the 1980s in the Women Against Pit Closures movement and the immense range of support groups which sprang up in the mining areas to feed and organise the pit communities. It is towards this view of the voluntary sector that local politics has turned the local state, so that people's initiative and ideas can be seen to be as legitimate and significant a part of democracy as the act of putting a cross at local and national election times.[18]

These fine-sounding words, however, need to be viewed in the context of Labour politics of the 1980s, which placed the more politically driven organisations at the forefront:

The 'voluntary sector' of the 1940s is barely recognisable today. No longer dominated by traditional councils of social service and local branches of national philanthropic organisations, the community movement has made locally rooted groups more assertive and confident. Often they join hands with more formally established organisations and pressure groups: Age Concern, Child Poverty Action Group, Friends of the Earth. They have also set up new regional or national organisations such as the Federation of Women's Aid and the Federation of Law Centres, and federations of Pensioners' Action Groups. Their significance extends beyond their influence on the single issues with which they may be concerned.[19]

The theory behind Blunkett's politics in the 1980s was returning Labour to its guild socialist roots as a means of reviving the community. Given, however, that the vehicles for that rebirth were local government, trade unions and organisations such as those mentioned above, the idea was doomed from the start, as he came to realise. Blunkett's political journey since then has been based on finding a workable alternative: the same intended outcome but with different machinery (or, to coin a phrase, traditional values in a modern context), as the subtitle of *Politics and Progress* makes clear: 'Renewing democracy and civil society'.

This was of a piece with his shifting views on public ownership. Happy to sign up to the 1983 Bennite manifesto (entitled, with unintentional irony, *New Hope for Britain*), which pledged a mass programme of nationalisation, by 1986 he had shifted to a softer-sounding idea, 'social ownership', which Blunkett promoted in a paper (*Social Ownership*), written with John Smith, which recommended cooperatives and municipal ownership as well as traditional Labour nationalisation. Blunkett had tried to put such ideas into practice in Sheffield, as he outlined in a Fabian pamphlet published in 1983, *Building from the Bottom: The Sheffield Experience*. The very title of the pamphlet was intended to show how different his style was from that of the traditional Labour local council leader. But the meat of it is in four central policy areas. First, Blunkett argues (with his co-author, Geoff Green, then Principal Strategy Officer in the Central Policy Unit at Sheffield council, a title that in itself is redolent of the politics of Sheffield at the time) for the pivotal role of local councils in planning the local economy and generating local employment. To that end, they should draw up industrial plans as a prelude to local authority intervention, conclude local planning agreements, direct local funds into socially useful projects, encourage research on the local structure of industry and devise ways in which industry might meet local social priorities. Council money, they say, should be used to generate employment, and councils' purchasing policies should benefit local firms. Although they recognise that these policies will not create private sector jobs, they say that councils' bargaining power should be leveraged to establish good working practices. And, for good measure, they argue also that socialist local authorities should aim to reform local social relations by establishing alternative forms of organisation which challenge the market economy: for example, the establishment and encouragement of worker cooperatives and by employing their own direct labour force.

Second, they say that this economic planning should be linked with environmental planning so that council land and property are used to promote community initiatives rather than private property speculation.

Third, they argue that councils should challenge what they describe as welfarism and centralist parliamentary benevolence, which have always been the foundation of Labour policy. Welfarism is, they say, redistributive socialism in which Labour governments have attempted to compensate for inequalities through the welfare state. But a socialist welfare policy should be concerned to prevent these inequalities by public control of production, distribution and exchange (Clause IV of the old Labour Party constitution). They argue that centralist parliamentary benevolence has meant that services have been provided in the past *for* people and not *with* people. Service delivery is most important, and they believe that decentralisation is one way to improve both political direction and accountability. The deprived (for example, inner-city residents) should also be involved in shaping their own lives; that requires positive discrimination in the delivery of services in favour of the deprived because universal provision benefits the privileged.

Finally, they propose a new socialist approach to bureaucracy. Rather than the traditional distinction between the committed, amateur politician and the neutral, specialist administrator, they argue that those who work for local authorities must have a commitment to the community; specifically, to the objectives as set out by the Labour-controlled local authority.

Speaking in the Commons in 1993, Blunkett outlined the broad thrust of his views:

Conservative Members have undermined the Beveridge principle that people who pay in should have a right to benefits – not a benevolence, something handed down by others or something passed across because they happen to be in distress. They have undermined the key principle of full employment and the ability of those who have a job to contribute back into the Exchequer as well as look after themselves and their families. They have undermined individuals' responsibility for themselves and their families to earn a living through hard, re-warding work in order to contribute to themselves and their loved ones, but also to put back into the community, through contributing to tax and national insurance, money that can then sustain decent public services. The crunch of the ideological difference between us is that Conservative Members . . . believe that public expenditure is bad and undermines the fabric and backbone of society. They believe that a free-for-all, free-market economy in which people 'do it your-self' in terms of gaining benefits and buying insurance is the direction in which this country should go. That mirrors in part the United States' experience, with insecure work, insecure prospects and a lack of stake in a community that values itself – a society in which people are threatened and their stability is undermined to ensure that they are willing to take lower and lower wages to manage to survive on the breadline. If that is the sort of society we want, we shall continue with the policies that were enunciated yesterday. But if we want to build a society that believes in itself and can use its intelligence, rational thinking and experience of history to build up public services, the community and a sense of belonging so that people value those around them and understand their interdependence with others, we shall turn instead to the policies enunciated by the leader of the Labour party and the shadow Chancellor today.[20]

Shortly after taking office in 1997, Blunkett had a correspondence with his long-time sparring partner, Roy Hattersley, in the letters pages of the *Guardian*. Hattersley, who had asserted in his credo, *Choose Freedom*, that: "The equality we seek is equality of outcome",[21] argued that "it is hard to describe New Labour as a democratic socialist party". He attacked Blunkett as exemplifying the worst of the new government's ideological heresies, specifically for saying in February 1997 that: "The truth is that any government entering the 21st century cannot hope to create a more equal or egalitarian society simply by taking from one set of people and redistributing it to others, as envisaged when the rich were very rich and the poor made up the rest." Blair and his acolytes had abandoned the belief that "the good society is the equal society . . . That ideological apostasy has freed egalitarians from the obligation to support all it does. Loyalty to the idea . . . not only justifies dissent. It demands it."[22] Blunkett replied with a letter: "You can give the poor some money for a period of time but they still remain poor." Instead, they should be helped to escape from poverty through, for example, education and training. The vulnerable, meanwhile, would still need support of the old kind.[23]

Superficially, the close relationship and shared political beliefs between Blunkett and Blair seem distinctly odd. Their backgrounds could not have been more different, both as children and politically. And yet, as Blunkett observes, there is a strange similarity: "Maybe my working-class community and Tony's public school had something in common because they both reinforced having to live with people; having to understand other people. Both afforded a sense of fellowship and mutuality."

One of the criticisms levelled at Blunkett is that he has an unrealistic view of the community and some people's ability to contribute: he has been so successful at overcoming his handicap that he cannot empathise properly with those who are not similarly driven or able to rise above their disabilities. He is aware of this himself:

When I have people who are disabled in my surgery, I have to get a real grip of myself. People come in and they say, 'You see, Mr Blunkett, I'm disabled,' and I say, 'Oh, I'm very sorry about that, sit down.' And they'll say they can't work because they've got ulcerous colitis, or irritation of the bowel: 'It's really bad and it causes me stress, you know, I can't take a stressful job.' Or they might say, 'You'll understand because you can't see.' And I think, 'Hang on a minute, I've got all of those.' But you can't say that. You would devastate somebody if you said, 'I don't know what the bloody hell you're talking about, I've got high blood pressure, I have had it for ten years, I've got ulcerous colitis and I can't see, so sod off.' So you have to see instead if you can get them on to the same positive trajectory of welfare to work, or taking a part-time job. An MP brought a letter to me about a woman who said she was being expected, as part of learning to live after the loss of her sight, to be able to boil a kettle and pour it into the pot, and she couldn't do it. Instead of saying, 'Don't be stupid,' I actually said, 'Well, what she probably needs to do is get a jug kettle, which is much more handleable than a spout.' And so yes, sometimes I have to take a step back; it's not going to be helpful to somebody just to rub their noses in it.

In an interview in the *Observer* he remarked that "I plead guilty, certainly in my earlier days, to not fully understanding how some inadequacies – some difficulties in life – make it more of an obstacle than it was for me, for some people to go out and fight for what they wanted. I was tempted to say, 'Look here, it's in your own hands. Do something about it.' When I went into schools, I used to say, 'If I can do it, you can have a crack at it.' I do have to restrain that element in me."[24]

3

"A strong, well-built boy"

David Blunkett was born on 6 June 1947 to Doris Matilda Elizabeth Williams, then aged forty-four, and Arthur Blunkett, aged fifty-five. It was both his parents' second marriage – Arthur was a widower and Doris a divorcée. Doris Williams's family moved to Sheffield from Leicester in 1903, when she was a baby. Because of a heart condition, she had had to leave school at thirteen and, although mentally strong, she was always physically frail. In her early twenties, she married and had a daughter, Doreen; she divorced soon after. Doris and Doreen then lived together, along with Doris's father (John Henry, 'Grandad Williams'), Doris supporting them both with various factory jobs. At the time she met Arthur, she was working for Stanley Tools, which had switched to producing tracer shells during the war. Her job was skilled, fine-spraying the tracer bullets; if it was over-done they stuck, and if it wasn't done sufficiently the bullets would not fire.

Arthur had been born in Egham, Surrey, in 1892. His father was a farmhand and young Arthur – together with his five siblings – soon moved to the Lincolnshire village of Wainfleet All Saints. As a young man, Arthur was something of a drifter, first running away to sea on a fishing smack out of Grimsby, then becoming a waiter before ending up in Sheffield during the First World War. He was a tall man – "straight as a die", as Blunkett puts it. And unlike Doris, he was extremely fit for a man in his fifties. Arthur was more than just physically upright; he believed in the importance of work and 'decent' behaviour. Other than a spell off with pneumonia, he missed not a day's work throughout his time with the East Midlands Gas Board. Although his family life was to change dramatically – he had seven children with his first wife, but living in the Sheffield slums meant that only four survived childhood – he spent the rest of his life working for the board.

Arthur and Doris met at the end of the war, introduced by a work friend of Doris's who thought it a good idea that after years on her own, she should make a new friend and settle down. Arthur and Doris married in April 1946 and moved into a two-bedroom council house in Everingham Road, in the Longley district of Sheffield, along with Doreen and the then seventy-six-year-old Grandad Williams.

Arthur and Doris were well suited, both instinctively believing in the value and importance of making the most of life and getting on with it.

Despite having worked in factories, my mother believed in behaving in a ladylike manner. She was not a snob – far from it. She simply felt that everyone should try to 'put their best foot forward' and make the most of themselves. She was therefore always tidily turned out, though never fashionably dressed because she did not have the means. Friends said she had been pretty in her younger days and, despite considerable hardship and illness, she remained good-looking in her later years. She was fairly short and a little on the plump side – cuddly, I thought – which was the norm then given the nature of the food and lifestyle.[1]

She was also a tenacious woman; when set a challenge, she would always meet it head on – a trait (which David inherited) which she was to demonstrate to the full as her son reached his teenage years. One contemporary describes her as "wittery – she would obsess over some things and gnaw away at them". (Blunkett recognises that he has inherited the same characteristic: "I sometimes get involved in detail when it is better not to. Sometimes it's the detail that irritates me more than the big things, politically and personally.")

Their only child, David, was born the year after they were married. Doris was in her mid-forties and they had not intended to have a child. In 1947 it was risky in the extreme to give birth at such an age, and the difficulty of the birth was compounded by Doris suffering a prolapsed uterus. Her recovery was not helped by the devastating news that she was told soon after the birth: as a result of a genetic mismatch between Doris and Arthur, their baby was blind. The optic nerves behind David's eyes had not developed properly and would not do so. The shock of the news had an immediate physical impact: Doris's hair was said to have turned white overnight. It took a lot of convincing to persuade her that her age was not a factor in David's blindness.

There was, initially, hope that David might have some – albeit very limited – sight, and he was prescribed glasses. Blunkett recalls being able to discern a large headline in an edition of the *Hotspur* comic and being able to make out some large shapes. But this did not last; the failure of his optic nerves to develop had a knock-on effect on other parts associated with the optic nerves, which were unused and thus withered away. The network of nerves behind the eye is renowned as the most delicate in the body: even with the advances in surgical techniques today, there is little that can be done for such a condition. His sight was soon reduced to the state in which it has remained: recognition of strongly contrasted light and dark, but nothing more.

Despite their living in an extremely cramped house without much money, Blunkett's early home life was happy. Doris spent a lot of time reading to him, mainly children's stories such as those of Enid Blyton and – these obviously had a great impact – extracts from the newspapers. "My mother taught me the importance of being able to read well; she had left school at 13 because of a heart complaint, but she taught herself and she read very widely, and she instilled in me the beauty and elegance of good writing."[2]

His mother and father's determination to push the young boy to stretch himself and to make the most of his life provided the foundation for his adult political beliefs, especially as Education Secretary, when he would bemoan the failure of many parents to do the same for their own children.

Arthur did not read much but he would spend hours playing with David, who would shoot at him with a rubber bow and arrow or a ping-pong-ball machine gun. He was a self-contained man. He rarely drank and did not enjoy pubs or clubs. His main pleasure was pipe tobacco or 'smokes', as he called it. He had one trait that embarrassed both David and Doris: whenever he met someone he took to be well educated, he would mask his Yorkshire accent. Blunkett's voice today, unlike his father's, is always proudly from South Yorkshire, the flat vowels the same in his constituency and the House of Commons.

Arthur had a mind full of general knowledge which he liked to pass on to his son and which opened David to the horizons beyond his immediate experiences. He would quiz the young boy on capitals of the world, geography and whatever popped into his head. "He had a breadth of knowledge and an understanding of current affairs which was phenomenal. He taught me the value of knowing things and not just learning them by rote."[3] This, too, informed the future Education Secretary's views: he has long expressed his belief in traditional rather than progressive education – not just the three Rs but a proper grounding in facts.

The third member of the household was Grandad Williams (David's half-sister, Doreen, had married soon after David's birth and moved out). He was a very traditional man: he did not believe in public displays of emotion or affection, held that parents should not over-indulge their children and that discipline and an ordered life were essential. He disliked modern inventions such as the television. Even the radio was something to be avoided. But he was a kind man and cared deeply for his family (he had supported Doris during the collapse of her first marriage, when other family and friends had condemned her) and took to David, spending much of his time reading to him from the *Daily Herald*, which David enjoyed and which, coupled with Arthur's general knowledge, instilled a keen interest in current affairs and events in the young boy. But Doris was forced to spend an increasing amount of time caring for Grandad. The burden seemed to fall unfairly on her; her siblings Eric and Joe, both of whom lived in Sheffield and were skilled craftsmen in machine-tool engineering works with regular healthy incomes, thought it women's work (their sister Mary suffered from mental health problems and was in no position to help).

Arthur's side of the family was full of characters. His father, Sanders Blunkett, had died before David's birth, at the age of sixty-seven, but his mother, 'Grandma Blunkett', was still around, an intimidating figure even though she was a frail woman in her eighties when David was a young boy. Rather like Miss Havisham, she spent her life in bed at her home in Wainfleet, five miles from Skegness. The family (minus Granddad, who did not like variety or change and so would remain at home) would have an annual holiday paying a visit to Grandma, for which Arthur would save all year round. Using Skegness as a base, they would take the bus to visit their many relations.

If this sounds like a normal childhood, it was. But there were two further components which transformed the normality into something altogether different and traumatic: school and Arthur's death.

When David was four, his parents were told that, in the absence of any appropriate local schools, he would have to be sent to board at Manchester Road School for the Blind (now called Tapton Mount), on the other side of Sheffield. They would be allowed to visit him on the school premises once a month, and he was to be allowed home for one weekend a month Arthur and Doris protested: it was inhuman, cruel and beyond their imagining that a four-year-old should be torn from his family like this, let alone a blind four-year-old. But the council were adamant: David must be sent to Manchester Road.

The story of his departure is heart-rending:

As if it were yesterday I remember passing the cathedral with my parents as we made our way through Sheffield city centre. The warmth of the late afternoon sun that Sunday in September was beginning to fade. The cathedral bell was tolling for the evening service. Everything felt as though it were happening in slow motion, such was the tension as we bustled along hand in hand, Dad on my right, Mum on my left, to find the bus to Manchester Road. We alighted at a strange place, somewhere I had never been before, and walked up a driveway with the scent of newly mown grass in the air. I shivered as we entered the coolness of what then seemed to me an enormous building. A peck on the cheek, 'Goodbye, son', and then they were gone. All I had ever known before was my home and garden, and a bit of the immediate neighbourhood. Now, for the first time, I was alone in alien surroundings, cast adrift, abandoned. The anguish I felt was heart-wrenching as I stood bewildered, fighting back the tears, in the assembly hall of Manchester Road School for the Blind. It was a boarding school. I was four years old.[4]

The regime was brutal. Parents were not allowed to remain even for an hour to help their children settle in, let alone take them to their dormitory: they were to leave immediately on depositing their child in the assembly hall. Not surprisingly, Blunkett recalls it as one of the worst experiences of his life. His parents were distraught, and – against the rules – remained in the grounds in the vain hope that they might catch a glimpse of their son. They did not. David was on his own.

The four-year-old David was given a uniform and marched to his dormitory, where there were nine other boys. It was a harsh – the word barely begins to describe it – introduction to school life. The boys were given no help; getting dressed, washing and finding their way around the school were all tasks that they had to manage for themselves. For the first few weeks, even months, there was a constant wailing sound at night. Some cried constantly, others wet their beds and then had no idea how to have the end product dealt with. They were helpless; physically, emotionally and intellectually.

There was one small alleviation to this otherwise all-enveloping misery: the 'house mothers', one in charge of each dormitory, whose job was to supervise the basic tasks such as washing. Even this was grim. The communal baths were in a basement which could be reached only via long, twisting, damp corridors. The house mothers were themselves still barely out of childhood – they were sixteen or seventeen years old – but they did provide a modicum of human warmth in an otherwise desolate existence: "How precious were the swift hug and goodnight kiss bestowed nightly on us as she tucked us up in bed – one of the few signs of affection we received at school. I desperately missed the hugging and affection of home, as did most of my companions, and there was no real substitute. Even the pets we were allowed to have later on could not fill the gap. This deprivation had a lasting effect on me well into adult life."[5]

The contrast between home, where David was loved and given all the affection he could want, and school, could not have been starker. Allied to this was the absence of any privacy. As a young boy, right through to when he left Manchester Road at the age of sixteen, Blunkett was never alone, always in the presence of other boys. He felt both alone and suffocated by the others. Although he eventually got used to boarding-school life, this feeling of never having privacy remained with him throughout his school years: "There was no quiet, private place to be alone or where one's belongings went unrifled. Privacy is therefore something I came to value greatly."[6]

As with any such experience, routine began to dull the impact, and as David grew used to it he developed methods of coping. After he had learned Braille, for instance, he would read late at night under the bed sheets. And the sports afternoons were a particular pleasure: as an only child he took full advantage of the new camaraderie to which playing in a team introduced him. The footballs contained ball bearings and the cricket balls bells. The blind versions were far more dangerous than the sighted; Blunkett's preferred sport, cricket, was particularly interesting. If a fielder got too close to a batsman he could be clubbed as the batsman played his shot, or hit in the face by the ball.

As the boys got to know each other and gained in confidence, they became ever more daring and adventurous in their activities. Blunkett had three favourite physical hobbies: riding his bike, go-karting and sledging. The problems with learning to ride were not merely about balance but also avoiding a crash every time he hit a bump and learning how to take a corner at speed. The go-karts were perhaps less immediately dangerous but more of a challenge. They were made from two flat planks with a pram wheel at either end. A cross-bar was attached with a length of string. In winter, the slope in the school grounds proved an irresistible allure. Dangerous barely begins to describe the antics of two blind sledgers. The young Blunkett suffered broken fingers and collar bones, all in the name of behaving like any other young boy. He has a large scar on his left knee to this day.

While school life may have been traumatic for the young Blunkett, at home things were good. The council had agreed to a transfer request from his parents and so when Blunkett was five the family moved into a house that had been built in the 1930s in Pollard Crescent on the Parson Cross estate, on the industrialised northern side of Sheffield. It was far more spacious than anything he had previously experienced. The bedrooms were tiny but there were three of them. Much as they wanted to let David have his own room, his parents could not afford the furniture required and so he continued to share with his mother and father; the third room remained empty. After a few months of this arrangement, they realised that David really did need space, and so they took out a hire-purchase agreement to buy a bed, a wardrobe and a locker, which meant David now had a room to himself – a huge and welcome contrast to the school dormitory.

Even more of a contrast were the picnics in Derbyshire which Doris, Arthur and David would take when he was home from school. Arthur and David would walk together, constantly chatting, Arthur describing the scenery and quizzing his son on general knowledge. Having been brought up in the countryside, he loved to escape there whenever possible. It was a love he passed on to David.

Nearer to home, the two would walk across the estate towards Ecclesfield and the Jewish cemetery to the north; they would also wander around Ward's Cemetery beside the railway line close to Hillsborough stadium, where David was sometimes taken for matches and where his passion for football – and Sheffield Wednesday – developed. They would sit on the wall behind the goal and David would be exhilarated by the noise of the crowd.

Much of their time together was spent gardening. Arthur had turned a small area of disused scrubland at the back of the house into an allotment and the two of them would spend hours working on it, Arthur teaching David the difference between plants and weeds and how to nurture the edible plants. After a hard afternoon's work, David would flop into bed and sleep for hours. His favourite treat was his mother's pickles, made from the vegetables in the allotment. When she came to cook carrots, she would joke with David that he would be able to see in the dark.

Doris insisted that David do his share of the chores, such as the washing up and drying, making sure that her son knew that he was the equal of any boy and as such as bound to do the less pleasant tasks as the next.

The move to a bigger house meant that David was allowed pets: at various times rabbits, white mice, a tortoise, a budgerigar and goldfish. His favourite mouse was Peterkin, who was housed in a cage built by his father and kept in the kitchen. Bimbo the budgerigar was an equally popular pet.

Despite the name, the budgie was not a young temptress but a male named after a popular ditty of the day, the refrain of which was 'Bimbo, Bimbo, why are you on your owneo?' Nevertheless, he was not the most macho of birds and was easily driven to hysteria by my grandfather. Whenever Bimbo was let out of his cage and was foolish enough to land on Grandad's shoulder or his chair, Grandad would shoo him away by vigorously waving his beret under the bird's beak. With a high-pitched squawk Bimbo would flap off in a panic. One day, whether by accident or design we never knew, he dived into the rectangular goldfish tank. Evidently he discovered he liked it because thereafter, whenever he was let out, Bimbo would fly straight for the tank, jump in at one end, flap his way through the water to the other end and then leap out like a miniature seaplane. Behind him he left a trail of bewildered goldfish gazing upwards through the rippling surface at Bimbo's fast-disappearing tail feathers, wondering what on earth had hit them. In the meantime, Bimbo, looking mightily chuffed, would perch somewhere to preen himself, all the while muttering defiantly, 'Bimbo, Bimbo'.[7]

At the age of ten, boys were allowed to keep a pet at school, and David brought a rabbit from home. An early manifestation of his later belief in community politics emerged in connection with the school rabbit. In theory, the boys were meant to take it in turns to look after the school pet. Blunkett felt sorry for the rabbit, which received almost no attention. He started to look after it; over time, he came to be seen as responsible for it, a metaphor perhaps for the political dangers of welfare dependency.

School lessons were difficult. The Braille writing frames, by means of which David was taught to write, were awkward and slow. Using wooden styluses, the boys not only had to learn to prick dots through special paper but to do so in reverse – in mirror image, so that when the paper was turned over the words would read from left to right. This process was aided by a large wooden frame which moved down a line at a time. Learning different methods of brailling was an ongoing task. When he was a few years older, he was taught to use the much faster Stainsby writing machine, which had six keys (which operated the stylus), plus a space bar. And then, when he was thirteen, he learned how to use an American machine – the Perkins Brailler, which could write from left to right and could be read at the same time.

Maths involved an indented wooden board, with metallic pegs of different shapes (representing different numbers) slotted into holes. The machine was fiddly and so Blunkett – along with most of his classmates – preferred mental arithmetic, a rigorous but, given the circumstances, in many ways easier discipline. The timetable also included geography, history, nature and wood-work. The latter left him with a permanent reminder. Wilf King, the woodwork teacher, had shown him a piece of wood with a nail in it. Blunkett felt it. King then told him he would show him how to hit a nail in it. Blunkett did as asked. But, taking the teacher literally, he did not remove his finger and so, instead of hitting the nail, King hit Blunkett's finger. It is still bent.

When David reached the age of twelve, in the autumn of 1959, it was time to move to secondary school, and a much bigger switch away from Sheffield to the Royal Normal College at Row-ton Castle in Shropshire. There was only one grammar school for blind boys in the country (Worcester College). But the head-master of Manchester Road, Mr Tooze, judged that David was 'unsuitable' even to be entered for the eleven-plus equivalent which determined entry to Worcester College. As he put it in his final report:

David's Intelligence Quotient was assessed at 104 on 9 December 1959 using the Williams' Test. The psychologist said he was a boy of undoubted average intelligence with a vocabulary associated with a higher intelligence quotient. David is a very co-operative, conscientious, hard-working boy. He takes a very serious attitude towards work which is shared by his parents. His standard of attainment is good for this school, and I am quite certain he is the right type of boy to succeed where hard work and application are required. His desire to make the best of himself is rather remarkable. He is certainly worth a trial at the Royal Normal College. He is a strong, well-built boy, well adjusted to his blindness, mobile and active.

No consideration, no appeal: just the arbitrary judgement that it was far more suitable for him to attend the less intellectually demanding boarding school at Rowton. Blunkett's later hostile attitude to selection was hardly surprising.

David thus prepared for the journey to Shropshire, dreading the distance from his friends and family and once again being thrust, as years before when he was first taken to Manchester Road, into an alien environment, all alone. Before he could leave for the new school, however, his life – and that of Doris – was plunged into a despair that made even his early days at school seem like nothing by comparison.

Arthur had, for forty-seven years, been a trusted and respected employee of the East Midlands Gas Board, reaching the position of foreman, operating the water gas plant which transformed coal into gas-created coke. In 1957 he reached retirement age, sixty-five. But because of his reliability and record, he was asked to stay on for a further three years to train new employees. Much as he wanted to stop the relentless grind of work and devote more time to his son (and to Doris), he knew that the family still needed all the money he could earn: David's needs would grow ever greater as he became a teenager and Grandad Williams was growing more frail: and he did, after all, enjoy his work. He accepted the offer.

In December 1959, two years after what should have been retirement, Arthur fell into a giant vat of boiling water. A fellow worker had not repaired a safety device. As he plunged into the vat, he managed to hold on to the rim with one hand and avoided drowning but he was horrifically burned. Although he made it to Sheffield Royal Infirmary, he died a month later on 7 January 1960. The remaining days as he clung on to life were traumatic in the extreme for David and Doris. They spent as much time as possible with him and to this day Blunkett recalls the exact time of his death – 3.34 p.m. – and the smell of burning flesh which pervaded the room. "It was a dreadful, agonizing end. At the time I felt tremendous hurt, anger and bewilderment at his unnecessary and painful death; in later years such feelings led to my involvement in the fight to improve regulations concerning health and safety in the workplace. But that January we were left totally bereft in more ways than one."[8]

As if the emotional trauma were not enough, the behaviour of the gas board took Doris's despair to a new low over the next two years. The board's position was that since Arthur was past retirement age, compensation was inappropriate; compensation is meant to replace income lost during a working life and Arthur Blunkett's working life was over. Worse, he had fallen behind with his union payments and the union (one of the small unions that later amalgamated into the General, Municipal, and Boiler-makers Union) initially refused to provide legal help for Doris. Eventually, after a mass protest by his fellow members, they backed down and accepted back payment of his dues from his former colleagues. The family had been poor enough even with Arthur's income. Without it, they were reduced to penury. A headstone, for example, was beyond Doris's means and so Arthur was buried in an unmarked grave in Burngreave Cemetery (when David started to earn money himself, the first thing he did was to erect a headstone). As Blunkett puts it:

Those who have never experienced real poverty are all too often very sentimental about it and about poor people in general. I have to smile at this and think: if only you knew what it was like, you would know all about aspirations and expectations, and why it was that, in the community in which I grew up, escaping the poverty trap and achieving success were the key aims. That is why I am so keen to give people ladders out of poverty: to give them a hand up rather than a hand-out. My mother, at one stage, only had bread and dripping in the house for us to eat. There is nothing even faintly romantic about being poor and hungry.[9]

When the case finally came to court two years later, both Doris and David were awarded a small amount, £1,500. The court decided that the money for David should be held in trust, rather than allowing Doris to use it to alleviate their immediate poverty, which somewhat defeated the purpose. Blunkett's attitude to the judiciary and the legal system was set in stone as a result of his mother's treatment at their hands.

David had always been close to his mother but inevitably the death of his father made him feel even closer to his surviving parent, not least because Doris refused to allow the pair to go under. She had always pushed David to succeed and to rise above his blindness – she taught him that there was nothing he could not achieve – and the trauma of Arthur's death only reinforced that determination. Blunkett himself was driven even further: he refused to fail, knowing how deeply upset she would be. He simply wanted her to be proud of him.

The switch to Rowton Castle would have been depressing and difficult at the best of times. Coming days after his father's funeral, it was almost unimaginably awful. David arrived three weeks into the spring term and was immediately aware that everyone else seemed already to have made friends and formed into groups. He felt lonely, miserable and as if his life consisted of a series of blows. He also felt self-conscious, since his mother could not afford new clothes for him, or long trousers. In his shorts, he was mocked by the other children. The experience may have been traumatic but it clearly toughened him. He soon learned to look after himself after a few slaps from the other boys.

Rowton Castle lay in 15 acres of grounds 7 miles west of Shrewsbury on the Welshpool road. The school building was originally Queen Anne, built between 1696 and 1704, and had been transformed into a neo-Gothic castle at the beginning of the nineteenth century. The school was part of what was known as the Royal Normal College for the Blind, later restyled the Royal National College because its odd name was misleading. The word 'normal' was derived from the French *école normale* to contrast it with the further education branch of the college at Albrighton, which was at one point largely a training centre for music teachers. As a consequence of this musical tradition, there were regular concerts by musicians of the calibre of Julian Bream and music lessons for the pupils. David was not gifted but could play a passable tune on the piano, the accordion and his favourite, the melodica (a wind instrument with a keyboard similar to that of an accordion). The castle, called the School Department, was for twelve- to sixteen-year-olds; further education was provided at Albrighton Hall, known as the Training Department, north of Shrewsbury (to which Blunkett later went). The dormitories next door were a series of modern red-brick buildings for boys and girls.

At the front of the castle was one of the largest (and thus oldest) cedars of Lebanon in Europe, over 18 feet high when David was at school; at the end of the driveway was another tree, known as 'Jacob's Ladder'. They presented an irresistible allure to the boys. But there are two problems that blind tree climbers face. First, although it is relatively easy to find a branch to cling on to above your head, the chances are that when you pull yourself up you will clobber yourself with one you did not notice. Second, you have to remember how you got up so that you can get down again. Step on a branch whose strength you have not already tested and you may well crash to the ground. Young David experienced this many times.

But tree climbing was the least of it – the teenage David would join his classmates in nocturnal expeditions over gates and hedges into the school grounds. One night he lowered himself slowly from the wall, ending up in a butt full of water. On another occasion – a jousting match that involved rolled-up braille magazines and standing on unstable wooden chairs – he lost most of one of his front teeth when he fell off a chair.

David's rowdy behaviour was hardly surprising given the traumas he had experienced. And his reports at the time were, consequently, hardly models: 'On occasions he can be a paragon

of virtue. At other times, he is rude, noisy and downright dis-
obedient'; 'Apt to grumble'; 'Uses his energy in talking rather
than in activity'; 'Shows off to gain attention'; and 'Makes too
much noise'. Doris knew well why David was finding it difficult
to settle, as she wrote to the deputy head on 24 January 1960:

Dear Miss Chapman

Thank you for your letter. I am pleased to know my son David
seems to be settling down to his new life and surroundings. I
expect it will take him a little while longer, having recently lost
his father, for whom we both had a strong affection . . . Pardon
my sending the doctor's note. In the year 1956 we had to seek
the advice of an ear specialist. After which David had an operation for sinus trouble, the specialist then advised no swimming
for the next two years. This time elapsed in August 1959. We
allowed David to swim in the sea and I am pleased to say no
ear trouble.

Throughout this period, Doris had been suffering from breast
cancer, which was diagnosed in 1956 – and was then far more
likely to be a killer than it is today. She had not been a well
woman for a long time, having earlier had an operation to remove her gall bladder. Unsurprisingly, the burden of caring for
her father eventually proved too much and Grandad Williams
was admitted, at the age of ninety-two, to the geriatric ward of
the Northern General Hospital. David spent much of his holidays
with his mother, visiting his ailing relative.

It was a heart-breaking experience. Though clean, the ward was large,
gloomy and depressing, dominated at one end by a huge television –
another irony, given Grandad's dislike of such appliances. All the old
people sat around or were propped up in bed, some trying to con-
verse with each other, some dozing, others going gradually senile.
The staffing levels were poor and many had no training. Without
wishing to disparage the kindness of those involved, the staff saw
their task literally as feeding and putting to bed old people who in a

sense had started to become children again. For my mother it was particularly sad because she had given so much of her later life to caring for Grandad, keeping him alert and comfy. In the end he died after falling down some steps in the ward. I swore then that if ever the chance arose to do something to lift people out of such conditions I would seize the opportunity with both hands.[9]

Geriatric care later became one of his obsessions on Sheffield City Council.

Grandad Williams died after three years in care. It is clear that the series of tragic events that marked his childhood was critical in forming the rage against injustice that drove the young adult Blunkett into politics. The adolescent David was a thorn in the side of the school authorities, always complaining when he believed he – and the other pupils – were being denied their rights, and never settling for shoddy treatment.

For all that he had been through, he did nonetheless have a lighter side; his ear was jammed next to the wireless whenever possible, among his favourites being sports reports, plays, the Paul Temple detective stories, *Life with the Lyons*, *The Clitheroe Kid*, *Hancock's Half Hour*, *The Navy Lark*, and *Beyond Our Ken* and *Round the Horne*. He also became an *Archers* addict:

It all started when I was about four. I think it was the music – that is the old music – rather than the country dialogue that caught my fancy. Every night of the week, on what was then the Home Service of the BBC, Mum and I would do a little jig in the confined space of our front room to the signature tune, 'Dum di dum di dum di dum, dum di dum di dum dum . . .' Mum laughed and I laughed too. I was hooked. Throughout my schooldays I would tune in each evening or catch the Sunday omnibus edition . . . I still listen, but not as avidly, and not every Sunday addictively as I did in the past.[10]

His real obsession, however, was an extension of his grandfather's reading to him of extracts from the newspapers: listening to the news. He was fired with enthusiasm by the energetic young

Leader of the Opposition, Harold Wilson, whose speeches he would listen to, transfixed with hope that the unfairness of life could be changed for the better.

What I heard on the radio and my reading of history encouraged me to become a fully paid-up member of the Labour Party. At sixteen I was not by any means a revolutionary and I was not at that time on the Left of British politics, although all my close family had always been Labour voters. But I wanted to change the world; instinctively I wished to see things improve. All too clearly I recognized what conditions were like where I was brought up, the tragedy of Dad's death, my mother's struggle to survive, how shabbily she was treated by the Gas Board, and the way my grandfather had ended his days. The lives of our neighbours were not much different. All this combined to make me very angry. Although at that stage I did not have an intellectual focus in terms of values and principles, I had already learned sufficient history to appreciate that through the ages there has been a constant struggle not only between right and wrong but also between those with power and wealth and those who have neither.[11]

4

The fight to be educated

1963 was an eventful year for Blunkett. Quite apart from turning sixteen, his grandfather died, he joined the Labour Party and he left Rowton for Albrighton Hall in Shropshire, the further education arm of the Royal Normal College.

Albrighton was as isolating an experience as Rowton Castle, both emotionally and physically. Buses to Shrewsbury were rare and the journey would have been a major expedition for ordinary boys of that age, let alone the blind. The regime was reminiscent of the worst kind of public school, devoid of intellectual or social nourishment, and seemed to be modelled on Dotheboys Hall in *Nicholas Nickleby* (although, unseen by the boys, it was in fact a splendid building that dated back to 1632 and is today an upmarket hotel). Blunkett enjoyed reading, football, table tennis and cricket, all of which were mainstays of school days, and the school grounds, with their birdsong and natural life, were a pleasant environment in which to walk. But all of this was over-whelmed by the feeling of imprisonment. The school timetable, with lessons on Saturday mornings, meant that there was no real time available for home visits. Blunkett did his best to overcome others' torpor, organising a sports and social club with outings to sports fixtures against other blind schools (and Shrewsbury, the public school). But the impact was marginal. It would be hard to conjure up a more bleak, isolated and depressing existence had it not been for Blunkett's earlier experience at Rowton.

Like Nicholas Nickleby, David refused to sit back and accept this state of affairs. The food the boys were given was, when it was not inedible, repetitive; after one week in which they were fed sausages four times, he led a delegation to protest to the principal, Dr Langdon. Tony Randall, one of his closest school friends, recalls Blunkett as forever arguing for what he believed to be right and protesting at what he considered wrong, such as "the endless Spam and mashed potato we received for our main meal of the day" and the refusal to supply more than one clean shirt a week – a protest that eventually paid off when the number was increased to two a week. Blunkett recalls an incident when he made a stand merely for the sake of it:

A new physical education teacher joined the staff of the College after leaving the Army. One Sunday evening a group of us seventeen- and eighteen-year-olds were relaxing in the lounge. In walked the PE teacher and ordered us off to bed forthwith, accusing us of being too rowdy. As it was only 9 p.m., we were naturally affronted at being treated like children so, when he left, we decided to get out some hymn books and render a few old favourites at the top of our voices. What could be more saintly on a Sunday evening? Of course, the PE teacher returned and ordered us to stop. When we refused, he stormed off to find the Principal and returned with him a few minutes later, demanding that strong action be taken. As a result, three students were actually suspended from the College and several of us were severely punished by being gated for an entire term, with the threat of suspension or expulsion if we misbehaved in the interim. All this because of what we considered to be a minor incident. Resentment simmered for months.[1]

Blunkett's maturity at an age when most of his contemporaries considered school something to avoid if at all possible is remarkable. The college principal was a caricature of the progressive educationist, believing that exams were not merely unnecessary but positively harmful, narrowing intellectual development. He therefore forbade pupils from studying for them. Blunkett, however, was already the Education Secretary manqué, realising that such an attitude could only condemn children – including him – to a life of frustrated achievement and limited horizons. As he puts it: "Such an attitude angers me to this day because he had a PhD. I wonder how he thought he could have become head of a college without qualifications."[2] Still more remarkable is the fact that he realised this for himself. For all his mother's determination that Blunkett should succeed in life, neither she nor anyone among his family and friends knew anyone who had gone to university. The idea of doing so was entirely David's.

Langdon's anti-exam regime was compounded by the poor academic grounding at Rowton and David felt that he was constantly playing catch-up. He was not, however, backward in coming forward and confronted Langdon with his worries, to be told merely that the principal did not 'believe' in exams. QED. But David was not one to take authority, and the limits it ordered, as read. With five other pupils who felt similarly certain of the need to sit exams, Blunkett went below Langdon's head and persuaded both his teachers and the local technical college in Shrewsbury, over 3 miles away, that they were capable of taking its course – and of doing it in one year, rather than the standard two – and enrolled for evening classes. Langdon was furious but presented with a fait accompli.

Langdon was nothing if not determined to do his best to wreck the boys' plan and went out of his way to make attendance as difficult as possible. He refused, for instance, to help with transport, so the six of them would, after a full day's school programme, collect their belongings and trudge along to the nearest bus stop, wait for one of the infrequent buses to take them into Shrewsbury, make their way across town to the college, have their lessons, and then do the same thing in reverse. Classes finished at 9 p.m. and it took an hour to return to the stop and catch the bus back at 10 p.m. It was an unusual night if they were in bed by eleven and the whole process was, to say the least, difficult. One of Blunkett's school friends recalls that they would have given up had Blunkett not kept reminding them that they needed exams to get on in life.

Matters eased slightly after the first year of such treks when a teacher from Rowton, Wilf King, volunteered to meet the boys at the tech and when Margaret Waddington, a retired teacher, arrived at Albrighton as a part-time English teacher for the commerce course that Blunkett was taking. "Some of us wanted to do English and she came along part-time. One day, she read some poetry and said, 'Do any of you boys have a clue who that was?' And I put my hand up and said it was Keats. She was so overwhelmed that I had the first idea that she took an interest in me."[3] She offered to provide the six boys with extra teaching for their O-level English language. The two became friends after Blunkett left school and he attributes his ongoing love of poetry to her inspirational teaching.

The six saw themselves as outsiders, egging each other on to succeed and studying while the other boarders were playing. Despite the temptation to join in, they kept each other up to the mark. Langdon refused even to help with basic matters such as providing them with space to study. There were no study rooms and the six had to scuttle around to find empty spaces – music practice rooms or, in the summer, a secluded corner of the school grounds.

The sight of six young blind boys wandering on their own across Shrewsbury was hardly normal and Blunkett soon experienced reactions from which, at school, he had been shielded. One afternoon, on his own, he heard two people approaching, an adult and a child. As they drew nearer, he heard the woman say to the child, "Come away, let's cross the road – that boy's blind":

My interpretation at the time was that she evidently believed that blindness was some form of contagious disease, and for a while afterwards I brooded about the incident . . . Following such a rare unpleasant encounter in town, I would return to College angry and depressed. I was pig-headed enough not to let such incidents bother me for long and I would soon bounce back. However, it would be easy for other young people, at such a sensitive age, to retreat into their shells and not venture out as often or as confidently as they would otherwise have done.[4]

Blunkett's education at Albrighton was not altogether useless. The upside of Langdon's belief that blind children needed commercial rather than academic education was that he was taught braille shorthand and typing, which stood him in good stead. Using an ordinary typewriter, his work could be read by teachers. But if he made a mistake he would have to start again; because it was not in Braille, he could not find his place to correct it. He learned shorthand typing in three years, rather than the usual four. In his next three years at evening classes, David took two O-levels a year: history and English language, geography and commerce, religious knowledge and physics, and in addition A-level economics.

Life was not entirely Dickensian. One of his evening-class teachers organised a week-long trip to Paris for both sighted and blind children. Blunkett had never been abroad but with his adventurous spirit was desperate to go and his mother used some of the small compensation for his father's death as payment. The trip did not live up to his romantic expectations: much as he enjoyed the new smells, sounds and feelings of the city, the group stayed in an orphanage on the very edge of Paris and the food was basic. Blunkett was also left with a strong impression of French attitudes to hygiene at a visit to a swimming pool: "the man in front of me in the queue had all too evidently come for a bath rather than to swim. I remember wondering at the time how Frenchmen came to have such a romantic image'.[5]

Like any boy of his age, he was starting to think about the opposite sex. Along with some of his school mates, David had attempted to escape the stultifying confines of Albrighton by joining a Sunday afternoon youth club run by Shrewsbury Methodist Church. Listening to the radio, he knew that the Swinging Sixties were happening. But they were passing him by completely. And he was well aware that his real experience of life beyond school and home was almost nil – most of it was gleaned from radio plays, hardly the most accurate depiction of real life. Not the least of the attractions of the youth club was the presence of girls. Other youth clubs also occasionally offered invitations for tea to groups of students and one Sunday afternoon Blunkett joined some Albrighton friends to visit the youth club run by the Congregational Church in Pontesbury, near Shrewsbury. Soon he started talking to a lively, friendly sixteen-year-old girl, Pamela Edwards. But it was not mere chance that they should meet. As she now recalls it, she had been asked to talk to Blunkett by the host: "Each member of the youth group was allocated one person. It was my job to look after David for the evening. I had met blind people before and I obviously didn't make him feel awkward. We discussed loads of different things."[6] The two hit it off: Blunkett found her fascinating and full of *joie de vivre*, and she was intrigued by this intense, earnest young man. Shy around women and racked with nerves, he nonetheless knew that if he failed to ask her out he would never see her again: "My intention was to ask her if she would like to go to the cinema with me, but so nervous was I that instead I heard myself blurting out, 'Would you like to come and look round the College at Albrighton?' It was a strange way of asking for a date but to my immense relief she accepted. Several days later, as we walked round the school grounds, at last I plucked up the courage to suggest a visit to the cinema. She said yes."[7] Pamela became his first girlfriend.

Their relationship was important in David's development; as the two became steadily closer, she opened him out, and gave him an even greater sense of inner confidence. Their friendship also offered him his first taste of family life since boarding, as he would stay with her family at weekends – a considerable effort of hospitality on their part, as they too were far from able to make ends meet. Pamela and David became very close: "We became serious about each other," says Pamela today.[8] David was, however, keener on Pamela than vice versa: "Pamela made me feel special, that I deserved to respect myself and that I could lead a normal life. Looking back, I realize that my Methodist upbringing, lack of experience with girls and a serious commitment to passing my exams at evening classes meant that I was not the most worldly boyfriend she might have had, but with Pamela I learned how to kiss and cuddle."

But it also had a devastating effect on him when they split up, at her instigation, after a year. For all that Pamela had put him at his ease, she left him for an older man who could drive her into Birmingham to see pop concerts and shows. She may have boosted his confidence initially but the upshot of their separation was that David could not but feel that he would always be at a disadvantage compared with others and his self-assurance took a big knock.[9] He started to become seriously depressed: "Life seemed to be passing me by. I would get up in the morning and ask myself, 'What the hell is it all for?'"[10] Given the obstacles he had already overcome, it is remarkable that he did not suffer more such bouts. His life was, friends apart, fundamentally lonely – made more so by the constant proximity of others in the eight-bed dormitories they had to share – and he had no one to spur him on. The only means of finding solitude was to row an old boat some 50 feet across an ornamental lake in the college grounds and then sit alone on the island in the middle, hiding with his radio behind a shrubbery.

Blunkett did have one pleasant distraction. Rather than wallowing in depression, as might have been expected after so hurtful a break-up, he decided in typical fashion to take the initiative – and found a pen pal through a pen-friend organisation. Maria Salerno lived in Malta and the two exchanged letters regularly, although Blunkett was careful at the beginning of their correspondence not to reveal that he could not see. As a seventeen-year-old boy, he did not want to admit to any weakness. The following summer, in 1968, he was invited by the Salernos to visit Maria. The visit was not trouble free. It dawned on Blunkett only on arrival that they may have had more than merely a friendly visit in mind, and were giving him the once-over as a potential husband for their daughter. But it became clear when he arrived in Malta that the Salernos had not fully grasped that he was blind. They were horrified when they realised that he was not the dashing young man they imagined, but a blind office clerk (as he had then become) with almost no income and still less in the way of prospects. The trip developed into something of a farce. Rather than staying with the Salernos, he was billeted with a couple originally from Lincolnshire, Eileen and Neil Doggett. Despite Maria and David being heavily chaperoned, the Salernos decided that their daughter and the young blind man were getting far too entangled and made sure that he spent more time with the Doggetts – total strangers – than with Maria. But in the end, Blunkett came to enjoy their company and they his. He returned the following year to stay with them.

He also had a second pen pal, Kirsty. The boy Blunkett was certainly father to the adult: their correspondence lasted only six months – he stopped writing to Kirsty after she told him in one letter that she had been taking drugs. "I'd never come across anyone who'd taken drugs. I was horrified."

Graduation, in the summer of 1967, was a release in any number of ways, not least because it meant that Blunkett could begin to function in the real world and escape the constraints of Albrighton. With his friend David Boyce, in August he set off pony trekking on the Isle of Skye. The two young men were not best prepared for what awaited them. Their journey – twenty-four hours, from Sheffield to Glasgow, thence to Mallaig, from there by ferry to Armadale and then by bus to Dunvegan – was just the start of it. As the two got off the train at Mallaig, their hands were full of luggage and so they were unable to use their canes. Blunkett started marching across the quayside to search for the ferry. Suddenly there was a yell from Boyce: "Stop!" Boyce could see a little and realised that Blunkett's feet were inches from the edge of the quay.

The rest of the holiday was something of a sitcom. The hotel in

Dunvegan was far more formal than either had ever experienced before. On their first night they were served a four-course meal.

We suspected our clothes were not smart enough for the rather formal atmosphere . . . Seeing we were totally nonplussed over which knife and fork to use, the friendly hotel staff inveigled the head of the pony-trekking firm to join us at our table and provide some tactful guidance on etiquette. Looking back, I wonder what other *faux pas* we committed. We were both rather brash and noisy, and perhaps because of this David and I were allocated a room in the annexe. Typically, I wanted a room in the hotel proper and I pestered the staff until, at the end of the first week, our rooms were changed for nicer ones in the main building.[11]

The hotel was the least of their adventures. The weather – hardly a surprise given the usual pattern for Skye in August – was cold and wet. But it was a happy time for Blunkett, one of the first when he was free of pressure and expectation and able simply to be himself in the company of a friend. They rowed on the loch – a "rash move", as he rightly describes it, but one that was fully in character; and the pony trekking was wonderful – sand and water, clean air, and no crowds. The rest of the time they wandered off for hours on end. On departure they were given a gift that kept on giving: a 6-pound salmon. Keen to take it home as a present for his mother, Blunkett found it had an alternative use – the pungent smell meant that they were left undisturbed in their train compartment.

On his return from Skye, Blunkett learned that he had passed all his exams – his final two GCE O-levels and A-level economics, as well as the tests for shorthand at 110 words per minute and Stage Three typewriting. For the first time since he had been dumped by Pamela, he sensed the truth of the lesson that his mother had instilled in him from birth – that he was as good as anyone else. The achievement was spectacular. If matters had been left to the school alone, he would not have been entered for the exams, let alone have passed them. Instead of a career within clear and confining limits, at the age of nineteen he now had a series of options open to him – albeit, as he puts it, "a leap into the unknown".[12]

5

A leap into the unknown: college and the real world

Blunkett was aware of the problems he faced when he returned to live in Sheffield. He had no friends of his own age, having been away at school, and had little sense of belonging to anywhere but his own home or to anyone other than his mother. And he missed his friends from school. The typical anxieties of a teenager, perhaps. Except that he was nearly twenty.

Yet within three years he was to be elected to the city council and on a fast trajectory to the very top of the political ladder.

But what to do now? His first idea was journalism, less out of any interest in writing than the need to think of something that would make use of his interest in politics and current affairs. After writing to the editor of the *Sheffield Morning Telegraph*, offering his services as a feature writer, he realised that perhaps he was not cut out for the job. The editor replied with a friendly letter but pointed out that before he could ascend to such grandiose heights he would need to start as a junior reporter and, preferably, take a course in journalism. The editor's letter itself was, as Blunkett calls it, "kindly", but behind it lay an assumption that provoked Blunkett's anger: that somehow a blind person could not be a journalist. "All too frequently other people make a judgement about what is possible rather than looking for ways round a difficulty and helping overcome the obstacles ... I learned two important things from this episode: firstly, that I must learn to express myself through the written word as well as verbally, and secondly, that I did not want to write about other people's activities anyway – I wanted to be active myself."[1]

The next step was effectively taken for him. Before he had left Albrighton, the Royal National Institute for the Blind's careers officer had approached the East Midlands Gas Board, in part because of Blunkett's father's death in their employ, and he was offered a job as a clerk typist on a wage of £12 per week. He was nonetheless angry, failing to understand how an RNIB officer of all people could ignore the importance of self-esteem and confidence. He did not want patronage; he wanted to gain a job on merit. But needs must; he needed a wage to look after both himself and his mother, and he took the position in the gas board's administration offices. It did not take him long to make his mark: within a matter of weeks he was elected a shop steward, and had persuaded his bosses to allow him to attend the local college of further education on day release (encountering far less hostility to the idea than he had at school). His week was now made up of a day and an evening studying for the National Certificate in Business Studies, with a second evening spent on A-level economic history. The next summer he passed with a B, resat his earlier A-level economics to gain a higher grade, and then took A-level law.

Blunkett's regular and rather dull routine was interrupted in the spring of 1968 by a trip to London for the FA Cup quarter-final between Chelsea and Sheffield Wednesday at Stamford Bridge. In theory, the trip made sense; he was to link up with Tony Randall after getting the coach from Sheffield and making his way to the ground, and the two would then go in together. All went swimmingly at first as he fell in with a crowd of Wednesday supporters who were only too happy to look after the eager blind supporter and get him to the stadium. Then reality dawned; how on earth would he find Tony amid the thousands of people? It had all the makings of a disaster. And yet, as he neared the football ground, he heard Tony's voice, shouting: "David, David, where are you?" The journey home was not as easy, however. In his first taste of London life, he discovered that, hearing him ask for directions, people would go out of their way to avoid him. Eventually he found another friendly crowd of Wednesday fans, who guided him back to the coach just in time.

Blunkett's life was developing a repetitive routine of work, study, work, study, work and study. His pen-pal relationship had come to an end and he had few friends in Sheffield – and few opportunities to meet new ones. Worse, he began to suffer from a form of agoraphobia – he could barely go outside without being seized by the idea that he was being stared at – which compounded his existing social awkwardness. The agoraphobia was in all probability a physical manifestation of the shyness that he often attempted to cover up with his (sometimes wayward) determination to prove himself as capable as sighted people – to wit, his trip to London for the quarter-final. His capacity for dealing with his own demons, however, was once again in evidence and he set about overcoming the problem by joining the local Methodist youth club attached to the church that he and his mother attended. The initial signs were not positive. He found the members cliquey and unwelcoming to the blind newcomer. The focus on dancing did not help; sight is a pretty crucial factor in dancing, not least to be able to copy what others are doing when learning how to dance. He tried, but never really managed it. Mostly he simply stood at the side. Indeed, things went from bad to worse. One evening he summoned all his courage to ask a girl to dance. "No, thank you very much," was the reply of the man he had approached. "Trudging home that evening with my heart in my boots, I wondered how I could ever set foot in the youth club again. Life seemed to comprise one long series of pitfalls from which I always emerged with egg on my face."[2]

On one occasion, immediately after his humiliation at the youth club, he was in a meeting at work and needed to leave an unfamiliar room to collect some papers. He ran his hand along the wall until he felt the door, opened it, said 'I won't be long' and walked into a cupboard. What might seem amusing was desperately upsetting for a socially uneasy young man: "The indignity made me want to retreat into myself and stay at home."[3] But still he pushed himself on: "I refused to be defeated." He returned to the club, forcing himself to go despite an overpowering feeling of embarrassment after his last evening there.

His life was soon to change for the better, however. At one of the regular discussion group sessions held after his church's Sunday evening chapel, he met Ruth Mitchell, a seventeen-year-old sixth-former at a girls' grammar school on the south-west side of Sheffield. At these discussion groups he was not the shy, awkward young blind man, unsure of his place in the world, but a self-possessed insider who knew what he thought and was able to express it. There was no immediate frisson between the two. They exchanged pleasantries but little more until, one evening, he found Ruth waiting for him when he left the office after work. Soon she started to do the same every day and the two would take the bus home together, she from school, he from work. Ruth was talkative, which David liked. She appealed to him because she seemed to like spending time in his company and did not appear to be put off by his blindness.

One day, he asked her to the cinema and it emerged that she was, if anything, even more unworldly than he; she had only ever been once. "In her company I felt more worldly wise than I truly was. Her lack of social experience appealed to me and presented a challenge. I would have liked to have taken her to some of Sheffield's emerging variety clubs to enjoy dinner and a show, but she was not interested in that sort of thing. Instead we went for walks, to the cinema or church youth sessions and generally spent quiet evenings together."[4] The two almost fell into going out, with Ruth initially making the move but David keen to accept the idea. What had put Pamela off – his earnestness – was what attracted Ruth. After she switched A-level subjects, on David's advice, to modern economic history, the two spent much of their time together working, Ruth reading David's National Certificate material and David helping Ruth with the A-level (in which she gained an A grade). The two were drawn closer by friendship and mutual interests. Whether it was the stuff of a sustained, loving and mutually attractive relationship was another matter.

Ruth's parents – her mother was a housewife and keen church-goer and her father, an engineer, was deputy head of Rotherham College of Technology – were not against the relationship but nor were they keen. Blunkett hardly seemed much of a catch: blind, shy, in a poor-paying position with no real promotion prospects. Blunkett's career was going nowhere in a deeply dull job.

One avenue that was still an option was the priesthood. At Albrighton the idea had been suggested, but was never taken that seriously. Given the lack of other opportunities, Blunkett began to give it more thought. He became a local preacher and started to conduct services. Clearly, although he did not realise it at the time, he was training not for the priesthood but for politics, as his sermons were very much in the spirit of the late-nineteenth-century radical Nonconformists, relating the Bible to social injustice. They were well received. One of his congregants recalls that his English was always precise and his argument logical rather than emotional.

It provided perfect practice for his later career as he taught himself not to read his speeches. "If you see most blind people delivering a speech, they read far too much of it, which is about confidence. But Braille is clumsy and difficult. So I'd make some very basic notes and make sure they weren't just a rant. I listened a lot to radio and my language reflected that."

As with the clichéd otherwise shy actor, Blunkett's awkward-ness and shyness vanished as soon as he stood in the pulpit – in part, because for the first time in his life he was in control of a situation; and in part because he was indeed the politician manqué, and felt he had important wisdom to pass on to his listeners.

Far more significant in the long run (but of a piece) was his decision after returning to Sheffield to become active in the local Labour Party. His first encounter with the Southey Green Ward branch was not, however, what he had expected. After crossing the large Parson Cross estate to the hut in which the branch met, he was disabused by the events of the first meeting of any notion that the local Labour Party was primarily a vehicle for social change:

First of all the minutes of the previous meeting were read out and were then hotly disputed for the following twenty-five minutes or so. Next we discussed correspondence received by the secretary and there followed a report on what had happened at the constituency management committee meeting. Politics were not mentioned. The occasion remains vivid in my mind because it made a profound impression – it was not quite what I had expected. I was twenty then, in 1967, and the other members all seemed to me somewhere over the age of ninety, although in reality they were probably only in their fifties and sixties.[5]

At this stage a career in politics was not on the agenda; it seemed unrealistic and was not necessarily what he wanted – there were more rewarding avenues to be explored, such as teaching.

Blunkett had applied to teacher training college while studying on day release and had met with a mix of responses, from "Wouldn't you be better off doing music?" or "Our premises are not suitable for blind people" to the more practical suggestion that he should first get a degree. It was a suggestion that he acted upon. Applying to Manchester University, he was told that the campus was too scattered to suit him but he was offered a place at both York and Durham to read sociology. He did not, though, want to leave Sheffield. He had already been away from his mother for most of his childhood and did not want to compound the problem by leaving Ruth, too. A solution presented itself when he was offered a place at Sheffield to read politics and modern history, with the emphasis of the course on political theory and institutions. Whatever else he was to achieve, this was in many ways his greatest triumph. His mother at first refused to believe the letter offering him a place, so unlikely was it, even without the additional difficulties of his blindness and his unusual education. Not only was he the first person in the family to go to university, he was almost certainly the first from anywhere near his home, so denuded of opportunities was the neighbourhood.

His time at university was not the magical idyll that some experience. It was above all practical, albeit with a wholly unexpected twist. Triumph though it may have been to be accepted, Blunkett's anxieties did not disappear during the first term. He was excruciatingly shy, almost paralysed with fear by the idea that he, alone among the student body, was unable to see and that he would be ignored by everyone else, left to fend for himself and without friends. For once, however, he had an alternative focus: Ruth. His anxieties at university pushed him even closer to her.

These anxieties were not eased by the lack of any specialist help for him. The library had no braille facilities of any kind. The arts faculty could be reached only by a footbridge across a moat-like structure; one foot out of place and he would be in the water. And then to ascend any of the nineteen storeys required either leaping on and off a paternoster lift or taking the many flights of stairs.

Blunkett had been persuaded that a guide dog would make life significantly easier. Throughout his teens he had been opposed to the idea, believing not only that the image they presented of blind people being unable to cope on their own was wrong but that their owners themselves tended to become too sentimentally attached to their dogs. But his school friend Graeme McCreath had acquired a dog – a German shepherd called Mike – and Blunkett saw from his capacity for work and his loyalty to his master that there was more to commend the idea than he had previously accepted. So in September 1969 he went to the guide dog training centre in Bolton, where he was introduced to Ruby, a golden Labrador. The training lasted for four weeks and they were to remain together for almost nine years.[6]

Ruby's appetite and her ability to locate and steal food while harnessed became a standing joke among Blunkett's friends. More often than not, victims of her theft were too polite to tell Blunkett. On one camping holiday in Bridlington she ate his friends' bacon and eggs out of the frying pan; and the cakes and buns on the bottom rung of the tea trolleys at the council offices and Barnsley Technical College were rarely left unmolested. One day, stepping off a bus, Blunkett heard a girlish yelp, swiftly followed by uncontrollable laughter. Having been the butt of unpleasant humour, he assumed that this person was laughing at him for some reason. Six years later, however, he was taking a council surgery when a constituent remarked that his guide dog had changed. Indeed, he replied, this one was Teddy. Ruby had retired. "Yes," the constituent remarked. "She was lovely looking, but very naughty. I remember one time when I was standing at the bus stop, you and Ruby got off. As she passed a toddler eating an ice-cream cornet, Ruby swiped the cone right out of the kiddie's hand, without a moment's hesitation. There one minute, gone the next. We could all see you had no idea what she'd done. The little kiddie's face was a picture. We had to laugh. You went off down the road blithe as can be. I cried laughing. Fancy a guide dog doing that, eh?"[7]

There were few concessions made to Blunkett's needs. Where he was helped was on paper. Given his odd educational background, he had never been taught how to write English properly – how to construct an essay or present an argument, how to express himself properly and even how to spell, skills that most of his fellow students had learned early on. Tutors gave him extra coaching and recommended books that his peers had all read but which he had never even heard of. As he got to know his fellow students, he realised, too, that his knowledge of current affairs was far more limited than he had imagined – for obvious reasons; they read far more newspapers and journals.

There was one further concession. It was agreed that he could record the lectures, rather than having to bash away on his braille writer taking notes and disturbing everyone. This had knock-on effects. It meant he was given his own study in which to work and he could use the tapes to barter with fellow students, persuading them in exchange to read other work aloud to him. Friends from his course (along with Ruth) devised a rota for them to read to and tape things for Blunkett, help that was increased immeasurably when Lorraine Simpson, a young mother of two children, offered to do brailling for him, as well as taking over much of the reading on to tape from Ruth. Blunkett's reading circle became the core of his network of friends. They tried their best to treat him like any other student and to invite him to 'normal' student activities but were fighting a losing battle; Blunkett simply disliked the typical student parties. "I felt very ill at ease amid the din of loud music, when I could neither see what was going on nor hear who I was talking to. At the few parties I did go to, people tended to be lying about on floor cushions or sprawled on beanbags, where I tripped over them. I infinitely preferred spending time with friends who invited us to their home for supper; a heated discussion would almost inevitably ensue across the dining or kitchen table but, despite vehement disagreements, the evening would end amicably."[8]

By virtue of his deafness he got to know Professor Bernard Crick, who was in charge of the course, whose family remained in London and who would travel down on Fridays, not returning to Sheffield until the following Tuesday. Blunkett came to hear about this routine, and asked the professor whether he would deliver and pick up tapes and books at the library for the blind in Bolsover Street, not far from where Crick lived in London. At the time, the tapes were sizeable discs (compact tapes were not yet available) and this required something of an effort on Crick's part. The routine brought the two men into regular contact. Given Crick's subsequent links with Blunkett in government, it has been assumed that he was somehow the *éminence grise* behind Blunkett's thinking. But Crick's influence on Blunkett has been over-stated: the two have never been, as is often recorded, close friends. Crick left Sheffield at the end of Blunkett's first year and they barely met again until Blunkett became leader of the council, and then again in 1987 for a jointly written paper on Labour's aims and values.

But Crick's political outlook – focused on practicalities, dismissive of revolutionary socialism and (later) of the Bennite 'socialism in 1,000 days' approach – clearly rubbed off on Blunkett. When he became council leader, he set up the Marx Memorial Lecture in a deliberate ploy to curry favour with the far and hard left, but gave the lectures his own twist. The first lecturer was Edward Thompson, the second Crick on Orwell. Blunkett knew exactly what he was doing in asking Thompson rather than one of "the dandy princes of the new Left", as Crick puts it. And Crick himself was not entirely to the taste of some of the hard left.

In his autobiography, Blunkett dismisses as 'myth-making' one of Crick's favourite stories of the time, that Ruby would bark every time the professor mentioned Marx. Crick says that he tried all sorts of tricks, such as calling him 'the German doctor', but that Ruby still barked. Blunkett insists the story is nonsense. Crick, however, insists it is true. Implausible as it seems, Ruby certainly had other similar habits. When she was bored, she would make plain her displeasure. More often than not, this involved rising to her feet just before the end of an hour-long lecture, grunting, stretching and yawning. Fellow students would be reduced to helpless laughter.

Ruby and Crick were together responsible for an incident that was to achieve national prominence. Blunkett and some fellow students had travelled down to London for a visit to the House of Commons and various government departments which Crick had organised. As the blind student reached the door at the St Stephen's entrance, one of the policemen blocked his path: "Sorry, sir, but you can't take the dog inside. They're not allowed in the Palace of Westminster." Blunkett explained that she was not a pet, to no avail: "I'm afraid she'll have to stay here with us."

Angrily, Blunkett left Ruby in the police cubbyhole beside the entrance. She immediately made her displeasure known by peeing on the floor. Blunkett opted for a less direct protest, contacting the Guide Dogs for the Blind Association and working with it to place newspaper stories on the incident (even as a first year undergraduate, he instinctively knew how to use the media to make a political point). As both the *Mirror* and *The Guardian* put it, 'Guide Dog Refused Entry to Palace of Westminster' – Blunkett had been denied his democratic rights. *The Times* ran a lengthy correspondence on its letters page. So great was the publicity that the Commons authorities changed the rules; Ruby became the first dog allowed into the Palace of Westminster.

(Later on during the day of the field trip, Blunkett and his fellow students had been granted a slot with Peter Walker, who had just been appointed Secretary of State for Trade and Industry after the Conservatives' general election victory in 1970. Some twenty minutes into the meeting in Walker's office, a loud snoring started to echo around the room. Walker stopped in his tracks and looked at his visitors. Everyone seemed awake. "I'm very sorry, Secretary of State," Blunkett confessed, "it's my dog." "Your dog? What dog? Where?" "Beneath the table." Walker looked startled but soon smiled and, after patting Ruby, resumed the meeting.)

Royden Harrison, another lecturer, also left at the end of the year to become professor of history at Warwick University but Blunkett stayed in touch and came to value his advice. He was "a reformed revolutionary who nonetheless comprehended the difficulties of practical day-to-day politics and pragmatism. He was always on hand with an appropriate recollection, piece of advice or political observation to ensure that values and philosophy were never forgotten. I respected him greatly for that".[9] The quality of his lecturers varied wildly but Blunkett especially enjoyed those of Ken Watkins, a right-winger whose lectures were by far the most entertaining and offered him a very different political outlook.

For the last two years of his course, his main influences were

Pat Seyd and Stuart Walkland. Seyd, who has had a distinguished academic career since, was then a young lecturer keen to make his mark and to support Labour. Walkland, Blunkett's tutor, was what he calls "a pink Conservative who had flirted with the Liberal Party ... A pleasant-natured man, he used me as a Labour Party benchmark during discussions and seminars. 'David,' he would say, turning towards me, 'what does the Labour Party think about this?' To which I would reply, 'Well, I really don't have a clue, but my view is ...' and then explain my ideas".[10]

Blunkett blossomed. He was in an environment that relished learning rather than sneering at it; he was surrounded by books, most of which were not merely new but on subjects he had barely been aware of; and he was there entirely on his own merit – despite, not because of, his previous circumstances.

A contemporary at Sheffield recalls that "he was very right-wing, in a 'practical' way. He was always cutting the others down by dismissing their grand schemes and ideas as 'not practical'. 'If you had lived in the real world at all' was one of his favourite put-downs". Students straight from school with grandiose theories of social change irritated him, not least because he was two or three years older than most of his fellow first-year students which, at the time, felt like a big gap. But this did make it easier for him to settle into a routine, treating university rather like office life. Sometimes he would stay late for a debate or the occasional social event but most often he would return home to his room at his mother's house after lectures or visit Ruth. He would rise early and be in his study room at college by half past eight. He was, after all, used to both a job and evening classes. On one occasion, Bernard Crick made a remark about the students' union being a youth club at public expense. As a contemporary remembers, "David was terribly pleased with that." Crick took some of his students away to Cumberland Lodge (a retreat in Windsor) and it was there that he first saw something more impressive than mere liveliness in Blunkett. "He developed the role of spokesman for the pack and the other students realised he knew what he was talking about so much more that they did. They were in awe of him."

That summer, he and Ruth got engaged. To Blunkett it seemed entirely natural. He had become closer to her than to anyone else and he could not imagine his life without her at his side. Although Ruth's parents were far from keen on the match, they did not create trouble. Blunkett's mother, however, had other ideas: "She was most decidedly against it and said so . . . She advised me to see the relationship in perspective over the long-term and to wait to find out what life might hold in store for us."[11] This had – when has such advice not? – the opposite effect. "The more forcefully she tried to dissuade me, the more determined I became. The more she urged me not to rush into such a major commitment, the more I felt she was clinging to me and that I must disentangle myself."[12]

They were married in July 1970 at Southey Methodist church in Sheffield. Immediately after the reception they went to York for the weekend, before travelling to Ireland for ten days. The honeymoon was not successful and was an ill omen for the rest of the marriage. They bickered constantly and their tour of the country was marked by a series of misadventures. The early years of their marriage were not helped by Ruth resenting the amount of time she was having to devote to her husband's career and studies. She had been dissuaded by her teachers from applying to university and was instead pursuing a teacher training course, and she began to feel that her life was being eclipsed by his.

There was one major plus to married life. They managed immediately to find an extraordinarily cheap (£2,750) terraced house near the university (it was cheap because it needed structural repairs). By 1974 it had already increased in value as the area became far more fashionable and thanks to the constant DIY-ing of Ruth's father – which came increasingly to annoy Blunkett, not least when he was studying for his finals. They sold it for £7,000.

But the marriage was never going to prosper: "Despite the best endeavours of Ruth and myself, our marriage was never a success in terms of our relationship . . . If we had had a less restricted social life with more opportunities for relaxation, perhaps we might have learned to be more at ease with each other. As it was, there did not seem to be much time to spare for having fun."[13]

Blunkett threw his energies – and his real commitment – into the increasingly successful side of his life: studying and politics. Politics became a substitute for his domestic life which, if not downright miserable, was joyless. Politics provided not merely public and professional acceptance but also most of his social life.

Despite the warnings of his tutors that his political activities would wreck his studies, he graduated in the summer of 1972 with a 2:1, missing a first by a whisker. He and his tutors were left to wonder how good a first he might have achieved had he been able to concentrate on his work. But a 2:1 was not merely good enough; it was a startling achievement, which meant that teaching became a real possibility.

Graduation day in Sheffield Town Hall, presided over by Rab Butler, the university's Chancellor, was the proudest day of Doris Blunkett's life. Much as she had willed David to succeed and had implanted in him the mantra that he was as good as anyone else, even she had not considered the idea of a degree. Ruby, however, was to have her own say on events: "Swathed in my freshly pressed gown and feeling exceedingly nervous, I followed Ruby up the steps on to the platform and approached the Chancellor . . . With a will of her own, she took me squarely to the centre of the stage and then sharp left down to the footlights. She wanted to enjoy her moment of glory. There was a vast audience and loud applause – for Ruby this meant taking a bow. With only inches to spare, the Chancellor caught me by the sleeve, thus preventing me from toppling over the edge and probably breaking a leg. The situation was redeemed and Mum's heart returned to its normal pace."[14]

For his teaching certificate in further education, Blunkett enrolled at Hollybank College in Huddersfield. His confidence boosted, he had few of the anxieties that afflicted his early time at university. And Ruth was now earning, having qualified as a geography teacher and started a job at Sharrow Lane Junior School.

He had other anxieties, however. Part of the course was teaching practice at a further education college and, not surprisingly, there was much scepticism as to whether he would be able to cope, not least with one of the classes he was allotted, known as 'Bricklayers I', for first-year students of bricklaying on day release from building sites. As Blunkett writes:

To these lads the idea of general/liberal studies was an open invitation to rebellion. As I entered the classroom for the first time I could sense that this group was going to be a challenge – a contest of Henry Cooper proportions – blind or not, they were determined to do me down. I was nervous to the point where my stomach literally knotted up. Every week it was to be the same. 'Get out your paper and pens, please.' 'We left them in the other room,' would come the reply. I had to make a judgement whether or not this was true. 'Stop messing about,' I would respond in my best Kenneth Williams voice. Raising a laugh was crucial to get them to do what I wanted. 'I want you to make notes on some slides I'm going to show you,' I might say. 'Please pull down the blinds.' 'They're down already,' came the instant response. 'Oh, so you've been sitting here in the dark, have you?' That would get them going ... Gradually we would begin to do some work, but then I would hear disturbances, such as paper darts hitting somebody, or worse. It was unfortunate that the class had to be held in a spare science laboratory, where the students sat on high stools at workbenches supplied with water and gas. Not a good idea. An outbreak of coughing and choking would be accompanied by the dread smell of gas. Once that had been switched off, someone else would start spraying water round the room. 'What on earth are you doing with that tap?' 'I'm washing me hair,' came the unlikely reply.

'What do you mean – washing your hair?' 'Jack's put chewing gum in me hair,' a mournful voice replied. Every session with Bricklayers 1 was a battle. A minor breakthrough occurred, however, when one day I took into class a cutting from the *Sunday Times* about an aircraft which had crashed in the Andes; most of the stranded survivors had eventually resorted to eating the bodies of their dead companions and there had been a lot of media coverage. I pointed out the moral and physical dilemmas inherent in the situation, and asked the class for their views. At first they reacted along the predictable lines of 'What's wrong with eating a nice bit of brain then?' But slowly I pulled them round to talking sensibly about this moral maze – what they would do, how they might feel – in order to get them to imagine the awful reality of such a situation. It was a struggle to sensitize them and persuade them to address the issues, but it was interesting and rewarding. At the end of each class I would stagger back to the staff room and slump exhausted into a chair. 'Are you still wanting to be a teacher?' demanded a couple of lecturers. 'Just,' I gasped. 'Well done! That class has finished off quite a few student teachers.' It gave me great satisfaction to prove to the doubting Thomases that I could indeed manage to control a class and even perhaps teach them a thing or two. The experience was an ordeal but at the time I knew I had to get through it and not admit defeat.[15]

His time at Hollybank was notable for one non-event. One evening, as he was being driven back to Sheffield with friends, the driver pulled up at a house shared by some fellow students. "We were lounging about, mulling over the state of the world, when I sensed that Ruby was becoming uneasy. She began to sniff and whine and despite my efforts she refused to settle. 'What on earth are you doing?' I asked one of the others. 'I can't get her to be quiet.' At this, one of them explained that they were dishing out marijuana and asked if I wanted to share a joint. I declined . . . Being a pedigree Labrador, a breed frequently trained to be sniffer dogs, Ruby was driven to complete distraction by the scent of marijuana."[16] Blunkett had pretty much the same reaction as Ruby. As he puts it: "I never felt the need to try drugs. Daily life seemed challenging enough without getting stoned . . . Although I often felt I was missing out on a lot of the fun fellow students seemed to be enjoying at both university and training college, the drug scene never appealed."[17]

6

Not the typical student:
The Socialist Republic of South Yorkshire

Blunkett was clearly not the typical student. The drive and determination to succeed that have characterised so much of his life were equally in evidence at university. When he was not studying or carrying out his Sunday duties as a Methodist lay preacher, he was devoting himself to the Labour Party. Something had clicked for him. He now realised that he was quite capable of getting on in any walk of life. Friends recall that he made no pretence about his ambition to be elected to public office, an ambition to which few of his peers would admit but about which he had no inhibitions – not least because he was openly critical of what he saw as the complacency and lethargy of the existing local council.

He did not have long to wait. Blunkett's first term at Sheffield began in the autumn of 1969. Within a matter of months he was a Labour member of Sheffield City Council. Michael O'Shaughnessy, one of the existing councillors in Southey Green, the ward to which Blunkett had moved back on his return from Shrewsbury, was deselected because, as one of those involved at the time put it, "he'd run out of steam". The obvious replacement was a young NUPE official, Stewart Hastings. Blunkett considered putting himself forward but realised immediately that Hastings's selection was a given and that there was nothing to be gained by standing – and quite a lot to be lost in goodwill for the future. The Sheffield Labour Party did not appreciate boat-rockers. But Blunkett had one of those strokes of luck that are so characteristic of those who succeed in politics. Less than a week before Hastings was due to be confirmed as the party's candidate, he was offered a promotion within the union – to a job in South Wales.

He took it. The search for a replacement suddenly became urgent and wide open. O'Shaughnessy considered that he had been given a second chance and moved heaven and earth to win back the nomination but the ward was not interested in reselecting a man they had deselected weeks before. Blunkett had been back in Sheffield and active for three years, and had developed the necessary 'iron bum', as party jargon had it (he had attended his fair share of meetings). But he was certainly not the obvious candidate. He was young, he was callow, he was awkward and he was blind. But as a fellow party member at the time puts it: "We needed new blood and some of us thought that David was the answer. He was – how can I put it? – different. And he had so much energy." Blunkett was approached by a group of branch members and this time leapt at the chance.

The selection meeting was on 8 February 1970. Blunkett describes the occasion:

Various members of the committee asked questions including the old chestnut, 'If Mrs Bloggs comes to you and says she's got a blocked drain, what would you do?' to which I replied, 'Well, the one thing I certainly won't do is put my arm down it!' . . . I then went on to say that being blind would not make any difference. I would simply go along to see her and talk about it, and then ring the public health department to get an inspector along to see it. They appeared satisfied. The combination of my evident commitment and enthusiasm, allied to the consensus in the local party that it was time for a breath of fresh air, seemed to swing the branch's decision in my favour.[1]

The selection was a risk. Not only was he blind but he was only twenty-two and still a student. No one really knew – least of all Blunkett himself – whether he could do the job. But since the other two councillors for the ward had served for many years (one of them, Winifred Golding, became Blunkett's mentor on the council) there was a feeling that even if he turned out to be a disaster, the position was salvageable. The defeated incumbent, O'Shaughnessy, called on Blunkett the next day, telling him that he would never manage it – that he would not be able to cope with the meetings and the reading. "We'll see," said the new candidate.

He had been offered a safe seat on the council, for which many seemingly better-qualified, more long-standing party members had already been waiting years. It was far from a disaster; Blunkett represented the ward for the next eighteen years.

The branch immediately discovered what had hit it. Since the ward was rock-solid Labour, the party had done very little canvassing or searching for new votes. On his first day as prospective candidate, Blunkett asked why a small section of the ward which was owner occupied was always ignored. He was told that they would all vote Tory anyway, so there was no point in canvassing there. Instinctively adopting a New Labour position, Blunkett replied that unless the party tried to change their minds, of course they would carry on voting Conservative. Instead of letting them go, they should target them with leaflets and visits.

Southey Green was 95 per cent council housing. With the neighbouring ward, it comprised the biggest council estate in Europe. Blunkett was determined that the 5 per cent of privately owned houses should not be written off as lost to Labour. His argument was simple: "Your interests are our interests, your concerns our concerns. The fact that you bought your home is neither here nor there – it doesn't change you, it doesn't change us!"[2] He knew without thinking what it took many in the Labour Party four general election defeats to discover: that if you attract the support only of your followers, you lose.

For his own election campaign, he was accompanied by a fellow student, Stuart Lowe, who was one of the circle who read textbooks and other course material out loud to Blunkett. Lowe was a soulmate beyond politics and student life. He would drive Blunkett around the ward in his decrepit Mini with a loudspeaker attached to the car roof and would then drop the candidate and Ruby in the chosen canvass spot.

'Find the gate,' I would say to Ruby. Having done so, she was instructed to 'find the door'. Having knocked on the door, I would then extend my hand towards the person who opened it and introduce myself. Sometimes my outstretched hand met with the face of a child, no doubt often dangerously close to the eyes. On other occasions a piping voice might respond to my greeting and I would ask in dulcet tones, 'Is your Mum or Dad in?' only to discover that the person I was addressing was a youthful parent. Canvassing provided so many opportunities for making a fool of myself that I really had to steel myself to continue . . . By the end of every hour-and-a-half stint of canvassing, we were both drained by nervous exhaustion. In the end Ruby became almost psychotic. For days after the canvassing was over, whenever I took her out, she would drag me through any gateway we came to, intent on the task of finding the front door. After a while, of course, she realized this was no longer what was required of her and life returned to normal, although she remained reluctant to get into Stuart's Mini.[3]

Blunkett's canvassing experiences did not end there. One Sunday he was at home when he heard a loud knock at the door. Answering it, he was met by a policeman, Superintendent Jones. Blunkett invited the policeman in, assuming that he had come in connection with council business. "I'm sorry to trouble you," he began. "I've been asked to come to see you on a serious matter. Do you drive a Mini?" "Of course not," replied Blunkett, somewhat taken aback. "I am blind." Superintendent Jones continued, "That's the significance of my enquiry. It has been alleged that you were seen driving round the Ecclesfield district of Sheffield." Blunkett was not sure whether to get angry or laugh. "Oh, really? I suppose my guide dog Ruby was sitting in the front seat next to me navigating?" Jones did not appear to have a sense of humour: "No, sir. According to my information, the guide dog was behind you in the back seat." Blunkett asked him when he had received the allegation. "Yesterday, sir." "Do you know," asked Blunkett, "what date it was yesterday?" The policeman said he did not understand the councillor's point. "It was, Super-intendent, 1 April – April Fool's Day."

Most of his department at university – with the exception of Seyd and Walkland – had advised him against standing and continued to warn him that he was likely to ruin his otherwise exceptional chances of a good degree by taking on too much. (One lecturer, Mr Thornhill, marked down his essays when they involved local government, on the basis that they were not accurate descriptions of his own experiences in Nottinghamshire two decades before.) His fellow students also regarded him with puzzlement. Since, in the late 1960s and 1970s, being a left-of-centre student meant by definition being a student revolutionary, a man such as Blunkett was regarded as plain weird: "Being a member of the Labour Party was considered deeply reactionary by the ultra Left and they regarded my involvement in local government as a peculiar and reprehensible diversion from theoretical politics. They seemed to feel I was soiling my hands by actually practising politics on local housing estates as opposed to devoting myself solely to reading Marx, discussing Hobbes or exploring the libertarian ideas of Mill. Such divergent attitudes led to many a heated debate, which I enjoyed immensely. It was life and soul to me."[4] But he did join the more obvious student demos, such as that at Old Trafford against the Springboks' tour and a number in London, such as that against the Industrial Relations Act in 1972.

The city council to which Blunkett was elected in May 1970 had been the archetypal Labour local authority of the 1960s, with councillors who had served for decades (a survey of its Labour councillors in 1967 showed that nearly two-thirds were over fifty-five and only one was under the age of thirty-five[5]) and to whom the idea of electoral defeat was unimaginable. One newcomer to Sheffield in the 1960s recalls meeting one of the councillors, a caricature of the breed: "There were six of them who were the Sheffield oligarchy. One of them said to me, 'Well, nothing can be done without team work. But mark you, one man has to give a lead. And that's all I will say for myself; not to blow my own trumpet.' They all had the same story."

Sheffield City Council had carried out an extensive programme of council house building, had been one of the first authorities to introduce comprehensive schools and had shown a strong commitment to libraries, galleries and museums. But as so often when a city is in the hands of one party for a generation, the political success bred complacency and covered up many problems. In 1967 the Labour group split over a proposed rent-rebate scheme which involved increasing council-house rents. This split – combined with Labour's national unpopularity – led, in the 1968 local elections, to the party's first defeat in Sheffield for thirty-six years, and only the second since 1926.

Blunkett's selection was part of a process of injecting new blood into the group which began after the 1968 election defeat and cleared out a large number of long-standing councillors. He was one of a group of new, young councillors who began their careers in the 1970s. (By 1980, nearly two-thirds of the Labour group had been elected to the council after 1970.[6]) But for all the changes in the Labour group's complexion, no one – other than the man himself – imagined that the rather gauche young blind man would end up as chairman of a council committee, let alone leader. They saw him rather as a useful exhibit – a walking, talking demonstration of how 'right on' they were in choosing a blind man as a councillor.

Labour was returned to power in 1970. The new leader was Ron Ironmonger, an exemplary old-style Labour council leader (who, rarely in those days, was awarded a knighthood for his services to Sheffield). Ironmonger would begin each day in the steelworks at seven o'clock in the morning, carrying out his job as a personnel manager (having started his working life on the shop floor). He would then leave for the town hall, where he would spend the rest of the day. He was, according to one former Labour councillor, "kind but robust". Unlike many of his colleagues in the immediate wake of Blunkett's election, Ironmonger made no political allowances for his disabilities. "If I got it completely wrong, he would cut me down to pieces inside the Labour group, and then come up to me afterwards and say, 'I needed to do that. You were entirely wrong. But' – and the but was always with an arm around my shoulder – 'don't go home and mope about it.' It was an act of respect for me that he would take me to pieces, because he needed to in order to win the argument."

Behind Ironmonger was Alderman Sidney Dyson, an enormous man in every sense of the word, who relished political fixing and, as full-time Labour agent in the Attercliffe constituency, was effectively a full-time councillor. According to Blunkett: "There was nothing he liked more than to stitch up deals behind the scenes, generally in the Town Hall members' quiet room, where he would recline in an armchair, his protuberant paunch reverberating in time to his *sotto voce* mutterings. Alderman Dyson could easily have been a character in a novel by J. B. Priestley."[7] There was no love lost between Dyson and Blunkett. Another contemporary describes him as "a malevolent figure; he didn't like young people, he didn't trust ideas and he felt that his generation knew best". Dyson thus had little time for a vocal left-wing new councillor who seemed to know it all but who was, as a blind man, plainly not up to the job. Blunkett should not, in Dyson's view, have had a safe seat wasted on him. This view was buttressed by an incident immediately after Blunkett's election, when he collapsed during a dizzy spell in the middle of speaking in the council chamber. The deputy leader and chairman of the Finance Committee, Isidore Lewis ("a likeable old warhorse")[8] had been present and realised that unless Blunkett's confidence was restored immediately, his reputation would never recover and Dyson would crow that he had been proved right in his hostility to the brash, blind left-winger. He thus proposed a rather bizarre idea: that Blunkett should move the vote proposing Dyson as Lord Mayor (a Buggins' turn honour), ostensibly as the youngest member of the council but in reality as a means of giving him a high-profile platform through which to show his ability – and, on Lewis's part, to wind up Dyson.

Came the day, the chamber was crowded with officials and dignitories dressed to the nines in their regalia. Blunkett rose to speak: "Lord Mayor, Lady Mayoress, ladies and gentlemen, I cannot think of anyone who could more amply fill the Lord Mayor's chair than Alderman Sidney Dyson." The rest of the speech did not proceed as planned. Blunkett takes up the story: "At that very moment events took a dramatic turn. Ruby made a sudden dash for freedom from beneath my seat, where she had been reclining, and took off round the council chamber at high speed. With ears flapping and tail swishing from side to side with excitement, she made two full circuits of the room before coming to rest with a painful-sounding thud on the stomach of the new Lord Mayor. There was an explosion of laughter from the assembly, while an outraged Sidney Dyson attempted to remove Ruby from his lap."[9] Blunkett somehow managed to turn a disaster into a triumph. After apologising, he eulogised Dyson with a fervour that he would not otherwise have demonstrated. "Dyson forgave me, my reputation as a speaker was redeemed and from that day on my life in politics went from strength to strength."[10] Ruby's lead was in future kept wrapped around Blunkett's leg.

The two men never reached more than an accommodation – a grudging mutual respect, but no more. One particular example of Dyson's narrow-mindedness still rankles with Blunkett:

He blocked Sheffield taking part in the development of the East Midlands Airport. And it was a really stupid thing to do because, had Sheffield taken part, we would have had an enormous stake in what later was sold at considerable profit by the counties – Derbyshire, Nottinghamshire and Leicestershire – which did invest in it. In his view, Sheffield should have its own airport, even though he had not the slightest idea where it should be or how it should come to pass. He simply ignored the evidence, which was that we didn't have the space for an airport which could accommodate large aircraft.

And it was self-evident that if you couldn't use large aircraft, including charters, you weren't going to be operating at a profit.

Blunkett had made an impact almost immediately on election. Paul Potts, a trainee reporter covering the municipal beat for the *Sheffield Star*, was interested in the new blind councillor and invited him for a drink. The two men met at the Norfolk Arms on the outskirts of Sheffield one lunchtime. As they walked into the pub, the landlord refused to serve them because of Blunkett's dog, Ruby. Blunkett and Potts protested, to no avail. The next day's *Sheffield Star* carried the story, bringing Blunkett to the attention of those Sheffield voters who had not already heard about him. The young Potts could spot a good source for stories, and thought to himself: "Great story; we'll have plenty more of these, thank you very much."

Blunkett had been taken under the wing of Winifred Golding, an old-style Labour councillor who knew every inch of her turf and fought hard to direct as much spending to it as she could secure. One of her proudest achievements was the building of a new library for which she had pressed, and she campaigned to have more public lavatories built. Blunkett's own view of his role was similar: "They weren't trivial – they were what being a councillor should be all about. Improving people's lives."

In his first year on the council, he likewise concentrated on issues of immediate relevance to his constituents: making safe a large derelict air-raid shelter and transforming a poisonous refuse-strewn field into a play area for children. (Golding in fact resigned as a councillor two months after Blunkett joined, having been elected alderman, but she continued to keep a motherly eye on her protégé.)

Blunkett had another mentor. Enid Hattersley, mother of Roy, (with whom he was to have a series of confrontations), was a remarkable figure in Sheffield politics and she too took Blunkett under her wing. Much of the hostility from Roy Hattersley towards Blunkett can be traced back to his mother's supportive relationship with him: "It must have been quite galling because she did go on about me a lot." Enid was a very strong personality and knew everyone and everything in Sheffield politics. As one of Blunkett's oldest friends puts it: "She guided him, encouraged him, took a great interest in him. She admired what he had achieved. She spotted him coming up through the ranks and encouraged him at every twist and turn. She admired somebody who with his very difficult background could have achieved what he had achieved in his studies, getting his exams, getting on buses." In fact, Enid Hattersley had first come across the young Blunkett when she was a governor of Tapton Mount School and recalled talking to Blunkett's mother and father in his early years (although Blunkett has no memory of encountering her until his election to the council). She remained an important figure throughout his time in Sheffield politics, the last of the great lord mayors occupying the judges' quarters and being fêted as a 'queen of Sheffield', and finally as chair of the Libraries and Arts Committee when Blunkett was leader. "It was a war of attrition with Enid," remarks Blunkett. "She'd ensure that you gave her a decent budget by ringing you so often that you really just had to give in." For all his confrontations with her son, Blunkett remained close to Enid. At the end of her life (she died in 2001) he would visit her regularly, take her a box of chocolates and keep her up to date with his career.

Blunkett earned a reputation over the early months as a fiery, committed left-winger but one with the will to buckle down to seemingly mundane matters. However, he blotted his copybook with an early example of the community agenda that he was to champion as leader, campaigning to stop the mass demolition of a group of perfectly good Victorian houses in Pitsmoor, an inner-city district that had gone Liberal because the Labour group were ignoring the interests of the local people, providing perfect fodder for the Liberals' community politics. He also helped launch *Pitsmoor News*, a local magazine that took on the council. Challenging the orthodoxy that the council always knew best, while serving on it, was viewed by the more conservative party establishment figures as a great betrayal.

After his early hiccup, he rapidly gained respect, such that at the beginning of 1972 he was appointed to a working party of councillors to draw up a draft Labour manifesto for the elections to the new South Yorkshire Metropolitan County Council (SYMCC), which was being created under the local government reorganisation. At the same time as becoming a member of the new SYMCC, he was elected a member of the Executive and Policy Committee of both councils, in effect local cabinets.

Other than parochial ward matters, Blunkett's early interest on the council was transport. Indeed, one of his main purposes in becoming a councillor was to push for a free or cheap public transport policy and the formation of the SYMCC provided the perfect platform for him to make his mark. With three similarly obsessive allies, he used the policy-making process to draft a transport framework that the party establishment regarded as radically left-wing. Local transport would be subsidised by the council to push down fares and thus move people from cars to buses and local trains. Blunkett proposed free travel within the city centre, a flat rate (2p per child and 10p per adult) within a 6-mile radius of the city centre and free travel everywhere for pensioners. His argument was based on a supposed virtuous circle: the greater the number of passengers, the greater the revenue, the greater the ability of the council to maintain and expand the service, the greater the number of passengers, and so on. It was a revolutionary policy for the conservative Labour group to agree to, the more so as the rationale behind it could only be speculation; such a subsidy had never been tried before. But Blunkett secured its inclusion in the manifesto, developing his political skills for the first time on a wider platform than his own ward. The party was committed to providing "free public transport for the elderly, the handicapped and the disabled as an immediate objective. *This will be regarded as a first step towards the ultimate provision of free public transport for all*", as the manifesto put it.[11]

He had to fight and win a series of internal political battles to see the policy implemented. Almost immediately after the new council was elected in May 1973, a number of council officers, including Ron Ironmonger (who had defeated the former leader of West Riding for the leadership of the new SYMCC), argued that it could not be afforded, in part because of genuine practical concerns and in part because they were worried it would subsume money from their own pet projects. Blunkett came up with an ingenious response, putting the manifesto pledges to a vote in both Sheffield council and the SYMCC, after changing the word 'Labour' to 'council'. Since Labour had an overwhelming majority, the motion passed. Blunkett then pointed out to the objectors that they now had to work to fulfil the manifesto commitments, since they were no longer a mere party pledge but council policy. Ironmonger's grace in defeat made a deep impression on Blunkett: he "did everything in his power to see that the policy was implemented efficiently. Observing his demeanour in such an awkward situation was a lesson I have never forgotten. He was close to my heart".[12]

Subsidised transport became the single policy with which Blunkett was most identified until he became a Cabinet minister. The fares were introduced at exactly the level proposed and were frozen until the abolition of the SYMCC in 1986, for most of the time in the face of both Labour and Conservative government opposition and attempts to force local fares to rise, and of a High Court judgment in 1984 challenging the subsidy's legality. The first problem arose in 1975 when Bill Rodgers, the then transport minister, announced that councils should not be free to use revenue as they saw fit – specifically, to subsidise transport – and that he was withdrawing the transport supplementary grant, thus removing £9 million at a stroke from the budget. The Labour group was split, with the leadership not wanting a confrontation with the government and worried that sticking to the policy might be *ultra vires*, but the more left-wing members, led by Blunkett, urging that the policy be maintained – an interesting foreshadowing of the disputes over rate capping that engulfed Blunkett as council leader. Blunkett won by three votes and then, as a constituency Labour Party delegate, proselytised for the policy at that autumn's Labour Party conference. (This was Blunkett's second speech at party conference; his first had been two years before in 1973, when he had seconded a resolution on the National Enterprise Board put forward by the APEX union.)

Speaking for the NEC, Shirley Williams attacked the fundamentals of Sheffield's plan as economically deluded (she espoused, Blunkett wrote a decade later, "a monetarist policy" against his plans).[13] "I am afraid she had not got a clue about transport and the conference overwhelmingly voted in favour of the SYMCC's policy. How could they not? It was not 'mere Socialism', as claimed by detractors. It was sound common sense."[14]

The real crisis came in the 1980s under Blunkett's leadership of the council. When the GLC launched its Fares Fair scheme in 1982 (based on the Sheffield policy), it prompted a legal challenge by Bromley Borough Council (which understandably objected to its residents having to subsidise the transport arrangements of non-residents). Bromley won on the grounds that the introduction of the policy had not followed the proper legal procedures. As in 1975, the SYMCC officers urged that their own scheme be dropped, too, but Blunkett took legal advice and was told that the ruling did not apply elsewhere. Whatever its fiscal merits or otherwise, the scheme was certainly popular. In January 1982, there were 100,000 signatories to a petition in favour of the subsidies in just under a week, and the petition soon hit 250,000.[15] During 1982–3, more passengers boarded per mile in South Yorkshire than anywhere else in the UK.[16] Even today, Blunkett is still widely associated – and praised – in Sheffield with what is remembered as a golden age of public transport.

What finally put paid to the scheme was the abolition in 1986 by the Conservative government of the metropolitan county council (along with the GLC). Under Blunkett, Sheffield City

Council continued to subsidise transport for a further year until forced to admit defeat and abandon the policy.

Blunkett was heavily committed. As a student he had had to use his study room as an office, since councillors were offered no secretarial or office support. After graduating he had become a full-time teacher at Barnsley Tech, although as his council duties increased he reduced his teaching commitments by four hours a week – which made barely a dent in his considerable workload at Sheffield Town Hall and the Barnsley office of the SYMCC.

When Alastair, his first son, was born on 27 March 1977, he decided that something had to give and so the following May he relinquished his position on the SYMCC's Executive and Policy Committee. But he was soon even busier. In May 1976 he was elected chairman of Sheffield City Council's Family and Community Services Committee (Social Services), a position he held until 1980, when he was elected as leader of the council. The city council met monthly, as did the committees and subcommittees, which meant he was attending three council meetings a week. Add to that the trusts, environmental groups and school governing bodies that he chaired, plus local party meetings, and his life was one long round of endless meetings. "There seemed little point ... envying those contemporaries who led more carefree lives. I was far too serious and politically motivated to dwell on such matters. On the contrary, I recognized how fortunate I was to have become a councillor at such an early age. It had allowed me to rise unusually swiftly, for those days, to the position of a committee chairman. In the seventies, particularly outside London, it was common for councillors to wait a decade or more for such promotion, whereas I had achieved it within six years."[17]

Blunkett's first action on assuming the chair was to change the rules and conditions under which geriatric homes were run – "virtually workhouse conditions", as he called them. His visits as a young man to his grandfather in the geriatric ward had left a deep impression on him and he was determined to do something about the conditions. He pressured the local health authority into closing some of the more decrepit units, such as Fir Vale, replaced them with care homes and increased the number of home helps available. Blunkett successfully pushed for flexible 'elderly person support units' in local areas, run by 'community support workers' to provide the whole range of services needed by the elderly, from occasional one-off help to give carers a break to comprehensive care programmes, aimed at giving the elderly a choice between staying in their own homes or going into a care home. He saw this as being of a piece with his more general economic and social views:

The market treats the elderly as it does other so-called non-productive groups – not as people, but as economic and social problems. Such problems are less acute for those who can afford the best institutions, or adapt their houses and pay for facilities. A rational approach to the economy and to collective organisation could ensure that wealth created during working years is returned over the whole of one's life. It is not simply a matter of 'caring for the elderly', but of ensuring that an increasingly active older population can contribute to society and tailoring necessary support accordingly, as strength and health fails ... The concept of home helps has broadened into one of community support workers. Jobs ... have been expanded – 800 people applied for 21 vacancies in the first unit. Those chosen were mostly local people, not professionals from 'the smart end of the city', as one applicant put it, although this is not to discount the effective professionalism which also made the scheme possible.[18]

Service provision for the elderly was an undoubted success and was widely recognised at the time as having become among the best in Britain. But there was a downside. There was a limited cake to be shared out and services to some other groups – especially children and the disabled – suffered from a consequent lack of resources.

Blunkett's position as a committee chair proved invaluable in a more practical way. As a ward councillor on a busy estate, he had mountains of paperwork, over which he would have to spend hours at his typewriter. The custom was that the secretary to the Director of Social Services would also help with the chairman's paperwork and Lynn Brown, the director's secretary, was happy to oblige and allowed Blunkett to dictate letters directly to her. He would sometimes bring Alastair with him into work at the town hall, at a time when such behaviour was extremely unusual.

Two years later, in 1978, Blunkett had a stroke of good fortune which, at the time, was heavily disguised. After a long illness, John Mendelson, the MP for Penistone, died, resulting in a by-election in what was a safe Labour seat between the boundaries of Sheffield and Barnsley. The nomination was wide open and Blunkett saw an early and unexpected opportunity to move into the Commons. (He had fought the safe Conservative seat of Sheffield Hallam in February 1974, winning 27.2 per cent of the vote.) He put his name forward. Penistone was very much National Union of Mineworkers' seat and there was some resentment of the pushy outsider who thought he could muscle in. But he was maturing into an impressive performer and, after securing a ward nomination with the help of his council colleague and friend Helen Jackson, he shone at the hustings. He lost the nomination by just one vote (beating the future MP Chris Mullin into third place). At the time, the defeat was galling. To have come so far and lost so narrowly was difficult to take. But with hindsight it was the best possible result. Had he won, he would have entered the Commons as merely another northern Labour ex-councillor. He would almost certainly have gone nowhere. As it was, he not only had his card marked for future selections, he was able to gain the most important experience of all, as leader of the council and an NEC member, so that when he did make it to the Commons he entered not as an unknown but as a national figure with a major party role.

As part of the by-election campaign, Blunkett was to introduce the Chancellor of the Exchequer, Denis Healey. Healey was driving up from London and Blunkett's job was to keep the meeting going until he arrived. Twenty minutes came and went, with no sign of the Chancellor. Thirty minutes; still no Chancellor. Forty minutes. After forty-five minutes Blunkett had plain run out of anything to say. Desperate, he confessed to the audience what was happening, and said how much he hoped for everyone's sake that Healey would arrive soon. A deep voice then piped up: "I've been here for twenty minutes, young man, but keep going – I am enjoying it."

Around this time, Blunkett began to realise that Ruby – who was now ten – was limping. She was diagnosed with arthritis and a replacement was needed. Ruby was allowed to stay with Blunkett as a pet – Ruth was spending most of her time at home with Alastair – and, miraculously, as soon as the dog realised she no longer had to work, her old energy returned and her arthritis seemed no longer an obstacle to her bounding over fences.

Ruby's successor, Teddy, was a very different character. For one thing, he was much bigger. "Here was a dog – a chocolate-coloured, curly coat retriever/Labrador cross – who needed brushing, but did not shed golden hairs all over the carpet, furniture and my trousers. Here was a dog who appeared not to be obsessed with food and took a genuine interest in where I wanted to go. My sort of dog. He was big and magnificent, and also extremely fast. Immediately we began training together I started to lose weight. Later it was to cross my mind that the hernia which had to be repaired in 1980 might have had something to do with Teddy's strength and the muscle power required in dealing with him."[19] He was also a far more dedicated dog than Ruby; where Ruby had thought of her master's needs almost as an afterthought, Teddy would always put Blunkett first. One day during their first winter together, this was to prove more valuable than Blunkett had ever imagined. The heavy snow meant that Bob Glendenning, who would normally give Blunkett a lift to his teaching job at Barnsley Tech, was stranded at home in Derbyshire. After three buses and a five-mile walk, Blunkett and

Teddy eventually reached their destination. Hardly anyone else had bothered to turn up and as the snow worsened he realised that, unless he set out to return to Sheffield straight away, he would not make it back. No buses were running and so he made his way to the station more in hope than expectation. A train eventually arrived and Blunkett got on. Not that this meant any real progress. After crawling along for a few miles, the train stopped and a message came over the Tannoy that it would not be moving. Three earlier trains were stacked up in front at frozen points. The passengers were told to disembark.

To get off the train required jumping six feet from the compartment into a steep embankment covered in snow. Teddy refused to jump, leaving Blunkett to do so alone. Eventually, after much persuasion, Teddy was cajoled into jumping. As Blunkett puts it, "The 'gentle giant' literally hauled me through the snow that icy winter's afternoon as I followed in his footprints up miles of totally deserted, snowbound streets to our home in Grenoside on the hill north of Sheffield. Whereas I had no clues where pavements ended and roads began, Teddy was sure-footed, strong and determined. Without him, I might well not have got home safely that day."[20]

Even if Teddy had been with Blunkett on a holiday in France instead of enjoying his own break at the GDBA centre in Bolton, he would not have been able to prevent what could easily have been a much more serious accident. The family arrived at their holiday complex just outside Bordeaux on a sweltering-hot August day and made a beeline for the beach. The sea was rough but Blunkett was lured in by the heat. In calm sea Blunkett can orientate himself through the sound of the waves lapping on the shore. In rough sea, however, the noise and conflicting currents make this very difficult. Within a few minutes he became totally disoriented and started swimming out to sea. Only the eagle eyes and prompt action of his friend and fellow councillor, Helen Jackson's son, Ben, averted a tragedy, as he swam after him and shouted directions.

Unlike in most city Labour parties, there was relatively little schism between the old guard and the newer activists who emerged across the Labour Party in Sheffield in the 1970s and 1980s. There was no palace coup such as Ken Livingstone had engineered in London, when seizing control of the Labour group on the GLC in 1981 – the day after Andrew MacIntosh had won the support of the electorate at the polls as the putative leader of the council. The younger generation – as Blunkett's own story shows – had been welcomed and assimilated into the party and had been given power and responsibility on committees. But a consequence was that the issues of party democracy that ripped Labour apart in the 1980s came to the fore in Sheffield much earlier, albeit with less of a struggle over the need for such things as reselection. "It was a much more gradual shift towards democracy," Blunkett wrote at the time.[21]

One of the first deselections in the country took place in Sheffield Brightside (later Blunkett's own constituency) in 1974, transferring the seat from Eddie Griffiths to Joan Maynard. Sheffield was ill-served by its MPs at the time. Most did not even bother maintaining a flat in the city. This suited the ruling powers on the council, as they would not face interference from MPs who had no real idea of what was going on in their nominal patch. For the younger breed of councillor, however, this was quite wrong and they sought to have Sheffield representatives who would truly represent Sheffield. Although the immediate cause of Griffiths's deselection was his dreadful relationship with the constituency Labour Party's General Committee, the underlying motivation was the idea of a new breed of MP who would see themselves as representatives of the party activists. Griffiths was a traditional, old right Labour MP; the activists were supporters of extra-parliamentary action and on the radical left. Maynard herself – 'Stalin's Granny', as she was known – although a figurehead of the new broom, was not from Sheffield either. But her selection ushered in an era when Sheffield's MPs were all local: Blunkett in 1987, followed by Clive Betts, Jimmy Boyce, Helen Jackson and Bill Michie.

There was a further factor. As Hilary Wainwright, author of a study of the Sheffield party, observes:

The Brightside deselection was an indication of the changes taking place in those few working-class constituency parties which were drawn into the industrial and community militancy of the late sixties, rather than bypassed by it. It was a case of a clash between youngish, mainly working-class activists radicalised through their union, the Amalgamated Union of Engineering Workers, or through the impact of a local tenants' campaign and rent strike and an ineffectual, conservative MP. In earlier days such an MP would have got away with it, through a combination of applied charm and his committee's deference.[22]

The Brightside deselection was a pivotal moment in Sheffield politics. Those behind it became the dominant group in the party (known in the city as the Brightside Mafia) and over the next few years Blunkett emerged as their leader. In 1975, the movers and shakers went away together over the spring bank holiday. Within a couple of years this had become a large annual event. With their families, the group eventually rose to almost two hundred. As a regular attendee describes it, "We would have this huge encampment in a circle, with campfires and continuous football games played in the middle. We'd stay up all hours talking politics."

But for all their dominance of the party, their influence on the council leader, George Wilson (who had taken over from Ironmonger), was limited. Wilson was a very different figure from his predecessor, with none of Ironmonger's personal warmth. His problem was that, as Blunkett puts it, although he had "a political nose and an instinct for how the land lay, he really couldn't cope with modern change". He was out of sympathy with the more radical element which was taking over the district party. For the first time in Sheffield Labour politics, a gap was emerging between the Labour group and the district party. By 1979, the Left had decided to mount a formal challenge to put down a marker for the future and to signal its unhappiness, and nominated Blunkett to stand against Wilson for the leadership. Blunkett's vote was sufficiently large (27 to Wilson's 35) to make the point and to establish him as the heir apparent. "We didn't actually think that we'd do it but we had to signal that we weren't prepared just to put up with what was going on and that there had to be a more radical approach." With local elections due in 1980 and candidate selections working in the left's favour – and thus towards a new balance in the Labour group – it was clear that the following year he would almost certainly win.

For the rest of the year, Wilson was in office but not in power, forced to accept the demands of the Left under Blunkett. A clear divide emerged between the fractured Labour group on the council and the constituency parties, with the Labour group in chaos and a party operation that was functioning well, as the elections were to show. When a new Conservative government announced its readiness to cut local government grants, the group decided that it had two choices: cuts or a massive rate increase. Not surprisingly, given their political views, they chose the latter and pushed through a 37 per cent increase, implemented on 1 April 1980 – a calendar month before polling day. As if that were not enough, Wilson then resigned on 30 April as leader of the group, denouncing Blunkett and the rate increase in the local media on polling day (he later joined the SDP). Neither, however, had the slightest impact on the result, Labour securing a majority of 33 on the 87-seat council.

When the vote for the leadership of the Labour group came, immediately after the elections, it was effectively a run-off between Blunkett as the 'soft left' candidate and Bill Michie (who went on to become Blunkett's Chief Whip) as the 'hard left' runner (to use the labels of the time). The result was never in doubt.

The year 1980 was one of enormous fulfilment for Blunkett. Not only had he been elected leader of the council in May, within ten years of joining it, the following July he was elected chairman of the Association of Metropolitan Authorities Social Services Committee, which gave him a national platform. And then on 13 July his second son, Hugh Sanders (named after his grandfather, Sanders Blunkett), was born.

Blunkett may have been seen as the least left-wing candidate for the leadership but his election still induced near-panic ("terror", as Blunkett remembers it) in the town hall: "They were going round saying, 'Oh my God, you know, this guy's going to be the leader, what the hell are we going to do?' I had to say to the chief executive and the senior team that a revolution hadn't taken place and that we actually knew what we were doing – we were experienced and had a clear idea." The impression that a revolution *had* taken place was, however, reinforced by the raising of the red flag over the town hall on Blunkett's first day in office: "A pure piece of gesturist nonsense, for which I plead entirely guilty. I didn't have then the political clout to stop it. And I wasn't going to waste capital on that and then go down on other more important things." By "other more important things", Blunkett clearly had in mind council-house sales. Sheffield council owned 45 per cent of the local housing stock in 1981. Blunkett saw straight away that fighting so popular an idea would be hugely counter-productive and went out of his way to force his colleagues to accept the policy, arguing that instead of opposing sales the council should dissuade tenants from ever wanting to purchase their homes through a combination of low rents and efficient repairs. It was a tough fight: he won by a single vote in the party and by just three in the Labour group.

Not that there were not other attempts at gesture politics, such as a proposal – successfully resisted by Blunkett – to ban KitKats from the town hall because of the unpopularity of their manufacturer, Nestlé, with the Left. But the council did twin Sheffield with the Soviet mining town of Donetsk (described by one official Sheffield council visitor afterwards as a 'hell hole') and the Labour group's manifesto for the 1983 election included commitments to promote world peace by "the introduction of peace studies into schools and colleges" as an "urgent priority", and to stop spending money on nuclear weapons.[23] One wonders what plans the Soviets had to counter the threat posed by Sheffield City Council's own independent deterrent. A further gesture that Blunkett refused to make was over the name of his third son, Andrew. A long-planned UN conference on apartheid and racism was to take place in Sheffield on 31 October 1982. That night, as leader of the council, Blunkett was due to make a keynote address at a formal dinner to an audience including luminaries such as Oliver Tambo, President of the American National Congress. Instead, he spent it at Jessop Hospital with Ruth, attending Andrew's delivery. The next day he was urged to name the boy after Nelson Mandela. He resisted (although his second name, Keir, was in tribute to Keir Hardie).

A decade later, he attacked his own time as council leader in a column in the *Daily Mail*: "I have been plagued by political correctness all my life . . . On the council, it began with simply changing the names of things . . . There was the ridiculous suggestion that words such as 'manhole' were no longer acceptable . . . My personal experience is similar. I am blind. It is a simple enough word for an obvious enough fact. Yet people want to call blindness anything but blindness . . . The puritanism that is part of political correctness seeks to instil guilt about simple, guilt-free things."[24] He now refers to many of his initiatives as leader of Sheffield as "zany".

Under Blunkett, Sheffield came to be seen as the vanguard for a new form of municipal socialism and was mocked as the Socialist Republic of South Yorkshire. But where in London and Manchester, for example, this new brand of Labour was marked by schisms and battles within the party, in Sheffield there was relatively little ill feeling. Blunkett's election was not a coup by one group, as with Livingstone in London, but a logical and relatively uncontroversial development. And the label was more about the myth-making that suited Blunkett at the time than the reality. His two most senior council lieutenants were Clive Betts, a

Cambridge-educated councillor who went on to succeed Blunkett as leader and then to become a fellow Sheffield MP, and the Reverend Alan Billings, a vicar who had been active in parish politics, chairman of the housing committee and budget subcommittee respectively. Although identifiably of the New Left, neither was remotely extremist and both would also have fitted easily into traditional Labour municipal authorities.

Sheffield was certainly at the epicentre of many of the key Labour battles of the early 1980s – opposition to rate capping, cheap transport, the 1981 steel strike and the 1984–5 miners' strike. Some of these were unavoidable Sheffield issues; the Hadfield steel works and the Orgreave coking plant meant that the city's politics would always have been imbued with the impact of the strikes. But others, such as the struggle against rate capping, were deliberately chosen as battles by Blunkett to demonstrate the council's – and his own – left radicalism, even if the reality of the council's day-to-day behaviour was far more mundane. Other similar cities adopted different, more pacific tactics. Blunkett and his allies chose confrontation. But Blunkett's behaviour was always calculated; unlike some of his more hotheaded colleagues, he was careful to provide himself, and his council, with the means of backing down without losing face – and still gaining credibility on the Left as a national figure. Even some of the more seemingly clichéd New Left initiatives, such as the council's Employment Department, had their directly practical side.

What separated Sheffield under Blunkett from other radical councils was that the local political leaders were, almost to a man and woman, born and bred in Sheffield and mainly working class. They thus remained much closer to traditional Labour supporters and avoided the excesses of the GLC's gesture politics. Ken Livingstone, for instance, then the leader of the GLC, was – and is – a very different figure from Blunkett. Livingstone tried to base his power on a so-called 'rainbow coalition' comprised of various minorities and middle-class wannabe working-class lefties. Blunkett may have pursued a seemingly Bennite agenda as leader but tactically he was very different, insisting the whole time on grounding his policies in traditional working-class priorities. As Blunkett puts it:

Sheffield was unusual in that I believe we managed to be radical without the lunacy which affected some Labour councils. We were certainly distinct from Militant Tendency, which advocated old-style dictatorial politics, where voluntary organizations were *persona non grata* and decisions were made centrally and applied no matter what the local people wanted. We in Sheffield kept the support of the electorate even when we inevitably made mistakes. Any politician who claims never to have made a mistake has never taken leadership or attempted to implement radical ideas or move in new directions; it is very easy to be a cabbage.[25]

This 'feet on the ground' approach is critical to understanding Blunkett's political development. Sheffield was lumped in the media at the time with the GLC as an example of 'loony left' council behaviour. Sheffield council under Blunkett may have been misguided in many respects but the comparison is flawed. Writing at the time of Blunkett's leadership, Hilary Wainwright put it perceptively: "There is a cautious, controlling strand in Sheffield's Labour Group; a wariness about raising expectations, which appears the opposite of the GLC's 'open up, accelerate and take off' approach."[26]

The seeds of Blunkett's later disillusionment with the Bennites, who in the early 1980s came near to taking the Labour Party over and pushed it almost to political oblivion, were also visible in this contrast. Tony Benn records in his diaries a meeting in Sheffield in November 1981 with Blunkett, Roger Barton, the deputy leader of the council, Richard Caborn, the MEP for Sheffield, Bill Michie, a councillor, and Keith Jackson, the vice-principal of Northern College: "To cut a long story short, they told me they thought I had made a mistake to make an issue of the North Sea oil compensation and thereby get myself thrown off the Shadow Cabinet. They were anxious that the Left shouldn't be blamed for disunity. They were nervous of what they thought was a sectarian London set dominating the strategy that I follow . . ."[27]

On becoming leader, Blunkett inherited his predecessor's personal assistant, Valda Waterfield. She remained with him until the end of 2004, running his Sheffield office. Although her role in sorting out his immensely complicated professional life was key, she also developed a close rapport with his new dog, Teddy. "She would often take him out literally for 'a run' while I was tied up in meetings. Teddy never walked. His legs were so long he always seemed to canter and Valda was pulled along behind. This did not pose too much of a problem except in winter when the pavements were icy and it was rather like making the journey on skis."[28]

That August, Blunkett, Ruth and the children went on holiday to Scotland with their close friends Helen and Keith Jackson and Clive Betts. It was not the best of weather: "One lunchtime, on an especially dreary day, someone had the bright idea that we should drive to the nearest pub for a wee dram and a bit of cheer. A couple of miles along the road, with Teddy breathing down my neck from the back of the car, a thought suddenly struck me. 'Where's [baby] Hughie?' I asked the others. And where was he? He was still tucked up in his cot back at the croft where we had left him. What guilt as we sped back to retrieve him!"[29]

Time-wise, Blunkett's life was beginning to get out of hand. As a lecturer, leader of the council and chairman of the Association of Metropolitan Authorities Social Services Committee, he was effectively doing three full-time jobs and as a consequence could not give any of them the necessary time. It was clear which would have to give. He negotiated a deal with Barnsley Education Authority, who let him go on secondment for three years (after three years they would no longer be required to contribute to his pension) to the council. Blunkett agreed to repay his councillor's allowances. He took a substantial pay cut but the benefits far outweighed that problem. At the very least, cutting out the repeated journey to and from Barnsley gave Blunkett far more time in which to concentrate on his real job: politics.

Election as leader meant that, on one level, he no longer had to prove himself; he had won the trust and respect of his peers. But on another, he had far more to prove than ever before; the idea of a blind man doing such a high-profile, high-powered job was still incredible to many, not least because, with Andrew's birth in 1982, he was also father to three young children.

Blunkett had a well-earned reputation for being, as he himself puts it, "strong-willed and bumptious". Having achieved so important a position, some might have expected him to relax. The opposite was true. In every position of power he has held, from leader of the council to Cabinet minister, he has been regarded by staff as one of the most demanding of bosses. Town hall officials did not know what had hit them. As one puts it: "We weren't used to it. We knew he had a reputation for being intolerant, but that was wrong. We had been used to a nice, gentle ride. It wasn't that he was intolerant. It was that he seemed on a personal mission to drive every one of us harder than we had ever imagined working. But if you did the job you were supposed to do, he remembered who you were, no matter how lowly you were. And if you didn't pull your finger out, he remembered that, too."

In his seven years as leader, Blunkett came to be seen by the media as one of the key 'hard' or 'loony' left figures.[30] His chosen label was 'firm' – "durable and reliable, without being inflexible" (to contrast with the more generally used 'soft', "which would have implied that we were malleable under pressure"[31]). Neither label properly explains Blunkett's positioning as leader. His aim was clear: "to steer a different route from, on the one hand, the old Labour tradition of paternalistic 'do as I say' politics, in which everything was determined by the Town Hall and, on the other, the Militant Tendency, which was rampant on Merseyside in the eighties. We endeavoured to create socialist policies which would be credible, viable alternatives to those of the Right of the Conservative Party as exemplified by Margaret Thatcher's monetarist deregulated market economics'.[32]

The election of a Conservative government changed the whole context of local government. During the 1960s and 1970s, local government was ignored by ambitious political figures and commentators. It was in most respects merely the local administrative arm of central government. This changed in the 1980s. After 1979, it was the only arena in which Labour activists could exercise power; and with the changing politics of Labour activists themselves, the Left was determined to use this to challenge not just the Tories but also traditional Labour policies, and instead to implement the range of anti-racist, anti-nuclear, feminist and radical socialist ideas that were becoming characteristic of Labour activists.

Many of the contradictions within Blunkett's ideas as a minister were first played out in his time as leader of Sheffield City Council. Blunkett talks a lot as Home Secretary about community. There is a direct line between his ideas today and those he first put into practice as leader of Sheffield council.

We tried to give people a greater say in their community and make them feel that the services belonged to them, not to the council. In our attempts to open up council policy to popular influence, we not only continued to hold regular ward surgeries but also increased the number of public meetings in order to air key issues, such as developments in our cheap-fares, integrated transport policy . . . [We] initiate[d] neighbourhood committees of tenants on council estates, providing them with environmental budgets to enable them to make decisions concerning their own patches. Long before it became commonplace, we were keen on local people serving as governors and managers of schools and colleges. Among other innovations, we also encouraged disabled and elderly people to become involved in the running of the day centres they attended.[33]

And yet for all the rhetoric and the professed aims, one of the most consistent and well-merited criticisms of Blunkett's time

as Education Secretary was that reforms were imposed from
above. The same is true of his time as council leader. Reforms
were sold as 'socialism from below' but they were usually marked
by a careful hold on real power. 'Opening up' meant wider
consultation. Council-house tenants, for instance, were simply
given a place on the area housing committees (although they
were given the right to spend a very limited amount of the
housing budget on items they themselves wanted). Consultation
only went so far. When the participants fell into traditional
Labour categories – council tenants and trade unionists – and
gave the right answers, then their input was welcome. But when
they did not speak as party activists expected, it was not. In
1981, for instance, the district Labour Party decided at its manifesto meeting to include a pledge to abolish both corporal punishment and uniform in Sheffield schools. After the council
election, a consultation exercise among teachers, parents and
pupils showed overwhelming opposition; their views were merely
ignored.

But this was not as simple a case of hypocrisy as it seems, at
least on Blunkett's part. The manifesto pledge was forced on
him – as well as the other senior councillors on the education
committee and the education officers, all of whom opposed the
abolition of uniforms – by the activists on the district Labour
Party. The episode needs to be seen in the wider context of
Blunkett's riding the Left horse. The consultation was specifically
intended by Blunkett as a means of prevarication and delay,
rather than to discover the views of parents, which were already
well known. But it was, all told, a pretty sorry mess. When
uniforms were indeed abolished, Joan Barton, the chairman of
the education subcommittee, told the *Sheffield Star* that "We did
explain at the outset of asking for people's views that this was
not a referendum. We didn't say we would decide along the lines
people voted for."[34] Blunkett's explanation at the time for going
ahead with abolition was not so much ingenious as bizarre,
managing – in the spirit of the 1980s municipal Left – to draw

on the behaviour of totalitarian regimes: "The council recognizes criticisms of those countries and regimes carrying out what we consider to be dictatorial and totalitarian actions, requiring uniformity and compulsion which we hopefully can manage to do without. The council therefore decided not to do away with school uniforms but to allow individuals and their families to comply reasonably with a standard of dress which was acceptable to the school."[35] Blunkett the parent voted in August 1995 to restore uniforms at the school attended by his sons.

Blunkett became a master at playing to the left gallery, stirring up his natural power base and keeping them behind him but ultimately accommodating their more dogmatic and ideological positions with reality. The futile opposition to rate capping was a case in point. Similarly, Blunkett was expert at working with the local party and was careful as leader to use the party as ballast to the workings of the council. The Employment Department that he set up, for instance, was run in accord with regular meetings with the district Labour Party's Employment Manifesto Committee, on which sat both trade union and party delegates. So closely did the Labour Party and the trade unions work in Sheffield that they were almost interchangeable, and with the dominance of union-based employment this meant that Sheffield labour politics were indeed representative of the wider population. But the economic and social composition of Sheffield was changing. In 1981, Sheffield had the third-highest employment dependence in the country on mining, iron and steel; by the 1990s, two-thirds of employment was in the service sector. The Labour Party and trade unions were becoming increasingly less representative of the city.

Blunkett provided his own account of what he was trying to do as leader in the Fabian pamphlet *Building from the Bottom: The Sheffield Experience*. The pamphlet was published midway through Blunkett's period as leader. The 'alternative economic strategy' – a conscious echo of the Labour Party's national platform – was meant to counter the impact of recession and preserve jobs. In 1981 the city council was reorganised, the existing Finance and Estates Departments being replaced by an Employment Committee and Department designed to implement the policies outlined in the pamphlet. In similar vein, senior appointments throughout the town hall went to those who were politically onside and a Strategy Unit (run by Blunkett's co-author, Geoff Greene) was set up as part of the chief executive's office, charged with ensuring a consistent political approach throughout the council. In addition, a copy of the full Labour manifesto was issued to every member of staff. The existence of a manifesto outlining the policy commitments of the Labour group was itself a departure; until Blunkett became leader, the Labour local manifesto consisted of a record of council achievement, with electors invited to vote for the party as an endorsement. In this respect Blunkett was a model Bennite leader. The process of drawing up the manifesto was seen as critical, designed to tie the next administration to a clear set of commitments that had to be implemented, regardless of bureaucratic conservatism. The 1983 Sheffield Labour Party manifesto was fifty-nine pages and over 25,000 words long. After the election, the manifesto was (as Blunkett had first learned to do over transport in 1973) formally incorporated into council business as part of the policy committee's agenda, with 'Manifesto Working Parties' drawn up to keep a check on its implementation.

Blunkett learned one particular lesson from his time as leader:

I learnt that unless you embed things in the system, so that the people delivering and the people receiving actually do believe that something is different – that they are operating differently – then when the drive from the centre goes, which it will at some point – the water closes over your head again. And that was self-evident in Sheffield: once the people who were engaged with decentralisation and new means of delivery moved on, then things just reverted back because we hadn't embedded the new culture deeply enough. This is still a major issue in running a Whitehall department – although it's different because as a minister I don't have anything like the constitutional role for change that I had as a leader of an authority.

(As Home Secretary, Blunkett has been heavily criticised for his own repeated criticisms of officials. In his autobiography, he blames the failure to transform services in Sheffield in large part on officials: "the changes met resistance from a number of officials and councillors who were frightened of allowing control of services to slip out of their grasp. They regarded the services with which they were connected as personal fiefdoms".[36])

By 1986 the Employment Department had over one hundred staff and an annual budget of £5 million. In terms of theory, let alone results, however, it is impossible to judge it as other than a failure. Between 1981 and 1986 local unemployment increased from 27,500 to 48,500 (from 9.3 per cent to 16.7 per cent of the local workforce).[37] Blunkett's Employment Department claimed to have created, or preserved, 2,000 jobs – a pretty paltry claim, even if true[38] – which failed to take into account the negative consequences of the policy of high rates, support for trade unions in local disputes and a determined pursuit of contract compliance with private contractors. And many of its interventions were decidedly reminiscent of a strand of employment policy that the experience of the 1970s showed was clearly counter-productive at a national level, but which remained popular on the Left: it invested in the development of new locally made products; it created its own services to replace those offered by private companies; it subsidised twenty-six Sheffield cooperatives; and it gave financial support to local trade unionists engaged in employment disputes. It also sought to attract new organisations to Sheffield. In 1983, it agreed a deal with Arthur Scargill for the National Union of Mineworkers to move to Sheffield with a grant of £500,000 from Sheffield and South Yorkshire County Councils, plus another £20,000 from Sheffield towards the cost of employing twenty workers.[39]

Blunkett argues that it was

correct in concept, but we underestimated the difficulty of the task of drawing in those with expertise in commercial enterprise. We recognized that Britain was working within a global economy and that the market economy was dominant, whether we liked it or not. We therefore tried to develop a middle course between old-fashioned command-planning economics, which we realized would fail, and laissez-faire Thatcherite economics. At one stage we sincerely did believe that we had found an effective alternative to Thatcherism: a decentralized municipal socialism which would provide a catalyst, drawing together business, commerce, trade unions, community groups and workers to save the declining steel and engineering industries. Funds were invested by us to help draw up alternative plans, but in the end we had to face the fact that even our investment in public services could not compensate for what was happening to our industrial base.[40]

Given that he was a council leader and not Prime Minister, this might charitably be termed 'overreach'.

As an employer of over 30,000 people, Blunkett was also in a position to practise as he preached. One of his first acts was to remove the differences in the conditions of employment between manual and non-manual jobs, by establishing single-status employment for all council employees, thus handing all workers the same pension and holiday entitlements and rights to paid educational leave. But he also learned that no employer can avoid disputes, however enlightened they may think they are being. In 1985, the introduction of new IT within the Housing Department provoked a bitter thirteen-week dispute with National Association of Local Government Officers (NALGO) members. The dispute was, in some ways, Thatcherite: Blunkett knew that he had to win and that any hint of weakness would be fatal to his ability to manage. He had form. As chairman of Family and Community Services he had faced – and beaten – an eighteen-week social worker strike, although that had been far easier to deal with because it did not affect many of the public. The

NALGO strike, on the other hand, impacted directly on the public. His tactics worked perfectly. His assistant, Valda Waterfield, contacted the more sensible shop stewards and arranged for them to meet Blunkett – by chance! – in a pub. Blunkett spelt out precisely what was on offer, most of which had been obscured from the shop stewards by the more politically motivated union leadership. The members agreed and the strike – after a series of votes – ended.

Yet in some ways the Employment Department was ahead of its time. According to Blunkett, "we were trying a version of the 'third way' before Giddens invented the term". The collapse in the city's economy (until 1981 unemployment in Sheffield had been consistently below the national average; afterwards, it was consistently above what was, until 1986, a rapidly growing rate) meant that the council faced a severe loss of business tax revenue because of factory closures, at the same time as increased demand for local services from the ever growing numbers of unemployed. This meant the council needed, merely to maintain services, either more money from central government or more income from rates. Since the former was ruled out, this left only the latter – unless the council itself could do something to boost the local economy. It thus established an enterprise and technology zone within Sheffield, and set up two enterprise workshops in which subsidised equipment and floor space were provided to help start-up projects. It also created dedicated, tailor-made training schemes for the unemployed, both managers and workers. All of these would – and do – sit happily on the policy agenda of a New Labour government.

The fundamental problem, however, was that the basic idea of a local alternative economic strategy was misguided. No such strategy could transform the structure of the local economy, having neither the economic nor the political power. Over the seven-year period of Blunkett's leadership, unemployment in Sheffield doubled. The council, Sheffield's biggest employer, announced a no-redundancy policy to try to offset job losses from surrounding industries. This ran the council into deficit, which it tried to overcome by refusing to obey the rate-capping legislation. Rates rose by 41 per cent in 1980 alone, and by 37 per cent in 1981.[41] Blunkett was determined that, budget squeeze or not, Sheffield would continue to pursue its own local agenda, the financial consequence of which was that, in 1984, it was one of eighteen local authorities designated by the Environment Secretary, Patrick Jenkin, to be 'rate capped' at the beginning of the next financial year, in April 1985. Rate capping became the defining issue of Labour politics in the 1980s. Blunkett entered the national stage as a result of the crisis.

Blunkett himself recognised the essential failure of his time as leader, given the objectives he proclaimed:

we only began to scratch the surface of persuading the general public to feel that the schools, libraries, transport, health and social services were theirs and not the council's. When I wrote *Building from the Bottom*, we were still struggling to stop people's houses all being painted the same colour. I was still overturning, as leader of the council, things which are unthinkable now in terms of command and control from the town hall – 'you get this or you get nothing'. It was the same with the big high-density, high-rise flats which Roy [Hattersley] built as chairman of Housing Management.

The year 1985 marked the end of the beginning for Blunkett. Rate capping had created tremendous fissures both between the DLP and the Labour group and within the group itself. Although he remained leader for a further two years, Blunkett was clearly focused on the national platform (he was already a key member of the Labour NEC) and his attention was increasingly drawn towards Westminster. Clive Betts was, for most of the next two years, de facto leader – to such an extent that when Blunkett formally stood down as leader in 1987, Betts was elected to replace him unopposed.

One of the episodes that most damaged Blunkett's reputation was the World Student Games debacle in 1991, which cost more than £147 million in capital spending alone, landing every adult poll tax and then council taxpayer in Sheffield with a £25 annual charge to be paid until 2013.[42] In 1986, the British Students Sports Federation invited bids for the staging of the sixteenth games. In November 1986 the Sheffield City Council policy committee approved a bid in the belief that the capital costs involved would be met by government grant and the costs of running the games by sponsorship and revenue. Misguided as both these assumptions were, the most astonishing aspect of the decision was that no cost–benefit analysis was carried out, the council simply taking as a given that the games would be worth it, generating employment, attracting tourists, giving the city a world profile and updating its sports facilities. None of these assumptions turned out to have any basis in fact. Why, however, Blunkett shoulders the bulk of the blame is something of a mystery. By the time the policy committee approved the bid (pushed for primarily by the chairman of the recreation and leisure committee) Blunkett had, although still leader of the council, stepped down from any day-to-day involvement, and the decision to bid was in any case far from irreversible. But even if he is still held technically responsible for a decision taken under his nominal control, by the time the city was granted the games the following year, he had formally left the council and had nothing to do with any of the planning – or lack of planning – for the games. Blunkett deserves to shoulder responsibility for many mistakes as leader; the World Student Games is not one of them.

Speaking in the Commons as Education Secretary in 2000, Blunkett looked back on his record as leader of the council:

I accept responsibility in respect of the city of Sheffield for the years 1980 to 1987. In 1985, a report by Her Majesty's inspectorate said that Sheffield's was one of the three best education authorities in the country. That was matched by an Audit Commission report that said that Sheffield's public services were 'a shining example'. I stand on my record on education and the comparability of Sheffield with other cities. If I had my time again, I would have introduced 15 years ago some of the measures that the Government are introducing now. The children of Sheffield would have had a greater chance of receiving a better education. However, at that time, we faced a Conservative Government who slashed public expenditure at every opportunity, denigrated public service, undermined the education system and encouraged people to go private. Anyone who looks back to those years should feel ashamed of the former Government's actions.[43]

The ultimate verdict on Blunkett's period as leader of the council rests with the voters. The Labour group maintained, and even increased, its support throughout Blunkett's period as leader: in 1980, Labour received 53.9 per cent of votes; in 1987, 51.2 per cent. Indeed, in 1984, at the height of his national prominence – or, rather, notoriety – the party won 54.5 per cent.

7

A *national figure: Labour in the 1980s*

By 1983, Blunkett was already a national figure. His position as leader of Sheffield council had given him a profile denied to all but a tiny number of party members outside Parliament. In 1982 he had made his first appearance on BBC1's *Question Time*, then an important programme. Blunkett's autobiography includes this account of his debut:

The prospect of making my first appearance on national television before an audience of millions made me nervous, so I was determined to be thoroughly prepared. My homework was comprehensive and it paid off. I remember in the course of the programme, during an exchange with Kenneth Clarke, then number two at the Department of Health, I stated how little low-paid health workers received as a basic wage – a figure which he denied. Counterclaims went on for several more minutes, at which point I pulled out of my pocket a hospital porter's payslip, which I asked Robin Day to read out. Kenneth Clarke was for once speechless. There was no answer. The audience enjoyed it and I believe it helped ensure that I was invited back on to the programme on subsequent occasions.[1]

(On his second appearance, Robin Day's introduction was rendered inaudible by the noise of Teddy lapping water from a bowl and the audience's subsequent laughter. And on another edition of the programme, which Blunkett – and, he sensed, the audience – was finding tedious, when asked by Robin Day, "Mr Blunkett, what have you got to say about this question?", he replied, "Well, my dog's gone to sleep." The audience burst out laughing.)

But although he was influential within the Labour Party, that influence was informal. Blunkett thus conceived the idea of standing for the National Executive Committee, the body that ran the party machinery and, during the 1980s, was the battleground for the volcanic debates over policy and party rules. Given the circumstances of the Labour Party in 1983 – out of power and ripped apart by battles between factions – any politician seeking to rise within the party wanted to be on the NEC. As Blunkett puts it:

The atmosphere at the time was like a state within a state. The NEC and party conference were a sort of bubble. It was almost as though – since in the world outside we'd been thrashed in the election, Mrs Thatcher was dominant and everything was falling apart – it was our cocoon. At that moment of absolute annihilation, the National Executive Committee mattered. And for those few years, being on the NEC was worthwhile. There were moments which I regret greatly of wasting my life, but I think there were some good things done and I learnt a hell of a lot. And we thought at the time that being on the NEC made us nationally recognisable figures. One conference, I was walking along the sea front at Brighton, when I heard a man say: 'It can't be, it is, it can't be.' I smiled to myself, thrilled to be recognised. Then he carried on: 'It is. It's a retriever.' "

With hindsight, it seems preordained that so popular a figure within the party should end up on the NEC. At the time, however, it was no such thing. Not since Harold Laski, professor of politics at the London School of Economics during the forties and party chairman in 1945, had a non-MP been elected via what was then the constituency section. Royden Harrison, one of Blunkett's tutors, who remained a close friend until his death in 2002, had previously tried to get on the NEC, to represent the non-parliamentary, non-trade union element of the party. He had, like all others who had attempted such a feat after Laski, failed, although he had done respectably, gaining 177,000 votes. As a fellow Sheffield resident, Blunkett knew that if Harrison could do that well then he, as leader of the council and a well-known figure within the party and the Association of

Metropolitan Authorities, could do a lot better. And given that local government remained the party's sole political strength, there would surely be many others who agreed with him that local government needed to be represented on the NEC.

Blunkett was lucky that his timing was perfect, since there were, very unusually, two vacancies: Frank Allaun had stood down, and Neil Kinnock had become leader. That meant not having to unseat anyone and offered delegates something of a free vote. They could vote for Blunkett without sending a statement that might be seen as shafting the leadership.

Blunkett remained on the NEC until the abolition of the constituency section in 1998. He was one of the more assiduous members, attending almost every regional party and local government conference and speaking at all sorts of events. Party officials knew that if they could get Blunkett onside on an issue, they were halfway to victory. For one thing, he was a draw; party members loved hearing him, as his speeches were always interesting – he would rarely be routine or bland – and the media were drawn to him. It was hardly a surprise, therefore, that his vote in the annual election was consistently high (which, politically, was an enormous weapon for him – an annual public endorsement by party members).

Blunkett's victory in 1983, when he received 322,000 votes, was nonetheless still a quite remarkable achievement, especially as he was not running on the Bennite 'slate', and given the Bennite hold on the local party delegations to the Labour conference. Just two years before, he had been – rightly – regarded as a down-the-line Bennite. In 1981, he had, as his Constituency Labour Party delegate, voted the straight Benn line. And he gave Benn his full support in his (successful) attempt to win the Labour nomination for Chesterfield.[2] "Looking back on it," he says today,

It seems bizarre that I was supportive of Tony [Benn]. He used to go round with a train of acolytes; it was almost like a medieval parade with the king moving about. I wasn't part of that but I was attracted by the very clear statement of thinking, the way in which he articulated what he'd got to say. It wasn't really until I was on the NEC and saw it for myself that I started to detach myself. The personality cult and the sheer arrogance were unsettling for supporters such as myself, as well as the inability to take on board that the world was changing. Tony was so good at understanding history yet so bad at interpreting it as showing the necessity to change and to move on. His grasp of the historic constitutional issues – on the Levellers and suchlike – was brilliant but we don't live in the time of the Levellers. Secondly, he didn't just back Militant, he believed that they were good, if occasionally mistaken. I'd cottoned on to how awful they were and what they were up to.

It took time, however, for Blunkett's hostility to Militant to emerge.

It was a uniquely eventful time to be on the NEC. The expulsion of Militant, the Policy Review and the more general modernisation of the party under Neil Kinnock gave the NEC a more direct importance than at almost any other time in Labour's history, and few votes were ever a foregone conclusion. Kinnock had to scramble to assemble a working majority on the NEC for almost all the major votes, which gave Blunkett an importance in the party's future direction which was denied even to most Shadow Cabinet members. The decisions taken on the NEC in the 1980s reverberate to this day.

It is easy to forget just how calamitous the defeat in 1983 under Michael Foot was for Labour, and how dire was Kinnock's inheritance. Its 28 per cent of the vote was Labour's lowest share since 1918. Worse even than the vote, the party seemed to be dying on its feet, the victim of changing times, a vicious civil war, inept leadership and a Conservative Party that appeared invulnerable.

Kinnock began the process of rebuilding in his very first speech as leader at the 1983 conference: "If anyone wants to know the reason why we must conduct ourselves in this fashion, just remember the old times and old temptations and remember how each and every one of you felt on that dreadful morning of June 9 and think to yourselves 'June 9, 1983 – never again will we experience that'." The next passage was a clear hint as to what was to be his first big battle, in which Blunkett was to be a pivotal figure – the expulsion of Militant: "Unity is the price of victory. Not unity for four weeks before the general election, not unity for four weeks before the European Assembly elections, but unity here and now and from henceforth, not a cosmetic disguise, but a living, working unity of people of a movement, of a belief and conviction, who want to win in order to save our country and our world."

Blunkett was, quite naturally, appointed chair of the newly created Local Government Committee at the beginning of 1984. It was not intended that the committee, or Blunkett, should be major players in party debates. In many ways it was designed to shunt Blunkett into a dead end. But as so often in politics, the law of unintended consequences came into play and with rate capping becoming the major political issue of the time, Blunkett had been handed a foundation on which he could build himself into a power within the party. (At the end of the decade, local government finance again gave him an unintended opportunity when, as local government spokesman, he eclipsed his boss, Jack Cunningham, on the poll tax.) Over the next eighteen months Blunkett became the de facto leader of the campaign against the government's legislation to limit council spending through 'rate capping', in part through his NEC position, in part also as chairman of the Local Government Campaign Unit, an organisation he had set up to draw together councils and trade unions (which later became the Local Government Information Unit, supported by over seventy councils) and in part as leader of Sheffield council. It is ironic that the campaign against rate capping which brought him to public prominence was, in the end, a total failure; the government won by the political equivalent of an innings.

As soon as he was elected chair of the Local Government Committee, Blunkett called a conference in Sheffield for Labour councillors and activists at which tactics would be decided by the likely affected authorities, to be held two weeks before the Environment Secretary, Patrick Jenkin, was due to announce which authorities would be capped. The political mood on the Left, as the leaders of the rate-capped authorities worked out their tactics, was fully behind those who favoured defiance.

Blunkett played a familiar game: to all outward appearances he was one of the most radical leaders of the resistance movement; but in reality he had a different agenda. Blunkett had two main concerns. First, he had to recognise political reality, which was that within the Labour Party – especially within local government – the only politically sellable policy was one of resistance. Any hint of compromise would have undermined his position fatally. After Labour suffered huge losses in the 1977 local elections, the unpopularity of the Conservative government was leading to the election of large numbers of new Labour councillors, selected in their image by constituency Labour parties and wards that were now dominated by the Bennites. Even where these new councillors broke party rules or defied the whip by voting against budget cuts, the chances of their being disciplined were remote given that the NEC Organisation Committee was chaired by Eric Heffer, a left-wing Liverpool MP.

Blunkett has always been expert at judging the political mood and he sensed that militancy was the order of the day. He was thus forthright in his opposition. As he put it at the 1983 party conference: "If this labour movement does not stand up and fight on this issue, then I am afraid we will be wiped out as a Labour Party, because local government is the only place where Labour representatives are taking decisions about the well-being and lives of ordinary people."

But as early as 1981, long before the specific issue of rate capping had arisen, Blunkett had marked out his opposition to the tactics of the more revolutionary leaders such as Ted Knight in Lambeth and Livingstone at the GLC. In *London Labour Briefing* in November 1981, for example, Livingstone had argued that councils should refuse to vote for "cuts in services or rent and fare increases, and rate increases under the Tories' new system. There is no way Labour councils can balance the books under the proposals",[3] with a similar argument also put forward by Knight. If necessary, councillors should risk bankruptcy, disqualification from office and personal surcharge. Blunkett, however, expressed a different view. In a memo to the Sheffield council Labour group he wrote: "Many of us would be delighted actually to be sent to gaol for our principles, but not ignominiously forgotten after disqualification and lingering surcharge if we failed . . . The clever complexity of the Government's proposals make simple stands extremely difficult."[4] What was needed, rather, were ideas that strengthened councils in their political battle and won the argument with the government, such as "A continual review of Sheffield's budget to eliminate waste or under-used resources" and "Scrutiny of any job vacancies arising to assess their priority". Blunkett was aware that services were often far from efficient, a message that was hardly consistent with the Left's prevailing theme of 'no cuts' (as the dispute with NALGO, the local government trade union, showed). Indeed, despite Sheffield's high spending (8.6 per cent more per capita than the average for metropolitan districts[5]), the council under Blunkett attracted the praise of the Audit Commission. The Controller of the Audit Commission, John Banham, remarked in 1985 that Sheffield was "a shining example" of an efficient local authority, from which many private sector organisations could learn: rent arrears were 3.4 per cent compared with an average of 4.6 per cent; cleaning costs in schools were 12 per cent lower than average; and school maintenance costs were 17 per cent lower than average.[6]

Blunkett knew well that victory was impossible but believed that stridency could perhaps bring Jenkin to the negotiating table and provide him and other less militant leaders with a face-saving means of retreat which would hold Labour together. The decision was taken to fight by refusing to set a rate for the following financial year. The view was that if the government was presented with a united show of defiance and strength the councils could prevail. So at this stage Blunkett remained to all appearances firmly on the side of non-compliance and coordinated the campaign behind it. At the 1984 party conference he put forward an NEC statement he had written, *Defence of Local Democracy, Services and Jobs.* "No individual council should be expected to stand in resisting government policy," he wrote. "Labour local authorities should not act as agents for central government even if the resulting budget is out of line with government policy."[7] Although it was deliberately ambiguous, it was interpreted by most speakers as a licence for civil disobedience. For most of the autumn the issue of resistance within the law versus law-breaking dominated party discussions. Blunkett's conference speech attempted once more to say two things at once: "In the last year, we have had tremendous support for the recognition, the old recognition that socialism will not come from parliamentary action alone. Socialism will come from the fight in the trades unions and in the community . . . We are standing up and fighting for those basic tenets of democracy which people gave all for. So, let us not be afraid of offering ourselves as elected members in the struggle ahead. Let us not pretend that breaking the law is the objective, because it is not. Being martyrs is not what we seek. Martyrs fail. We intend to succeed."[8] High-class rhetorical gibberish.

Kinnock had other ideas. Sitting on the fence between the law-breakers and the law-observers was not an option. One participant recalls a heated meeting around the Shadow Cabinet table when Blunkett, Margaret Hodge and other key local government figures were told in no uncertain terms that illegality was not on the agenda. At that stage, Blunkett seemed to Kinnock to be the archetypal Left council leader. One Labour member of Hackney council at the time, who voted to set a rate, bitingly recalls having been escorted by police into the council chamber for the vote "because we were voting against what David and Margaret [Hodge] wanted to happen". It was only as the campaign panned out that he and Kinnock came to realise that Blunkett was riding two horses at the same time and was managing, somehow, to pilot them both in the same direction.

There was a second concern: the issue itself. For Blunkett, the Conservatives' policy struck at the heart of local government. If central government was to be able effectively to decide the budget of every local authority in the country by determining both rate and budgets, that meant the end of any independence. To think this did not, of itself, imply a revolutionary left agenda of the sort espoused by many of the local government figures working with Blunkett; plenty of Tories came from, and supported, local government. Blunkett's task was somehow to "ride the tiger", as he put it: to keep his credibility with the Left, while fighting a winnable campaign to preserve local government independence. By 'winnable', Blunkett did not envisage defeating the government: he was always realistic about what could be achieved. What he did think possible was a score draw; to be able to say to his colleagues that the government had eased the capping criteria and left authorities with room to breathe.

His hand was not strengthened by the earlier apparent success of Derek Hatton and the Liverpool Militants in appearing to have faced down the government, which encouraged others to feel that victory was possible. Despite Liverpool spending as if it was about to go out of fashion, the government's response was to fudge, rather than take the council on. There was one important way in which this worked to Blunkett's advantage in dealing with Jenkin. Because some felt that victory was indeed possible, they were encouraged to behave themselves in private meetings rather than grandstand, which – if they had believed the whole campaign to be a charade – might have been their more natural position. "We had to say that when we went in to see Patrick Jenkin we would speak with one voice: mine. I would determine before we went in what the line was going to be and we would stick to it. That shook Patrick. We got on rather well [Jenkin chaired the Commons working group that determined the extra resources granted to Blunkett on his election in 1987, just two years later] and he told me that the Tories were flabbergasted that we were able to hold a degree of discipline. They thought we'd be a shambles."

The campaign, however, collapsed almost as soon as it was put into effect. It became clear after the first couple of meetings that there was no chance of victory and that Jenkin would not give ground. The defeat of the miners' strike had utterly changed the terms of political trade. This meant that there was another force pushing towards discipline: the need to avoid all-out humiliation. In March 1985 the GLC resolved that in the real world it had to comply with the law; over the next few months the rest of the opposition to rate capping crumbled. Within the Left caucus on the Sheffield Labour group there was a clear division between what became known as the 'accommodator' Left of fourteen councillors, who would only defy the law up to the point of personal surcharge and disqualification from office, and the twenty-two councillors who refused compromise of any kind and actively sought confrontation with the government. A week before the critical budget vote, due on 7 May 1985, Blunkett addressed the district Labour Party, arguing that the council should set the maximum legal rate and combine it with a deficit budget in the (vain) hope that later in the year central government would make more money available. His advice was rejected by 81 votes to 48. But at the eight-hour council meeting itself on 7 May, twenty Labour councillors voted with Blunkett (and the Liberals and Conservatives) to set, by 46 votes to 38, a legal rate.

The rebellion against rate capping collapsed in spring 1985 as every rate-capped council bar Lambeth and the Militant-dominated Liverpool knuckled under and set a rate. (There was one very minor victory, based more on the government's logistical difficulties than any political problems. The government changed the criterion for determining rate capping from one that was universal to one that was concentrated on picking off the most extravagant spenders.)

This was a pivotal moment, not just in Blunkett's career but in the Labour Party's future. Coming at the same time as the collapse of the miners' strike, action against Militant and the solidity and increasing confidence of Kinnock's leadership, it marked the beginning of a new mood within the party and the end of extremism, similar to that in 1926 when the failure of the General Strike demonstrated to all but a small number that revolution was not the way forward. Looking back, Blunkett can see the crux of the change. "Orgreave [scene of one of the most bitter and violent disputes in the miners' strike] is only half a mile from where I live. The city council gave over £100,000 to the miners' families. I was steeped in that solidarity side of the Labour Party, but in a way that didn't keep me from being able to see and tell the truth about what was going on. Because we weren't under any illusions that Scargill should have settled in August '84. We'd no illusions at all – we all said so privately – but we were still prepared to try and help those families that were just falling apart. It was a terrible mess. Never again. We were determined. Never again."

Blunkett's independence – he was not part of any grouping or on any slate – meant that he became a pivotal figure. When he joined the NEC it was assumed by Kinnock and his lieutenants that he would be another strident Left voice – and vote. His leadership of the rate-capping campaign initially confirmed this assumption. But his handling of the more hot-headed elements showed that the caricature was off beam and that there was a depth and subtlety to his politics and positioning that Kinnock had not appreciated. That he had been able to maintain his stature with the more radical activists while steering them clear of illegality was an impressive achievement which Kinnock realised pointed to someone who could make up his own mind and prove useful in winning the support of the sensible left. Kinnock knew that without Blunkett's support – and that of two others from the left, Tom Sawyer, the newly elected deputy general secretary of the National Union of Public Employees, and Michael Meacher, Shadow Health and Social Security Secretary (who had been defeated by Roy Hattersley for the deputy leadership in 1983), both of whom were seen by the Kinnock camp as biddable – very little could be done. So as a matter of course he would solicit their support before meetings and votes. (This is usually referred to as a triumvirate of Blunkett, Meacher and Sawyer, but the voting records show that Sam McCluskie of the seamen's union, a former party chairman and later treasurer, was just as much a part of the alliance, as Blunkett confirms: "He needed cover, because he was a trade unionist and a Scot who was pretty well out of it, but you could rally him so he was in it as well." McCluskie was, however, from a very different political background.)

But Kinnock still had a lot to learn about party management. His first proposed reform – One Member, One Vote for parliamentary selections – was put to the vote at the 1984 conference. It was a miserable failure. The union leaders, who had most to lose, lined up their block votes alongside those of CLP delegates who, in those days, seemed to view their role as providing the internal opposition to the party leadership. But embarrassing as the defeat was, in the long term it was an important step forward. Kinnock realised that appealing to loyalty was not enough. Only one thing counted: stacking up the votes in advance.

Moreover, it was not enough merely to win. Unless his victories were emphatic, the press – and the hostile elements within the party – would portray him as essentially powerless, at the mercy of the NEC's whims. Thus he made the formation of a leadership-supporting alliance his priority. Given the hold that the Bennites still had on the party organisation, this was not as easy or obvious as it might sound. The right-wing unions' partially successful attempt to take back the NEC in 1982 was a major help, but Kinnock's main good fortune was that those who had previously been slavish devotees of Benn were beginning, slowly, to see that they – and the party – were getting nowhere. Blunkett had been invited on his election to the NEC to attend the left caucus, which controlled eleven of the twenty-nine members, but he instinctively reacted against the assumption that his vote was in their hands, not his own.

Those changes were given concrete form in the foundation of the hard-left Campaign Group, designed to challenge the soft-left Tribune Group (which had been Kinnock's initial power base) in Parliament, and the Labour Co-ordinating Committee, which, as the soft-left's constituency organisation, soon came to be the most important such grouping in the party. Within a year, by 1984, those divisions began to be reflected on the NEC. As Hughes and Wintour put it: "Three distinguishable blocs emerged. The right-wing was led by Gwyneth Dunwoody and Roy Hattersley, the left by Tony Benn, Dennis Skinner and (initially at least) Eric Heffer. But a new Labour Co-ordinating Committee/Tribune-oriented group – sympathetic to the miners' cause, but privately uneasy about the failure to ballot NUM members – was beginning to mark out distinctive ground in the middle. The primary achievement of the first period of Kinnock's leadership was to weld that newly-emergent soft-left grouping into an alliance with the right. That isolated the hard-left, and forged a new, centrist unity in the party."[9] Step forward David Blunkett, whose role on the NEC was henceforward critical.

Blunkett himself puts it like this:

At this time, the task of leading the Labour Party was very difficult, owing to the continual splits and divisions. I like to think I played my part in trying to act as a bridge between the non-Militant Left and the leadership . . . I did my best to put across the message that we were in one party, even though we had our differences and genuinely held alternative points of view. In some respects, this position of holding the balance, even for a short time, probably gave me an inflated sense of my own importance, but it also engendered in me a real appreciation of the political responsibility we were carrying. The situation certainly gave me an opportunity to exercise influence in a way which would not normally have been the case.[10]

Not everyone agrees that Blunkett's role was quite so pivotal. A Kinnock ally at the time disputes the idea that

David represented the soft-left in a serious discussion with the party about where we ought to go. There were a number of iconic figures at that time, of whom in the Shadow Cabinet Cook and Prescott were a pair. David was an iconic figure, Margaret Hodge was an iconic figure. Michael Meacher, in a funny way, was an iconic figure. There were a series of people who played roles around this time. But it was Neil's leadership which moved the party in the direction that it needed to go. Without Neil's leadership it wouldn't have happened, and the question that individuals of the types I've just described had to face up to was whether they were going to back Neil's leadership or not, at times of great difficulty. None of those people made a constructive contribution to changing the party towards the direction in which it had to go.

Despite – and because of – his standing with party members, Blunkett was far from universally popular. One NEC member recalls that he was "despised by the old right on the NEC, who viewed him as out for himself – predatory. He was pushing his own agenda and his own profile. The atmosphere on the NEC could be pretty poisonous then". Kinnock's office considered Blunkett to be fundamentally untrustworthy. They believed that his motivation was simply to shore up his position within Sheffield, with a view towards being selected to fight Sheffield Brightside. Only once he had secured that nomination did he start to nod in Kinnock's direction, and even then he continued to face both ways politically, one day a Kinnock ally and the next an opponent.

Another fellow NEC member at the time argues that Blunkett "was always the slowest to jump, always asking for time to

reconsider. He never took a lead. He wasn't particularly cour-
ageous at the time. Nothing like as brave as Michael Meacher.
At the 1985 Brighton conference Meacher voted for Kinnock
against the miners. That was that – he knew that meant he'd
lose his NEC place, and he still did it. That is not something
that Blunkett would ever have done".

One reason was that he had his own pressures. Whereas Tom
Sawyer had his union behind him, Blunkett was always having
to balance the views of his constituency with his own wishes, so
he was playing a very delicate political game. He had, for
instance, a very difficult time with Joan Maynard, the Brightside
MP, who regarded him as a traitor to the Sheffield left.

An NEC ally explains Blunkett's problems thus: "He was a
provincial politician adjusting to being on a national stage. He
was also on the Left adjusting to getting on and being in the
centre." Kinnock, however, was unsympathetic, and would often
complain to Sawyer about the amount of time that he had to
spend trying to pull Blunkett round. Blunkett would moan on
the phone to Sawyer that Kinnock was going too far; Sawyer
would tell him to buck up and that really he had no alternative.
Kinnock, however, had little time for him. He thought Blunkett
was a populist and that he courted the Left for his own ends.

As a more sympathetic colleague at the time puts it: "Take
the red flag flying over Sheffield; it was all gesture politics. It was
all to make the Left think that he was one of them. But he did
not actually believe in it. What he really wanted was office for
himself and for the Labour Party, and one of the reasons why he
was part of the alliance that backed Kinnock was that he realised
that the only way to get on in the Labour Party was to back
Kinnock, both because he was the leader and also because Kinnock
was the only answer to the Labour Party's problems."

For all Blunkett's importance as a crucial swing vote on the
NEC, the very fact that he was seen as so useful by Kinnock's
office meant that they were more inclined than they might otherwise have been to boost him and his prestige. It served Kinnock's

purpose to build Blunkett up. For all his ostentatious truculence over Kinnock's various proposals, he would almost always – defence being the one exception – cave in when push came to shove. Had he been more recalcitrant and less supportive on crucial votes, he would have found the leader's office starting to undermine him. It is a moot point whether Kinnock needed Blunkett more than vice versa.

The Blunkett/Sawyer/Meacher alliance was most crucial, and most solid, over the Militant expulsion, which was the most important test of Kinnock's leadership. The three would meet prior to NEC meetings in the Royal Festival Hall café (where they were sometimes joined by another NEC member, Jo Richardson, then the MP for Barking), partly to discuss tactics but partly also to gee each other up and stiffen their resolve. Since the late 1960s, members of Militant, an extremist hard-left organisation, had steadily infiltrated the party. They denied they were 'members' of anything; they argued that there was no organisation of which to be members; Militant, they said, was merely a newspaper. With the national party sliding from one crisis to another during the 1970s, and a party machine that had been left to rot by two prime ministers, Harold Wilson and James Callaghan, who were preoccupied with the problems of remaining in office, Militant had been pushing at open doors in the areas in which they chose to operate – mainly constituency Labour parties which the Right had taken for granted and neglected. By the 1980s, they dominated the youth wing of the party. Although the genuine Left of the party shared neither their tactics nor their views, they nonetheless resisted the idea of a purge, in part because memories were still alive of the purge of Bevanites in the 1950s. Others, such as Blunkett, were simply in denial about both the extent of Militant's entryism and the ends they pursued. And Michael Foot, the party leader between 1980 and 1983, was, in some ways intentionally, weak on matters of discipline.

Kinnock had a very different approach. The new leader

realised immediately that unless Militant's hold on so many parts of the party was broken, the idea of a Labour revival was a non-starter. It would also have the twin bonus of showing to the electorate how serious he was about change and how much the party was changing. Because of the neglect of the problem in the past, Militant's tactics had never been put to any real test. The way Militant-run Liverpool council operated was not merely wrong, it was inept. It vastly overplayed its hand in fighting rate capping and when the rebellion collapsed, Kinnock was handed the perfect opportunity to launch his campaign.

The Liverpool crisis arose from the government's attempts to curb local authority spending by means of the Rates Act, passed in 1984. Mrs Thatcher was determined to control local government spending by reducing the annual grant to over-spending authorities and by using the District Auditor to determine when expenditure was illegal. Where the situation was especially grotesque – in Liverpool and Lambeth – legal proceedings were initiated against specific councillors who had refused to set legal budgets as laid down by the government. The penalties were swingeing. Their behaviour was ruled by the courts to be 'wilful misconduct' and the councillors were individually surcharged, threatened with bankruptcy and disqualified from holding office.

The Labour leadership was thus put squarely, and nimbly by the government, in the middle of a crisis. If it did not condemn the councillors, it would stand accused of supporting illegality. But by condemning them, it would guarantee an internal party split which could have catastrophic consequences for the unity that Kinnock had made his mandate. But Liverpool council scored a series of own goals that handed Kinnock the sort of victory that could have been, if the Militant councillors had behaved more sensibly, a fatal defeat. Instead of proving their point and then looking for a way out, they ploughed on, assuming that they would be the leaders of a nationwide rebellion. But support died away once the courts had spoken. Few Labour members, let alone councillors, have ever believed in illegality, still less revolution, which the Militant councillors effectively proposed.

The NEC, under Kinnock's determined leadership, condemned the council. Blunkett's attitude was, at this stage, far from hostile. In May 1984 he had proposed a motion at the NEC, seconded by Heffer, which pledged support for the Liverpool councillors in their refusal to set a rate and which had been agreed by the party's Local Government Committee. Benn's diaries show the extent to which, at that time, Blunkett was behind the councillors: "Blunkett said, 'Liverpool is behaving responsibly.' Heffer pointed out that the Liverpool Council, under its present leadership, had received over 50 per cent of the popular vote, and even the Liverpool press were now coming out in favour of Liverpool's case. We then had a heated discussion about the whole Liverpool problem."[11]

Blunkett was slow to recognise the Militant threat, not least because he had very little experience of it in Sheffield and that which he did have was very different. There was just one known Militant, Paul Green. He was, according to Blunkett, "A nothingness. He wasn't an evil man, he'd just been caught up, as people often are when they become zealots. It was like a religion. Militant gave people certainty in a world of uncertainty. It gave them a bible. It gave them a kind of cloying comradeship which gave them security."

(There had in fact been an earlier Militant presence in Sheffield: Hatton himself. In the late 1970s the future Militant councillor in Liverpool had been a community worker in Sheffield, in Enid Hattersley's ward. "She came to see me, and said, 'I've got this lunatic called Derek Hatton who's a community worker, who's causing me absolute havoc. Can you sack him?' I pointed out that I needed more than her enmity to cause me to sack him. Then he went back to Liverpool. He made no impression whatsoever when he was in Sheffield, none at all. He was just ignored as a loony.")

Famously, Kinnock devoted a large part of his 1985 party

conference speech to an attack on "the grotesque chaos of a Labour council – a *Labour* council – hiring taxis to scuttle round a city handing out redundancy notices to its own workers". It was obvious how the speech would play to a media that delighted in Labour splits and hated Derek Hatton and the other Militants. What was far from obvious was how the speech would go down in the party, especially among the soft-left represented by Blunkett, whose NEC vote was so important. The hostility of the Bennite left was a given. Eric Heffer's theatrical departure from the conference platform typified the reaction. But the soft left could react either way and Kinnock had no way of knowing for certain in advance, since much would depend on the atmosphere in the hall. If they supported his confrontational tactics, it would in effect seal the permanence of the NEC alliance that he had built. If, however, they considered that Kinnock had gone a step too far in so publicly, and so strongly, attacking fellow Labour Party members, then Kinnock's leadership strategy might be permanently destroyed.

Blunkett's reaction was not what Kinnock, or anyone else, expected. The next day, Wednesday, 2 October, Blunkett was scheduled to speak in the local government debate, moving the NEC statement calling for reimbursement of councillors who had suffered financially through rate-capping legislation. The NEC had agreed its statement at the pre-conference meeting on Saturday, 28 September. Kinnock had put forward a resolution distancing the party from the Liverpool councillors. Eric Heffer had then moved an amendment "to support the demonstration taking place today in Liverpool, to praise the courage and determination of the Liverpool and Lambeth councillors".[12] Seeing himself as the one to reach a compromise, Blunkett then proposed his own amendment, which blamed the government for the situation. As Benn describes it: "He said the only question was whether this helped or hindered our prospects of victory."[13] Kinnock's unamended resolution won and it was that which was put to conference later that week. Blunkett's determination to reach a compromise was not, however, spent. It was not for nothing that he was known to some at the time as the Great Amender; he never seemed satisfied with the wording of a resolution, and would always seek to find his own, better version.

Blunkett was riding high at that year's conference, topping the NEC constituency vote and displacing Benn, who had come first for the previous eleven years, a vote that with hindsight can be seen as heralding the decline of Bennism and the rise of the soft left. (Although Blunkett had first won election to the NEC in 1983 without being on any slate, in 1984 he had been supported by the Campaign Group and had thus received a much greater vote. He was then elected top of the poll for eight years until Kinnock, standing as the ex-leader, beat him to first place in 1992.) Not a man to underestimate his own importance in events, he determined that he ought to take a hand in the main events of conference. Immediately after Kinnock's speech on the Tuesday, he went for a swim to unwind. "The more I thought about it, the more I thought, tomorrow I've got to do something fairly spectacular but I've not to hold him under the water because, apart from anything else, I'll then be dead; but also because we need to move this on. There's no point in doing what Heffer did in walking off the platform. I've actually got to engage with it. So that's what I did."

Blunkett took umbrage at Kinnock's all-out assault. The party nationally and at local level had become deeply split. Local government was seen, as Blunkett puts it, "as a problem; not as a potential but as a problem. We were all lumped together. What really got me in his speech – the rest of it was brilliant, about enabling government, but that all got lost in the 'scuttling around Liverpool' – was that it felt as if we were all being lumped together, whereas of course we were very different. I was trying to keep things going for local government despite Ken [Livingstone], who was causing havoc in London, and Hatton and Co. causing havoc in Liverpool. And now it felt as though we'd all been smeared." Coming from his local government background, he resisted what seemed to be an increase in central party control, with the NEC – and London – determining what went on across the country. As a fellow NEC member at the time puts it: "They didn't want the party interfering in how they ran their local power bases." Blunkett also believed that Kinnock's tactics would be counter-productive, turning Militant into the victim and tarring all local government with the same brush. Better, he thought, if independent observers could show that the Liverpool councillors had ignored a sensible means of balancing the books; the case against Militant would be made stronger. He was not alone. Larry Whitty, the Labour Party general secretary, also thought that Kinnock's attitude to Militant was over the top and that he did not seem to appreciate the need for due process.

When Hatton had spoken at conference earlier in the week, introducing his own motion supporting Liverpool, he had argued that if Kinnock had been there to see for himself the calamitous financial situation faced by the council, he would not have spoken as he did. Kinnock should, he said, "come to Liverpool, look through the books, and if you can show me any other option where jobs are safe then fine, we'll do it".[14] Why not use that claim against him, thought Blunkett. Much better for party unity if Hatton could be hung out to dry by his own misdeeds, rather than by mass expulsions. Tony Benn describes the scene in his diary: "There he was, this Christ-like bearded blind man, standing on the rostrum appealing to Derek Hatton to withdraw his Liverpool resolution asking for industrial action in support of councillors 'not prepared to carry out Tory cuts'. 'Will you do that? Will you do that, Derek?' He stood there waving his hands into the darkness. So Hatton, who is a bit of a smart alec, ran towards the rostrum in his neat suit, got up on to the rostrum and said, 'Yes, in the interests of unity, Liverpool will withdraw its resolution.' There was an explosion of applause. I believe the right wing were angry with Blunkett for having done that."[15] Blunkett, of course, had no idea that Hatton was running to the front of the hall. The one thing Hatton, the self-publicist showman *sans pareil*, could not stand was being outperformed. Blunkett had presented him with little choice but to accept the offer, as some of the more politically shrewd Liverpool delegates realised, shouting 'no' as Hatton ran to the podium.

The story had thus moved in less than twenty-four hours from that of a strong leader ripping out a cancer from his party to a senior party figure, still regarded as being on the left, offering an olive branch. Kinnock thought Blunkett had wreaked havoc by changing the atmosphere in the hall and letting Militant off the hook. He was incandescent: "I was bloody furious because we'd painstakingly put together a Conference majority to defeat the motion and show that Militant had left Liverpool bereft."[16] He walked up to Blunkett and told him, "You're bloody good at skating on thin ice."[17]

At that night's Tribune rally, still then the main soft-left meeting of the week, Blunkett was greeted with a standing ovation: "All the groupies want to know you, everything's fine, you're a great hero. But you know that actually that won't last, that's just ephemeral." Indeed, in his speech to the rally he described his position with some accuracy: "Hero today – traitor tomorrow". He was certainly a hero to most of the party, who wanted nothing more than peace and quiet and hated the idea of a witch-hunt. But he was already a traitor to the Kinnock camp, who to this day remember what they see as a combination of grandstanding and treachery.

For many people in the Kinnock camp Blunkett's behaviour was par for the course. One key figure at the time describes the "constant tension" over "the role of David throughout the 1980s, through the rate-capping disputes, through the Militant events, through the conference where he did his bit with Derek".

At the NEC meeting immediately afterwards, at teatime that Wednesday, Gwyneth Dunwoody, who was fully supportive of the drive against Militant, channelled her indignation into a complaint that Blunkett's proposal was unconstitutional. Blunkett describes the meeting: "One of the old trade unionists who was in the chair during the debate didn't know what was going on and agreed to Hatton withdrawing his motion, which wasn't in the constitution. Gwyneth was beside herself. She raised it at the NEC the following day as an outrage to the constitution. But I had the rest of them with me. The reaction was 'Sod off, Gwyneth, we've got these shysters to agree to open the books'."

The inquiry which then took place under Maurice Stonefrost, the former GLC Comptroller of Finance, turned out to be perfect for Kinnock. The Militant-dominated council had been forced to open their books and to reveal how catastrophic their handling of the city's finances had been. The result was clear. The council could certainly have escaped its financial chaos if Militant had not been determined to use Liverpool as a vehicle with which to confront the government. Worse, when the inquiry team proposed a sensible rescue package combining a 15 per cent rates increase with a cut in the house-building scheme, the council rejected it and borrowed £30 million from Swiss banks to fund a stepped-up package of spending.[18] This wilful extravagance swung the doubters firmly behind Kinnock. As a result of the inquiry, Blunkett became convinced that Kinnock had been right all along, although he remains adamant that his proposal for a financial inquiry was critical: "It was a road-to-Damascus moment. But had I not done what I did [at conference], they would have been able to hide behind the smokescreen of the hard-done-by council that was struggling to build houses and look after their people, because my speech opened up that financial inquiry, which blew the lid off of it." He had run a tight ship at Sheffield, and the 'grotesque chaos' of Liverpool's financial affairs demonstrated all he needed to know about the reality of Militant's behaviour. Not only should Militant be excised from the party but those party members – especially those on the NEC – who were unwilling to go along with that excision must themselves be quarantined. Blunkett did not shy away from following through with his newly firm attitude, deciding to go to Liverpool on 4 November to speak at a rally of the Liverpool left and tell them straight that they must implement the inquiry's proposals. In an era when party meetings were always intimidating and often violent, this was no exception – indeed, those who were there remember it as by far the worst of their political careers. Blunkett's blindness helped him get through it: "I'm not susceptible to visual intimidation. It has to be verbal or physical to work on me, and since the cameras were there they could not do that. But I could feel John Hamilton [the nominal leader of the council] physically shaking next to me. It was one of those moments that you never want to go through but it was seminal. It was when the Left outside Militant decided that it was prepared to take them on."[19]

Years later, Blunkett spoke in a Commons debate on Liverpool.

I was a visitor to Liverpool. I knew what the situation was and I examined its budget. The decision was taken to instruct the Labour party in Liverpool to balance the books. My hon. Friend the Member for Copeland (Dr. Cunningham) and the then leader of the Association of Metropolitan Authorities, Sir John Layden, wrote to all members and enclosed a report that I had written, extracted from the Stonefrost committee's report [the NEC inquiry] ... I said: 'A failure now to meet the responsibilities of the council to the people of Liverpool would not only be insane' – I appreciate that these are strong words – 'but a deliberate sabotage of the whole Labour movement.'"[20]

Later that November, Tom Sawyer suggested that the NEC send a team to Liverpool to investigate infiltration and intimidation by Militant, a proposal that Blunkett seconded and which, at that month's NEC meeting, was passed by 21 votes to 5.

Today he recognises that Kinnock's tactics were right all along: "I don't think he had any choice. I think he had to create a massive wave to carry it through, because he would not otherwise have had the momentum to break it. I wasn't quite as far ahead of the game then as I am these days. Neil was. I saw the problem but I didn't think it was a major one. Neil had a perspective I hadn't. I was a local authority leader, he was leader of the Labour Party with advisers, support systems and a network. He got the information, I didn't. I was too busy running Sheffield."

Blunkett was not alone in becoming more convinced of the need to remove Militant the more he was exposed to the facts. Tom Sawyer, one of the eight inquiry members, heard more than enough evidence of Militant's organised, systematic entryism (covert takeovers of local party branches) and witnessed at first hand their intimidatory tactics. As he told the conference of his own union, the National Union of Public Employees (NUPE): "In an atmosphere of intimidation fuelled by parading security guards and hundreds of non-delegates, Nupe representatives were threatened and intimidated because they would not toe the Militant line. Some of the things I saw as a member of the Liverpool inquiry have more in common with the extreme right in European politics than with the left."[21] In February 1986, the NEC considered the inquiry's recommendations for reform of the Liverpool party and the expulsion of ten members of Militant, which it passed 19–10.

By May, the NEC had moved on to expelling the members of Militant. The hearings were awful occasions, as Blunkett recalls. "It was the most gorgeous end of May, people were going on Spring Bank Holiday, the sun was blazing down and we were stinkingly sweating it out for twelve to fourteen hours on the most ghastly sandwiches."

Even by this stage, when Blunkett was in no doubt about Militant's grip, he was still loath to go the whole hog. Peter Kilfoyle, who as Labour's regional organiser in the North-West between 1986 and 1991 was a key figure in the drive against the entryists, records that "some within the legitimate left were still reluctant to grasp the expulsion nettle. They wanted to believe that these were wayward comrades, loyal but misdirected". To wit, he writes of the "David Blunkett/Michael Meacher argument at the NEC that Hatton should be debarred from 'office, delegacy and candidature' but not expelled".[22]

Blunkett seemed to annoy Kinnock even when he had no wish to. It appeared to happen naturally. Kinnock had planned that the Tony Mulhearn and Hatton cases should be dealt with at the NEC on 21 May. But as the day dragged on, with the wily Mulhearn – "the best barrister you will ever meet", according to Blunkett – running rings around the committee members, a tired and frustrated Blunkett said: "I really do think we should adjourn at 9.45 tonight and meet again at 9 tomorrow."[23] The motion to adjourn was carried 11–10. But Kinnock was, as Benn puts it, "in an absolute panic that he wouldn't be able to carry it [the expulsion] out. So during the next break, which lasted for ten minutes, Kinnock did a lot of canvassing, and when we met again at 6.50 he proposed that we go on after 10. So there was another motion, which was carried, that we return at 10.30 after the vote in the House".[24] In the end, the hearing carried on into the next day, when a decision was taken by 13 votes to 7 that Mulhearn was a member of Militant, and by the same figure that he had broken the rules of the Labour Party.

The following day saw some light relief with the case of Councillor Harry Smith from Liverpool. Smith arrived accompanied by "a sallow-faced man with dark hair who kept whispering in his ear".[25] Smith introduced him: "I should introduce the man I have brought with me. His name is George Nibbs – of course, that's only his pen-name."[26] The room collapsed with laughter. The whole tone changed and carried on in that vein as Smith gave his statement: "What would happen if I walked out? I am very nervous. Ian Lowes has been done in and I'm afraid you are going to do me in too. It's like two murderers before a court. The judge says, 'We've hanged one now, we'd better hang the other.' I'm going." Asked by Kinnock whether he felt angry towards Militant for taking advantage of him (he claimed that he had only ever spoken at meetings when asked to do so by the local party, rather than by Militant), he replied: "I'm easy-going. My wife says people take advantage of me, and perhaps they do. My school report says that if I had given more attention to my work I might have been a brain surgeon."[27]

Smith was charged only with Militant membership, not with rule-breaking or malpractice. According to Blunkett: "After agonising I decided that the real factor that counted in his favour was that he was the only 'accusee' who had a sense of humour. It was difficult to accuse someone with a genuine sense of humour of being a hardened central committee man of Militant." And so, with McCluskie, Kitson and Meacher also resolved that they would not vote to expel him, Kinnock made clear that he would not push for expulsion.

Paul Green, the Sheffield Militant, was later expelled by 14 votes to 13, despite Blunkett's urgings that he was harmless. Benn told Blunkett that he had only himself to blame since he had started the "witch hunt"; Kinnock then told Benn that he was suffering from a "hallucination".[28] The expulsion had a further impact; when Blunkett tried to persuade the Labour group in Sheffield that the NEC's authority had to be upheld and thus Green excluded, he was almost defeated, managing a majority of just 4 votes.

Internal party matters, however important to Labour's future, are not the reason able politicians enter politics. At the same time as he was dealing with the Militant imbroglio, Kinnock was attempting to restate the party's aims and values – a seemingly enduring task through the 1980s and early 1990s. Initially, in the spring of 1986, this took the form of a campaign – Freedom and Fairness – focusing on health, education and welfare, which *Tribune* called a "welcome return" to "bread and butter issues . . . presented in a modern, attractive and relevant way".[29] It was not just the Labour press which welcomed the shift to a degree of normality by the Party. The *Financial Times* wrote in its leader columns that "The British Labour Party is again beginning to look like a credible party of Government – at least in the sense that it wants office, and may achieve it."[30] Well received it may have been; but Freedom and Fairness did not meet with Blunkett's approval. He wrote on 2 May to Peter Mandelson, then the party's Director of Communications, with a copy to Kinnock, that it was "value-free" campaigning on "isolated and unconnected policies". It had spurned "strong and clear socialist policies" in favour of "saying things which people like". Kinnock did not hold back in his reply, saying he found Blunkett's criticisms "astonishing":

You suggest that we may 'fall into the trap of merely presenting isolated and unconnected policies'. In fact the campaign deliberately selects symbolic policies – such as under-5s provision, cervical cancer screening, a ban on lead in petrol and home improvement grants – to illustrate our commitment to general values ... The reason for this approach is very simple: the extensive research we did before the campaign launch showed that, in the abstract, people found it difficult to see how our values related to their daily lives. Linked to particular policies, those values came alive ... This campaign is one of the most successful we have run so far which explicitly presents strong and clear socialist policies in a way which the vast majority of people find very attractive. You have consistently – and rightly – argued for such an approach and I hope that – on reflection – you will realise that your remarks simply do not do justice to the campaign.[31]

Blunkett's views were aired at a meeting of the Campaign Strategy Committee in Kinnock's office on 19 May 1986, which was focused on a presentation by the Shadow Communications Agency, the group put together by Philip Gould and Peter Mandelson to professionalise the party's communications. Benn's diaries record the meeting: "It was a real management presentation with words and phrases being flashed up on a screen, like 'qualitative research', 'hypothetical solution', 'targeted'. This went on for ages, and Blunkett asked, 'What about democracy?' 'We haven't got round to that.' They continued, 'We must be credible, our promises must be backed by machinery. We must have sympathetic values. We must be able to answer the question "Where will we get the money from?" "[32]

Blunkett had a similar reaction to the now infamous Hugh Hudson-directed 'Kinnock – The Movie' party political broadcast during the 1987 election campaign which focused entirely on Kinnock as if he was a presidential candidate. Watching it at a meeting of the campaign committee, Gerald Kaufman remarked that it was so good the party should use it twice. Blunkett turned to Tom Sawyer and, in a stage whisper, asked him to pass a sick-bag.[33]

By the time of the 1987 election defeat, Kinnock had determined that a root-and-branch review of policy was unavoidable. Under the auspices of Tom Sawyer (a former Bennite and a future Labour Party general secretary), chairman of the NEC Home Policy Committee, the policy review took priority over almost everything else over the next two years. Blunkett was, along with Jack Straw, joint convenor of the 'Consumer and the Community' review group. With Straw as Shadow Education spokesman, Blunkett was left to take charge of every other aspect of the wide remit of the group.

The task was key to Labour's electability: how to square the circle of adapting to the changed political landscape, after eight years of Mrs Thatcher, while holding on to Labour's traditional values. Blunkett was the ideal convenor for such a group. With his local government background and the respect this gained him in the party, he could suggest ideas that might seem too outré from other sources, and he could use this background to face up to Labour's failures. Labour had been routed in local government after the rate-capping fiasco, which had given rise to some harshly self-critical analyses by the more thoughtful local councillors. As Hughes and Wintour put it, "Councils who were running 'Save our Services' campaigns suddenly discovered that a large body of voters did not believe the services were worth saving."[34]

Blunkett himself and other senior local government figures such as Margaret Hodge in Islington had already realised that

Labour needed to do some serious thinking as to how it could hold on to its support if it was not to suffer even worse losses, let alone attract new voters. The re-election of a Conservative government gave further impetus to such thinking as it showed how, contrary to the fantasy of many in the Labour Party, voters were not longing to be freed from the yoke of a vicious Conservative Party; their real anger was directed at Labour. A Labour Coordinating Committee pamphlet (*Labour Councils in the Cold*), published in early 1988, reinforced this message, arguing that Labour councillors had forgotten about their core task of managerial responsibility. Beholden to local authority trade unions and professional groups, they ignored their real masters: the electorate.[35]

The 'Consumer and the Community' report was entirely consistent with the development of Blunkett's beliefs as leader of Sheffield council and those he holds today. From his first days as a local councillor, through to his time as Education Secretary, central to his thinking has been the idea that socialism is about the empowerment of individuals and that key to this is the local community. It was what he then called 'socialist consumerism'.

I wasted quite a lot of my life on 'Meet the Challenge, Make the Change'. Tony and Gordon, who were then working hand in glove, were absolutely brilliant, because they'd worked out that you only needed to turn up to the drafting meeting at the end and determine either something you wanted added in or something you wanted taken out. They were right. It was mugs like me who sat through all these interminable meetings, believing that every line counted, every amendment had to be won. But we were formulating concepts around 'the community' – what one whole section is actually called – in which I was genuinely interested. The world was changing rapidly and the party was coming to terms with the global economy. But it wasn't coming to terms with new social models. Could we recognise that people weren't bound into any model of delivery? They were interested in what they got and whether it was of a high enough quality. People of all dispositions and of all social classes were going to buy education if they could afford it, if their kids were getting a crap state education. And that was true with health, too. We just weren't coming to terms with that and we needed to. Nobody was much interested; it was not an agenda within the party for the '92 election. We were taking ourselves from 1945 up to about 1985, rather than the twenty-first century. That's what we were doing in the party generally at that time. It wouldn't have made any difference to winning; we weren't going to win.

Blunkett saw the report as a means of making clear where the party needed to travel (hence it was by far the longest of the seven policy review reports; over 27,000 words initially, reduced to 17,000 after editing by Patricia Hewitt). Labour could, he believed, turn the Tories' championing of the voter as consumer in its favour by concentrating not on who owned a service but on the level of quality it provided (a view that is remarkably similar to the Blair government's philosophy). The report argued that quality and efficiency were far and away the two most important measures of a service (thus the Audit Commission would become the Quality Commission) and that, instead of relying on the market, consumers would have most control if they had the power to penalise local authorities that did not meet the required standard of service delivery. As well as fixed-term contracts for council officers, the report also proposed performance-related pay (which has become a Blunkett hallmark, forming a central part of his teaching and police reforms in government).

The report shied away from dealing with one of the most controversial areas: share ownership. Blunkett argued that the government's privatisations had had the same effect as council-house sales – assuring the loyalty to the Conservatives of a new group of voters who might otherwise have been natural Labour supporters. By appearing as if it wanted to confiscate such shares, Labour was attacking the very people whose votes it needed –

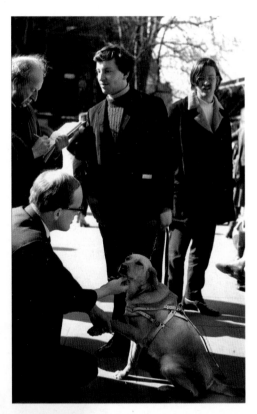

'I'm sorry, sir. You can't bring that in here.' David is told that he can't take Ruby into the Palace of Westminster (1971).

A fresh-faced young socialist (with Ruby) addresses the Labour Party conference (1973).

The candidate. Councillor Blunkett stands for Parliament in 1974.

The leader's women: David with Enid Hattersley (left) and Ruth (right) (1981).

NEC member
David Blunkett at
the 1986 Labour
Party conference.

David about to be
sworn in as an MP for
the first time, with
Teddy (1987).

The first Labour Cabinet for eighteen years, 8 May 1997.

Here's one I painted earlier. The Prime Minister and the Education
Secretary take a lesson at a Brighton primary school, 1997.

The Education Secretary at the dispatch box, 1998.

So close yet so distant: Blunkett and Brown during the 2001 election campaign.

Will no one rid me of these turbulent judges? Blunkett's *bêtes noires*: the Lord Chief Justice, Sir Harry Woolf (left), and the Lord Chancellor, Lord Irvine (2000).

With the Commissioner of the Metropolitan Police, Sir John Stevens (2002).

No tanks at Heathrow, just armoured vehicles (2003).

All friends together: Boris Johnson, Kimberly Fortier and David
(with private secretary Jonathan Sedgwick obscured) at the
Spectator party in 2004.

Getting away from it all: David (with Paul Potts), on holiday
in Italy as news of his relationship with Kimberly Fortier
emerged. (August 2004)

What might have been? David outside No. 10.

aspirant Southerners, often in key swing marginals. An idea that started to emerge in party think-tanks was that, instead of rena-tionalising, it should offer to turn every user of a utility into a shareholder – 'citizens' shares'. Blunkett gave strong support to the proposal, expanded in a paper presented to the review group by Peter Hain (then a union researcher).

The idea encroached on the territory of Bryan Gould's Pro-ductive and Competitive Economy review group. At the start of the review process, the two agreed that Gould would concentrate on regulation, Blunkett on consumerism. This did not last long – not, that is, beyond Blunkett's embrace of the citizens' shares idea. At the penultimate convenors' meeting, designed to smooth out such clashes between groups, Gould argued that the idea was worthless and it was taken out of the final report.

Blunkett had also advocated another alternative; Labour could take back the utilities by issuing bonds. The idea was instantly written off by both Gould and John Smith (in a rare example of unity between the two men) as not merely impractical (the money would still count as government spending) but also little more than a vehicle for Blunkett's grandstanding, letting him appear to activists as more left-wing than the other members of the review teams.[36]

The rest of the report has a decidedly clichéd 'Labour 1980s' ring to it. Consumers, in the form of consumer councils, would be represented on company boards. A string of utility councils would be overseen and funded by a new Department of Con-sumers' Affairs.

The long-standing feud with Roy Hattersley also began to have an impact. At an NEC meeting convened to go through the reports, Hattersley objected to the idea of the head of the new department having Cabinet rank (ironic, given that his own elev-ation to the Cabinet was as Secretary of State for Prices and Consumer Protection). Blunkett was stuck at the House of Com-mons and was informed on his late arrival by Jack Straw what Hattersley had been up to. Blunkett then launched into a speech in which he argued that what unions had been in the nineteenth and twentieth centuries (representing ordinary workers and giving them strength through collective membership), consumers' organisations would be in the twenty-first century. Kinnock suggested that the wording should be changed to 'a minister of Cabinet rank', to be met with the comment by Dennis Skinner, who was chairing the session, that 'I think we've settled that'. Quite what 'a minister of Cabinet rank' might be, if not a member of Cabinet, will always remain a mystery.

There was one critical area in which Blunkett actively did his best to frustrate and defeat Kinnock: defence. Blunkett has always been – and remains – a unilateralist. As a senior member of the government today, he rarely talks about defence, not least because he is still an implacable opponent of nuclear weapons, believing them to be morally indefensible: "I was and I still am, very much. It's passed; it's gone now. The cold war's over, the Soviet Union's collapsed, but I have never changed my mind. It is a moral issue with me. I understood the argument of multilateralism and the balance of terror. I just thought that we were wasting billions of pounds given that we were actually under the umbrella of the US anyway and our Polaris capacity was a bite on an elephant's backside."

In June 1988, following a TV interview in which Kinnock began the process of ditching unilateralism, Blunkett both wrote to the leader warning him that there would be a "great debacle" at conference that year if he persisted with his revisionism[37] and then took the astonishing step on the same day of issuing what amounted to a public reprimand, spelling out in a statement that "If an unnecessary and devastating split in the party is to be avoided, the leader needs to make clear that his words were not an abandonment of his long-standing commitment in which so many of his allies have placed their trust".[38] Kinnock saw nothing to be gained from rebuking Blunkett, knowing that he had to proceed carefully but that victory was in sight.

Blunkett was fundamentally opposed to the aim of the defence policy review group, convened by Gerald Kaufman, which was – at the very least – to neutralise defence as an issue; and, if politically possible, to ditch Labour's unilateralism. Instead of decommissioning Polaris and cancelling Trident, as existing policy would have it, the review argued that only three of the scheduled four Trident submarines should be built and that British nuclear weapons should be included in negotiations. Dull as it may seem now, it was, in Labour Party terms, seismic, since it marked the abandonment of the unilateralism that was a shibboleth for so many party members. Indeed, *Tribune* published on 31 March a 'Disarmament Appeal', signed by figures such as Blunkett, Margaret Beckett, Jo Richardson, Joan Ruddock, Clare Short and Chris Smith. Within six weeks of the 'appeal', the NEC had voted to seal off its unilateralist blind alley.

The matter was so important and so fraught with danger for Kinnock that he devoted most of his political energies to securing his NEC majority on defence. On other matters, by this time, he barely needed to bother. But on defence, many of his loyal union supporters were bound by their organisations' policy resolutions. So if the soft-left unilateralist NEC members, such as Blunkett, Robin Cook, Joan Lestor, Clare Short and Margaret Beckett, refused to support Kinnock, his majority would disappear.

The night before the defence paper was to be debated at the NEC in May 1989, Blunkett called a meeting of his soft-left allies. Not everyone attended. Diana Jeuda, a representative from USDAW, the shopworkers' union, said that her union had changed its policy so she could not come. Joan Lestor said her loyalty to Kinnock overrode all else. Robin Cook agreed to attend, provided Joan Ruddock did not. (Oh, the joys of comradeship.) In the end, there were five: Blunkett, Cook, Beckett, Richardson and Short. The meeting was a mess. Hughes and Wintour describe it:

The first pub they entered did not like Blunkett's dog and they ended up sitting outside at a pavement table at a pub round the corner. Cook, a long standing unilateralist and one of the sharpest minds in the Shadow Cabinet, told them he had seen Kinnock earlier that morning and reached agreement over an amendment of his own: 'If the beginning of Start II is subject to long delay, and there is good reason to believe that these negotiations will not make the progress we require, a Labour Government will have the option of initiating direct negotiations with the Soviet Union or with others.' . . . Blunkett had been to see Kinnock in the leader's office at 9.15 that morning. Pressed to explain why the document did not set out a strategy to remove US bases, Kinnock simply replied: 'Trust me. It's manageable.' It was almost a courtesy call. 'I know you don't need my vote or you would have been on the 'phone by now', Blunkett joked. He stated his case and left, sensing defeat. Blunkett said Cook's amendment did not go far enough. There had to be a timetable, with a deadline for the removal of Trident set at the lifetime of a parliament. Cook, to Blunkett's surprise, said he could not support such an amendment; he had struck a deal with Kinnock and would not go back on it. Clare Short said Blunkett was right; the Kaufman draft had no failsafe strategy for the removal of Trident . . . She said she would be putting a series of hastily prepared amendments of her own on the dangers of proliferation, the uselessness of nuclear weapons as a deterrent, and finally a proposal not to commission Trident pending negotiations.[39]

The meeting was useless. There was no agreement between them as to how to vote or how to act. All that really emerged was that their chances of success were negligible, if even as high as that. The following day, Blunkett proposed an amendment setting in concrete a timetable for removal of Trident. A Labour government would take "independent steps to remove nuclear weapons and bases from our soil" if after five years negotiations had not secured a nuclear-free Europe.[40] It was defeated by 16 votes to 9. Kinnock then outlined how the world had changed; so, he said, should party policy:

If we had the opportunities for nuclear disarmament in the '80s that we have now, I would not have needed to advance the unilateral argument then. If we get the full support I firmly expect for this new policy, we will gain the credibility necessary to promote nuclear disarmament and stop the nuclear rearmament being undertaken by the present Conservative Government. The choice now is between a nuclear-disarming Labour government, renewed negotiation, or a re-arming Tory Government whose policies will set back all the progress, all the development we have seen since Gorbachev came to power. Gorbachev wants partners in negotiation to secure nuclear disarmament – not only the US, but also France and China too. Out of power we don't have the opportunities of unilateral or any other sort of nuclear disarmament. We only have the chance to talk about it. In power we can act, and make dramatic progress. My pledge is that the Labour Government will do that, and do so unstintingly, and I want your support for that.

When he had finished speaking, he was applauded. (His words were then passed to the journalists waiting outside by Peter Mandelson.) The policy review paper was passed by 17 votes to 8, with Blunkett joined by Benn, Skinner, Beckett, Richardson, Sawyer, Haigh and Hannah Sell, the Young Socialist representative. Short abstained.[41] As Blunkett told *Tribune* that week, 'There was not a gesture to the rest of us.'[42]

(On the second morning of the NEC, Blunkett arrived to discover that "overnight some guileless member of the TGWU had disposed of my Braille copy of the meeting document and all my Braille notes, as well as a good set of earphones."[43])

For some reason, which Kinnock had certainly not indicated, Blunkett believed that there would be some sort of sop to the unilateralists. Quite the opposite; the whole point of the exercise was to show that Labour had ditched the electoral albatross. The press coverage the following day focused on just that, precisely as Kinnock intended, prompting Blunkett to write an angry letter to Kinnock: "Someone, somewhere, is promoting the idea that there is a sea change in views rather than a reappraisal and updating."[44] Blunkett thought – correctly, since that was Kinnock's purpose – that spin doctors were deliberately flagging up the end of unilateralism.

He took this as a betrayal. As he put it in a later interview:

At the May 1989 NEC, Kinnock made a brilliant speech, but it didn't touch me at all. Not that it wasn't a good argument. It was. It simply meant that nobody could ever trust him again. I had been trying to be helpful, arguing that we could use Britain's nuclear weapons in multilateral discussions. As a 'first strike', let's divest ourselves of nuclear weapons. To kick start the process, let's be the first in. At the start of the correspondence, Neil Kinnock reassured me, and he continued to reassure me until directly afterwards, when Gerald Kaufman wrote an article saying, in effect, that we had completely ditched the unilateralist nonsense which he had never believed in. So we went into the 1992 election committed to pay for a fourth Trident. That is the issue on which I fell out with Neil Kinnock, and never fell back in.[45]

In tandem with the policy review process, Kinnock had also launched into a restatement of the party's aims and values via a document by Kinnock and Hattersley presented to the Shadow Cabinet in early 1988, entitled *A Statement of Democratic Socialist Aims and Values*. Kinnock intended this to give a philosophical underpinning to the policy review by embracing the mixed economy. It was not met with universal acclamation. Cook and Gould argued that it was an abdication of Labour's core aim of the redistribution of wealth. And by accepting that market forces were 'generally satisfactory' as a means by which goods and services could be allocated, it also worked against the idea of intervention in the economy.

It was ironic that Kinnock had first been persuaded of the merit of such a restatement by Blunkett, who became one of the harshest critics of the end result. In 1985 he bowed to Blunkett's urgings that the party needed a governing, inspirational idea with which it could take on Thatcherism, which had benefited from having such an ideological touchstone. Blunkett himself favoured participatory democracy, which formed the basis of his policies as leader of Sheffield and stemmed from the same root as his Consumer and Community review group proposals. By participation, he meant that every citizen should be involved in the decisions that affected his or her life, whether that meant what day the bins should be emptied or whether the country should have a nuclear deterrent. And it meant that public services should operate in the consumer's, rather than the producer's, interest.

An NEC committee was established in 1985 and papers were drafted by Geoffrey Hodgson, the professor of politics at Newcastle Polytechnic, Geoff Bish, the party's head of research, and by Bernard Crick. Crick, who had a high public profile as a result of a regular slot in the *Observer*, had been picked up by Kinnock during his leadership campaign and asked to form a small group of people not interested in office who would do some basic thinking about the future of Labour and the party's fundamental values. (Kinnock had also asked Richard Hoggart to do the same thing but had, embarrassingly, forgotten this earlier request.) Crick drafted a paper.

The process became farcical, however, with drafts criss-crossing London and appearing to make no progress towards a final version. The penny dropped for Crick when at one face-to-face meeting with Kinnock he was told by the leader exactly how the document should be changed – which was precisely how it had been written. It was clear to Crick that Kinnock had not read it. Not wanting to waste what had been a considerable work undertaking, Crick asked Charles Clarke, Kinnock's chief of staff, whether he could publish the paper himself, keeping secret its background.

With an eye for publicity, and with Blunkett a rising star, Crick sent the paper to his erstwhile pupil for comments and a view to publication and joint authorship with Blunkett. The 1987 election (and Blunkett's elevation to the Commons) came and went and, as time passed without a satisfactory conclusion, the idea of a statement came to serve a different purpose, as the bedrock of the policy review. Kinnock turned to Hattersley, who began by studying Crick and Blunkett's most recent version. He was, he told Crick in a letter, unimpressed.[46] The arguments over the paper centred on the role of the market and individual liberty. As Hughes and Wintour put it, "What the episode actually proved was that, when it came to words in black and white, each leading Labour politician had an intensely strong personal understanding of the socialist creed, accompanied by an equally strong conviction that theirs was the proper understanding of that creed."[47] Crick and Blunkett, meanwhile, published their joint paper, *The Labour Party's Aims and Values, An Unofficial Statement*,[48] off their own bats.

8

Westminster:
"a good fight with a worthy opponent"

With Joan Maynard announcing in 1985 her intention to retire
from the Commons, attention turned to the question of a successor. In normal circumstances, a figure with Blunkett's record
would have been a shoo-in. But despite having been leader of
Sheffield council for five years, with a place on the Labour NEC,
and thus a pivotal figure in the party's reconstruction, he was far
from that. Nothing in Blunkett's life has ever been obvious; what,
for most people, is the standard career path to the top – Labour
Party activism, election as a local councillor, followed by a seat
in the Commons, promotion, and then ministerial or Shadow
office – has been, at every stage, a battle to prove the doubters
wrong. Councillor? Well, perhaps. So long as he knows his limits
and doesn't go beyond them. Leader? As if! Hmmm; he's done
remarkably to cope with the council. Good on him. But be realistic.
He's surrounded by friends. He has his family. He'd be eaten alive
in Westminster. It just wouldn't work. Too many obstacles. NEC?
Maybe . . . stick to rallying the members and he'll fit in fine. So
yes, he may indeed have become a nationally known figure, he
may indeed have been key to the removal of Militant, and he
may indeed have topped the NEC poll, but it's one thing being
a big fish in a small pond; national politics is a step too far. Just
as Blunkett has faced a battle at every stage, however, so has he
won each – backed, crucially, by his local party.

Quite apart from being a national figure, Blunkett was not
just a wannabe MP. He was also, as a major figure on the NEC,
on the Labour Party's campaign team. Up to the 1983 election,
this would have been significant. By the 1987 campaign, however,
control over strategy and tactics had passed from the NEC to

another group, the inner circle around Kinnock. The campaign team meetings every two or three days were simply rubber stamps for decisions already taken. The received wisdom today is that – despite the party's heavy defeat – the actual campaign run by Labour in the 1987 election was a success. Blunkett took a rather different view:

While the campaign appealed to the media, it did not appeal to the ordinary potential Labour voters. The notion that 'the medium is the message' is nonsense. Certainly the public's perception of a political party and the nature of a political debate can be influenced through sustained, broadly based efforts by both print and broadcast journalism, but Margaret Thatcher was living proof that conviction and clear appeal to an identified segment of the population can be extremely effective . . . The people's interests have to be our interests and vice versa. But the small matter of how to bring about change and how to challenge those who always resist change, unless it is in their own interests, were questions we in the Labour Party failed to address at that stage. It was to be another ten years before we won over the electorate. So it was that in 1987 one could palpably feel that Labour were not making progress in winning new voters, no matter how hard we tried or how slick the party political broadcasts.[1]

(By which he meant the infamous Hugh Hudson 'Kinnock – The Movie'.)

Other than the joy of election to the Commons, 1987 was awful for Blunkett. Earlier that year, he and Ruth had decided to separate, an inevitable decision after they had been growing apart for so long. Ruth, Alastair, Hugh and Andrew remained in the family home; Blunkett found another house, large enough for the children to stay in at weekends. As a national figure and a controversial council leader, Blunkett was used to press criticism and exposure but he was taken aback by the press reaction to a personal story that involved no third party and no recrimination from either wife or husband. The northern edition of the *Sunday Mirror* ran the story as front-page news.

As if that was not enough, within weeks of his arrival in London he was struck down with illness and suffered for the next few months both in and out of hospital. In November 1987, just after entering the Commons, he had to have his gall bladder removed. This was compounded when, soon afterwards, he went down with viral pneumonia and had to stay in hospital until March 1988.

The illness was not entirely to his detriment. His absence from the Commons for much of his first year spared his fellow MPs from over-exposure to the rather brash new MP from Sheffield; Blunkett has never felt the need to keep his opinions to himself. What would have been seen as inappropriate bumptiousness from a new member would not have helped his reputation at the critical early stage in an MP's career. Used to being a big fish in his own pool, he would have found it difficult to stand quietly back. Instead, he was able to settle in much like any other newcomer.

Blunkett was lucky that, because of his blindness, he was allowed to make his maiden speech early – the first by a Labour MP in the new Parliament after Kinnock. If he had not, his illness would have meant that he would have made no contribution for the rest of the year. It was, for a maiden speech, notably confident and composed. He argued that under the Conservatives, British democracy was being superseded by that of "the bank balance and of the privilege that comes with wealth and property . . . [I]f the symptoms of the present decay of inner city areas are not allowed a democratic outlet, the government will be forced into even greater authoritarianism in order to suppress those symptoms".[2]

Unlike his fellow local government alumnus, Ken Livingstone, who was never able to carry the House's attention in his time in Parliament, Blunkett seemed relatively at ease when speaking in the Commons chamber: "I came to recognize that the mood in the Chamber can change swiftly and sometimes unpredictably. If misjudged, the resulting outcome can sap self-confidence. It is particularly daunting when a member is being barracked mercilessly from all sides as sometimes happens when a speaker has lost the support of his own party and there are mutterings of a 'poor show'. The other side then feeds on this and attacks more vigorously. If on the other hand, a speaker is on form, then the barracking can be invigorating. I relish a good fight with a worthy opponent."[3]

The sensitivity to atmosphere and environment that is such a crucial part of Blunkett's modus operandi is especially useful in the Commons chamber. Given that one of his skills is judging moods, he has been able to adapt better than some might have expected to the unique atmosphere of the Commons, where judging the chamber's mood can be critical. And his superb memory and quick wit also help in an environment in which speech-reading is frowned upon. As he wrote shortly after being elected:

> Too much I read of that which I have written
> And if not written, wished that I had.
> Too oft I hear the echo reflected
> From the wall that I myself have built
> And fail to recognise the words
> Which bounce back in my face.

In January 1988, Blunkett was appointed by the Labour whips to the standing committee set up to scrutinise the first draft of the Local Government Finance Bill, which replaced the rates with the poll tax. Given his background, he was a natural for the job. Over the next two years, the poll tax was to propel him into a national role. Blunkett began his domination of the issue in a committee that was, even by the usual complex and intricate standards of local government finance, both phenomenally technical and hard fought. The committee would often sit until three or four in the morning as individual clauses were taken apart word by word, with Blunkett seizing the early opportunity he had been given to prove to the doubters that he could master the most intricate detail.

Teddy was by now eleven and his health was declining, even though he still seemed to have an appetite for work. The decision was taken by the vet and the Guide Dogs for the Blind Association (GDBA) that he should carry on for as long as he seemed inclined but that they should prepare for his retirement. One hot, humid day in May 1988, however, Teddy started to pant. As the day progressed, the panting grew worse and Blunkett immediately took him to the nearest vet. Teddy's heart and circulation were both failing and he had only a few weeks to live. Cancelling all his engagements, Blunkett took Teddy back to Sheffield, where he left him with Valda to be cared for. On 5 July, Blunkett was handed a message in the Commons chamber. Teddy had collapsed and had lost the use of his legs. The vet told Blunkett that Teddy should be put out of his misery. Taking the next train to Sheffield, Blunkett arrived at the surgery to be greeted by the heart-rending sound of Teddy trying to get to his feet and failing, his paws flailing on the lino floor. Determined that his friends' days should not end in such an anonymous environment, Blunkett took Teddy home, put him on his favourite rug and waited for the vet. When he arrived, Blunkett took Teddy's head in his lap and held him as the vet put him to sleep. He commemorated him with a poem:

> He was a gentle giant of a dog,
> Running magnificent through the woods,
> A huge branch clamped between his teeth,
>
> He was a soft, lovable lion of a dog,
> Full of sniffs and a nuzzling nose,
> Touching against the hand
> To say thank you for walks
> And for fondling of ears.
>
> He was a *Guinness Book of Records* dog,
> First ever in the Chamber,
> Ensuring the noise and bad behaviour
> Of the 'schoolboys',
> And the medieval ritual of the Mother of Parliaments.

He was a TV star dog,
Sleeping through *Question Time*,
Lifting his head only when it was time to go,
And bringing a smile to millions
And joy to those who knew him well.

A child could climb upon his back
Or pull his ears without fear or threat,
For Teddy was a dog of love, you see,
Who cared for others as he cared for me.

Guiding me, wherever I needed to be,
Full of keenness, enthusiasm and love of life,
Working to a record age
And giving of his best, wherever we might be.

Being superb – my guide dog gave his all
In those twelve years, you see
All of us who knew him
Will remember him with gratitude,
And with love and much affection.

Among the many letters of commiseration Blunkett received, he was most surprised by one from Margaret Thatcher. She understood, she wrote, what a great loss it would be, not only for practical reasons but also because of the enormous affection owners have for their guide dogs. Whenever she had passed Teddy in the Commons she had stopped to pat him on the head.

The GDBA later set up a fund for Teddy, who had become known to the public for his teamwork with his master. It raised over £7,600 towards the training of other dogs, one of which was also named Teddy.

In August 1988, Blunkett was summoned to the Middlesbrough GDBA centre to meet his new dog, a German shepherd/golden retriever cross called Offa.[4] In a rare concession to Blunkett's commitments, the GDBA consented to his attending for only eight days' training rather than the normal four weeks. Offa was a lively dog – too lively, in fact, for Blunkett, as he would run off at a rate of knots with his owner clinging to the harness for dear life. Back at Westminster, Offa soon managed to find his way around and make friends; not least with Blunkett's fellow Labour MP Michael Meacher, with whom Offa associated getting a lift home. Offa had an appealing nature – always keen to please – but he also liked to be the centre of attention. If someone appeared to be taking too much attention away from him, he would start to fidget and grab his master's attention back.

For the next few years, Blunkett's life was dominated by the poll tax. The 1988 Labour conference was memorable not just for Offa's first public appearance but for a difficult task which Blunkett had been given wearing his NEC hat. The main issue of that year's conference was whether or not Labour should endorse non-payment of the poll tax, a tactic that the more hot-headed, extremist party activists favoured. There was, of course, no possibility that the leadership of a major party could back such illegality but passions were raging and the group within the party which favoured non-payment was sizeable and vocal. Blunkett's task was to tell the party to be sensible – the same job he had done a few years before over rate capping. The atmosphere in the hall when Blunkett came to the rostrum was electric. There were moments when he could barely be heard above the heckles and jeering. But he stood firm: "What we are sick of in this party is sectarianism that turns in on ourselves and campaigns against the party and not for it . . . If we advocate something that we know will fail, the people will not turn on the government, they will turn on us for misleading them."[5] In the end, the NEC's position was backed by a majority in the conference hall – the votes had been assembled with care by Kinnock's office – but only after a raucous, politically damaging debate which showed Labour once more as internally split.

Jack Cunningham, the Shadow Environment Secretary, had been a target of the civil disobedience, non-payment brigade during both the rate-capping dispute and now over the poll tax.

As one of the more politically astute Shadow Cabinet members, he could see the advantage of having Blunkett on his team and so asked Kinnock to promote him to the front bench. Cunningham was respected by Kinnock and, for all the disagreements that Kinnock had had with Blunkett over defence policy and his frustration at some of Blunkett's behaviour on the NEC, the leader well understood that Blunkett had the best local government network in the party, as well as a public profile that could only be to the party's advantage. There was, however, one voice against his appointment – which, for a man less than two years in the Commons, would be a remarkably speedy promotion: that of Roy Hattersley, driven, it appeared to some, by jealousy of the younger man's success.

The job of local government spokesman is always important, especially when, as was then the case for Labour, local government is the sole avenue for exercising power. But Blunkett was fortunate to be handed the biggest domestic political issue of the entire Thatcher period, the poll tax, and given the opportunity to run with it. It was a fantastic challenge for him to sink his teeth into, not simply because it gave him an even greater national profile than he already enjoyed but also because it positioned him as a "left realist", as one of his fellow team members describes it. He faced two sets of pressures: from the Left he was denounced as a sell-out because he was not leading the 'can't pay – won't pay' campaign; from the other side he knew that he had nonetheless to keep the party with him whilst avoiding being too closely identified with the culture of protest. The upside was that having to take on certain sections of the Left earned him a respect in the Parliamentary Labour Party that he had not previously enjoyed.

He was helped practically by being given special funding for his new position from the Commons authorities and from NALGO (the local government trade union), which he used to employ a total of five staff, including Mike Lee, who remained with him until 1994, (and went on to become public affairs director of UEFA, the governing body of European football, and a key figure in the London Olympic bid for 2012). He had far more staff than other junior shadows, but some of their tasks were simply creating tapes, processing material and reading newspapers and papers – a basic survival mechanism.

Blunkett's front-bench debut was on 14 December 1988. He began as he meant to carry on, asking the Environment Secretary, John Selwyn Gummer, "how much money he intends to spend on profligate propaganda publicising the Government's case on the poll tax?"[6] Blunkett's contributions to the debates on the poll tax legislation were commanding and fellow MPs were impressed by his competence and debating skills. His confidence at the dispatch box belied his junior status; when Chris Patten was promoted in July 1989 to take over from Gummer, Blunkett behaved towards him as if the two were equals, rather than one a senior Cabinet minister and the other a junior opposition spokesman. Welcoming Patten to his new post, for example, he remarked that he hoped that "he has greater fortune than his predecessors – although, perhaps, promotion out of chaos might be catching . . . by anybody's description the Bill is in chaos with more than 600 amendments having been tabled . . . Those who have been promoted have left behind them – if my canine friend will forgive me for saying so – an absolute dog's dinner. It must be a message for the hon. Gentleman – if he makes a big mess, he could end up a contender for the premiership".[7] Blunkett had been in the Commons for only two years, but was already being talked up by colleagues, the press and – most importantly for career advancement – the whips.

It was not only the personal imbalance in stature with Patten which Blunkett overrode. On so complicated and technical an issue as local government finance, the opposition would usually be struggling to keep up with the civil service. Viscount Palmerston remarked that there were only three people in the country who understood the Schleswig-Holstein question: "One of them is mad, one of them is dead and the other one is me and

I have forgotten." Most people felt the same way about local government finance. But as the founder chairman of the Local Government Information Unit, Blunkett had access to first-class researchers who could match, and sometimes beat, the civil service for expertise and so demolish the legislation clause by clause. Patten claimed, for example, that 'transitional relief' (a central government subsidy to local government) would ensure that no one would be more than £3 a week worse off after the poll tax's introduction. In November 1989, however, Blunkett was able to publish fully detailed figures showing that the £3 figure was nonsense, since it relied on the implausible notion that all councils would stick to government spending guidelines. As the debates progressed, he was able to release a series of similar figures and predictions, all backed up with firm, clear reasoning. He impressed his immediate opposite number, Michael Portillo; on polling day in 1992, Blunkett was taken aback to be called by him and commiserated with on another Labour loss and another period in opposition.

For a shadow local government minister – who at that stage was technically just number four in the team – Blunkett had, as one of his staff at the time puts it, "open-door access to Kinnock's office and to the policy unit", in part because of his NEC position but also because he was already viewed as a campaign asset. Cunningham had a schizophrenic reaction to his junior's success. As the man who had selected and fought for him, he was pleased that he was performing well. But as an ambitious politician who had little false modesty, he became resentful of Blunkett's domination of the issue. Cunningham was an old-school politician, naturally jealous of the blanket coverage given to a man who was, after all, not even in the Shadow Cabinet. Add to this Blunkett's prickly self-confidence and there was a recipe for ill will on both sides. This is confirmed by Cunningham's successor as Shadow Environment Secretary, Bryan Gould, who inherited Blunkett and kept him in post. "David was someone I knew only slightly. He had had some problems while doing the same job for Jack Cunningham and I was a little apprehensive as to how we might get on."[8] But they got on extremely well; so well, in fact, that Blunkett became Gould's campaign manager when he ran for the party leadership in 1992. Gould was a very different character to Cunningham. He writes of Blunkett: "His blindness gave him a special sensitivity which was both a strength and a weakness. He had a unique insight at times and a suppleness of mind which was a great advantage. He needed, however, constant reassurance that nothing was happening without his knowledge. We established an excellent relationship of mutual trust – something which stood us in good stead in the difficult times to come."[9]

Working to put the details on Cunningham's plan for a replacement for the poll tax, Blunkett outlined a complicated twin-tax system, combining a revised rates system based on house values with a local income tax. It was both technically difficult and politically off-putting; not only could few people understand it (including MPs, which led to Cunningham almost being voted off the Shadow Cabinet in 1989, coming eighteenth out of eighteen in the annual ballot), it was almost impossible to explain to voters. And the few who were aware of it saw it not as Labour promising to scrap the poll tax but as Labour proposing to introduce two new taxes. There was strong opposition to the idea from John Smith, the Shadow Chancellor. Smith thought that any alternative had to be simple, clear and easy to understand. Gould agreed. Smith's media flag-wavers created the impression that 'Sensible Mr Smith' (as a *Times* leader put it[10]) had used his authority as Shadow Chancellor to block the idea of a property revaluation based on capital values. In fact, the decision to dump Cunningham's idea had been one of Gould's first acts as Shadow Environment Secretary. Working in tandem with Gould, as he had been unable to do with Cunningham, Blunkett devised the final policy. As Gould writes: "The truth was that John had no ideas at all on the subject and never made any proposals."[11]

There was also a significant body of opinion within the

Shadow Cabinet which held that Labour did not even need an alternative and should simply go back to the rates – a view that Smith held; the poll tax was so unpopular that Labour stood to gain votes merely by opposing it. Any alternative would open Labour up to attack from the losers. Blunkett rejected the idea. Bad as the poll tax was, the old rates system too was unfair on those such as pensioners who lived alone in houses with a high rateable value. And the rateable value itself was a nonsense, based on the rent that a property would fetch if let out. But such a figure was entirely unrealistic, since the private rental sector had collapsed. Even the more obvious solution, basing rateable value on sale value, had its difficulties, with a raging housing market changing values almost by the week.

Blunkett considered every conceivable alternative, such as a 'floor tax', based on the size of a property. No sooner had a paper been written on the pros and cons of the respective proposals than a news story would appear, 'revealing' that the latest idea was the one that Labour would adopt. More often than not, the leaks were deliberate – an 'off the record' briefing to a journalist designed to secure column inches that would show Labour (and Blunkett) in the positive light of a party thinking in detail about policy, preparing for government. What Labour said now mattered. In the late 1980s, the more general unpopularity of the government and of Mrs Thatcher, fed by the overwhelming hostility to the poll tax, meant that the prospect of a Labour government seemed, for the first time in a decade, realistic.

The plan that both Blunkett and Gould favoured was to use the computerisation of the Inland Revenue to calculate automatically an adjustment of liability to rates, based on taxable income. This would, they felt, deal head on with the main objection to rates: that those on low incomes, such as pensioners, could be saddled with enormous bills because of the value of their property. John Smith and his allies argued that this was, like the earlier Cunningham proposal, too complex, would "frighten" voters[12] and would pose a problem of confidentiality.

The end result, which Blunkett revealed in July 1990, was a compromise, designed to be implemented over the course of three years. First, a return to the rates, with rebates for those worst affected. The next year, new rateable values would be calculated, based on a series of notional market prices. In the third year, the Inland Revenue computers would enable a combination based on property value and ability to pay. The plan was called 'Fair Rates', to show that it was a return to something akin to rates but without the anomalies. Politically, this worked. By being able to talk about positive proposals, Blunkett and Gould could deal with comeback from the Conservatives on their own policy and could concentrate on an all-out attack on the poll tax.

As if the difficulties of drawing up the policy were not enough, however, Blunkett was caught up in the crossfire between Peter Mandelson, the party's Director of Communications, and Gould. Mandelson had little time for Gould. Since Gould was one of the earliest 'modernisers', one might have thought the two would get on well but Mandelson considered him to be unreliable – code, perhaps, for not being pliable enough. Gould was a supremely intelligent man; as an Oxford law don, he had practically invented the now widespread study of modern administrative law. He did not take well to the attempts of a spin doctor to interfere. As Gould puts it: "while we were trying to bring our plans to fruition, Peter Mandelson was briefing the press regularly (there was intense media interest in our plans) and they were clearly being given an account which suggested that my views were likely to be rejected by my colleagues. When this turned out not to be the case, Peter reacted by trying to prevent me from talking to the press about our conclusions. He presumably feared that I would be able to demonstrate that the briefings they had been given over the previous few months were simply wrong".[13]

Blunkett made veiled reference to these internal problems in a Commons debate on 22 May 1990: "No one could ever accuse the Labour party of not engaging in full and open debate on its policies. We are notorious for that. We have lost the past three elections in our endeavour to engage in open and democratic debate. We shall certainly not engage in it again."[14]

(Mandelson's successor, John Underwood, was a far less prickly character. He might, however, have got off on the wrong foot with Blunkett. Writing at the end of 1990 to all the Shadow Cabinet and to front-bench spokesmen, he introduced himself and offered them autocue training. Blunkett replied that, while he had every faith in Underwood's ability, this did not extend to expecting him to work miracles and give him sight.)

Blunkett thought he had parked the issue for good, especially when the council tax was introduced. But over a decade later, in 2004, council tax 'hikes' became a major political issue and he dusted off his proposals, which, at the time of writing, look like forming the basis of the alternative revenue-raising tax to which Labour will turn. In 1990, the computerisation of the Inland Revenue may not yet have been able to cope with the complexities of the proposed hybrid system. By 2005/6, it ought not to cause any problems at all – in theory.

The relationship between Blunkett and Gould was strong and the two became friends as well as colleagues. Gould gave Blunkett far more scope than most shadow secretaries of state did to their junior ministers, with a broad set of responsibilities. A former colleague ascribes Blunkett's collegiate style as a minister to his experience under Gould: "The contrast between working for Bryan and working for Jack, whose styles were polar opposites, was enormous, and he learned that one works and one doesn't. And it stood him in very good stead, even when he's had difficult and uncooperative team members."

So when Gould decided in 1992, after Kinnock's resignation, to run for the leadership, it was natural that Blunkett should be his campaign manager. "I was his number two in the shadow Environment team and I felt a sense of loyalty to him. But I actually did want to reform. I wanted us to do something. I didn't just want us to be what we'd been in the past, but better.

Bryan was the modernisation candidate. Apart from his views on Europe, where John [Smith] and he were vehemently apart, the difference between John and Bryan was that John wanted to stabilise the moment, whereas Bryan wanted genuinely to address the future."

Gould knew well that a Smith victory was a given. "He had for so long been written up not only as the next but as the preferred leader that an unstoppable expectation had developed. This expectation had been reinforced throughout the election campaign, during which John had been treated as our trump card. Great emphasis had been placed on his qualities of prudence and trustworthiness. The failure of the campaign, and particularly of our tax initiatives, did nothing to dent this confidence in John's virtues. Images, once set, are often remarkably impervious to the facts."[15] But if Smith declared his candidacy first, no one serious would challenge him and risk humiliation. So despite having endured a fourth election defeat in a row, the party would have opted for a safety-first leader, without any form of post-election self-examination. Gould felt that there needed to be a proper debate as to the future direction of the party and he alone seemed willing to provide one.

Blunkett's advice was that "there was not a chance in hell of winning, but if he came out with some dignity he would have both influenced events and placed himself in a decent position for the future". Things did not turn out like that. In the event, the debate was muted to say the least. From the off the predictions of a Smith walkover seemed, if anything, an understatement. One of the campaign team at the time recalls: "The frustration was that Bryan was largely an ideas man and the question of the nuts and bolts of running the campaign, of pinning down the trade unions, of pinning down the party, of being realistic about your numbers and knowing your strength and weaknesses were all left hanging. In the end that showed in the result." Rather than providing a voice for those who felt the need for a debate, Gould struggled to be heard, his challenge dismissed by most of the party and all of the press as an irrelevance. Blunkett was unhappy with Gould's conduct of the campaign: "All he would want to do was to slag John off to other people around him. Of course that meant that they were going to get their own back on him."

While the relationship between Gould and Smith became even worse, leading to Gould's eventual departure from politics, Blunkett demonstrated deft political skills in distancing himself from Gould – despite privately, and repeatedly, urging him to withdraw from the leadership contest and to concentrate on that for the deputy leadership (advice also given by Cook, Smith's campaign manager).

Gould ignored the advice and paid the price in a humiliating defeat. Smith received 229 votes out of the 297 cast by MPs and MEPs, compared with 68 for Gould – a majority of over four to one. All but five of the twenty-two Shadow Cabinet members voted for Smith. Gould won just twelve of the 597 constituency Labour parties. In the final result, Smith received 90.9 per cent to Gould's 9.1 per cent. As Blunkett recalls:

It was a tragic moment for me because he fell out with me for not going with him into oblivion, and for taking a Shadow Cabinet post when he was resigning. Well, apart from the fact that I didn't have New Zealand to go to [Gould, who had emigrated to Britain from New Zealand, returned to his home country soon after to become head of Auckland University], I didn't want to go into oblivion. We'd fought a campaign and we'd engaged a lot of good people in that campaign – a lot of reformers who are around today. Tony and Gordon were able to piggyback on it. They were astute politically in keeping out of it at the time, but they were able to piggyback on it, and it helped with the reform agenda of the mid-1990s.

In October 1991, Blunkett almost lost a still more important partnership – with Offa. Running around in the garden at Sheffield, Offa was shocked by a firework going off, jumped over the fence and ran off. For hours there was no sign of him, until a phone call from the GDBA informed Blunkett that someone had reported Offa lying injured in the road (his GDBA ID number was on his collar). Rushing to the spot, Blunkett found no sign of Offa. He and his friends searched through the night, to no avail. The local radio station agreed to broadcast an SOS asking the public to look out for him but, fourteen hours after he had gone missing, the police rang. Offa was in the garden of a house 300 yards from the main road, so badly injured that he could not stand. No bones had been broken but according to the vet he was badly bruised and traumatised. Only after six weeks did he regain his normal walking speed; and it was a further three weeks before he could go back to work.

But the problems were not over. One weekend in March 1992 he started to vomit. The vet could find nothing wrong and after a few hours he seemed fine. Then, campaigning in Wales and Bristol ten days before the general election on 9 April, Blunkett booked into a hotel for the night. Within an hour of going to bed, he was woken by Offa panting. The hotel helped find a vet who would see Offa straight away and they raced to his premises. Even though the journey took only a quarter of an hour, by the time they arrived Offa seemed on the verge of death, barely able to breathe. He had, the vet diagnosed, gastric torsion, in which the stomach enlarges and rotates, causing damage to the internal organs. Too weak to be operated on, he was put under sedation and a tube was inserted into his stomach, with a drip pumping fluids and drugs into his blood. He was operated on the next day, his stomach being untwisted through 270 degrees and the damaged portions of his stomach wall removed. The vet considered it almost a lost cause. For the next three days it was touch and go. Finally, after another four days, he began to show signs of recovery. Ten days later – the Saturday after Labour's election defeat – he was well enough to leave the surgery.

9
The Shadow Cabinet: the making of a player

Like many in the party, Blunkett had for a while convinced himself that Labour would win the 1992 election. But as if the bad vibes he felt when out on the campaign trail were not enough to demonstrate otherwise, he was receiving regular, depressing private polling news from Mike Lee, who was based at Labour's Walworth Road HQ. Blunkett rang Lee in the middle of the now infamous Sheffield rally, barely able to believe what was unravelling before him. If he had any remaining doubts that the campaign was heading into oblivion, the rally removed them.

The year was not all gloom, however. The election may have been lost and Bryan Gould's leadership campaign a fiasco but in July Blunkett was elected to the Shadow Cabinet for the first time (one of only two from the 1987 intake, the other being Mo Mowlam), a result primarily of his success in opposing the poll tax and a recognition from his Parliamentary Labour Party colleagues that he was not merely a coming man but one who had already arrived. Only Gordon Brown had risen quicker in the time Labour had been in opposition, reaching the Shadow Cabinet in four years to Blunkett's five. Blunkett had been disappointed not to get into the Shadow Cabinet earlier. He thought that Kinnock was not properly rewarding the loyalty he had shown on the NEC at no small risk to his positioning on the Left and not doing enough to get him elected to the Shadow Cabinet. Given the speed with which Kinnock promoted Blunkett to the front bench, recognising his talent and utilising it in a key, high-profile position even after his awkward behaviour in the 1980s on the NEC, this says more about

Blunkett's sense of his own abilities than it does about Kinnock's treatment of him.

For all his party position on the NEC, it was the Shadow Cabinet which really mattered now that, for the first time in over a decade, Labour looked like a serious party of government. In what seemed at the time like the eternal opposition of the 1980s, power in the party lay with the NEC; once government looked possible, the centre of power shifted to the Shadow Cabinet. Blunkett's arrival there signified that he was held in high esteem – especially as, unlike many Shadow Cabinet members who owed their position in large measure to their ability to socialise and massage their colleagues' political erogenous zones (Gerald Kaufman, for instance, was said to keep an index card with details of PLP members' families and interests, and to utilise the information in the run-up to election), Blunkett did not find it easy, or sometimes even possible, to do such 'schmoozing'.

There was some talk that Blunkett might be made Shadow Education Secretary. The idea did not meet with universal approval, however; his sons were so concerned that they decided to write to Smith and implore him not to appoint their father because he was keen on homework and discipline and would make their lives a misery. After a stern word from their parent, the letter remained unwritten. Blunkett was in any event given the health portfolio, one of the major positions. (They were not to be so fortunate two years later.)

Smith was generous in his behaviour towards both Gould and Blunkett. Although he was widely thought to have humiliated Gould by offering him the inconsequential post of Shadow Heritage Secretary, this was in fact Gould's own choice; Smith had telephoned him and offered him the choice of Education, Health or Heritage. That he chose Heritage was but another demonstration of Gould's poor political judgement.

Despite the health portfolio being the sort of subject that should be meat and drink to Labour politicians in opposition,

Blunkett never gave the impression of being fully comfortable in the role. Although he was to demonstrate ease and clear-sightedness at Education afterwards, there was rarely any sense of command at health. Robin Cook, his predecessor as health minister, had been a brilliant opposition spokesman but had barely bothered with positive proposals. Blunkett responded with a long policy statement, Health 2000. Unlike most pre-Blair policy statements, which were swiftly dumped when Blair took over, Health 2000 was a precursor to the Labour government's initial agenda, concentrating on prevention and public health, although, like Cook's proposals, it was devoid of real detail. Blunkett focused, as he had as leader of Sheffield council, on the consumer, rather than the producer, of public services, concentrating on the need for more GP facilities and widening the role of nurses, and thus taking on the rigid demarcation limits on which the British Medical Association insisted. He also proposed a complete ban on tobacco advertising and sponsorship – which was not quite as controversial then as it later turned out to be. (Blunkett raised this in the Commons in October 1992 when he asked the health minister, Brian Mawhinney, if he agreed "that the £100 million spent on tobacco advertising not only influences those who already smoke but has a direct impact on the lives and well-being of those who, against their will, are passive smokers? That is a consequence of others being persuaded to buy a product that damages their health. The industry continues to spend a large amount of money inducing smokers to continue damaging their health because that is good for their profits".[1])

The exchanges between Blunkett and Virginia Bottomley, the Secretary of State, were remarkably empty of content, even by the low standards of political debate at the time. Blunkett's main tactic was vituperation ("This is a shoddy statement from a Secretary of State who is a spent force. We shall expose, attack and denigrate the fraud that is inherent in the statement this afternoon"), followed by Bottomley's usual (and merited) rejoin-

der that "We always know what the hon. Gentleman is against
... But none of us on this side of the House is any the wiser
about what he is in favour of."² Bottomley was on shaky ground
herself, however; although she had to attend the Commons for
statements, and thus had to answer Blunkett's questions, she
refused to debate with him. After a debate in January 1993 in
which she was mauled by Blunkett, she never again risked a
repeat. By the time Blunkett was moved to Education in October
1994, he had gone nearly two years without being given the
chance to debate with Bottomley.

Blunkett had never been close to John Smith but had got to
know him much better since joining the Shadow Cabinet and
then, in October 1993, becoming Labour Party chairman (a
Buggins' turn position based on time spent on the NEC). For all
their previous differences over the poll tax replacement, Blunkett
– like most of the party – respected Smith's decency and the aura
of competence he emitted. But although Smith pushed through
the important internal party change of 'One Member, One Vote',
reducing the role of the unions, he had put a block on any
fundamental policy thinking, believing in the 'one more heave'
approach – that, after Black Wednesday, the next election was
now Labour's to lose, and that the party should not run the risk
of frightening the horses (leading one MP to write that the party
was in fact 'sleepwalking to oblivion'³). It made for a desperately
frustrating time for any Labour politician who wanted to think
about where the party was going wrong. As Blunkett puts it:
"We'd all been shocked at the scale of the defeat in '83; we'd
been quietly shaken by the fact that we'd run a good campaign
in '87 and still lost massively. But to have lost in '92, when hopes
were so high, was a real culture shock. It enabled Tony Blair and
Gordon Brown to see that we weren't going to shift anything if
there wasn't a different kind of momentum; a different type of
agenda from that John Smith was delivering." They may well
have seen that. But, under Smith, they had no chance to do
anything about it.

One night in the spring of 1993 Blunkett had, with other Shadow Cabinet members, gone to Smith's Barbican flat. The evening prompted a poem: "On occasions of this sort, I try to build a picture not only of those present but also of the surroundings. I asked various colleagues to describe what they could see across the city from such a vantage point. Their comments and my own feelings of soaring in the lift as floor after floor swept by I combined into a poem which I was never able to show John, but which I feel sure Elizabeth would understand:

> Challenger Three, I thought,
> As the lift soared
> Ten, fifteen, twenty, thirty, thirty-five floors.
>
> Doors open on to a landing,
> Still, eerie, silent.
> Then, from a door beyond,
> The sound of voices.
> People, laughing,
> Conversing about little or nothing,
> Here in the sky.
>
> Is this, I ask myself,
> A vision of the future?
> Capsules circling the earth,
> Distant from human life
> Freed from London's traffic din,
> But freed too from reality on the ground.
>
> For thirty-five floors high
> In the Cromwell Tower,
> No birds are heard to sing,
> No leaves to scatter in the wind.
> Views are wondrous, yes,
> But like gazing down
> On a Lilliput of life.

Here you meet no one,
And no one meets you.
Alone in the sky
On the thirty-fifth floor
You could disappear from the world
And never be noticed,
Until, your bills unpaid,
Reveal you have gone
Into orbit forever.

Lost to the world of men
And the love of womankind.

The poem was eerily prescient; the following year Smith went 'into orbit forever'. On 11 May 1994, the night before Smith's death, Blunkett had sat next to Elizabeth Smith at a Labour Party fund-raising dinner. The two got on well. She – like her husband – was gregarious and good company. Smith made a fine speech, in which he pledged that "We will do our best to reward your faith in us . . . Please give us the opportunity to serve our country. That is all we ask." The next morning he was dead.

As party chairman, Blunkett spoke for the entire party when he said on the day of Smith's death that he had "given his life for the Labour Party". Looking back, Blunkett believes that "It was almost fate that John should have died, because [if he hadn't] we'd [still] have won the '97 election, probably with about fifty or sixty seats. But nothing drastic would have changed in terms of education, health or the law and order agenda. I knew that from my experience as Shadow Health Secretary, and I had heard what he'd said about education." Things were to be very different under the next leader.

The leadership contest which, as party chairman, Blunkett oversaw was not as straightforward as he wanted. Margaret Beckett had won near-universal acclaim within the party as acting leader, fronting the European and local election campaigns which were in full swing when Smith died. But there were few who saw her as permanent leadership material. Had she chosen to remain deputy leader, she would have been elected unopposed. Perhaps understandably, however, she felt that, having done so well as acting leader, she had every right to run for the leadership. Blunkett has always maintained that he knew immediately that Blair was the obvious man to succeed Smith, not least because both he and Blair had the same instinctive belief in community as the governing idea behind the future direction of policy. But his actions at the time belie that notion. He may have realised, once the final contenders had emerged, that Blair was the only plausible choice, and he may have acted strictly impartially throughout the campaign, but in the immediate aftermath of Smith's death he had another leader in mind: Robin Cook, who was widely regarded as the party's best Commons performer and who came from a similar soft-left perspective. Blunkett contacted Cook early on to urge him to stand.[4]

Blunkett sought to tread the fine line between remaining above the fray as chairman of the party and also doing his level best to ensure a clear, uncomplicated contest. Once Beckett had declared for the leadership, however, both positions were clearly up for grabs. In the end, there were three leadership contestants: Beckett, Blair and Prescott.

There was another significant event for Blunkett that year. Back in 1992, after Offa's stomach operation, he had agreed with the GDBA that he would be retired when a suitable replacement could be found. Offa was clearly not himself, slowing down in little ways and showing much less enthusiasm for work than he had in the past. The GDBA found two new dogs for Blunkett to consider. One was clearly unsuitable – he was too easily distracted. Another, a collie/golden retriever cross, seemed promising and was taken to Westminster to look around (and was introduced to John Smith in the cafeteria) but on his second day he chased a cat while still on harness. That put paid to him. Eventually, in March 1994, Blunkett was told that a first-class candidate had emerged. Lucy was an eighteen-month-old black curly-coated retriever/Labrador cross. As a test, Blunkett sneaked her into the Commons chamber behind the Speaker's Chair. She settled instantly, despite the noise of Prime Minister's Questions, made even worse than usual by a call by Conservative MP Tony Marlow for John Major to resign. The test was passed effortlessly. Offa retired at the end of May, and Lucy – along with her trainer, Peter Smith – joined Blunkett for on-the-job acclimatisation on the European election trail.

Blunkett knew what lay in store for him. Lucy's puppy walker, Mrs Smith, had written to him with some of her experiences:

Lucy was my second puppy-walking assignment. My supervisor suggested that I might like to try something more challenging than my previous dog. One glance at Lucy at the Bolton training centre proved what an evil sense of humour she has. She was much taller than the two Labrador puppies that were with her, with uncontrollable legs and ears. She was busily organizing the bewildered pups in a game of leaf chase, and convinced herself that the pup cowering in the corner loved being dragged by the ears to join the game. I stood in silence with my eldest son and several other puppy walkers until someone mentioned that Lucy looked 'something of a live wire'. At first she did not welcome the suggestion that she might become a guide dog one day. She felt her real forte was operatic singing and she practised her scales every night for five weeks. Then she found a new career in furniture design with a special penchant for three-legged chairs. My sons thought she was brilliant and called her 'the naughtiest puppy ever'. We used to introduce her as 'Lucy, short for Lucifer'. She was such a characterful puppy that when she was going back to Bolton for training, I remarked to my supervisor that she would need a lot of brain activity to keep her out of mischief and she should preferably go to someone with a sense of humour! But please beware of muddy ditches. I hope you have not discovered her enthusiasm for hurtling through them, nose down, throwing the water over her head . . .[5]

Lucy was indeed a live wire. But Blunkett was instantly impressed. As soon as she was harnessed, she switched into work mode. She coped like an old pro with her full-time debut in Westminster. She was the top story on the BBC's children's news, *Newsround*, and a main story on every other news programme that day.

Blunkett had been concerned with finding a retirement home that would give Offa the environment he needed. The ideal solution presented itself when Paddy March, the vet who had saved his life in Bristol, offered to take him once a replacement had been found. Offa would be perfect for March's three children. Offa stayed with March until June 1999, when he had to ring Blunkett to tell him that the dog had finally come to the end and needed to be put down, at the age of twelve. Later that year Paddy March committed suicide. As Blunkett has written: "I know that the hurt and distress that he felt about allowing Offa to die in peace had taken its toll on this gentle and kind man who had saved his life. If I had had any inkling of the suffering Paddy was going through, I would have done anything to have helped him. But, I suspect, as his family have assured me, that there was nothing that any of us could have done to prevent such a tragedy occurring."[6]

Throughout the campaign to elect Smith's successor, Blunkett acted neutrally in accordance with his obligations as party chairman. But he knew exactly what to do once the need for impartiality was removed. In the interval between the polls closing and the result (a foregone conclusion in favour of Blair) being announced, he was careful to place on the record (via a piece in the *Daily Mirror*) his shared belief with Blair in the values of community, which Blair had stressed in his campaign and which had, indeed, long formed the cornerstone of Blunkett's beliefs. Although the two men would not seem at first glance natural soulmates, coming not just from very different upbringings but with entirely separate party backgrounds, they had much in common politically. Both had an instinctive ability to speak to voters in language that resonated, and had caught the modernisation bug – albeit in very different ways – before it became fashionable. Immediately on becoming leader, Blair told Tom Sawyer (soon to be appointed general secretary of the Labour Party) that Blunkett was the ideal Labour politician and that he intended to promote him to a major post. Blunkett then received an early invitation for dinner at Blair's Richmond Crescent home, "to see what I'd got to say and what I was prepared to offer", as Blunkett puts it. Blair asked Blunkett what job he would like. "Given your relationship with Gordon," he replied, "I know I'm not going to be offered the one I'd really like. But I would like to do either education or employment." He was handed education; when the Conservatives amalgamated the two, he ended up with both.

Blair shared Blunkett's evangelical idea of the community, without any of the baggage carried by the former leader of Sheffield City Council. Blunkett discovered how much that mattered, and appreciated for the first time the importance of Blair's signals to the electorate, over the ditching of the commitment in Clause IV of the party's constitution to common ownership of "the means of production, distribution and exchange", which Blair announced in the autumn of 1994 at his first conference as leader. For all his keenness that Labour should change, Blunkett disagreed with Blair's move, thinking it a pointless stirring up of internal party antagonism. The trajectory of Blunkett's views on this are reminiscent of his behaviour over the expulsion of Militant. Initially he believed Kinnock was making a big and unnecessary mistake. As time passed and he began to see both the positive effect and the objective need for such a move, he changed his mind. The same thing happened over the removal of Clause IV. As the debate moved on, he realised that it had a far greater impact outside the party on voters. "I understood then the importance of signals. The signals to the electorate that we really were something different mattered; I've understood the signals ever since." Blunkett was himself to become the master of signals.

Blair's first act as leader – on the Monday after his election – was a huge political signal of the changes that the party was about to undergo, marching into and taking control of a press conference by Ann Taylor, the then Shadow Education Secretary. Taylor was, in effect, the National Union of Teachers' Westminster spokeswoman, representative of a tradition in which Labour's education policy was in thrall to the teaching unions and the education establishment, of which the NUT was by far the most antediluvian example. Taylor was also politically ineffectual. Despite John Patten's near-calamitous tenure as Education Secretary, she seemed to spend all her time in consultative meetings with the NUT working on her would-be masterwork, *Opening Doors to a Learning Society*, a policy statement which trotted out the usual themes of expanding nursery education, smaller class sizes, ending selection and introducing 'home–school contracts' (one of Labour policy-makers' obsessions at the time). Blair's actions made it perfectly clear that things would be changing, effectively dismissing the very document that Taylor was supposedly launching at the press conference and then removing her from her post in favour of Blunkett.

The respective educations of Blair and Blunkett could hardly have been more different, Blair having followed one of Scotland's leading public schools, Fettes, with Oxford. Both, though, had similar views on the basics. And there could be few better demonstrations of the ability of education to transform lives than Blunkett's own story. He had long believed that the most important issues, bar none, were literacy and numeracy. Ann Taylor and those around her had seemed almost fearful of talking about standards, as if they were somehow encroaching on Tory territory. When Blunkett took over education, the Conservative reforms – the most important of which were the introduction of the national curriculum, beefing up the schools inspectorate, grant-maintained schools and the publication of examination results, allowing parents to see by means of league tables how successful (or not) their local schools were – were still relatively new. But with the first national curriculum results coming through, with appalling results in literacy and numeracy and

Ofsted (the schools inspectorate) starting to find out what was really going on in schools, Blunkett had a clear choice: adopt a knee-jerk hostility to Conservative reforms simply because they had been introduced by the Conservatives; or build on them. He chose the latter.

Fundamental to literacy and numeracy success was, of course, teaching quality. The Ofsted reports revealed, at the very least, significant pockets of bad teaching. Any worthwhile policy for literacy and numeracy would have to deal with what went on in the classroom. The inspection regime introduced by the Conservatives was all very well but there was little follow-through after poor findings. Coupled to this was the need for discipline. (As Blunkett put it in the Commons in November 1996 when school detention was given specific legal status: "Some of us are slightly taken aback to discover that, after 18 years of Conservative government, detention is not compulsory. If I had known that when I was at school, I could have saved myself hours of difficulty sitting through it, but I welcome the belated decision to ensure that, after all those years, people will not be prosecuted and locked up for having held me in detention."[7])

For all the hopelessness of Taylor's period, Blunkett had at least some recent foundations on which to build. Jack Straw, Taylor's predecessor, had been careful not to damn the Conservatives' reforms out of hand, denouncing the chaos that the "lethal cocktail" would supposedly cause but backing the aim of higher standards. His purpose – pursued to far greater effect by Blunkett – was to "establish Labour beyond doubt as the party of standards."[8] The policies on which the party fought the 1992 election under Straw, however, did not give the National Union of Teachers fright: grant-maintained schools would, according to the manifesto, be "brought together with City Technology Colleges into the mainstream of the local school system"; local management of schools would be reformed out of worthwhile existence; all selection would be abolished; and the assisted places scheme would be ended.

Blair's belief in "education, education and education" as the three top priorities of the next Labour government (a phrase he coined in his speech to the Labour Party conference in 1996) chimed with Blunkett's outlook. Both were traditionalists who gave short shrift to the progressive theories that dominated the educational establishment. Instead of concentrating on structure, both believed that all that really mattered was what went on in the classroom. So what if grant-maintained (GM) schools were not regarded as socialistically pure? They comprised fewer than 1,000 of the total of 24,000 schools. And why waste so much political energy on the 160 remaining grammar schools? Politically, too, it was suicidal; many of the GM schools were (quite deliberately) in Conservative-held marginal seats – the very constituencies that Labour needed to win. During the leadership contest, Blair had given an interview that effectively summarised the approach which he and Blunkett adopted over the next seven years, first in opposition and then in government:

For the vast majority of parents, they want to know their kids are brought up in a school where there is proper discipline, where they are given homework and are expected to do it, where the teachers are highly motivated, where you know how well your kid is doing . . . I think it is an absolute scandal that we have a large number of children leaving primary school and they cannot even read or write. These are the things that need tackling . . . Parents, of course, must have a choice of school. I would like to see them given the fullest information. I would like to see them know exactly how well their kid is doing and I would like them to be able to demand and expect high standards of performance throughout our education system . . . Of course you have got to be able to compare schools, but it has to be on a basis that is fair to the school and is accurate.

As for GM schools: it was "manifestly absurd for Labour to criticize parents who want to send their children to one".[9]

Blunkett made his first formal statement on education in October, saying that "standards, achievement and opportunity" would be his "watchwords in developing policy". The following month, he went on the BBC's *Breakfast with Frost* and began to flesh out the specifics and to ram home the message that Labour had changed. The school league tables, which the Conservatives introduced in 1993, had been fundamentally opposed by most Labour members. Blunkett saw the party's attitude to them as a perfect demonstration of what needed to change. The tables were "far from perfect but they are a lot better than the previous system, where parents 'in the know' could find the results, but those who needed the information most were left in the dark". He told Frost that a Labour government would continue to publish the tables, though it would expand them to include a measure of 'value added'. The following month he wrote in *The Times* that "without such comparisons it is difficult to judge objectively the progress of one's child and the school's success rate".[10] The teaching unions responded with anger (their usual reaction to any change). But, as they would soon discover, this was barely the start of the changes that Blunkett would introduce.

Blunkett had been in post only for a month when the London Oratory affair broke, a crisis that could easily have sunk him at the very start. Blair had decided to send his son Euan to the Oratory, a Catholic GM school. Although the story had first broken in June in the *Daily Express*, it took off only when confirmed by Blair in November. Blair's defence, however, turned a potential disaster into a sign that he was a different kind of Labour politician: "That's our choice as parents and I wouldn't want to deny that choice to other parents. Any parent wants the best for their children. I am not going to make a choice for my child on the basis of what is the politically correct thing to do."[11]

But what did this mean in terms of party policy? A few days before the Oratory story broke, Blunkett had already told the *Times Educational Supplement* that GM school policy needed to shift. GM schools presented a major political problem. Anything that seemed less than outright hostility and an unambiguous policy of abolition would (and later did) arouse the hostility of some of the most influential, and loud-mouthed, party figures. "We are", he said in response to the Oratory story in a letter to the Parliamentary Labour Party on 2 December, "opposed to schools opting out and remain committed to the pledge to bring such schools back into a local democratic framework. There is no plan to have a paper on GM schools, nor is there any intention that GM status should continue." But this was being decidedly economical with the truth. Outside the party and the educational establishment, they were popular – not least with parents. A pledge to abolish GM schools would have sunk at birth any idea that New Labour had a different outlook from that of its former incarnation, and in strategically placed areas with small Conservative majorities it would have had a direct political cost. The task that preoccupied Blunkett was finding a means of pacifying the party opposition to GM schools yet at the same time neutering the damaging political consequences of outright abolition.

Almost immediately, the word went out that Blair was distinctly unimpressed by his new Shadow Secretary of State's political footwork. On so deeply personal an issue for the leader, Blunkett had in effect slapped his wrist. There were whispers within Westminster and stories, sourced from within the leader's inner circle, to the effect that Blair was already considering moving Blunkett to a less important post.

Before he had time to recover his footing, Blunkett was in further trouble. In an interview in *The Sunday Times* on New Year's Day 1995, he remarked that the next Labour government would "consider" putting VAT on private school fees. Not only should Blunkett have realised that this was giving out exactly the wrong sort of signal – the whole Blair agenda was based on winning the support of the upwardly mobile – he had also – unusually – not done his homework and had not realised that Gordon Brown, the Shadow Chancellor, had explicitly ruled out such an idea. Humiliatingly, he had to go on that day's *The World This Weekend*, the Radio 4 lunchtime news programme, to contradict himself: "The Shadow Chancellor and the leader think it is helpful to rule out that possibility in order to avoid confusion."[12]

The fallout from the VAT issue, while awkward and embarrassing, did not linger too long – unlike the GM schools issue, which dominated Blunkett's thinking and strategy throughout 1995. About a fifth of schools had become grant-maintained, the attraction being not merely the extra funding but also more independence over admissions and employment of teachers, and the absence of direct Local Education Authority control. The policy document *Diversity and Excellence*, published in June, was the end result of a process designed to pacify the party's more unreconstructed elements but at the same time neutralise the issue as a potential vote loser.

Under Taylor, Labour had simply opposed GM schools in what one Blunkett aide calls "the most extraordinarily sterile campaign – designed to pander to Labour activists but no one else". Blunkett's attitude was that, as he put it in his first Commons appearance as Shadow Education Secretary, in November 1994, the GM "experiment has failed. It is a sideshow that is completely irrelevant to the future of our children and of education".[13] But instead of simply attacking them he looked at why schools wanted to have GM status in the first place, what it was about GM schools that worked best, and whether that could be expanded to other schools. To that end, he and his staff worked closely with three prominent local government figures (officers rather than politicians) from Local Education Authorities where the majority of schools had gone, or were going, grant-maintained.

Blunkett's chief aide, Conor Ryan (who had a background in education, having been a press officer at the Inner London Education Authority), made sure that he was in regular contact with the Association of Grant Maintained Schools, whose key figures he saw every six weeks, to ensure that they would be able to live with Labour's eventual policy. Midway through the process, a private seminar was organised for over a hundred head teachers from GM schools. At every stage, keeping the GM schools on board was paramount. For the schools, the sticking point was the imposition of governors from LEAs. The eventual policy was, just, acceptable to the schools. All schools would, as was the case before the introduction of GM status, be funded locally but they would all have far more autonomy than hitherto. Existing GM schools would be renamed Foundation Schools and employ their staff directly but – as a sop to the Local Education Authority lobby – would have two governors appointed by the authority.

Although with hindsight this seems like a rather dull, technical issue – hardly the stuff of political earthquakes – at the time it was explosive. Opposition to GM schools had been a core part of the attacks on Conservative policy, and it was difficult to find a party member who saw them as anything other than iniquitous. And even though the teaching unions were not, as was often mistakenly thought, affiliated to Labour, the party was in effect the political wing of the teaching movement. At the 1995 annual conference, 60 per cent of delegates were teachers or governors.[14] As Blunkett puts it: "The seam runs very deep in terms of the struggle for comprehensive education in the 1960s. People who are now in senior positions in the party, and their friends and relatives, grew up with it. It became an article of faith, linked with all the other issues relating to equality of opportunity. Also, there are more teachers in the Labour Party per square inch than there are bristles in a hedgehog."[15] Blunkett himself was, of course, one of them.

There was a real possibility of defeat at that year's party conference and Blair needed to be certain that Blunkett's formula would work. To that end, he summoned Michael Barber (an educationalist who had started working with Blunkett), David Miliband (then head of policy for Blair), Alastair Campbell and Leisha Fullick (formerly director of education in Lewisham) to a secret meeting – of which Blunkett and Ryan were both unaware – at his Islington house for a rigorous examination of the policy.

After two hours of searching questions, Blair was convinced. Speaking at the end of the meeting about the absent Shadow minister, he remarked, "I wish I had five or six like him".

Diversity and Excellence was, however, far more significant than merely as an attempt to ditch the GM problem. It proposed that LEAs should focus, above all, on monitoring and supporting standards, that comprehensives should become 'community schools' and that the voluntary-aided church schools should become 'aided schools'.

Diversity and Excellence was to be by far the most important and controversial component of the 1995 conference, since it married what many in the party saw as an unconscionable acceptance of the fundamentals of the GM schools' self-governance with what was intended as a clear sop to party members: a commitment to abolish selection. But even that was not quite what it seemed. Abolition of the 160 remaining grammar schools "would only follow a clear demonstration of support from the parents affected by such decisions", as the policy document put it.[16] That failure to pledge outright abolition of selection led to an almighty public row which continued to haunt Blunkett throughout his time as Education Secretary.

Roy Hattersley saw himself as keeper of the progressive education flame. He seemed to expend much of his political energy on opposing Blunkett. Hattersley had long been a passionate opponent of selection and had made his name as a junior education spokesman in the early 1970s. His opposition was so strong that he had been denied the post of Shadow Education Secretary by both Foot and Kinnock. To Hattersley, as to the overwhelming majority of Labour members, a belief in the local comprehensive was a touchstone of socialism.

Hattersley launched an all-out attack on the proposals, using every media and party avenue open to him over the summer to arraign Blunkett on charges of betrayal, attempting to cause so many political problems for him that he would be unable to gain sufficient support at conference. Foundation Schools, he argued,

were merely "grant-maintained by another name". The notion
of parental choice and a variety of types of school, so critical to
Blunkett and Blair's attempts to shift the perception of the party
as being in hock to the teaching unions, would lead to "social
selection". Hattersley was, however, playing straight into
Blunkett's hands. Nothing would more clearly demonstrate how
the party had changed than a set-piece dispute with the man
who, on education, was as Old Labour as they came. As Blunkett
wrote in the *Guardian*, responding to one of Hattersley's attacks:
"The quality of education is what matters. We can and must do
better if we are to succeed in the new century." There was no
point in pursuing dead-end fights over GM status. All parents
were interested in was how Labour would improve teaching and
standards. So, as Education Secretary, Blunkett would

work with LEAs and the profession on schemes of teacher appraisal,
and to improve management training for heads. We are examining
ways to enable good teachers to continue teaching, as teacher pro-
fessors, and to improve the ratio of pupils to adults in the classroom
to tackle the problem of class sizes . . . We will build on the success
of reading recovery and other programmes to tackle illiteracy. We
will work with LEAs to develop plans where schools are failing to
enable them to improve, and we will intervene to turn schools around
where closure seems the only alternative . . . And, finally, we will
explore ways to use new technology more effectively so that its
benefits are available to every school. We must recognize the social
and economic benefits to our nation of well-educated young people
and a well-educated workforce.[17]

Everything pointed to an old-fashioned conference row at
Brighton in October. Not only was there a danger of defeat, but
the message that the vote would send out to voters would be
critical in persuading them whether or not the party had
changed. Blunkett was an experienced conference speaker, who
had been charged with a series of tough assignments, from asking
members to pay the poll tax to paving the way to the expulsion

of Militant. But this time it was different. This time there was a real danger of defeat.

Hattersley's speech was a barnstormer, tickling the delegates where they loved to be touched. He was cheered repeatedly as he derided Blunkett's proposals for Foundation Schools as "opt-out schools by another name", saying that they were "absolutely beyond understanding . . . For God's sake, let's stop apologising for comprehensive schools". His speech met with a heartfelt standing ovation – somewhat unusual in the context of Hattersley's record as the social democrat the party hated to love. (Indeed, Blunkett had himself dressed down the then deputy leader, Hattersley, at the opening of the 1986 party conference, warning him not to go "mad over moderation" by avoiding tax increases on those earning less than £28,000.[18]) Blunkett knew that he had to make one of the speeches of his life. He had told friends in advance that he wanted to "have it out with Roy", and he did. He accused him of playing into the hands of the Conservatives. "Those who did not come up with solutions should not turn on those who have," he said. He spoke of his own childhood and how he had struggled to succeed and how above all he wanted to ensure that it was children who would otherwise be left behind who were given the opportunity to succeed by the next Labour government.

Blunkett was aided in his attempts at persuading delegates of the socialist passion behind his proposals by having recently bolstered his standing with the Left on the NEC. A far-left activist, Liz Davies, had been selected by the Leeds North East Constituency Labour Party as its prospective parliamentary candidate. As with all candidates, her nomination had to be approved by the NEC and Blair was determined that she should be barred from standing. Blunkett had been reluctant to expel Militant until the very end; so, too, he found it difficult to reject Davies, and refused to vote against her candidacy.

This helped to persuade some of the delegates in Brighton who might have rejected his words out of hand to listen to what he had to say about GM schools. His conciliatory tone worked. The document itself, and thus the new policy, passed – despite Hattersley's urgings. Crucially, the constituencies voted in favour; if they had not, the victory would have been pyrrhic. Blair, sitting alongside Blunkett on the platform, looked visibly relieved.

Blunkett's speech, in which he argued that concentration on GM status was "a diversion", was, however, remembered more for an entirely different subject: selection. Cut a cross-section through the average Labour Party member and you will discover two core beliefs: that the NHS is morally superior to any other healthcare system; and that selection is morally wrong. The evidence to the contrary about both from the Continent is irrelevant. The belief is heartfelt and runs deep. Thus when Blunkett promised – "read my lips" – that there would be "no selection, either by examination or by interview, under a Labour government", he was rewarded with a thunderous standing ovation, clearly genuine rather than staged. Hattersley himself could not have asked for more. Yet the statement was bizarre. The party was certainly *de jure* opposed to selection but the very policy that conference had just approved stated, explicitly, that the future of the few remaining grammar schools would be a matter of "local agreement". The words would return to haunt Blunkett. They were, clearly, a mistake. It is inconceivable that Blunkett would not have realised they were nonsense. The only sensible conclusion is that he did, as he has claimed, leave out a critical word. Blunkett himself says that he meant to say "no *further* selection by examination or interview" – the words he used at the 1996 conference. That is certainly possible. Others close to him, however, suggest that the word he left out was 'more'. 'No more selection' would have had the virtue of being (deliberately) ambiguous. It could have meant no further selection, which would have been the meaning ascribed to it after conference, but in the heady conference atmosphere Blunkett could have traded on it being taken to mean 'an end to selection' – the meaning of the words he ended up using.

The concentration on standards was continued in the next policy document, *Excellence for Everyone*, published in December 1995. The paper was intended to address the worries of parents about standards across the board, which meant new twists on what Alastair Campbell, Blair's press secretary, later called "bog standard comprehensives", such as specialist schools, with an emphasis on the need to stretch brighter pupils. Blunkett had a vested interest in the subject: all three of his boys were educated at a local comprehensive school.

Excellence for Everyone was the first product of Blunkett's consultations with two of the men who were to be crucial to the development and implementation of Labour policy, Tim Brighouse and Michael Barber.

Barber was a former teacher who had been at various times the NUT's head of education, chair of education in Hackney, an adviser at the Department for Education and Employment under the Conservatives, and dean of new initiatives at the London University Institute of Education. At the time he was professor of education of Keele University. Although working in Whitehall under the Conservatives, Barber had been invited to write a speech on education for Blair during the 1994 party leadership contest. A few months later, in January 1995, he took part in a seminar on education organised by David Miliband, then Blair's head of policy, in the Commons. This meeting marked, in effect, the beginning of the Labour education revolution. In attendance, alongside Blair, Blunkett and Miliband, were Conor Ryan, Barber, Tim Brighouse and Leisha Fullick. The foundations of the New Labour education agenda were decided at the meeting, encapsulated in a phrase invented at the seminar by Barber: "Standards matter more than structures", a mantra that neatly deflected attention away from the most controversial aspects of policy within the party and which was reflected in the new approach to GM schools. Instead of adopting the old Labour stance of abolition, the new Labour position was to accept the reality that they delivered the goods and thus to find a compromise policy that neutered the abolitionists.

Barber was due to give the annual *Times Educational Supplement* lecture in March, regarded as a keynote platform amongst educationalists. Working on his own initiative, he titled his lecture "Imagining an End to Failure" and floated the idea of closing down failing schools. Blunkett distanced himself from what was, so soon after his being given the education portfolio, too radical an idea to be endorsed just yet – especially immediately after his difficulties over the Oratory and VAT. But within a matter of weeks Blunkett decided to use his speech to the annual Association of Teachers and Lecturers (the most moderate of the teaching unions) conference in Harrogate to propose just that: "A school identified as failing would be closed and a new school opened on the same site for a new school year. The new school, with a new governing body, teachers and head-teachers, would be able to offer pupils a fresh chance."[19] Barber was soon able to put his idea into effect; he was appointed by the Conservative Education Secretary, Gillian Shephard, to a task force dealing with the notorious sink school, Hackney Downs. Barber was careful to balance his loyalties to his current boss, Shephard, and to his Labour roots and kept Blunkett in the loop. Blunkett could have made political capital out of the project – it was, after all, based on turning round a school that had failed under a Conservative government – but was keen to see if the Hackney Downs experiment could work. He told Barber that he wanted to "let the deed be done".

Brighouse, who successfully sued the former Education Secretary, John Patten, for calling him a "nutter", was director of education in Birmingham, having done the same job in Oxfordshire during the 1980s. He went on to become professor of education at Keele (where he was succeeded, on his departure for Birmingham, by Barber). Unlike Barber, who was in the vanguard of a new educational realism on the part of Labour, Brighouse remained an unapologetic 'progressive' and was regarded as 'the enemy' by many parents who believed that he and his like had been responsible for much of the educational vandalism over the past two or three decades. When, in May 1997, Blunkett appointed him as joint vice-chair with Chris Woodhead, the chief inspector of schools, of the National Schools Standards Task Force, there was much laughter from the press and education commentators: quite apart from their fundamental difference in approach to education, the two men had spent most of the past two years rowing in public over the testing criteria used by Ofsted.[20]

Excellence for Everyone concentrated on improving teaching standards via continual assessments of performance, homework recommendations, smaller class sizes, lessons in parenting skills, home–school partnerships and reading recovery schemes to push up literacy levels. But the most newsworthy aspect (the document was launched by an article by Blair in the *Daily Mail* in December 1995) was the promise of "tough" measures to deal with failing schools – and to sack poor teachers. Blunkett had regained the initiative earlier in the year after the VAT fiasco by turning to this theme, criticising the "culture of complacency" in schools, opposing the teaching unions' strike calls (this time over class sizes) and outlining, for the first time, Barber's idea that failing schools should be closed. This idea was extended in February 1997 when Blunkett announced, also via the *Daily Mail*, that he would, as Secretary of State, take over the running of failing Local Education Authorities, imposing an Ofsted inspector, an educational expert and a Chief Education Officer from another, successful, LEA.

At the core of the battle that Blunkett had to fight within the Labour Party as Shadow Education Secretary was the tension between the political dogma that much of the party adhered to, which pointed towards mixed-ability classes, progressive teaching methods and other hopelessly ill-founded beliefs about the best form of education, and practical evidence about what did, and did not, work. In February 1996, Blunkett used a Social Market

Foundation seminar to argue that "diversity is essential for the renewal of comprehensives", a key part of the New Labour approach. "For me", Blunkett has written,

there had to be a distinction between the all-ability intake of a comprehensive school and how lessons were organized in schools. Those who pioneered the comprehensive system never expected it to adopt the dull uniformity that it often unfairly came to symbolize. Susan Crosland was later to confirm that her late husband, Tony Crosland, who had created many comprehensives as Education Secretary in the sixties, saw things this way. Nor did those pioneers expect every pupil to be taught at the same pace, regardless of ability. While this remains controversial in some party circles, most headteachers have long accepted these realities.[21]

The message was received loud and clear that Labour was changing. Indeed, Blunkett's opponents continually played into his hands. Every Easter, the three main teaching unions – the Association of Teachers and Lecturers (ATL), the National Union of Teachers (NUT) and the National Association of Schoolmasters/Union of Women Teachers (NAS/UWT) – hold their annual conferences. (There are three other teaching unions, and two for head teachers.) Since it was his first year in the job, Blunkett felt that he should speak at each. It was, on one level, not the most propitious of beginnings to his relationship with the unions. He was greeted by ATL members gathered in Harrogate with silence – a bad enough welcome for any speaker but for a blind speaker who has no idea how many people are in the hall, even more so. (Two years later, they extended the silence to his entire speech. And the ATL was the most moderate of the teaching unions.)

The speech was in many ways seminal:

I was determined to show that Labour would put the interests of pupils and parents first in the drive to improve school standards . . . So when I reached the International Centre for an early evening session I said to the assembled teachers that it was not enough to identify failure in schools; something also had to be done to improve those schools dramatically or they should close. That often meant a new headteacher and a change in staff. But there needed also to be proper financial support and help from the local authority. I believe that those receiving rather than delivering services must be our primary concern, and while those delivering the service are crucial to achieving this, their interests are not paramount. Quite simply, we wanted to ensure that those who couldn't teach and were letting down thousands of young people left the profession, and those who couldn't lead either retrained or found a job elsewhere.[22]

Times and attitudes change quickly. Today, such a statement would be commonplace to the point of being dull. Then, however, it was seen as near revolutionary – especially by the unions. As an aide at the time puts it: "all hell broke loose". Peter Smith, the ATL's general secretary, and John Monks, general secretary of the TUC, were both withering in their responses. Monks argued that a football manager wouldn't be sacked if his team was bottom of the league – a somewhat bizarre analogy, since that is precisely what would happen. The Friday papers were full of the row over Blunkett's comments and served to increase the temperature in time for Blunkett's debut at the most rowdy conference, the NUT's. The NUT was, and is, by far the most unreconstructed teachers' union, with a regular, sizeable Socialist Workers Party presence at its annual conference. The events of that afternoon have become legendary, Blunkett being reportedly bundled into a broom cupboard to take refuge from screaming militants. As *The Sunday Times* put it the next day:

BLUNKETT BESIEGED AS TEACHERS LAMBAST BLAIR'S SCHOOLS POLICY

Left-wing demonstrators mobbed David Blunkett, Labour's blind education spokesman, yesterday as members of Britain's biggest teachers' union vented their anger at the party's firmer stance on standards and strikes. As Blunkett arrived at the National Union of Teachers' annual conference in Blackpool to warn against striking, he was surrounded by 40 protesters, many waving Socialist Workers' Party banners and shouting: 'Sack the Tories, not the teachers.'[23]

The truth is rather more mundane. The NUT newspaper, *The Teacher*, had a small office near the hall and Doug McAvoy, the NUT's general secretary, guided Blunkett, Estelle Morris, Peter Kilfoyle (a junior spokesman) and the rest of the party into it while the fuss – a small number of angry, chanting SWP members – died down. It would have to have been a rather large cupboard to have accommodated the entire party around Blunkett.

Ryan had been waiting with Estelle Morris for Blunkett to arrive at the front entrance. Mistakenly, Blunkett's driver had taken him to a back entrance, so he wandered off to look for the rest of his party. Harry Smith, the ITN reporter, spotted him, shouted "There he is" and suddenly several TV crews, followed by the rest of the media pack, caught up with him and filmed him being bundled into the office – pictures which, on a slow day, led that night's news. After twenty minutes the militants lost interest and wandered off. The scene did not come close to the level of hostility that Blunkett endured during the expulsion of Militant. But on television it looked like a major incident – and one which rebounded entirely in Blunkett's favour, providing a political story of which he could only have dreamed, demonstrating at once both Blunkett's own political courage and the veracity of the idea that the teaching profession needed a thorough clear-out. It was also a stark illustration of the journey on which Labour had embarked, with the teaching unions reduced to spluttering, impotent rage.[24] The NUT leader, Doug McAvoy – who was to be one of Blunkett's most implacable opponents over the following years – realised immediately the self-inflicted wound: "This is a sad day for the union. The image of the mob will live with me for a long time."[25] As if to prove all Blunkett's points about some teachers, not one of the rabble was later disciplined by their school.

Opponents of Labour's previous attitudes were increasingly aware of what was going on. Melanie Phillips, for instance, who had written a withering critique of the progressive attitudes that Blunkett was dumping,[26] wrote in her *Observer* column that "this was Labour's social policy Clause Four. It underscores the line Labour is drawing under its past, a message that has to be rammed home to Middle England. Not for nothing did Blair raise the standard of this crusade in last week's *Daily Mail*. If they are not careful, the teachers could become Blair's Militant Tendency, to be used, as Neil Kinnock did in a different context, to demonstrate his toughness in defence of the interests of ordinary people".

The flow of policy papers continued ceaselessly throughout the next year. In opposition, this constant drip – more of a flood – of policy statements was a brilliant media tactic. It was, however, to become part of the New Labour DNA and, as such, to cause immense problems when policy papers were translated in government into initiatives and directives, as Blunkett was to discover. *Aiming Higher* dealt with sixteen- to nineteen-year-olds' education, both academic and vocational; *Target 2000* outlined a plan to ensure that all under-twenty-fives had at least the equivalent of five GCSEs; *Lifelong Learning* pledged to widen access to higher education and reform the student loan scheme; *Learn as You Earn* introduced the idea of Individual Learning Accounts, contributed to by both government and employers, which would fund ongoing education and training (and which turned out to be a disaster when introduced by Blunkett as Secretary of State, mired in organised fraud and abolished after less than three years after costing £273 million[27]). By the time of the election, there was barely a dot or comma of the ideas later pursued in government left to be written. When Labour took office in 1997, it was better prepared than any other government before; and of the various departmental teams, Blunkett's education team had by far the most detailed policy proposals, outlining the core themes – and specifics – of the agenda.

The sum of these many parts was the draft manifesto *New Labour, New Life for Britain*, published in summer 1996, approved by that year's Labour conference (when Blair first used the formulation that was to define the party's election campaign: "Ask me my three main priorities for government and I tell you: education, education, education") and then supported by a vote of individual party members in November.

It was not just policy papers. Barely a set-piece speech went by without an announcement of some sort. In May 1996, for instance, speaking to head teachers at the National Association of Head Teachers' annual conference in Torquay, Blunkett announced the establishment of the Literacy Task Force, to be chaired by Michael Barber.

The national curriculum was all very well but literacy and numeracy levels were shameful. Because of the domination of teacher training colleges by the ideologically driven progressive education establishment, many primary school teachers had no idea that phonics – teaching children to recognise the sounds of individual letters – was by far the most successful method of teaching children to read. There was a similar problem with numeracy teaching; the evidence showed that children needed to be taught first how to calculate simple sums in their head before they could go on to anything more complicated.

Barber gathered together a team of head teachers and open-minded academics to develop a literacy and numeracy strategy that Labour could implement immediately on taking office, referred to by Blunkett as a "reading revolution". Their conclusions were published in February 1997 and recommended a structured daily literacy hour. David Reynolds, an educationalist at Newcastle University, developed a similar numeracy hour. Immediately after publication of his report, Barber took what he saw as a calculated risk by meeting Sir Michael Bichard, Permanent Secretary at the DfEE, to take him through the details of the proposals. Given the purpose of the task force – to work out the specifics of a strategy in opposition so that Blunkett could begin reforming the system on day one – it was important that the civil service knew what it was likely to be implementing. By the time of the election, copies of the report had been sent to every head teacher in the country to prepare them for what was coming.

Blunkett and his advisers had been spending a lot of time with Bichard. The two men hit it off immediately, Blunkett warming to Bichard's 'can do' attitude and Bichard respecting Blunkett's thought-through approach. Bichard's attitude was critical. As the first year in office was to show, the department was far from on board for the changes being introduced. Without Bichard's backing and managerial abilities, the entire project would almost certainly have come crashing down.

The best-laid plans, however, almost always come unstuck in politics. While the nitty-gritty of policy-making was proceeding with remarkable success, political problems repeatedly threatened to derail the process. Blunkett may have thought that, after the Oratory controversy had passed, he would be free from being hulled by Labour politicians' school choices. On Friday, 19 January 1996, however, Harriet Harman, the Shadow Health Secretary, was called by the headmaster of the school that her son was due to enter that autumn with some news. The *Mail on Sunday* had discovered that she had chosen a grammar school – St Olave's in Bromley, a grant-maintained grammar school in a Conservative borough 10 miles from her Southwark home. Over the weekend the news was dominated by the story, which Labour's all-powerful news management skills seemed powerless even to dampen, let alone kill. The teaching unions scented blood and went for Harman with a personal ferocity that they have unleashed on no other Labour – or Tory – politician before or since. The decision to send Euan Blair to the Oratory (the school attended by Harman's eldest son) may have been hated but taking on the party leader was of a rather different order of magnitude to taking on a health spokeswoman who was already unpopular in large parts of the party for being one of what John Prescott referred to as "the beautiful people".

The unions were not alone in their attitude. There are few more heinous offences within the Labour Party than support for selection and Harman had betrayed that most basic principle, compounding it with her hypocrisy in seeking to deny to others what she wished her own child to take advantage of. For a time, her support within the Shadow Cabinet seemed to have drained away and the expectation was that she would be forced to resign her post. It was, until the impact of the Iraq War, the most serious party crisis faced by Blair and Blunkett was caught square in the middle of it. The Oratory's status could be fudged (Blair repeatedly called it a "state comprehensive" which, technically, it was; by sending his son there, he became the first prime minister to send his child to a state school). St Olave's could not. It was a grammar school, plain and simple.

Blunkett was placed in a difficult position. He had no doubt that Harman had been a hypocrite and was firmly of the view that she ought to leave the front bench (a view which, although he shared it with confidants, he did not communicate to Blair). But, understandably, this was the last thing Blair wanted, especially with an election possible in a matter of weeks. And Harman had, after all, only done what Blair himself had done – put his child first. But the charge of hypocrisy was too powerful to be met by such a rebuttal and argument raged. Once Blair had determined that Harman should stay, however, and had made his decision public, Blunkett had no choice but to defend her. As he told Peter Mandelson (who had coordinated Harman's media defence) afterwards: "Your job was to look after her, mine to look after the party."[28]

The affair was, in the end, yet another demonstration of the unions' impotence. Despite their all-out assault, Harman remained in place. The only policy impact of the imbroglio was that Blunkett was forced, against his better judgement, to flesh

out precisely how Labour would deal with the remaining grammar schools. The plan was a direct contradiction of his 'read my
lips' pledge, just weeks after it was made. If opponents of an
existing grammar school could secure a specified threshold of
signatures in favour of a ballot, then a vote would be held among
parents of children at all local primary schools. It is almost
impossible to imagine a scheme less likely to lead to a vote for
abolition, since parents would be required to vote against the
continued existence of a good school for their children to attend.

Blunkett was plainly regarded by Blair as one of the most
reliable Shadow Cabinet members. Blair's biographer, John
Rentoul, writes that "Blair was impressed with Blunkett's old-
fashioned emphasis on basic literacy, numeracy and homework
– and sometimes even taken aback by how far Blunkett would
go".[29] Only he and Brown were publicly promised that they
would perform their respective jobs in government. The agenda
was clear: the literacy and numeracy strategies in primary schools
as the foundation; adopting at root the approach which – challenging previous Labour policy – stated that poverty is not an
excuse for failure; and addressing the most glaring under-
performance – that among boys.

The 1997 manifesto proclaimed education as the putative
government's "number one priority". It included Barber's original phrase, coined for his first meeting with Blunkett in 1995:
"Standards matter more than structures". "Labour will never
put dogma before children's education," it promised. "Our
approach will be to intervene where there are problems – not
where schools are succeeding. Labour will never force the abolition of good schools whether in the private or state sector." As
for specifics, it pledged to introduce a year's pre-school education
for everyone, funded by the abolition of nursery vouchers; class
sizes of fewer than thirty for five-, six- and seven-year-olds (paid
for by the ending of the assisted places schemes); focusing on
the three Rs in primary school by means of literacy and numeracy targets and summer literacy camps; minimum homework

requirements for seven-year-olds and above; 'a target of' five GCSEs at grades A to C for all pupils; and four out of five sixteen-year-olds should stay at school. Added to this mix was the 'fresh start' policy for failing schools, the Foundation Schools policy, and the notion that grammar schools could remain if parents did not vote for their abolition.

10
Shaking the trees: Education Secretary

For many of those who had been working to secure Labour's first election victory since 1974, the triumphant night of 1 May 1997 was marked by the party of all parties on London's South Bank and a more private celebration in the party's Millbank HQ. For Blunkett, the celebrations were more muted; he was in the "dreary surroundings" of Sheffield Town Hall.

The work started more or less immediately; unlike others in the Shadow Cabinet who did not know which – if any – department they would be given, Blunkett had already, with Brown, been confirmed in post. Early the next morning, therefore, as Blunkett was driven to Sheffield station for the journey to London, he spoke to the new Chancellor to arrange a meeting. On the journey down he sat with aides trying to grasp the fact that he was no longer 'Shadow' anything but the real thing: Secretary of State for Education and Employment.

On arriving at St Pancras, Blunkett did not head straight for home. He found a park where Lucy could be given a good run around. As the dog was bounding about, Blunkett's mobile rang. It was the new Prime Minister's chief of staff, Jonathan Powell, asking the new Secretary of State to come to Downing Street to have his appointment confirmed.

It was with a mix of humility and pride that I entered Number 10 Downing Street, which had a Labour prime minister again in residence after eighteen years. I'm afraid my stiff and formal words seem rather feeble in retrospect. 'Thank you Tony,' I remember saying. 'I am very grateful and I will do my absolute utmost that we make a success of education and employment.' At least I had the benefit of a few hours' sleep. Tony was extremely tired but clearly elated, having been up all night, and flown from the north-east of England to ask his memorable question at the Festival Hall: 'A new dawn has broken, has it not?' We certainly felt we could start making a difference.[1]

Blunkett was driven immediately to Sanctuary Buildings, his department's office in Great Smith Street, Westminster. He – along with Lucy – was greeted with the traditional applause. The department had already made preparations for his arrival; the lift now had braille signage.

That night, along with Sir Michael Bichard, Michael Barber (who was immediately appointed a special adviser and, soon after, head of the new Standards and Effectiveness Unit) and Alan Evans (Blunkett's new private secretary), he dined at Shepherd's, the Westminster restaurant. The meeting was seminal; they went over the work they had done in the previous three years, "plotting" (as one participant puts it) how they would change British education over the next few years.

One of the first topics for discussion was the planned Standards and Effectiveness Unit. Hand in hand with individual policy initiatives, Blunkett set about restructuring the department. The creation of the SEU was designed not just to do a specific job but also to act as a catalyst for changing the culture of the department from managing decline to pushing for success. (Blunkett faced a similar, still more pronounced, task in the Home Office.) The unit was small by Whitehall standards and staffed mainly by existing civil servants. As it evolved, the present staff were joined by others who – a first for the DfEE – had hands-on experience in the classroom. It was the first time an attempt had been made within the department to set up a mechanism not merely to introduce an idea but also – again a first – to push for change throughout the system. The civil service had little truck with the idea of 'delivery'; civil servants considered their role over once legislation had been passed. Blunkett saw one of his key tasks as being to change this culture so that the civil service would see the delivery of a policy on the ground to be as central a part of the job. Worse still, until the creation of the SEU, implementation of any new policy had been left to the Local Education Authorities, many of which were themselves the problem. LEA inspections (similar to those conducted by Ofsted on schools) became one of the most important levers for change, providing for the first time an incentive to LEAs to become more cooperative and to improve. This clash between local independence and central initiative was to create much tension over the next four years.

Bichard's support was crucial if the unit was not to take months to become reality and to be dragged down in turf wars. A typical civil service response would have been to point out all the problems associated with such a new body within the department. Bichard was not, however, a typical civil servant and the unit took shape within a week, backed also by Blair. (The Prime Minister had to insist that the Cabinet Secretary, Sir Robin Butler – who resisted both the creation of the unit and Barber's appointment to it instead of a career civil servant – overcome potential opposition from other departments which would fight such a revolutionary precedent.) The concept of a small, dedicated unit, headed by an outsider, within a department, was a model that Blunkett later used as Home Secretary with the formation of the Police Standards Unit under the former Commissioner of Police in Boston, Massachusetts, Paul Evans.

As the dinner talk became less formal on the first night, Alan Evans became fascinated by the practical questions of how his new Secretary of State coped with his blindness. Blunkett opened up about a subject he often felt uncomfortable discussing. He talked about how he had developed a sense of what lay behind what people were saying and how he could tell when people were lying. As one of those present puts it: "He put the fear of God into us".

As the main policy adviser, Michael Barber had a non-stop series of meetings with the junior ministers and officials over the bank holiday weekend after the election, preparing for the first real day of work, Tuesday, 5 May, and concentrating on the agreed priority: the literacy and numeracy strategies. A few days later, Blunkett and Bichard went out of the department for dinner alone. Bichard realised the scale of what had happened politically when, as the two of them walked along Horseferry Road, some young men caught sight of Blunkett and crossed the road towards him. They wanted simply to congratulate him on Labour's victory. A lot had changed since Blunkett had been on Brighton beach and it was his dog which had been recognised.

Blunkett secured a high-powered ministerial team. Estelle Morris and Kim Howells, the parliamentary under-secretaries, were responsible for the school curriculum and teacher training and 'lifelong learning' respectively, with Baroness (Tessa) Blackstone as higher and further education minister. Morris, MP for Birmingham Yardley, entered the Commons in 1992, was state school educated and, before becoming an MP, a teacher – despite not having any A-levels. She had been on the education team since 1995. Howells, MP for Pontypridd since a by-election in 1989, was a grammar-school-educated former NUM official who became one of Arthur Scargill's most vocal critics during the miners' strike. He was a media favourite, with a penchant for stirring the pot. Blackstone had a long background in academia and policy-making, but was strikingly unpopular among colleagues, who found her arrogant and cold.

By far the most important appointment was that of Stephen Byers as minister of state. He and Blunkett had known each other since 1984, when Byers was deputy leader of North Tyneside – both running authorities which, in response to rate capping, decided to flirt with not setting a rate, and both travelling a long way politically to end up as key New Labour ministers.

Immediately after the election, Blair instructed each department to draw up a presentation outlining their plans. Blunkett, Byers and Bichard arrived at Downing Street as one of the first teams, within two weeks of the election, having prepared a detailed outline of the main threads of policy and legislation. Blunkett was to speak for five minutes on the big picture, with Byers following up with specifics. The three spent hours rehearsing the presentations and answers to any possible questions from Blair. Blunkett's notes had been put into braille on a new machine that the department had discovered which could translate dictation tapes and documents directly into braille. The three men arrived, nervously, in the Cabinet room – the first time (other than at Cabinet for Blunkett) they had seen Blair since the election. As Blunkett rose to begin, Byers poured himself a cup of coffee. Within seconds of starting, however, Blunkett simply stopped, handing over to Byers. The minister of state did his best to make it appear as though everything was normal but he was thrown by having to remember what Blunkett was supposed to say. The presentation, while not a disaster, was hardly smooth. On the way out, he asked Blunkett what had happened. He turned to Byers: "My bloody braille's in Swedish." The machine had four settings: German, French, English and Swedish. Not surprisingly, no one in the department knew what Swedish braille looked like, and thus that the machine was on the wrong setting.

Byers had not been part of the education team in opposition and was surprised to be appointed to such a key post. But his instincts had long been in tune with the Blunkett agenda. In 1981, he was chairman of the North Tyneside education committee. Confronted with the recurring problem of school windows being broken at the weekends, he decided to give head teachers the power to spend fifty pounds to hire a local glazier to make repairs. The response of the council direct labour unions was to threaten strike action. Such work was their monopoly and the fact that it was taking a minimum of six weeks for each repair was deemed irrelevant. Byers stood his ground and won an early New Labour battle.

Throughout his time in government, Blunkett has always sought out strong personalities as his junior ministers. Where some look for those who are weak, will always keep their counsel, will never ruffle any feathers and will remain fearful of disturbing a mouse, Blunkett has consistently had as junior ministers politicians who have gone on to the Cabinet: Stephen Byers, Charles Clarke, Tessa Jowell, Estelle Morris, Hilary Benn, Paul Boateng, Andrew Smith, Charles Falconer.

Byers is a case in point. Potentially he was a difficult minister of state to have in post since he had many of his own ideas and a determination to implement them quickly. But Blunkett was keen to have him as his schools minister and specifically asked Blair for him. Blunkett then gave him a great deal of discretion. From the first, the two men agreed the narrative they wished to follow and Byers was then given the authority to get on with things, without being micro-managed by Blunkett.

Typical of this was the policy on the private sector. Blunkett agreed with Byers on the need to utilise the resources of private schools; where they parted company was over Byers's determination to create a viable private sector that could take over the functions of public sector institutions such as Local Education Authorities, and to do this as soon as possible. Hence the idea of Education Action Zones (EAZs), which were intended to be trail-blazers for an extension of the role of the private sector, providing an opportunity for the private sector to gain expertise and then be in a position to take over a Local Education Authority or a group of schools.

The problem was that EAZs were pretty much doomed to fail, since the private sector had no expertise at running schools or helping schools to run themselves; the only organisations that did have such experience were the LEAs, the very bodies that Byers wanted to replace. Blunkett gave Byers the freedom to introduce EAZs but his reluctance to allow full-blown private sector involvement – he saw this as too much, too soon – meant that they were tepid, with the rules constraining and severely restrictive. The failure did not come cheap. Even in 2001, by which time the idea was clearly a failure, EAZs were costing £60 million.

EAZs were intended to provide companies with the know-how to take over the functions of those failing Local Education Authorities which were an active block to improvement in schools. On one level, they laid the foundations of a transformation; by the time Blunkett left the department in 2001, twenty LEAs had either contracted out their functions or were in the process of so doing. In February 2001 Blunkett announced a £1.8 million project aimed at "encouraging LEAs to develop innovative ways of working with the private sector and other partner organizations" and he had introduced legislation – which came into effect during Estelle Morris's tenure – under which 85 per cent of LEA funding was devolved directly to schools.

It was appropriate that the first LEA to have its powers transferred was Islington, a borough that was seen as the spiritual home of metropolitan New Labour but which failed on every measure to deliver a decent education. Cambridge Educational Associates, a for-profit company, signed an £11.5 million contract to run Islington's schools and pay its teachers. Blunkett had stepped in where even Mrs Thatcher had feared to tread, and his actions seemed to herald a revolution.

But the real picture was rather different. The fact that twenty LEAs were contracted out was more an indication of failure than success. The process of bidding for a contract was so horrendously complicated and expensive that, *ab initio*, a number of suitable companies ruled themselves out. The Leeds experience was typical. Ofsted's report, which was damning, was met by the LEA with accusations of political bias and outright rejection of any criticism. If ever there was a case for full-blown privatisation, it was Leeds. The result, however, was a fudge. A company "wholly owned" by the city council was set up to run educational services in Leeds, "advised" by Capita.[2] The LEA staff, roundly criticised by Ofsted, were simply transferred to the new company.

After Byers's departure in 1998, the push for LEA reform came from the Downing Street Policy Unit and was met with resistance from Blunkett, who could not see the point in making enemies of vast swaths of Labour councillors. Number 10 felt that LEAs were, more often than not, failing to do their job properly; they were either coasting or in some schools actively making the situation worse. Blair and his education adviser, Andrew Adonis, wanted to have a sufficient weight of evidence to be able to force wholesale reform on a reluctant department. Thus, as a first step, Ofsted was asked to step up its programme of LEA inspections so that, by the time of the next election, every LEA would have been inspected and the extent of the problem would be clear. Just as it had taken Ofsted school inspections to bring home the degree of failure, so it needed a similar study of LEAs.

There was a downside to Byers's impatience and determination. For every worthwhile reform, there were others that took time, money and political capital for no real benefit. EAZs were one example, the General Teaching Council (GTC) another; fine in theory as an attempt to inculcate a greater sense of teaching as a profession (akin to the doctors' professional governing body, the General Medical Council) but in practice a talking shop. Byers's previous portfolio, which involved deal-making with trade union leaders, left its mark on the GTC. Barber had persuaded Blunkett that the GTC could be a counterpoint to the teaching unions; Byers had little enthusiasm for the idea and wanted to get it out of the way with as little effort as possible. He gave reserved seats to the unions, who were determined to strangle at birth any idea of the GTC as an alternative teaching voice, so negating from the start its intended purpose. As Chris Woodhead pointed out: "The GTC line is identical to that of the unions. The National Curriculum and the National Literacy and Numeracy Strategies have driven the fun and professionalism out of teaching."[3]

There was a further flaw: any chance the GTC might have had was ruined by, as one central figure puts it, "very poorly drafted legislation". A Whitehall truism is that officials resist establishing bodies that have power. Although the GTC was viewed internally as a counterbalance to the unions, it was never given the strength to act as such. And membership was voluntary, which meant that it lacked credibility as a genuine professional body and was never seen as more than a minor player.

The first chairman of the GTC was David Puttnam, the former film producer. Puttnam had been working informally for Chris Smith, then the Shadow National Heritage Secretary, drafting Labour's cultural policies. As part of his brief, he had had dealings with Blunkett but the two men were not close. A fortnight after the election, however, he received a phone call out of the blue from Conor Ryan, asking whether he would be interested in working as an adviser at the department. Puttnam had decided anyway to leave the film industry and leapt at the chance.

Although he was formally attached to Estelle Morris, Puttnam's *de facto* role – before the setting up of the GTC – was to act as a 'teachers' spokesman' both within and without the department: within, focusing on how to restore teachers' morale via such ideas as the national teaching awards (which Puttnam proposed on his first day in the department); and without, as something of a licensed jester, providing an alternative to the harsher rhetoric that Blunkett needed to use. His outsider status and already high public profile positioned him at an apparent distance from the politicians which, in theory, would help win support from the profession. Puttnam spent much of his time out of the office on a marathon tour of schools, visiting some 350. Initially, Labour's victory had been greeted with near-euphoria by teachers. "Ninety-four per cent of teachers voted Labour and we saw the result as something near to the second coming," according to one union leader. This turned swiftly to disenchantment as it became clear not only that their *bête noire*, Chris Woodhead, was to remain in post as Chief Inspector but also that Blunkett was to be almost equally critical of poor teaching. Puttnam's role was to act as a softener to Blunkett's detergent.

(Within a week of being asked to join the department, Puttnam received a call from Jonathan Powell, Blair's chief of staff, asking whether he would be interested in becoming a life peer, taking the Labour whip. Puttnam replied that he certainly would but that the call was too late; he had just agreed to work for Blunkett. "Don't worry about that," replied Powell. "We'll talk to David." June went by, then July, and then most of August. Puttnam had heard nothing since the phone call. And then on 31 August he bought a newspaper while staying at his home and saw that he had been created a life peer. Blunkett took to referring to Puttnam in meetings as My Lord Puttnam.)

The double act of Blunkett and Byers was widely seen as the most effective team in government. Unlike some other ministerial teams, which seemed to spend most of the first year acclimatising, Blunkett and Byers made their presence felt immediately. The two men agreed on the need for a big bang; the system had to be picked up by the scruff of the neck and given a good shake. Byers was only in post for fourteen months before being promoted to Chief Secretary to the Treasury but in that time he dovetailed perfectly with Blunkett.

Byers had been given a clear brief from Blair: "It's the big issue; you've really got to go for it and just do whatever you need to do." The pace of those fourteen months was intense, with the foot deliberately on the accelerator. As one of Blunkett's closest aides puts it: "It was a big electric shock through the system, but I think that's what the system needed. You can see that from the problems we've got now. The foot has been taken off the pedal and schools are not under the pressure they used to be under. So standards in primary schools are falling back. The changes in secondary schools are still a long time coming through, and the improvements just aren't happening as they should."

Blunkett had two immediate advantages denied to most of his fellow ministers. First, as a former council leader, he had already run a big organisation. Those who wondered whether a blind man could cope with the pressures of leading a department seemed to forget that he had previously led a council. He had a still greater advantage; being confirmed in post by Blair so far in advance meant not only that he had spent years preparing for this moment, it also meant that he had built up a working relationship with Sir Michael Bichard, the department's Permanent Secretary (and, although later events were to show that this was not to prove as beneficial, with Chris Woodhead, the Chief Inspector of Schools). It also meant that there was a detailed body of policy documents for the civil service to get to grips with in advance of Labour winning power. Ministers in other departments found on their desks a series of dusted-down civil service proposals. The education team, however, had a clear agenda which had already been worked through with the civil service.

The relationship between Bichard and Blunkett was unique in Whitehall. Bichard was not a typical mandarin. His background was in local government, as chief executive of Brent and Gloucestershire before taking over the Benefits Agency. The two men had not only a personal chemistry (as one civil servant puts it: "Michael was devoted to David, absolutely devoted to him") but a similar drive to change both the department and educational standards. Blunkett was the chairman to Bichard's managing director. "The two came together at just the right moment in time for both of them," the civil servant continues. "It caught both of their careers at exactly the right moment. The fact that Michael left when David left says it all – he could see that it wouldn't be the same without David."

Blunkett had a further advantage: Lucy. Whenever he visited a school – which he tried to do at least three times a week in term-time – pupils would more often than not ignore the bearded middle-aged man and focus instead on his dog. She was not only an ice-breaker but also a source of wisdom. On one visit to a nursery school in Tower Hamlets, it became clear straight away that some of the children were afraid of her, so Blunkett decided to sit down immediately on a tiny child's chair. Lucy pulled as if to say "Don't sit here". Blunkett ignored her, and stayed put. He then put his arm round the person sitting next to him. "And how old are you, my dear?" he asked. "Twenty-three," replied the nursery nurse.

Lucy was not always so sensible. On 11 March 1999, when Blunkett had finished speaking in the Budget debate his shadow, David Willetts, rose to speak. Lucy marked the occasion by being sick on the floor of the Commons.

The first Queen's Speech of the new Labour government, on 14 May 1997, promised two education bills. The most immediate was one to abolish the assisted places scheme. ("The education of young people will be my Government's first priority. They will work to raise standards in schools, colleges and universities and to promote lifelong learning at the workplace. They will cut class sizes using money saved as a result of legislation phasing out the assisted places scheme"[4]). This would be followed by a bill in the autumn to be based on a forthcoming White Paper on standards, with new powers for the department over failing schools, a series of new targets, improvements in early-years provision and vocational training, LEA reform, Foundation Schools, student loans, and the introduction of the GTC. ("A further Bill will contain measures to raise educational standards, develop a new role for local education authorities and parents, establish a new framework for the decentralised and equitable organisation of schools, propose reforms to the teaching profession, and respond positively to recommendations from the National Committee of Inquiry into the future of higher education."[5])

This meant that Blunkett's first major task – publishing the White Paper, *Excellence in Schools*, which would outline the direction of policy over the first term – was immediate. It was put together in a record-breaking sixty-three days. Byers chaired a series of meetings with Barber, Miliband (head of the Policy Unit at Number 10) and the relevant officials, who drafted individual sections to be sent to Blunkett for approval. It was in his response to these chapters that officials – and junior ministers – received their first taste of what became a familiar Blunkett modus operandi. He would respond with long demanding notes, sometimes dismissing entire chapters and asking for them to be rewritten.

Officials – and ministers – in the department soon got used to receiving what they called the Blunkett Note, which he would send around, ticking people off, issuing instructions or requesting information. One early instruction was that nobody was to speak to anyone from Number 10 without prior approval from the Secretary of State (an early indication, too, of the tensions to come in his relationship with the Prime Minister's Policy Unit). The note was not fully obeyed; both Barber and Ryan simply ignored it.

The relationship between the DfEE and Number 10 has been caricatured as that of a unified department engaged in a battle with the Prime Minister's Policy Unit – specifically, Andrew Adonis, then Blair's education adviser – to resist what Blunkett felt to be the more extreme suggestions emanating from Downing Street. Much of the difficulty arose from Blunkett's determination not to be pushed about – to be clearly and unambiguously in charge of education (a theme that re-emerged over immigration policy in 2004 when, with tabloid headings screaming for action, Blair made clear that he was taking charge of the issue). Adonis was often referred to in the press as 'the real education secretary'; such a description – inaccurate anyway – was almost tailor made to rile Blunkett, the more so given that both Adonis and Blunkett were, in their different ways, close to Blair. On many issues Blunkett and Adonis were as one – City Academies, for instance, which Blunkett championed and persuaded sceptical Labour MPs to support despite much opposition from Labour LEAs. Conor Ryan, too, was sympathetic to a lot of the ideas emanating from Adonis, and there was agreement on the broad thrust of policy. But there were also genuine, stark theoretical differences with Adonis, notably over the role of LEAs, which Adonis was keen to pare back, and selection, about which Adonis was far more relaxed than Blunkett.

So there was certainly tension, with Number 10 tending to feel that Blunkett was dragging his heels and not reforming fast enough. But it took the form more of a negotiation than a confrontation. Much of the tension came from what Blunkett and his advisers saw as Adonis's alliance with Chris Woodhead, the Chief Inspector of Schools, whom Blunkett would not, left to his own devices, have kept in post. One Blunkett adviser argues that "there were times when Andrew was his own man – and there were occasions when you could just see Chris behind him; the two had clearly been speaking". Blunkett and his advisers talked of the "Adonis–Woodhead alliance". But far from agreeing on everything, Woodhead thought Adonis was all talk and little real action, and Adonis would often despair of Woodhead's abrasiveness. They did, however, need each other politically. Without the support of Number 10, Woodhead would not have been kept on in 1997, let alone had any influence on policy; and without Woodhead, Adonis and Number 10 would have had to be far more confrontational with Blunkett – Woodhead acted as a lightning conductor for the anger.

Woodhead thus came to be seen as a touchstone for both sides. Blunkett knew that Blair was determined that Woodhead should stay on, since if he had left it would have sent out the worst possible signal – that Labour did not want to, or was simply unable to, work with a man whose public profile was as the main force in the country pushing for high standards and identifying failure. This would have neutered the claim that Blair and Blunkett had been making since 1994, that Labour was the party of high standards. Keeping Woodhead in post was a critical symbol to that end.

But Blunkett felt that Woodhead was a liability and too much of a loose cannon. Most of their aims were similar but Blunkett thought that Woodhead had made a conscious decision not to cooperate but to fight – a cardinal sin in Blunkett's book. Woodhead could certainly be useful to Blunkett; he gave a voice to some arguments that needed to be made but which Blunkett did not want to air in public. In Blunkett's view, Ofsted had broken the back of decline by identifying failure, but it was not Ofsted's – or Woodhead's – job to deal with the problems. That was Blunkett's. But, as one adviser to Blunkett puts it, "instead of Woodhead seeing his role as to help, to engage in the debate and to work with the Standards and Effectiveness Unit, he took the view that Ofsted and the unit were outright competitors". Blunkett could not understand why Woodhead regarded the SEU as a competitor. In Blunkett's mind the two were not in competition but complementary. (In June 2004, Charles Clarke, Blunkett's successor, abolished the unit – the one element within the department that included people with experience of teaching. Blunkett was unhappy about the change of tack under Clarke: "They've taken their foot off the accelerator. They've gone soft. They've produced documents called *Excellence and Enjoyment*. The next one will be called *Smiley and Fun*.")

Saddled with Woodhead by Downing Street, Blunkett sought to neuter him straight away by appointing both him and his polar opposite, Tim Brighouse, as vice-chairmen of the new Standards Task Force in May 1997. Chaired by Blunkett, the task force's remit was supposedly to "Unite the various educational interests in the new drive to raise standards in schools; Be advocates for the spread of good practice to achieve higher standards; advise the Secretary of State on the development and implementation of policies to improve school standards; keep the Secretary of State abreast of best practice nationally and internationally; work with the national agencies and others to achieve the national targets for literacy and numeracy".[6] It was, in other words, a talking shop.

To say that Woodhead and Brighouse were hardly natural bedfellows is to understate a deep-seated enmity. A flavour of the fundamental difference between them comes in Woodhead's book, *Class War*: "I will never forget the documentation Tim Brighouse supplied us with when Ofsted inspected Birmingham LEA. It was not the bulk, the grandiose ambition of the many different initiatives, the unintelligibility of much of the prose. It was the statement in black and white that no school, however effective, could remain successful without the support of its local authority. I have no idea whether Brighouse still believes this, but, sadly, I suspect he does. It says it all."[7]

Woodhead was not backward in proclaiming what he believed to be right, both inside the department and in public. He is a mild-mannered man, quietly but resolutely determined that when he is right he should make it clear. A critic within the DfEE recalls one meeting at which Woodhead reacted to Barber's contribution by "putting his feet up on the table, stretching and yawning. His body language made it clear what he was thinking: 'Why are we having to listen to all this rubbish?'" In all likelihood it was indeed rubbish, but Woodhead's behaviour ensured there was little chance of his being able to influence the discussion. What Blunkett saw as Woodhead's refusal to play ball, Woodhead saw instead as Blunkett's refusal to engage with him. One aide characterises the resentment against him thus: "He had a huge ego problem: he hated seeing other people get credit for things in which he was involved." Another adviser remarks that Woodhead "tended to see problems where there weren't any. He had the potential to influence things, such as the literacy and numeracy hour. But instead of working with us, he played leader of the opposition to Michael Barber – a battle he would never win".

More often than not, communication with Woodhead was made via Byers, who got on much better with him than did Blunkett. The two would have long policy discussions and found that they had far more in common than not. Byers seemed better able to deal with a man who could be as prickly as Blunkett. But while Byers was happy to be the point man for relations with Woodhead, he was aware that Woodhead had a further agenda in dealing with him; he thought that he could detach Number 10 and Byers from Blunkett.

At the beginning, Woodhead seemed content. Frustrated, yes,

that his specific agenda was not adopted wholesale but sufficiently content to stay inside the tent. Naming and shaming of
schools, fast-track sacking of poor teachers and arguing that
LEAs did not have a God-given right to run education were
all classic New Labour themes which chimed equally well with
Woodhead's views. The problems started when Byers was promoted to the Cabinet in October 1998. His replacement, Estelle
Morris, was a far more cautious politician than Byers, with less
drive and more concern lest she upset any of the education
establishment with which she had to deal and from which she
had come. She neither liked nor respected Woodhead, whose
modus operandi and personality were very different to her own;
and Woodhead felt the same about her. With Byers, Woodhead
believed that he had an ear inside the department. When Morris
took over, he began to feel frozen out. The burden of communication switched to Barber, but since Woodhead had fought, and
lost, a battle to downgrade the influence of Barber's Standards
and Effectiveness Unit, their relationship was never better than
correct.

Blunkett had lived with the confirmation in 1997 that Woodhead would remain in post. Given a clean slate, he would have
removed him but he could see the political benefits of keeping
him. He was, however, determined that Woodhead's contract
would not be renewed when the time came for reappointment
in 1998. Number 10, however, thought differently. Woodhead's
reappointment was the only clear Whitehall defeat for Blunkett in
his time at the DfEE. Adonis, via Blair, won, the Prime Minister
ordering Blunkett to keep Woodhead. As one close adviser to
Blunkett puts it: "David went ballistic. I have never heard him
swear so much. 'What is the bloody point of my being here?' he
screamed. 'Who is the Education Secretary, me or Adonis?' Even
to the civil servants, he never made any bones about the fact that
he was put in an impossible position."

With Woodhead foisted on him not once but twice, he gave
David Puttnam licence to act as a semi-detached internal

opposition to Woodhead and as a public face of that internal opposition. The consequence, however, was that the government was running two directly contradictory policies: Woodhead-style 'telling it straight'; and Puttnam-style cuddles. One speech by Puttnam, at the Association of Teachers and Lecturers conference in Bournemouth, illustrated the problem. Puttnam spoke about his concerns that creativity was being damaged by the focus on rigidly prescribed literacy and numeracy teaching. That afternoon's *Evening Standard* featured a headline saying that a government adviser was attacking the obsession with standards.

Blunkett's handling of a potentially damaging situation illustrates the strengths and weaknesses of his tenure at Education. He told Puttnam that he well understood that the story was misleading – Puttnam's speech had been far more subtle. And he acknowledged that Puttnam had a point. But, he finished, "I can't have two messages coming out from the department. Your background allows you to make perfectly legitimate comments about the importance of imagination and creativity for the development of young people. But you must let me criticise you for saying so." Politically, of course, Blunkett's was a sensible approach. But it meant that there *were* two messages, and two sides, to the most important of all issues: teaching.

It could not last. Neither side was happy. Every yin was met with a yang, Woodhead becoming more public with his criticisms and far more difficult as a partner. On 11 October, Woodhead was called to a meeting with Blunkett, who had discovered that the Chief Inspector had been in secret talks with the *Daily Telegraph* about a new job. It would not have been that difficult to discover his plans – Woodhead had been talking about an alternative job for months and was waiting to pick his moment to leave. He ended up not having that choice; although the meeting was described by one observer as "cordial", once rumbled by Blunkett he had to resign.

After his departure in November 2000 (and then after the three months he was required to wait), he wrote a series of articles for the *Daily Telegraph*. The language was harsh but the substance was pretty minor. The worst allegation seemed to be that Ryan had leaned on him to soften some of his public criticisms. As Woodhead has written: "Conor Ryan, who was David Blunkett's press guru, would phone me up, for example, to offer ever-so-nicely, in his soft Irish brogue, suggestions as to what might be included or changed in speeches and reports. Michael Barber, the then head of the Standards and Effectiveness Unit at the DfES, would express his disappointment if we were to criticise one of his cherished initiatives. David Blunkett himself would on occasion fire over a terse little letter. Great care was taken, of course, not to overstep the mark, but it was pretty clear which side felt that they should be calling the shots."[8] Ofsted under Woodhead was far from the caricature, however. In his 1998 report, for instance, Woodhead wrote: "The performance of teachers and pupils stands in sharp contrast to that of four years ago. Teachers are now teaching better and pupils, as a consequence, are learning more." And in his final report, covering 1999, he began: "The steady improvements that I described in my last Annual Report have continued."

Blunkett's most used form of expression within the department was a trenchant note, expressing a clear determination to proceed in one direction. It was also his negotiating style with other departments: bombarding them with all his demands, sticking avidly to them and giving no grounds at all, refusing to compromise – and then at the last moment making a concession, having secured most of what he wanted. One Treasury civil servant involved in the public spending round says Blunkett would "at first be absolutely adamant, would not give an inch, would fight like a tiger and would leave it to the last possible moment. And then at that moment – on the final day of the public spending round – he would agree a compromise, would be absolutely happy with that compromise and would work with that compromise completely". Treasury officials would remark after each public spending round that Blunkett had an absolute mastery of numbers, often better than that of his own finance officials. One journalist close to New Labour described Blunkett as "the only Cabinet member who can beat the Chancellor in an argument over detail".[9] The Treasury would repeatedly brief against him but some of those involved at the time now acknowledge that they disliked him primarily because he was formidably good in negotiation. He was also helped by Brown having his own commitment to education and the New Deal. Brown wanted to see money going to schools. The New Deal was, however, a double-edged sword; Brown wanted ever greater control of how the funds were spent, involving the Treasury in every detail.

Relations between the two became progressively worse as Blunkett's standing increased. When columnists and reporters started to talk him up as a figure of growing stature within the Cabinet, even as a possible successor to Blair, Brown's aides started to brief against Blunkett not over policy, as in the past, but personally, implying that he was unable to master either his brief or his department. This was compounded by Brown's penchant for trampling on other departments' territory. In May 2000 he marched on to Blunkett's patch by attacking Oxbridge admissions, citing the case of Laura Spence, a state schoolgirl who had applied to Magdalen College, Oxford, to read medicine and was rejected. Brown weighed in at a conference on financial inequity: "It is time for an end to old Britain, where what matters more is the privilege you are born with than your potential," he said. "It is now time that the older universities open their doors to people from all backgrounds. I take the view that it is an absolute scandal that a young teenager, with the best A-level qualifications you could have, should be turned down by Oxford University by an interview system that is more reminiscent of the old boy network and the old school tie than genuine justice in our society." Blunkett was enraged less by the specifics – he had very little instinctive sympathy for Oxbridge and shared many of the Chancellor's sentiments – but rather by the fact of his blundering in, encroaching on Blunkett's terrain, and by the ineptness of Brown's intervention. Not only had he got his basic facts wrong – Spence had not been rejected because she had come from the state system, nor had 'her' place been taken by a public school pupil – he had created a media maelstrom with which Blunkett, not Brown, had to deal.

It was far from the only difference Blunkett had with the Chancellor. When the Labour spin machine was exposed for inflating the spending rises agreed in April 1999 into a supposed 'bonanza' of £40 million over the three years of the Comprehensive Spending Review (a figure that was achieved by counting the first year's money three times, the second year's twice and then adding these to the third year's total), the real increases that Blunkett had secured were obscured by the media reaction against such cack-handed behaviour: the longest sustained increase in funds since the early 1970s, with spending planned to rise by an average of 6 per cent a year in real terms from 1999 to 2004. In his final spending round at the department he succeeded in negotiating a capital budget of some £3 billion for 2003/4, compared with the £683 million he had inherited in 1997.[10] Blunkett had warned Brown – whose idea the hype was – that it would be counter-productive, a warning that turned out to be prescient in the extreme, as Labour ever after suffered from the perception that its figures and announcements cannot be believed. But Blunkett's warning came to nothing and he was forced, once Brown's idea had secured Blair's enthusiastic backing, to proclaim that he had secured a £19 billion education increase. Blunkett had promised in opposition that Labour would spend 5 per cent of GDP on education. By the time he left in 2001, the figure was as near as dammit – 4.98 per cent. By March 2001, schools had received an extra £300 per pupil real increase since 1997.[11]

On taking office, Blunkett and Byers knew that a big story straight away could define and set up the entire first term. Just as the Chancellor seized the headlines and made a pointed statement about how different this New Labour government was from its predecessors with the announcement of the Bank of England's operational independence, so Blunkett was keen to make a similar impact. Byers suggested that, since the main message they needed to impart was that under-performance and failure would no longer be tolerated, they needed something that would ram the message home. They needed, he told Blunkett, not only to make an announcement but to engineer a row of some kind to ensure that everyone knew just what they had announced.

The policy on failing schools that emerged from Barber's Greenwich lecture in opposition provided the perfect vehicle. The Ofsted reports indicated that around eighty schools were failing beyond all hope of improvement. Byers instructed his officials to go through the reports to identify those which had been repeatedly weak and had shown no improvement over the past year. From that list, Byers chose eighteen that seemed beyond salvation. With these schools in mind, he went to Blunkett suggesting that they be publicly put on notice: if they did not turn themselves around within, at most, two years, they would be closed.

The idea pressed all the right buttons and became the main preoccupation of the two men and their staff over the next three weeks. The culture shock to the department was enormous. As one adviser puts it: "There were huge barriers from the departmental officials, who hated it, absolutely hated it. They did everything they could to frustrate it. It went against everything they believed."

Blunkett announced the eighteen schools on 20 May 1997. They would, he said, now have to work with the department's new "special measures action recovery team" on plans to turn themselves around. If, by September, there were insufficient signs of progress, staff might be replaced. And if there was still no progress then, once the legislation had come into effect, they would be closed and reopened with new names and new staff. "The decision to name these schools has not been taken lightly," said Blunkett. "But persistent failure will not be tolerated by this government in any one of the 25,000 schools in this country. Our children only get one chance to go to school. If their school is failing it denies them opportunities to which they have a right . . . There is no easy way of turning round a failing school . . . However, I want to see schools and education authorities taking responsibility for raising standards and clearly demonstrating that everything that can be done is being done."

Writing in that day's *Times* he argued that "The government was elected on a manifesto with education at its heart. The prime minister has made it clear that our priorities are 'education, education and education'. Having been given this important brief, my priorities are standards, standards and standards. The aim is to infuse everyone connected with education – teachers, parents, governors and business people – with ambition and purpose."[12]

It had precisely the desired impact, receiving a welter of virulently hostile criticism from the education press – clearly demonstrating that this was a very different sort of Labour Education Secretary. The head teacher of one of the schools 'named and shamed', as the media put it, wrote in that week's *Times Educational Supplement*: "A government that cannot see the difference between punishment and correction is unlikely to gain the confidence of the half-million teachers that voted for it."[13] Roy Hattersley weighed in as usual with a column in the *Observer*: failing schools "needed quiet help, not parading through the streets, unjustly branded as wilful failures". The failing schools initiative, he said, was "a carefully contrived signal sent to confirm that the Department of Education aims to get tough". Hattersley's analysis of the motivation behind the announcement was, of course, spot on. Where he was wrong was in opposing the idea. By 2001, when Blunkett departed, four out of five schools that had been put on special measures had been subsequently deemed successful by Ofsted.

Fresh Start was introduced for those schools that managed less than 15 per cent five A*–C passes at GCSE over three years and were considered to be beyond redemption, involving new 'super-heads', new furniture and a new ethos. The first was George Orwell School in – where else? – Islington, closed and then reopened as Islington Arts and Media School. Unfortunately, however, the idea did not always work: the new headmaster in Islington resigned, unable to master the culture of failure and violence that still infected the school, even in its new guise.

Given Brown's pledge to stick to Conservative spending plans for the first two years, it is possible to view almost everything emanating from the DfEE through the same prism. The series of programmes designed to raise standards in primary schools generally, and to tackle under-achievement among below-average-ability children, were designed specifically to grab the headlines and give a sense of drive and busy-ness that would belie the lack of extra funding available. What little extra money was available from the abolition of assisted places was already ring-fenced to fund the manifesto commitment to cut primary school class sizes to a maximum of thirty. Whatever the merits or otherwise of a pledge that was remarkably similar in intent to the NHS waiting list commitment, it proved extremely difficult to implement. Despite being described as an 'early' pledge, it was only just met by the time of the 2001 election, and then only by forcing schools to increase the number of mixed-age classes – a perfect example of how the fixation on targets that is characteristic of New Labour can distort sensible ends. There is almost no evidence that supports the idea that class size is a key determinant of educational achievement. There is, however, plenty that shows that mixed-age classes lessen it. But in order to fulfil an arbitrarily determined figure for overall class sizes, the number of mixed-age classes grew. (Blunkett had managed to persuade Blair before the 1997 election that the intended pledge – a maximum class size of twenty-five – was too tough. As he told a colleague: "Then we really would have been screwed."[14])

There was a further problem. A health secretary can dictate

what happens in the NHS, hearing, as Aneuran Bevan put it, the clang in Whitehall every time a bedpan is dropped in a hospital ward. But there is no National Education Service for an education secretary to run. They have, instead, to operate on the components of the system, rather than its foundation: inspections, salaries, exams, training and suchlike. So Blunkett did just that, and never let up. The constant stream of initiatives, however, came at a price: teachers and schools started to be buried by the mound of papers, to such an extent that the department and Blunkett were the progenitors of a new word, 'initiativitis'. This conflict between central control and allowing those on the ground to get on with the job is a theme throughout Blunkett's time in government (as his spat as Home Secretary with the Chief Constable of Humberside and the Humberside Police Authority clearly demonstrated). On one level Blunkett's push from Whitehall was understandable. With Labour having come into government for the first time in eighteen years, the natural response was not to relax the grip on the levers of power but, on the contrary, to grasp them more strongly than ever – to force the pace and direct change.

Both Barber and Brighouse had been influenced by a paper published by the Center for Educational Outreach and Innovation at Columbia University entitled *Re-Centralization or Strategic Management?*,[15] which argued that the "old dichotomous view" that "local is good, central is bad or vice versa" was now redundant. "Top managers" and "local educators" all have "a unique and important contribution" to make. The "former holds the big picture, the benchmarks across settings, access to external resources, and the authority to intervene when things go wrong ... Meanwhile, the delivery units (schools and classrooms) – having the close-up picture and the best knowledge of students and families in their schools – are free to determine means and proximate ends, leaving final, summative assessment to those at the top of the system." This became the basis of the department's actions. Dig through the forest of jargon, however, and what emerges is the central flow of funds, and central initiatives. But the consequences of the ever increasing flow of directives and central control of funds became self-defeating. There were initiatives and directives on everything. In 1998 alone, his first full year in charge, Blunkett sent out 322 directives to schools and LEAs.

Blunkett's main worry was balancing the conflicting pressures of the need for a raft of reforms and the need to ensure that the system did not seize up under the pressure. But although this might have indicated a slowing up in the pace of reform, it tended to manifest itself in ever greater central control, to ensure that changes were implemented. This initiativitis is usually held to be Blunkett's worst failing as Secretary of State. But, as one adviser puts it: "We were blamed for initiativitis – bombarding schools with initiatives – but that was almost entirely a product of Number Ten's interference." More perhaps than any other departmental minister, Blunkett was seen from the outset as carrying the imprimateur of Number 10 because he was in charge of a department that was so pivotal to Blair's agenda. Given Blair's slogan that his top three priorities were "education, education and education", he did not merely want a secretary of state whom he could trust fully; he – through the Policy Unit – demanded a full input in policy, again perhaps more so than with any other department. Most of the tensions that arose were ones of pace – the inevitable impatience of a prime minister over the pace of reform – rather than, in the early stages, of policy itself.

The real problem was a more subtle extension of this initiativitis. The nature of bureaucracy itself, in the context of the department's special fondness for rules and procedures, meant that perfectly straightforward ideas and instructions would, unless carefully checked, end up as long, complicated documents. Typical of this was one on school governors which also showed the department's unwillingness to change. One of the proposals was modest but symbolic: increasing the number of parents on governing bodies. Such an instruction might, at most, necessitate a page. The document, when it landed on the desk of Conor Ryan, came out at just over sixty pages. Ryan rang the official concerned to ask why sixty pages were necessary. The problem, he was told, was that the instruction had to include all the more unusual types of school such as grant-maintained and church schools. Ryan suggested sending separate documents to the grant-maintained and church schools and a simple instruction for the 90 per cent of schools that only required this. Not possible, he was told; the document was going to the printer. Ryan then had to suggest that there were two alternatives available: either a discussion in Blunkett's office; or doing what was requested. The instruction was changed.

"I believe", Blunkett said just before the 2001 election, that "it is important for schools to be self-managed and for head teachers to have the flexibility to improve education at a school level. Over the last four years, they have had increased financial autonomy". In the 2000 Comprehensive Spending Review, Brown had announced that schools would be handed up to £70,000 each to do with as they saw fit, free of any Whitehall or LEA control – and this on top of the previous year's 'windfall' grant for repairs, followed in November by further money for capital work (worth £17,000 for a typical secondary school and £5,500 for a typical primary).[16]

Yet it was Blunkett who had introduced many of the very regulations that he then proudly boasted he was reducing towards the end of his time in Sanctuary Buildings, such as the billion-pound 'Standards Fund' which, by getting head teachers to compete for their share of the money and to demonstrate how they would use it to apply the various departmental initiatives, was designed deliberately to give the department direct leverage over how money was spent. The £235 million spent in 2000–1 on reducing class sizes was a typical example of central control, since it was to be allocated irrespective of whether schools themselves wanted to reduce class size.

Blunkett was wary of being isolated by the department or by

those pushing their own agenda. To avoid this, he maintained around the country a network of contacts among head teachers and others, independent of the usual Whitehall and party channels, on whom he could call to ask what was happening on the ground, so that he was not simply listening to what he was told by civil servants. He would regularly call them up, often out of the blue, to ask what he should be looking out for – problems that they had noticed on their own patch and which needed attention. They, too, knew they could call him if and when they felt the need. As Blunkett learned in Sheffield, officials tend to avoid telling politicians of problems until they have to, by which time they are often full-blown crises.

There was a more fundamental, structural problem with the department. It was not just Education but Education *and* Employment – two pre-existing departments that had simply been lumped together, with two very different cultures, two very different mindsets and two very territorial sets of officials. This had a direct impact on policy. Within days of arriving, Blunkett ordered that childcare and nursery education, which were covered independently by officials from each of the former departments, should be dealt with by the same team. It took over two years to merge the two and to establish an Ofsted inspection regime to ensure that nursery schools were doing more than merely acting as drop-off points for working mothers.

The theory was that a decent school system works as from the earliest years. If primary schooling fails, secondary schooling is doomed also to fail. And primary schooling is helped if nursery schooling is plentiful and stretches children. Councils were thus told to come up with plans to spend the money that had previously gone on nursery vouchers, backed by new funds, to fulfil the manifesto pledge of a nursery place for all four-year-olds. In September 2000 that aim was extended to all three-year-olds.

The employment brief meant that the implementation of the New Deal also fell to Blunkett. As a consequence the Treasury, which was already beginning its transformation into the all-enveloping department that Brown was determined to create, became far more involved in day-to-day decisions than had ever been the case before – an early cause of the tensions between Blunkett and Brown which were to develop over the next few years.

The reaction to the department's targets for school exclusions was typical. Initially, the new Social Exclusion Unit proposed a series of measures designed to reduce the level of exclusions. Blunkett, who saw discipline as one of the key blocks in the rebuilding of educational standards, disagreed with the very notion of exclusion targets. But in the early years of Labour's first term, the Social Exclusion Unit was viewed throughout Whitehall as being an arm of Downing Street, with the full authority of the PM behind it. Politically, ruling out targets was simply not on. Blunkett realised that this would be a fruitless battle and moved instead to have the Social Exclusion Unit's suggestions reduced to a level that he thought would be a workable compromise and would not interfere with schools' ability to discipline unruly pupils. But within four months of the target being implemented, the feedback he received from his contacts was so wholly negative that he eased the guidelines (a decision that did not come into effect until after the 2001 election, and was thus erroneously attributed to Estelle Morris).

One of the pivotal issues in Blunkett's time as Education Secretary was over the use of phonics in the literacy strategy. Woodhead's view that phonics – particularly synthetic phonics, whereby children are taught a series of letter sounds very rapidly and shown how to blend the sounds together to pronounce unfamiliar words, generally before they are introduced to books or reading – needed to form the core of the literacy hour, was shared by some of Blunkett's closest advisers, and although the final form the hour took was not wholly to his liking, it was one of the few areas of policy that Woodhead was happy to defend in public. As the central thrust of the drive to increase primary school standards (which itself was placed ahead of reform of secondary schools), the National Literacy Strategy was pushed through quickly. The literacy and numeracy hours ended up as a conscious attempt to blend both traditional and progressive teaching methods. The form the literacy and numeracy hours eventually took – two hours every day devoted to the three Rs – when they were introduced in, respectively, September 1998 and September 1999 was initially viewed by most teachers as being far too prescriptive, exemplifying the worst aspects of Whitehall control. The 18,500 English state primary schools were required, from September 1998, to teach reading and writing through phonics. Pupils were to be taught to discriminate between the separate sounds in words; read words by sounding out and blending their separate parts; and write words by combining the spelling patterns of their sounds. The legislation was positively Napoleonic. Primary schools should introduce a daily English lesson in which pupils were taught for the first half of the lesson as a whole class, reading together, extending their vocabulary, looking at the phonetics of words and being taught grammar, punctuation and spelling. For the last half of the lesson pupils were to work in groups or individually with the teacher focusing on one group.

Unpopular as they were with some teachers initially, within a matter of months they became part of the furniture. In 1997, only 60 per cent of eleven-year-olds could read to the official standard; within a year of the introduction of the literacy hour the figure had risen to 71 per cent. By 2001, the figure had reached 74 per cent – six percentage points, nonetheless, below the target that Blunkett had set at the outset, and the level on which he had staked his job. Blunkett argues that he did not, as was reported at the time, pledge to resign if the target was not met, but rather to put "my head on the block". In the usual political fashion, by the time the 2001 figures were announced, Blunkett was *in situ* in another department and the credibility problem was no longer his. He was well aware of the political trap:

We were a bit bound in by the advice we received. We did ask what would be a tough but manageable target. That's why we ended up with eighty per cent on English and seventy-five per cent on maths. But we underestimated the time it would take. We thought that four or five years would be enough to make the shift. And even to get to where we got, we had to drive it like hell. That's hundreds of thousands of youngsters who did better than they would have done, so it was worth it. Had I remained in education, I would have really upped the ante on getting the literacy-numeracy target met. I still think it was possible. But if I'd been there, where would I be now if I hadn't met it? Kenneth Clarke moved on every eighteen months in order never to be pinned on anything until the final throw of the dice.

Blunkett was nonetheless especially proud of the literacy hour. Indeed, criticism in the Commons in July 2000 by a Conservative MP not especially renowned for his intellectual gifts, David Tredinnick, provoked Blunkett to lose his temper and come up with a rare piece of unparliamentary language: "I have just spelled out that there was a 15-point improvement in literacy, from 56 to 71 per cent. I do not recall the exact figures between 1994 and 1997, but there was certainly not an improvement from 41 to 56 per cent. If there had been, we would have adopted the policy that Opposition Members were then following – which was to do sod all."[17] Not that there were not huge problems remaining. By the time Blunkett departed in 2001, half of all eleven-year-old boys could not write to the official standard for that age.[18]

Blunkett regarded the two main teaching unions, the NUT and NAS/UWT, with contempt, not least because they opposed all change for no other reason than for the sake of it. The only teacher's union leader for whom he had any time was Peter Smith, leader of the more moderate Association of Teachers and Lecturers, who was seen as interested in talking rather than oppositional strutting. But while he may have regarded the teaching unions with contempt, he was well aware of the importance of teachers (he had, after all, been one himself). Even after a pay award in 2000, a teacher could still earn only £23,958 a year from teaching (although extra money could be earned from "responsibility outside the classroom"). Public spending restraints for the first two years meant that the enormous sums that would be needed to transform salaries, and stop the jibes about paying peanuts and getting monkeys, were out of the question. How, then, to attract the new teachers who would be required – one estimate suggested 10,000[19] – to make possible the commitment to reducing class sizes? Blunkett introduced £6,000 bursaries for student teachers (and a further £4,000 for maths, science and IT teachers) but, sizeable as these were, they were not enough. By September 2000 acceptances for places at teacher training colleges were up by only 2 per cent compared with the 20 per cent needed.[20]

There was a further problem. Blunkett had not shied away from acknowledging the existence of poor teaching and poor teachers. It would look bizarre in the extreme if his next action was to offer teachers, good and bad, a massive salary increase. He needed a mechanism that could lead to substantial increases in income but which was targeted at the best. Thus the 1998 Green Paper, *Teachers: meeting the challenge for change*, proposed a form of performance-related pay – 'Modernising the teaching profession', as it was called. But PRP was, in the form it took, a waste of time and political capital. Blunkett's aim was straightforward: to reward and motivate good teaching. The unions wanted to kill any such notion. The result was a victory – of sorts – for the unions: almost every one of the 197,000 teachers who applied to go through the 'threshold' qualifying for reward received an extra £2,000, with no annual reassessment or categorisation of the best and the worst teachers. It was a funny kind of performance-related bonus when 80 per cent of teachers qualified for the money. As Woodhead puts it: "Game, set and match, in fact, to the unions,"[21] at the cost of a further £737 million on salaries. (The NUT's reaction was a perfect illustration of their malign influence. Having won the battle, the union then sued the government over the details, delaying implementation until the following year. As Blunkett said at the time, it was the first time a union had sued with the object of not being given a pay increase.)

But it was not as simple as that. Blunkett was well aware that politics is, in large measure, the art of the possible. Even to launch this scheme involved a monumental battle and it is difficult to see what was really achieved. The principle, yes; but the practice was very different – simply handing over more money to teachers, regardless of merit.

In July 1997 Blunkett gave his response to the massive Dearing Report on higher education, to which he had given bipartisan support in opposition. Tuition fees had been a political killer (Jeff Rooker had broached the idea and been sacked by John Smith for his trouble). Blunkett knew that he would have to make a decision early on in government and persuaded Blair that he needed a clear policy. In a Commons statement three hours after Dearing was published, he said that he was "accepting" it, and then proceeded to announce his own, rather different, ideas. It was very much Blunkett's scheme: there had been no discussion at Cabinet.[22] Tuition fees would indeed be introduced but they would be means tested against parental income rather than funded by loans as Dearing recommended. Fees would be paid in full, 'up front', by one third of students; a further third would have to pay a contribution to the fee; and the rest would pay nothing. Student grants would be abolished, to be replaced by loans.

It was not Blunkett's finest hour. His mind was preoccupied with school reforms and he did not develop a proper strategy for dealing with what was clearly a political hot potato. There was no attempt to smooth over the inevitable opposition – and not, as with schools policy, because this was part of the tactics. There were no tactics. Blunkett announced, matter-of-factly, what was perceived, albeit mistakenly, as being the end of 'free' university education. Blunkett's failure to explain the policy properly – the impression left in many minds was that poor students would have to take on enormous debt to pay fees, which was not the case – was eerily similar to the government's later failure to explain top-up fees in 2004.

That the mess was probably attributable to the policy not having been properly thought through was corroborated by a remarkable mistake. Close study of the proposals showed that, with the scheme due to start in the 1998–9 academic year, the status of students taking a gap year between school and college had simply been forgotten; over the summer, Blunkett back-tracked and announced quietly that the gap-year students would not have to pay and would be dealt with as if they had begun their course in 1997.

The failure over Dearing was all the more striking given the obvious skill with which Blunkett dealt with other policies that may have seemed guaranteed to invoke the ire of parents and the media. Both the abolition of the assisted places scheme and the transformation of Grant Maintained to Foundation Schools passed off almost without any controversy – the result of the formidable preparations that had been made in advance to achieve precisely that end. The assisted places scheme paid for 30,000 children to attend a private school; one would have expected a major fuss. In fact, there was no opposition of any note until 1999, when Blunkett was called to account by the courts for the loose wording he had used in opposition. When first announcing the plans, he had said that pupils currently benefiting from the scheme would be allowed to finish their education – an obvious political necessity. When he came to implement the policy in government, however, Blunkett refused to include within this pledge the 1,500 children in private junior schools attached to secondary schools. In July 1999 he was held by the High Court to have been entitled to withdraw funding for children at the "natural break" between their primary and secondary education, even at private "through schools" that provided education up to eighteen. But the judge, Mr Justice Kay, criticised Blunkett for "a sorry state of affairs" in which the Education Secretary had had to "explain away his own letters as mistaken or unclear, and a statement by the Prime Minister as an incorrect representation of policy, taken out of context".[23] The following month, the Court of Appeal ruled that Blunkett had handled the affair with "incompetence" by mis-stating government policy and giving the impression that state-assisted junior pupils at combined primary and secondary private schools would continue to be funded until the age of eighteen, but that the mis-statement had been corrected within weeks and the government was not bound by it or by its pre-election pledges to the same effect.[24] The criticism was, by comparison with what Blunkett would face as Home Secretary, footling.

Blunkett's deft political footwork was again in evidence over grammar schools. The pledge that he made in opposition – that no selective school would be abolished unless parents voted in favour – was itself a demonstration of that nimbleness, designed to ensure the survival of good schools and thus to assuage supporters of grammar schools, but doing so by giving the vocal opponents of selection within the Labour Party the idea that they could – at least in theory – achieve their aim. The fact that parents are the last people who would want to have good schools closed meant that the chances of a negative vote were almost non-existent. And when the ballot rules were published in November 1998 such a possibility became even less likely, with eligibility to vote being confined to parents of children at feeder primary schools (defined as schools that send five or more pupils to the grammar school in question, and which must have sent pupils within the previous two years). When the first (and, so far, only) ballot was held in March 2000, on the future of Ripon Grammar School, there was a two-to-one majority in favour of maintaining its selective admission criteria.

Blunkett had a long history of interest in ideas of citizenship and political literacy. The week before polling day in May 1997, he called Bernard Crick, a long-standing champion of political education, out of the blue and told him that he intended to put citizenship on the national curriculum. Crick replied, "How marvellous, after all these years we will get political education." "No," retorted Blunkett, "citizenship." "Ah, very wise politically," replied Crick. "No, it's more than that," said Blunkett. "Political education is too narrow. We've got to look at the voluntary sector. Your work in the 1970s was too focused on politics. We need to be much broader."[25] Did Crick want to be responsible for this and to chair the task force? He accepted immediately. "I had a hand in the remit, but it was polishing and sharpening. The gist of it was there from the start, from David."[26] It was crucial to make sure that the proposals would not be seen as being party political and attacked by the Conservatives as indoctrination. Crick had had a number of dealings with the former Education Secretary, Kenneth Baker (through their role in the Hansard Society) and the two men began the process of wooing him – two lunches and a dinner – to join the committee.

They hit a problem almost immediately. For all his team's political acumen, Blunkett's appointment of Crick to head the committee had not been formally communicated to William Stubbs, the head of the Qualifications and Curriculum Authority, who had already been asked to set up a group by the civil service and was proposing to offer the chair to Chris Woodhead. "Remember, this was early on; David's political advisers were not used to working the channels and I think they just thought that because David had decided then somehow that meant all was agreed," recalls Crick.[27] Stubbs was extremely irritated to be confronted with a *fait accompli*, which he then tried to water down into "a mish-mash of personal and social health, hygiene, environment and God knows what", as one committee member puts it. According to Crick, "He was saying, 'Well, there isn't room for citizenship in the national curriculum.' And I said, 'Haven't you heard there's been a change of government?'" The civil servants, following Stubbs's lead, thought that citizenship was a New Labour gesture but that implementation would be kicked into touch because the national curriculum was already far too overcrowded. Blunkett's response to the report that Crick's committee produced surprised everyone, not least Crick: Blunkett asked Crick to remain as a departmental adviser on citizenship. "I thought, 'That's nice. I'll pop down to London every week or so.' Within two weeks there were four part-timers and an official from the Lord Chancellor's department to head the team. But as with all such initiatives, departmental inertia was never far away."

A few weeks before the 2001 election, Barber booked time with the Secretary of State. Blunkett was on his way to another department and it was important to take time to reflect on the lessons of the past four years. They reached a broad conclusion: before Blunkett, no other secretary of state had been judged on the performance of pupils; they had been judged, rather, on their political nous and how they had managed the department. From now on, all secretaries of state for education would be judged against the only standard that matters: how pupils do. Indeed, Estelle Morris's resignation in October 2002 was a clear demonstration. She went because the Key Stage 2 results were not as good as they should have been (a fate that Blunkett had avoided by being moved to a new job).

Blunkett's tenure at Education was the making of him. When he arrived in 1997 he was not regarded either within the party or by observers as a major player. Education had always been regarded as a mid-range department; important, but not in the same league as the Foreign and Commonwealth Office, the Home Office or the Treasury. By the time he left in May 2001, Blunkett had not only transformed his own reputation, being seen as one of the few genuine heavy hitters in the Cabinet and a possible successor to Blair, he had also, more importantly, transformed the department itself into a recognised major portfolio.

II

Criminals, terrorists and louts

Speculation had started regarding Blunkett's future towards the end of 2000, with the Home Office seen as the most likely destination. This was fuelled by Blunkett's own comments. Speaking to journalists off the record that autumn, he had had no hesitation in dropping heavy hints about how much he wanted the job of Home Secretary, pointing to his constituency's need for policies to deal with anti-social behaviour and his long-standing, albeit less catchily formulated, belief in being tough on crime and tough on the causes of crime. At a private lunch with journalists, Blunkett had stressed the need for government to provide "stability, security and order, in order to provide a backdrop for progressive politics" – as clear a statement of intent for the job of Home Secretary as could be imagined.

Commentators were united in regarding such a move as certain. Blunkett, too, behaved as if it was, holding a farewell drinks party for his staff at the DfEE in April 2001.[1] But although he had been told by Blair long before the 1997 election that he would be given the education portfolio, the Home Office brief remained mere speculation until the week before the 2001 election, when Blair and Blunkett were travelling together on the campaign trail. Blair had two reasons for giving Blunkett advance notice of his next job. First, he was already thinking beyond polling day. He wanted Blunkett to be able to use the first weekend after the election not just for settling in but also for focussing the media on crime policy. Second, there was a purely practical issue. If preparations within the Home Office had not begun before Blunkett's appointment, there would have been a three- or four-week interregnum while he and his advisers caught up.

His Braille equipment took time to set up, documents needed to be put on tape and the Home Office civil servants needed to work out how they would provide the necessary support services.

Blunkett thus spent most of his time during the election campaign as he travelled between events listening to recordings of the bigger documents with which he would have to deal as Home Secretary, most notably the Halliday Report on sentencing which was being readied for publication in July and which was to provide a focus for a major strand of Blunkett's policy outlook.[2]

Jack Straw had been told by Blair of Blunkett's appointment and was happy to cooperate with the necessarily secret arrangements, using his aide, Ed Owen, to liaise with Blunkett's team. Happy, that is, until the day of Labour's manifesto launch on 16 May 2001. The *Sun* had prepared a damaging story for that day's paper which Alastair Campbell was keen to kill, lest it undermine the positive message of the manifesto. Campbell and Trevor Kavanagh, the paper's political editor, reached a deal: Campbell would provide Kavanagh with a big exclusive and the *Sun* would drop the hostile story. The story that duly appeared on that day's front page was that Blunkett was to be the next Home Secretary. Straw hit the roof, livid and deeply upset that, despite being cooperative and helpful, he should be so publicly undermined – indeed, humiliated. Straw had been increasingly annoyed by the stories that had been appearing for months regarding Blunkett's desire for his job and by the widespread belief that he would get it. He was convinced that the *Sun* story was a result of what he saw as Blunkett's continuing self-puffery. Far from it; having had his post confirmed by Blair, there was no mileage for Blunkett in planting such a story. For Campbell, however, it was a perfect operation, killing off a bad story and replacing it with a wholly positive one.

The *Sun* story made for a difficult train journey from London to the manifesto launch in Birmingham, a journey made farcical by Blunkett being deposited by his driver at the wrong end of the train at Euston and so having to walk through every carriage to reach the cordoned Cabinet carriage in which Blair, Brown, Prescott and Straw were closeted.

On the Saturday after polling day, Blunkett and the other senior ministers went to Buckingham Palace to exchange the seals of office. The Queen had been at the races, so her ministers had to wait until her early evening return for their audience. As one of those present puts it: "We were dead on our feet because we'd been campaigning for three weeks. We'd had the excitement of the reshuffle the day before. And of course the adrenalin had stopped flowing and we were all absolutely knackered. We were dog tired, all of us." It was not the most propitious of beginnings to the second term. Prescott walked to the Queen, nodded, kneeled, recited his oath and walked away, forgetting to take his seals of office with him and leaving the Queen holding them vacantly. Straw followed, mangling his oath. Next up was Blunkett. Since he finds it difficult to kneel without assistance, Straw led Blunkett to the dais. But Straw has always been – like many people – slightly uncomfortable when steering a blind person. Blunkett kneeled and recited his oath. There was just one problem. Instead of Blunkett facing the Queen, Straw had positioned the new Home Secretary at 45 degrees to the monarch. He faced not the Queen but a statue of George IV, to which he addressed his oath. At the end of a shambolic series of events, the Queen looked at her new senior ministers and addressed them: "I hope you run the country better than you've managed over the last fifteen minutes."

Blunkett had very little time before becoming Home Secretary, compared with his appointment as Education and Employment Secretary, to think about what he wanted to do. As he puts it: "For obvious reasons, not least normal courtesies and diplo-macies, it's very difficult to prepare for a job in government that you haven't actually got. There is a wider issue about the transfer of posts in government that is never addressed. People see the transfer and the change in culture and direction, even if it's only modest, but there's not been enough thought about how you take on a new agenda in government." But he was still able, on the Sunday after polling day, to publish a manifesto in *The Sunday Times* for his tenure of the Home Office, a piece that had been prepared over the previous week and which contains the seeds of almost every policy enacted during his time as Home Secretary:

My first task is to . . . get to grips with problems that affect social cohesion. We will work towards eradicating organised exploitation and intimidation of vulnerable people and neighbourhoods by criminals and towards the ending of trafficking in drugs and in people.

Tackling crime and protecting the right of every one of us to feel safe in our homes and to enjoy public spaces must take priority.

[W]hat horrifies me is the knowledge that entire communities appear to be almost resigned to crime. There is nothing acceptable about dangerous streets and rundown estates where drug dealers and thieves prosper at the expense of their neighbours. No government can resolve in isolation the great challenges we face. Tackling crime and the fear of crime in our most bedevilled neighbourhoods is dependent on mobilising the community.

. . . The standards and effectiveness unit that I set up at the education and employment department has made a huge contribution to driving up levels of achievement in schools. Its work has been to identify and disseminate good practice and to develop and implement national strategies based on what works. That is why I propose to establish a new standards unit within the Home Office to provide, for the first time, a consistent approach to standards and the sharing of best practice to every police force and every divisional command in the country.

. . . There is no possibility of pleasing everyone. There are those, for example, who advocate uncontrolled immigration. But the impact on their lives would be limited. It is the lower-paid workers who, having just achieved a minimum wage, experience at first hand the impact of illegal immigration on their communities and on their striving to earn a decent living. The gang masters who ply this illegal trade do not care about the impact of their actions on local jobs, but they throw down a gauntlet that cannot be ignored. Connecting the work permit system with the needs of the economy will pull the rug on the gang masters and provide a controlled but legal route for people who seek work to fill Britain's skill shortages.[3]

Blunkett saw his role as being more fundamental than merely reacting to events, a view of the job which most home secretaries share on taking office but of which they are quickly disabused. Speaking for the first time in the Commons as Home Secretary, he told how he had been given a video of a BBC programme, *How to be Home Secretary.* "It frightened me to death – it was all about clouds appearing in blue skies and being overtaken by events. I was quite worried the other morning when someone pulled up alongside the kerb. I thought for a moment that my security men might have to intervene, but it was Lord [Kenneth] Baker, who leaned out of the window to say, 'Remember, it's events, dear boy, it's events'. So I am truly warned."[4]

Tackling the underlying issues of crime and order meant, in Blunkett's view, changing the relationship between government and governed, a theme that has been constant throughout his career. Government could no longer pretend that all the major social problems could be resolved simply by better policing, a clampdown on drugs and more robust criminal justice procedures. Issues such as citizenship and nationality were as critical in rebuilding society and confidence in government as, in the long term, dealing with clandestine asylum seekers. If government was seen as dealing properly with such problems then this would in turn breed confidence that other areas could be tackled.

Blunkett described his objective at an early meeting with his Home Office officials. As he put it at the time:

Regeneration, community activism, engagement and citizenship are critical. That needs to be at the front of our minds in everything we do. That's true in terms of a proper managed migration policy, of making sure that people at local level have confidence in the criminal justice system, engaging with witnesses and giving people who are prepared to come forward the confidence to do so. And that's also true in mentoring people coming out of prison, with community punishment and working with young people in terms of anti-social behaviour. It's a balance between enforcement, with the signals that sends and the culture it breeds, and engaging people by offering solutions and a way out, and then insisting they take it. So it's not just something about rights and responsibilities; it's also about consequences.

But this meant changing the very *raison d'être* of the Home Office, long regarded within Whitehall as possessing the least able, least effective and least interested civil servants, a byword for inefficiency and torpor. Blunkett respected one of his predecessors, Michael Howard, who was the first home secretary to try to reshape the culture of the department from being focused on slowing down the increase in crime to reducing it. But under Straw, he felt, things had not progressed as speedily as they should. Blunkett and his team had been aware of the received wisdom that the department was still a long way from working effectively. But they were nevertheless shocked at just how chaotic and inefficient it was. "Nothing had prepared us for it," recalls one adviser. "It was worse than any of us had imagined possible. God alone knows what Jack did for four years. I am simply unable to comprehend how he could have left it as it was. At least Howard had the alibi that he was attempting a wholesale culture shift. In the Home Office, doing nothing means going backwards. It was a mess. A giant mess."

Speaking to Blair for the first time since the 2001 election, Blunkett described the management and competence of the department as "abysmal". Unlike many ministers, who see management of their department as a time-consuming burden, Blunkett came into government having already run an enormous organisation, Sheffield City Council, and having seen at a young age the impact of good and bad management. He was well aware that, difficult as it would be, his first task would have to be restructuring the department. He told a friend that "we've just got to turn it around. If we don't, you'll soon be reading my political obituary". That comment was particularly apposite, given the problems that he was later to encounter over immigration.

Given the chance, Blunkett would have replaced the civil servants from top to bottom. One of the officials typified the department, according to one adviser: "She should have taken up psychotherapy because she used to sit with ministers for ages, absorbing all their frustrations and making them feel a lot better. She'd sympathise deeply with them and say, 'It's dreadful, isn't it.' And then do absolutely sod all." But Blunkett knew well that there was only so much change he could manage without producing a backlash. John Gieve, for instance, the Permanent Secretary, although an able, smooth, archetypal civil servant, lacked the drive and passion of Sir Michael Bichard, Blunkett's Permanent Secretary at Education. But throughout his career Blunkett has been a past master at picking fights where necessary and backing off when appropriate. Replacing Gieve, well liked by other permanent secretaries and by Sir Andrew Turnbull, the Cabinet Secretary, would have been a bridge too far. Reorganising the department was one thing; political suicide quite another. But alongside him there would have to be a new team, persuaded by Blunkett "that their future and not just mine is dependent on change. Because otherwise they just see us off because we come and go".

As a fellow minister puts it: "It was a very difficult line to tread. These people can do you in. David was mindful of that. He felt, 'If I try and have too much of a clear-out of people who aren't doing enough, then they can bring me tumbling down quite easily.' So he acted to strengthen the existing structures rather than to have more of a clean sweep."

When he took over Education, Blunkett had effectively had two and a half years to build a policy and to work out how the department should be restructured. He had a week to do it for the Home Office. And the mess he inherited was far worse. As one civil servant supportive of Blunkett's criticisms of the department puts it: "Neither Jack Straw nor Richard Wilson [the previous Permanent Secretary, who then became Cabinet Secretary] did anything. Wilson was hopeless. Straw presided over some important reforms and falls in crime – and some of the steep ones have levelled out under Blunkett – but they were inherited from Howard. Structurally, and in the whole feel of the department, you could tell it hadn't been modernised for a long, long time." When Blunkett started at the DfEE, the Employment Service was a moribund, uninspired institution; but it was at least a functioning organisation. The Immigration and Nationality Directorate was, however, beyond chaotic. And for every day that passed without improvement, Blunkett's political stock would take a greater dive.

At Education, Blunkett had the support of Bichard, who helped drive the departmental reforms through. Such changes, which can look obvious to outsiders, are especially difficult for politicians to bring about if they are done against the wishes of senior officials. At the Home Office, Blunkett had to proceed far more cautiously, with the result that the pace of reform was far slower. It took almost two years for him to clear out the dead wood and to bring in new officials and the new structure. Martin Narey, chief executive of the National Offender Management Service (the prison service) and Leigh Lewis (Crime, Policing, Counter Terrorism and Delivery) joined Gieve as permanent secretaries. A Group Executive Board was set up in 2002 to "lead the Home Office Group, including its agencies, to ensure that it delivers on the aims set by Ministers, builds its capability for the future, and maintains high standards of propriety".[5] Non-executive directors from outside the civil service sat on the board, with similar functions to private sector equivalents. As one civil servant describes what happened: "Large numbers of people at lower grades found themselves leaving the department or being put into backwaters."

Blunkett has had strong views about the relationship between officials and politicians since his Sheffield days. For him, politics is about politicians. It is the politicians' job to do the politics;

the officials' role to ensure that their ideas are implemented. That sounds straightforward, but it is deeply shocking to a strand of civil service tradition, exemplified by the Home Office, which holds that delivery is none of its concern. Once a bill has passed into law, its job is over.

Blunkett's view has strengths and weaknesses. A strength is that he is willing to take on the reorganisation and management reforms necessary to make delivery possible. A weakness is that he can lose patience with those who do not deliver. Blunkett has, for instance, repeatedly aired his criticisms of immigration officials in public – a habit repeated by Beverley Hughes as immigration minister, and which cost her her job. As one adviser remarks: "The civil servants feel it and some of them will then take their frustrations to the press, as they did with Bev. David should have been a little bit more private with those things. But he has a very different, clearer view as to how they are supposed to function than a lot of other people and I think that's reflected in his determination to do things."

The civil service is constitutionally structured to stop politicisation and to prevent politicians taking charge of the machinery. But this has a consequence: it also stops rapid change. This seemingly dry topic – the machinery of government – has a direct impact on policy implementation. Tony Blair has spent much of his time trying to change the machinery of government, from his building up of the policy-making capacity in Number 10 through to the creation of the Delivery Unit, run by Michael Barber (Blunkett's former head of the Standards and Effectiveness Unit at the DfEE), charged with policing the success – or otherwise – of individual departments' implementation of policy. Barber was not originally a civil servant when brought in by Blunkett; other figures (such as Geoff Mulgan, former head of the Strategy Unit in the Cabinet Office) were also brought in from outside to take on what were traditionally career civil service jobs. As Blunkett puts it:

This is rarely, if ever, written or spoken about, partly because it's dangerous territory and partly because previous Labour ministers thought the problem with the civil service was that it is political. But it's nothing to do with politics at all. It's to do with the culture of the service, which acts as a defence mechanism. That's what has really got in the way of radical change. The party doesn't give this proper attention because it still believes that if you pass a resolution or a bill, things happen. But in modern politics, what are needed are subtle new influences and new ways of changing political direction. Change is no longer brought about by dramatic, seismic shifts in policy such as nationalisation but by cultural changes.

Beyond the need for competent civil servants, Blunkett is heavily dependent on his political advisers; more so than most ministers. But initially he found the Home Office resistant to listening to them.

I don't know how, in a modern government, people are able to do their job without advisers. Not because of the political advice, because political advisers aren't political advisers in that sense. But as the outreach – my arms and legs – and being able to speak with my authority. It took a while before they accepted that. It's always been accepted in the Treasury; they speak as though their masters have spoken. It certainly was worse here than it was at Education and Employment, because the immediate senior staff in Education and Employment not only knew what was coming but saw their engagement with it as part of the success of their job.

That was certainly not the case at the Home Office.

As one adviser puts it: "It was a department in which people had been trained to write fluent submissions and to draft legislation and, other than the Prison Service and the Immigration Directorate, which had even worse problems, it didn't regard itself as a 'delivery department'. You could feel it in the ether." Blunkett himself is caustic about the civil service:

The one thing I wasn't prepared for was incompetence and inefficiency. Twenty years ago, I believed the Tony Benn/Barbara Castle version that it was really a political conspiracy and the people were against them because of their politics. I don't believe that now. It was just incompetence. They mistook what was really just muddle and an inability to administer properly for political blockages and resistance in the system. Outside, they think the civil service is a Rolls-Royce machine and it's only the interference of politicians that gets in the way of it working really well. And that's the real problem. Constitutionally, we don't have control over the management. Any hint of that is attacked as politicisation. I can persuade and I can manoeuvre to get them to accept that they must move people, but I can't order them to. I could as leader of Sheffield City Council. The people inside the Home Office didn't believe that we would do what we said. And they had a policy of their own. I've never experienced anything quite like the first few months here. We were running parallel policies. There were my policies and there was what officials called 'Home Office policy', and that was what they worked to. I had to say to them over and over again, 'There is only one policy and it's what we say it is.' At the edges we're still struggling with that.

Blunkett's initial view was that "the Home Office was reactive, an absorber of punishments. All home secretaries whom I have ever seen interviewed talked about things coming out of a blue sky and hitting them". Like every home secretary before him, and no doubt every home secretary who will succeed him, Blunkett was determined to do otherwise and to change the very nature of the job:

There are moments when you make the opportunities and you change the ether, and therefore you create the space you need in which to operate. The knack is knowing when the space is big enough to get through. That's the real art of politics – when to pick up the ball and run with it. Lenin did it. He stayed in Switzerland a long time before he went to Russia. You have to make the climate and make the atmosphere in which you will be judged, not by what was there in the past. Take Harold Wilson in the 1960s; he created an environment in which he was going to be judged on the balance of payments. So you've got to be careful not to create the wrong environment for yourself in which you're judged badly.

Just as Blunkett had introduced citizenship on to the curriculum as Education Secretary, so as Home Secretary he took citizenship and the community as his central theme, on which all other policies would hang:

That includes nationality and the immigration debate, and developing the idea that on policing, crime reduction and drugs, the community and the role of the citizen are the key elements. Underpinning everything is the belief that without security, stability and order, progressive politics can't flourish. That's the basis of everything. When people see me doing tough things, they misinterpret it completely. They say, 'Oh, you're illiberal.' But it's those actions which make other things possible. It's about a sense of trust that we know what we're doing, that we've got the right balance, that we're not going to be taken for granted and made fools of. But also that we are prepared to open up whole new vistas such as granting 200,000 work permits a year.

Blunkett's first months as Home Secretary were, as one adviser puts it, "a firestorm". Riots in the North-West and the release of Jamie Bulger's killers would have marked the period as exceptional. But all that was soon dwarfed by an unimaginably transformative – and horrific – event.

All the planned policy priorities and organisational changes had to be redrawn when, on 11 September 2001, two planes were flown at the World Trade Centre, another at the Pentagon and a fourth brought down by its passengers. A wholly new, unexpected and controversial dimension was added to the debate over citizenship and community – that of individual freedom and the protection of rights, and whether they are undermined or buttressed by the extra security measures introduced in response to 9/11. As Blunkett puts it: "I had to take a PhD on this between 11 September and making my statement to the House on 15 October. I've never read so much and absorbed so much before, because I knew I'd be taking on lawyers. It was a fascinating experience; it taught me a hell of a lot. It made me think from first principles about the philosophy that we were carrying through."

Blunkett treated the passage of the Anti-terrorism, Crime and Security Bill as a game of chess, conceding on the less important points but manoeuvring to keep the principal objectives. All legislation is a balance. This was the ultimate balance between two diametrically opposed views of the central purpose of demo-cratic politics: the protection of liberty. Some thought the bill did not go far enough, others that it was an unjustified attack on basic civil rights. Blunkett himself considered the bill another example of the twin-track approach: "It is that balance again; all the time just trying to do the two-hander, doing what is necessary without going over the top."

But the bill was full of measures that the Home Office had been trying to secure for years, as Blunkett now concedes. "The Tories were right. We did stuff things in that needed to be done anyway to correct anachronisms and sillinesses from the past, so I was guilty of 'Christmas-tree-ing' the Bill [hanging all sorts of unrelated measures on to a central spine], as Robin Cook used to call it." Politically and procedurally, however, the passage of the Bill, from its introduction at the beginning of November 2001 to its third reading on 14 December was, objectively, a triumph. Blunkett had steered a deeply controversial bill through and had secured all he wanted, and more, by political sleight of hand. But it did not seem much of a triumph at the time. For all his wiliness, Blunkett made a basic political mistake. At that year's Labour Party conference in October he had won massive applause by announcing that he would legislate to create a new offence of incitement to religious hatred. But over the next few weeks, the idea was unpicked across the media and in represen-tations to the Home Office by people from a range of stand-points. Such was the head of steam behind the opposition to the clause that Blunkett was forced to abandon it. "It was the bill or the clause, because of our stupid constitution. If it had been possible to bring it back in the next session, the opposition wouldn't have mattered; we could have used the Parliament Act. But because it was an emergency bill and I had to get it through, the Lords knew that they could scupper the whole bill." The Liberals joined with the Tories in opposition to the clause and Blunkett realised that he had no choice but to drop it.

Blunkett had, as he put it in the Commons, "already reached agreement on 98 per cent of the Bill".[6] On that one clause, put in as a sop to the Muslim Council of Great Britain and Labour activists, and about which Blunkett had no strong feelings, he had been defeated in the Lords. He announced to the Commons that he was dropping it: "Coming from Sheffield, I am familiar with the old nursery rhyme about the grand old Duke of York. So I have marched myself up to the top of the hill and I am about to march myself down again."[7] His words were met by a wall of jeers and cheers from the Tories and Liberals. Blunkett then made the fatal mistake for a politician of losing his temper:

Every decision that we take – be it this House, the House of Lords or people in their individual lives – has consequences. Some people's attitude is, 'We really agree with this proposal and we think that in the long term it would be a good thing to do, but this is not the time for the bill and we did not agree with every word so we will reject it.' Those people will need to reflect in a year's time on where the new Bill is, not least those Liberal Democrats who are heckling me. After all, they have suggested that we should re-examine every aspect of this Bill, to the point where no time or space would be available to table a separate small Bill on incitement to religious hatred. That is the consequence of the enthusiasm demonstrated by hon. Members – on the Opposition Benches and on my own side as well – at the fact that the provision has been removed from the Bill. We all understand that the House should concern itself with construction, constructive change, improvement and building on proposals. What I have never understood is the great joy and cheer at the destructiveness of removal.[8]

Speaking later, when upbraided by the Conservative Sir Brian Mawhinney, for his sour tone, Blunkett said that, "If someone blows a raspberry in my ear, I am inclined to blow my mouth organ slightly louder. A raspberry was blown by Members when I announced that the clause was to be dropped."[9] The reality was that outlawing incitement to religious hatred had nothing to do with the central purpose of the bill: fighting terror. Blunkett had gained almost everything that mattered, at the expense of an irrelevant clause. And he had outmanoeuvred the Liberals and Tories on almost every other clause. But the only story the next day was his defeat, and his reaction to that defeat. "I just saw red," as he put it later.

For all the pointlessness of Blunkett's reaction to losing the clause, it was in some ways appropriate. Race politics would always have played a large part in Blunkett's time at the Home Office but the impact of 9/11 was to make it far more prominent. Without the measures in the bill and the refocus on fighting terror, Blunkett would have been seen as a very different home secretary to the prevalent image of a populist authoritarian. The 'talk tough and act tough *and* liberal' approach, which was his favoured *modus operandi*, would have been far more to the fore.

Anti-terror issues may have forced a refocus of the initial agenda on which Blunkett had expected to concentrate but he was still able to drive it through. Police reform was a typical example. The White Paper published in 2001 set out a series of reasons why reform was needed: clear-up rates falling an average of 40 per cent to 18 per cent in two decades; an increase in already large variations in response times and detection rates across the country; a lower level of public satisfaction with the police than almost anywhere in Europe; and a rising fear of crime.

The Police Federation conference in May 2002 would be a

critical staging post in selling the reforms, which were proving deeply unpopular within the force. On pay, Blunkett proposed raising all annual pay scales by £400 and introducing an extra performance-related pay tier ('competence-related', in the jargon) paying a bonus of £1,000. But overtime rates and allowances would fall and officers would have been required to work more flexibly; added to that, a new breed of 'civilian warden' and more centralised control over chief constables (which was to come into play in June 2004 when Blunkett and the Chief Constable of Humberside engaged in a protracted legal battle over Blunkett's insistence on his suspension) combined to raise the hackles of the last public service to be exposed to reform.

Driving down on the morning of his speech, Blunkett heard a recording from the previous year's conference on the BBC's *Today* programme. Jack Straw had been barracked, slow-handclapped and booed. "I thought, bloody hell, what am I walking into?" He knew that the best he could hope for was a respectful ear. But even that would be something of a triumph, given the ferocity of some of the attacks on him in the course of the new police contract negotiations. His keynote speech could make or break the reforms and thus his home secretaryship. But Blunkett had done his preparation. With the help of a senior Police Federation member sympathetic to his ideas for reform, he and his special advisers had drafted a speech to play to the organisation's wishes. Starting out with an admission that he had failed to explain his proposals properly, he turned on the charm. He apologised for going too fast. He should, he said, have taken longer to consult. And then, as he got farther into the speech, he played a surprise card.

Shortly before the 2001 election, Blunkett had visited a school and community centre in Swindon. Waiting for a train back to London, he was approached by a young woman. "Excuse me," she said, "are you David Blunkett? I am Emma Blunkett – David [his cousin]'s daughter." The two wings of the family had fallen out of touch, but David Blunkett the politician remembered the other David Blunkett, whom he had visited on holiday as a child. He especially remembered the family chip shop – and the fact that the other David had, as a young man, become a policeman. Once the election was out of the way, the two men renewed their acquaintance. For the next year the story of the Home Secretary's policeman cousin remained a closely guarded secret. Blunkett's announcement at the Police Federation conference that his cousin, David Blunkett, was in the audience was a perfect piece of political theatre, all the more valuable for the fact that not only did the two men look alike, they thought alike: both David Blunketts believed in the need for reform.

It worked. He received a civil response, which was to be important over the coming year as the arguments over police reform became ever more heated. The following year, the Prison Officers Association had a new leadership. Blunkett saw, and grabbed, the opportunity, making a conciliatory speech that was tailored specifically to the new broom. A hack politician would have been reminded by his civil servants that he had had a poor reception the previous year and would have reacted accordingly by going through the motions and reading a predominantly civil-service-prepared speech – "and it's ten to one on that the civil servant wouldn't have got the nuance about the new leadership's willingness to listen, and that that needed a different speech", as Blunkett puts it.

But even when the Police Reform Bill passed into law, there were still no levers by which chief constables or divisional commanders could be made to do what the Home Office wanted. The parallels with Education are obvious. As Education Secretary, Blunkett was most pointedly criticised for pushing as hard as he could from the centre to compensate for the institutional barriers on the ground, instead of allowing change to come from the bottom up. It was even more difficult at the Home Office. Forcing Local Education Authorities and schools to change is one thing; forcing chief constables, who are responsible not to the Home Office but to their own local Police Authorities, quite another.

Change rested upon persuasion, and persuasion takes a lot longer than diktat, although Blunkett showed his determination to impose himself within days of taking office when, on 25 June 2001, he called for Sussex Police Authority to consider sacking their Chief Constable, Paul Whitehouse, after an unarmed man was shot dead in a police raid. Whitehouse promptly resigned.

One Home Office minister knew the flaws in the policy even as it was being implemented: "Our mistake was not to have put in mechanisms that changed the nature of police authorities and to drive from the bottom up. So we're having to drive again from the centre. Even though we all know that real change can only take place locally, we're still having to drive it ourselves because the machinery won't respond to local push."

There was a more personal problem: Blunkett's frayed relationship with Sir John Stevens, the Metropolitan Police Commissioner. Blunkett considered Stevens to be a weak Commissioner, lacking in judgement. He could talk a good game but was rarely able to deliver. Stevens's response to the incident when, in June 2003, the 'comedy terrorist', Aaron Barschak, made it past the police's supposed watertight security into a Windsor Castle party, solidified Blunkett's view. The Commissioner promised root-and-branch reform and strong disciplinary action against the offending officers. And yet eleven months later, in May 2004, there was a similar security breach.[10] Clearly, Stevens had failed to do what he had promised. Blunkett called the Commissioner, pointing out that both their jobs were on the line; it was only by a stroke of good fortune – the Commons Speaker's refusal to grant a Private Notice Question (a means by which a minister can be forced to make a statement) on the subject – that the story had not taken off. Blunkett was not impressed with Stevens's response: more bluster, as he told his colleagues, and more empty promises. As Blunkett put it to his advisers: "That man [Stevens] needs to start feeling the pressure he is under."

Blunkett was initially prepared to give Stevens the benefit of the doubt and for the first two years their relationship had ups as well as downs. One incident, however, destroyed the relationship for good. In February 2003, tanks were deployed at Heathrow in response to a detailed intelligence warning of an al-Qaeda attack. Most security warnings are general. This time, the advice was that there was a specific and identifiable danger. Meeting at Number 10 under Blair's chairmanship, Dopit I (the relevant Cabinet committee) was asked by the Metropolitan Police's anti-terrorism branch for authorisation to bring in the army. The committee agreed, although Blunkett insisted that he clear the statement that would be issued on the day, a normal procedure.

Come the day – 11 February – Blunkett was in his office with his advisers. The news was on in the background. When the pictures from Heathrow came on-screen, a voice piped up: "David, I think we may have a problem." Instead of the restrained, proportionate presence agreed at Number 10, Heathrow looked as if it had been taken over by the military, with tanks everywhere.

The media reaction was near unanimous. Blunkett was clearly attempting to scare the public in order to bolster his own desire to introduce draconian anti-terror measures. He was accused of cynically manipulating the fear of terror for his own base political ends. The truth was rather different. Blunkett knew straight away that having tanks at Heathrow was a PR disaster. "They [the police] used their operational freedom to go over the top. I found out from the television. Because you're not operationally in charge, then, once you've agreed the principles of the policy, the police have operational freedom. That makes sense, not having politicians second-guessing every move, sitting there like Hitler with things on a board deciding what to do."

Blunkett went through the roof. Enraged, he called Sir John Stevens, who told him with patronising annoyance that there were no tanks at Heathrow. None. The Home Secretary was quite wrong. There were, however, some 'armoured vehicles'. Blunkett pointed out that to the rest of the world they were one and the same thing and that the message that they sent out was one of sheer terror. Stevens was uncomprehending: they weren't tanks, they were armoured vehicles. Blunkett summoned Stevens and his senior colleagues to his office. "I had them all in. And they said [again], 'They're not tanks.' They didn't know what we were talking about. It was male, macho, silly laddism. *Boy's Own* comic stuff. They couldn't help themselves."

Stevens had a further response: no other home secretary had ever wanted anything to do with such things. Blunkett could barely contain his anger at Stevens's insouciance. "That", he told him, "is because they wanted to hover above the problem and say it was nothing to do with them. Well, you can't do that. If the impact is bad, you've got to stop it, not to say, 'Nothing to do with me, guv.'" Blunkett insisted that the armoured vehicles, which weren't tanks but looked like tanks to everyone bar Stevens, should be withdrawn. Stevens, reluctantly, agreed.

It was a real learning curve. I said to Tony [Blair] that he had to give me authority to say to the anti-terrorism people, and to the Commissioner, 'You are operationally free, we are not interfering politically, but you've got to read back to us what you're doing, because we have to answer for it.' These things are very sensitive. The message you send out has to be one of positive reassurance, that we know what we're doing, we are in charge. Yes, we will put more patrols on the streets or in a particular area, but we won't do something so stupid that it actually worries people. When things are really bad I don't want people to think that we've cried wolf before. I want them to know that if we say that something is really bad, it is.

Blunkett is opposed to a minister for homeland security for a similar reason: "His whole job would be to frighten people to death. No Cabinet minister is going to avoid appearing on television or appearing in the House. It's like having a job to scare people." An adviser to Blunkett agrees that "Tom Ridge, in the Homeland Security Department in the United States, is wasting tens of billions of dollars on things that are just an irrelevance to actual security." In a similar vein, Stevens's warning after the

Madrid bombings in March 2004 that "there is an inevitability that some sort of attack will get through" in London prompted a rare public rebuke from the Home Secretary to the Commissioner. "There has", Blunkett told an interviewer, "to be a balance between telling the truth and reassurance."[11] The word 'inevitability', however, would make people "jumpy without it having a good effect".

Osama bin Laden was not the only one to create unplanned crises for Blunkett. Derry Irvine was also a persistent problem. The roots of Irvine's departure from the government in the 2003 reshuffle lie in the dispute between the Home Secretary and the then Lord Chancellor. Blair had made clear immediately after the 2001 election that Blunkett's Home Office agenda – especially the twin-track approach combining tough sentences for crimes the public felt needed severe punishment with community sentences for lesser offences – was to be a priority for the government (the *Sunday Times* article immediately after polling day was intended by Blair and Blunkett to convey this). Blair's intention was to ensure that the usual inter-departmental rivalries were smoothed over. To fight Blunkett was, ministers soon learned, to fight Blair. ("I used that in full," says Blunkett. "I always do.") But one minister stood apart: Lord Irvine – the only minister who felt that he could fight Blair as his superior. Blair became increasingly frustrated with his Lord Chancellor and former pupil-master's blocking of the Home Office programme, a frustration that swiftly turned to anger after an interview on the *Today* programme, ostensibly about reform of the House of Lords, which Irvine gave without any consultation or prior notice on 6 January 2003.

According to Irvine, the public was "sophisticated enough" to understand that community sentences worked more effectively than prison terms in rehabilitating offenders, a comment that came less than a month after a decision by the Lord Chief Justice, Lord Woolf, that first-time, non-professional, non-violent domestic burglars should no longer be sent to prison. Lord Irvine told the BBC that he had "no difficulty agreeing with the Lord Chief Justice" on the guidelines. "I don't accept that people are disturbed at first-time burglars or even second-time burglars – where there are no aggravated elements in the burglary – not going to prison." The prison population of 72,000 in England and Wales was "insupportable". He did not stop there. Traditional civil liberties, he went on, had been eroded after 9/11 by David Blunkett's anti-terror laws.

Blunkett was incandescent and knew instantly that Irvine's "buffoonery", as he called it, would unravel everything he was trying to achieve, well beyond the specifics mentioned by Irvine. Take immigration. Blunkett's main priority was to get a grip on the machinery, instil some order and demonstrate that he was tough. Only when he had done that could he begin to persuade a sceptical electorate of the positive benefits of legal immigration. The tactic – specifically agreed with Blair – was adopted across the range of Blunkett's responsibilities: tough rhetoric, backed by tough action, demonstrating that Labour meant business. The idea was to convince the electorate that it was on their side and to show that the twin-track approach worked best, laying a foundation on which more liberal policies could be built, such as the extension of alternative sentences and pushing 50,000 prisoners towards basic skills qualifications, where there was none in 1997.

For eighteen months the tactic seemed to be working: "We'd done it well. And it was working, people were getting the message. We're tough on dangerous, violent sexual offenders, life means life, all of that. We got sentencing policy across to the public. We were beginning to get it across to the judiciary and magistrates. We were beginning to turn the corner. We'd got a balance between tougher sentences for violent, dangerous sex crimes and first-time offenders being community sentenced. And then Derry does his bit upon the *Today* programme, completely out of the blue." Everything was undone.

Irvine's comments would have been damaging at any time. But

his timing could not have been worse, coming days after the shooting of two teenage girls in Aston, Birmingham, with the crime statistics due later in the week, and just before the policeman, Stephen Oake, was stabbed to death during a counter-terrorism operation in Manchester. Irvine had destabilised – "blown apart", to use one minister's words – the carefully constructed agenda of nearly two years. It was a fascinating political episode, demonstrating how one mistake can destabilise things to the point where the can opens and the worms start to spill out.

There was little love lost between the two men long before the *Today* programme interview. As one ministerial colleague recalls, "In some meetings we had on asylum which the Prime Minister chaired, David would get really pissed off at Derry's supercilious, condescending tone. He'd say things like, 'Well, I have already had a presentation like that from your officials, David,' implying that David didn't know about what was happening in his own department. Or he'd say, 'You've misunderstood the law.' He'd play that card all the time: you're not on top of your brief or you're not intelligent enough. I'm the master of all I survey, I'm the intellectual, you're nothing. That really pissed David off." Irvine was public – and patronising – with his criticism. In March 2003 he told MPs: "Maturity requires that, when you get a decision that favours you, you do not clap. And when you get one that goes against you, you don't boo."[12] Blunkett (and his junior minister, Charles Falconer) seemed to be engaged in a permanent, all-out battle with Irvine (and his ally, Peter Goldsmith, the Attorney General). The end result was always the same: they would turn to Blair to sort out whatever was at issue and Blair would come down in favour of Blunkett. Blair was increasingly frustrated – and angered – by what he saw as Irvine's obstructiveness.

Irvine did not learn from the *Today* programme debacle. Three months later, in a round-robin letter to the Cabinet, he criticised Blunkett's measures to combat anti-social behaviour as "an extreme example of the nanny state". When the letter, inevitably, leaked, Blunkett replied with a statement that "those who had no experience of the misery that anti-social behaviour can bring should not get in the way of those prepared to introduce measures to do something about it".[13]

Irvine was sacked two months later, prompting a chaotic series of changes to the Lord Chancellor's Department and wholesale confusion over the role of his successor, Lord Falconer. Blair had decided to use Irvine's departure to hive off the Home Office's responsibility for criminal justice to a new Ministry of Justice. Blunkett, unsurprisingly, did everything in his power to resist, arguing to Blair that such a move would not only be counter-productive – the job needed to be done (and seen to be done) by a Cabinet heavyweight – it was also misconceived. He then made a thinly veiled threat to resign to ram home the point that Blair should ditch the idea. Having lost Alan Milburn through the Health Secretary's decision to spend more time with his family, he knew that Blair could not afford another departure. As a source close to Blair puts it: "Tony needed David more than ever and David made full use of that." The compromise was to replace the Lord Chancellor's Department with a Department for Constitutional Affairs, a rushed and ill-thought-through decision that caused no end of chaos in the following weeks, as even Lord Falconer himself did not know whether he was still Lord Chancellor or Secretary of State for Constitutional Affairs – or both.

Irvine had represented all that Blunkett saw as wrong in the criminal justice system: utterly removed from the concerns of ordinary men and women, cloistered and patronising. The scars from his mother's fight to gain compensation for his father's death remain deep inside Blunkett; at every stage she was blocked by the arid arguments of lawyers. As he put it somewhat drily in the Commons in a debate on double jeopardy: "There are lawyers whom I like very much." He went on to make a deliberately ambivalent defence of the judiciary: "There are people who sometimes suggest, mischievously, that judges live in a cocoon, a different world. I am not one of them, as I believe that judges could be influenced, if they were not careful, by what they read and heard."[14] There was little love lost with the judiciary, a feeling which was well reciprocated. In September 2003, Lord Woolf, the Lord Chief Justice, wrote in an article in the *New Law Journal* that he was "appalled" by the Criminal Justice Bill, which was based on "a totally erroneous assessment" of the consequences of the proposed new tougher sentences for serious criminals. "For parliament to set the guidelines and interfere with sentencing in this unprecedented manner is particularly inappropriate." Blunkett's plans to double some of the existing minimum sentences for such criminals "demonstrate the consequences of the involvement of politics in sentencing", a line of attack he had started four months earlier in a Lords debate when he had spoken of the deleterious effects on the judiciary of "increasing political involvement"[15]. It was not just Woolf: Lord Ackner, a retired law lord, remarked that "this is about as bad a situation for the independence of the judiciary as there has been".[16]

Even on the record in a newspaper interview, Blunkett found it difficult not to reveal the extent of his anger at Woolf's interference in what were matters fundamental to democratic politics:

I accept that Harry Woolf believes that. And I understand the right of judges to challenge us when we step outside what parliament has laid down. What I don't understand is the assertion, made by the former industrial relations judge, Donaldson, that somehow there is the right of judges to be engaged in perpetually checking and overturning processes which a democratically elected parliament lays down. The judges are saying that they want to remain in the political debate. They are opposed to us removing them from the House of Lords. They want a supreme court which has the right to overturn the will of parliament . . . Judges have their role. I have my role. Their role is to defend what they see as their part of the constitution and to defend their independence. My role is to speak for the people I represent. People in my constituency do not believe that they are getting justice. They see how often the perpetrators are the ones whose rights are upheld. If people don't have their voice represented through democratic politics, they will turn to something different – including the British National Party.[17]

One case in particular enraged Blunkett: a ruling by a High Court judge, Sir Andrew Collins, that immigration officials were being unfair in their application of new rules that required asylum seekers to lodge their claim on arrival or lose benefits, one of a series of defeats for Blunkett in the courts. He was outraged, telling the BBC that "Frankly I am fed up with having to deal with a situation where Parliament debates issues and the judges overturn them".[18]

Blunkett was not going out on a limb in these attacks on the judiciary, as many commentators at the time assumed. Far from it. Blair was increasingly annoyed with a judiciary that he felt was one of the most culpable "forces of conservatism" (a phrase he had used at the 1999 party conference. Blair himself was considering an all-out attack on the judiciary, and was happy to let his Home Secretary wade in first). Blair had explicitly asked Blunkett to take on the judiciary, and Blunkett was keen to oblige.

It was not just Irvine's interview which started to unravel the Blunkett agenda. That was merely one of a series of events which, cumulatively, undermined the impression of a tough home secretary, in control of events, such as the murder of two girls in a shooting at Aston and the stabbing of Stephen Oake, a policeman attempting to arrest an illegal immigrant. At the same time, the directly hostile approach of the *Sun* under its new editor, Rebekah Wade (announced by a campaign on asylum and an editorial that Blunkett accused of racism and "stirring up hysteria", prompting the unusual spectacle of the *Sun*'s political editor writing a column in *The Times* attacking the Home Secretary[19]), brought an intensity to the feeling that Blunkett was losing control of the agenda.

The Irvine interview coincided with a collapse in the plans to neutralise immigration and asylum as an issue. Blunkett's idea had been that if asylum numbers could be seen to be declining – both in absolute terms and in terms of clearing the backlog in processing applications – then not only would a critical political problem be managed, it would also provide a more reasoned atmosphere in which the advantages of legal immigration could be sold to the public.

There was a fundamental flaw in the strategy. No matter what he achieved, the media would never pat him on the back, say "well done" and move on to another issue. Managing immigration and asylum as a political issue will always be like pushing water uphill. Blunkett realised that, whatever the policy arguments about the rights and wrongs of immigration, the political problem was asylum, with the tabloids making hay with a constant diet of stories about how 'asylum seekers' – the new bogeymen and women – were running out of control.

To that end, his first priority was dealing with the Sangatte refugee camp, 2 kilometres (1.2 miles) from Eurotunnel's La Coquelle terminal near Calais. Barely a day passed without a story about how asylum seekers and illegal immigrants were stowing away and crossing the Channel via the tunnel. In a camp originally designed to hold 500 asylum seekers, there were soon over 1,200, with about 400 attempting to stow away each night. Since its inception in October 1999, over 67,000 people had passed through Sangatte by December 2002.[20] The French government was turning a blind eye, refusing to exercise proper control; after all, once the refugees escaped they became a British problem. When Blunkett met his opposite number, Nicolas Sarkozy, it immediately became clear that there was a possibility of progress. As one official puts it: "The two of them just clicked. There was a real personal chemistry. They're both outsiders in their own way and they're both complete 'doers'. Both have the same restless ambition to do things. And Sarkozy's daughter was at Sheffield University, which helped." One minister remarked wistfully that "it was depressing in a way – we got absolutely nowhere with Jospin [the socialist French Prime Minister], our supposed political ally. And then all of a sudden Sarkozy came in and within weeks we were talking about closing Sangatte".

The closure of Sangatte was a triumph for Blunkett. His negotiating hand had been almost empty. As one official closely involved in the negotiations puts it: "He had to put something on the table in return, but what? We couldn't send the Iraqis back to Iraq [most of the inmates were Iraqi], nor could we send the Afghans back." All he could do, if he wanted to secure a quick closure, was to accept people who were otherwise going to come illegally. And so over a fraught dinner with Sarkozy at the French embassy, Blunkett agreed to mass evacuation of the camp, bussing inmates across the Channel and housing them. It was a gamble: playing the victory of closing Sangatte against the defeat of having to take in the refugees. That night, driving back from the French embassy, Blunkett turned to his special adviser and said, "If I take more than a thousand people I'm dead." He knew that he had taken a terrific risk. The following day, 2 December 2002, he announced the closure in the Commons:

To ensure that we play our part in getting Sangatte closed immediately and, of course, for good, I have agreed that up to 1,000 Iraqis can come to the United Kingdom, not as asylum seekers but on work visas. This is a one-off exercise. They will be temporarily housed for up to three months while we undertake job matching ... In this way, we will ensure that those who might have reached Britain clandestinely will now pay taxes and national insurance and will not be subject to continuing support from the British taxpayer. We will also take a limited number of Afghans under family reunification, determined by the United Nations High Commissioner for Refugees. The remainder of the Sangatte population, together with those with whom the French have already dealt, as well as anyone subsequently arriving in the area, will be handled by the French authorities ... I do not today pretend that we have reached the end of the road. We have only just passed the new legislation and we have only just reached agreement with the French . . . This is a substantial step forward, however, which no one predicted just six months ago.[21]

The deal was, inevitably, given a mixed press; but politics in the real world meant there was no choice if the French were to agree to the closure of Sangatte.

Sangatte was both symbolic and practical. Other measures, such as benefits changes, the stationing of UK immigration officials in French (and later Belgian) ports, fingerprinting of asylum seekers, greater control of student visas and moves to detain suspected terrorists did not receive the same publicity but were, in the long run, far more important.

Although Blunkett received a large number of letters from his constituents – his permanent private focus group – he knew that he had settled Sangatte as an issue as he went into hospital before Christmas for an operation on his oesophagus. The operation received little publicity. Even his colleagues assumed it was to deal with a minor complaint, since Blunkett had made little mention of it and had passed it off with a smile. In fact, it was a major procedure to deal with a life-threatening condition. Blunkett had had digestive problems for many years; his gall bladder had been removed in 1987. He had become used to a painful, burning sensation after eating, especially after cheese and red meat. By 2001, just before becoming Home Secretary, the problem had got so bad that he was finding it difficult to sleep and was becoming far more irritable even than usual. Sent by his GP for an endoscopy (an internal examination of the gullet, stomach and duodenum), he was diagnosed with reflux oesophagus, a condition where a valve at the bottom of the oesophagus is too weak and allows acid in the stomach to flow back into the gullet. The antacid that was prescribed to deal with the problem did no more than mask the symptoms, and in June 2002 a further endoscopy revealed that the reflux oeso-phagus had caused a still worse condition, Barrett's oesophagus, which occurs when abnormal cells develop on the inner lining of the lower oesophagus and which can lead to oesophageal cancer and serious lung damage.

The advice he received, which Blunkett knew was unsatisfactory, was simply to double his intake of antacid pills. By chance, however, he had dinner a few weeks later with the chairman of a company that produced keyhole surgery equipment, who pointed the Home Secretary in the direction of Professor Michael McMahon, one of the country's leading gastrointestinal surgeons. McMahon was one of the few specialists in the world able to perform a rare technique, Nissen Fundoplication, which specifically dealt with Blunkett's condition. The fundus of the stomach (the top portion) is wrapped around the back of the oesophagus until it is in front. The portion of the fundus that is on the right side of the oesophagus is sutured to the portion on the left side to keep the wrap in place. This creates a one-way valve in the oesophagus which allows food to pass into the stomach but prevents acid from flowing into the oesophagus.

Four weeks later, McMahon saw Blunkett and recommended surgery. Working within the NHS to find a time that would cause least disruption to his schedule, Blunkett was admitted to Leeds General Infirmary on 8 December 2002. The operation lasted two and a half hours and was a complete success. For the first time in decades, Blunkett spent four days – his time in hospital – without newspapers, on the advice of his staff, who were only too well aware of the impact of the media on his blood pressure. He returned to work a month later on 6 January 2003.

He needed to be at full strength on his return. Out of the blue he was presented with a new political problem when, in an interview on *Newsnight* on 6 February 2003, Blair announced that asylum applications would be halved by September: "I would like to see us reduce it by thirty or forty per cent in the next few months and I think by September we should have it halved." Figures released later that month showed applications reaching a record 100,000 in 2002, up from the 2001 figure of

92,000. The new measures that the Home Secretary had put in place meant that a reduction would follow.

Blunkett was incandescent. When news emerged of Blair's remarks in an interview pre-recorded earlier that night, he demanded an immediate meeting with the Prime Minister. In an extremely tense conversation, and doing his best to hide his anger, he made it clear to Blair that he was not prepared to be crucified over a pledge he himself would never have made and which the projected figures did not support. Managing a reduction was one thing. By giving specific figures, Blair seemed to be doing his best to ruin what little positive press there might be from a reduction, making 'success' dependent on hitting an entirely arbitrary figure conjured out of thin air.

Worst of all, Blunkett told Blair, the Prime Minister seemed to have a basic misunderstanding of what was happening. The various measures that Blunkett had set in train – the suspension of appeals and the agreements with other countries – would not help achieve a target figure. That was not their point. Their purpose was to achieve a measure of stability and confidence in the system which would help to win public trust. But they could not possibly have any impact on the actual numbers claiming asylum, at least until the message that Britain was no longer a soft touch had seeped through. The numbers were simply a measure of those claiming asylum; as soon as anyone touched British soil they could claim. What mattered was how they were dealt with once they did claim. Blunkett was thus presented with a target that he had not agreed, and over which he could have no control.

As a result of the meeting, a semblance of agreement was reached, albeit an unsatisfactory one. The damage had already been done. Blair could call it a "firm commitment"; Blunkett would simply say that he was keen to meet it.

The nature of the Home Office, however, is that even if ministers are able to spot elephant traps in advance, something will always ensure that a problem nonetheless manifests itself.

Blunkett argues that this goes beyond "events" and is a product of systemic failure. "On so many fronts we are ahead of the game and on every single one of them, the inertia and the problems of working across Whitehall have actually stopped us achieving our goal. Take the gang masters. [The issue of 'gang masters' blew up in February 2004 when nineteen cockle-pickers died in Morecambe Bay.] We were working on it months before the cockle-pickers died. We tried to get agreement to put something in the Asylum Bill but it was blocked by the DTI."

The problem is not merely a lack of joined-up government, to use the jargon, but the civil service itself. "They say, 'We can't really agree to this, Minister, there's a lot more thought needs to be done on it.' What they're really saying is 'We can't be bloody bothered to engage with this issue; it's not a crisis'. Because civil servants love crises. If it's a crisis, it's wonderful. Everybody runs around. It's a burst of energy . . . followed by death. Absolutely bonkers."

The issue of possible immigration from the ten new EU member states in 2004 is a further illustration of how such topics get mangled by internal Whitehall bungling – and also shows the subtlety of Blunkett's position on immigration. Early in 2003 Beverley Hughes raised the issue, arguing that there was no logic in attempting to ban such countries' citizens from automatic admission to the UK, given the government's explicit policy of managed migration and that the very point of the EU's free movement of labour was . . . free movement of labour. It was a big decision with major political ramifications, and so it went to the Cabinet's DA (Domestic Affairs) committee for approval, which it received in October 2003. But, well aware that the residence test for benefits was "ridiculously" loose, Hughes contacted the Department of Work and Pensions, with Blunkett's support, to work out a more sensible arrangement – the last thing that Blunkett or Hughes wanted was the tabloid nightmare of unemployed eastern Europeans turning up and claiming benefits. As Blunkett puts it: "We clearly needed to get a grip of benefits. We knew there was a problem because we'd already had hundreds of Roma [gypsies] claiming asylum."

They hit a brick wall. As one of the ministers most closely involved in the issue recalls: "We found it very, very difficult to engage the Department of Work and Pensions [DWP]. Our officials just got stonewalled by their officials saying there was nothing legally we could do about it." And so no action was taken until, by February 2004, the press had started to hone in on the accession issue and to worry about a potential army of immigrants from eastern Europe. According to Blunkett: "And then it started to be a panic. Over that fortnight we had hell on earth." After he had raised the issue with Blair at one of his regular 'stock takes', and driven by the media panic, agreement was finally secured with the DWP to restrict benefits. The press reported the decision as a chaotic last-minute arrangement – which it was. But it was an issue that Blunkett and Hughes had been pressing for over a year.

But there was a further problem. According to one minister: "Jack Straw and the Foreign Office just completely flipped on the position they had held before. Jack went into hysterical mode about what he now saw as the impending consequences of accession. He started making dramatic predictions of what would happen – completely the opposite of what he had wanted about five minutes earlier." For months, Straw had been "the man who said everybody was welcome to come and draw benefits", as Blunkett puts it. Come the moment of accession, however, Straw "suddenly decides he's in a terrible panic and he doesn't want anybody here at all. And so we're going round in circles". According to Blunkett, "this is actually a Foreign Office problem but the Foreign Office have done absolutely nothing. So Jack's just intervened at the very last minute and we've got his spanner in the works. And of course, from Tony's point of view, what Jack's whispering in his ear sounds very attractive politically: stop them coming, suspend implementation for six months [refuse to allow them to work, in other words, as other EU members had decided] and all this garbage".

Blunkett decided that he had to go public to make clear where he stood. As he put it at the time to one journalist: "I want to restrict the benefit entitlement, otherwise we'll have race riots. But I want people to come here freely and I want them to work rather than go into the clandestine economy. We are having a row about it."

For all the intensity of the onslaught over accession countries and asylum, Blunkett seemed to be managing to keep ahead of the game, if only just. The issue began to unravel only in the spring of 2004 with the crisis that led to the resignation of Beverley Hughes. At the very least, it showed that his basic strategy – if he could deliver some success, the issue would begin to dissipate – was wrong. Blunkett had started to get to grips with the Immigration and Nationality Directorate (IND) and with the asylum backlog. But no matter; whatever he managed, he would not have got to grips *enough*.

Hughes resigned over a specific mistake: in an interview on *Newsnight*, the BBC2 news programme, she had denied having any knowledge of supposed problems with fraudulent visa applications from Romania and Bulgaria until they had been brought to light by David Davis, the Shadow Home Secretary, a few hours before her interview. Did she know about them? she was asked. "Of course not, of course not. These allegations were not made until tonight." Later that night, however, the government's Deputy Chief Whip, Bob Ainsworth, sought Hughes out. Did she not remember, he asked her, that when he was a Home Office minister they had exchanged letters on visa scams in eastern Europe?

The following day Hughes ordered her private office to conduct an audit of the paper trail. The trawl continued as she and Blunkett were in the Commons taking part in a debate in which Blunkett spoke passionately in her defence. "I absolutely reject any suggestion that she has misled the House," as he put it in a written statement to the Commons. Earlier that morning he had told the BBC *Today* programme that the row was "naked politics

. . . The message to the right-wing press is look somewhere else, because you are not getting a scalp from a minister in my department".

The previous night Hughes and her husband had had dinner with Blunkett to celebrate her fifty-fourth birthday. The papers had been found, she told Blunkett over dinner. The news was bad. The statements she had made in the media "might have been in conflict" with the letters from and to Ainsworth, who had told her in 2002 that British diplomats were "demoralised" by having their carefully considered recommendations over-turned. Although Blunkett still thought he could salvage the situation, Hughes had realised that her position was unsus-tainable and she would have to resign. Blunkett hoped that Blair might persuade Hughes to stay. As Blair prepared for Prime Minister's Questions, he was informed of the contents of the Ainsworth letter. He summoned Blunkett and Hughes to Number 10 for a 4 p.m. meeting. In the hours before the meeting Blunkett and Hughes went over the options once again. Blunkett did not want to lose his protégée, a minister he rated as exceptional. Her misleading remarks were, he argued, unintentional. Resignation was out of all proportion. When they met the Prime Minister, however, it was clear that resignation was the only option. Her position was untenable. But they should all, Blair suggested, sleep on it.

Far from sleeping on it, Hughes stayed up all night; she knew she had to go. At 8.15 on 1 April she arrived at the Prime Minister's office in the House of Commons and tendered her resignation.

The proximate cause of her resignation was, however, mislead-ing. Her problems were more fundamental and went to the heart of the problems with Labour's immigration policies and the Home Office's civil servants. On 7 March, *The Sunday Times* had published allegations by an official in the IND in Sheffield, Steve Moxon, to the effect that he and his colleagues had been told to wave through applications from EU accession states, plus

Romania and Bulgaria. An internal inquiry in the wake of the allegations cleared Hughes of responsibility for such an instruction and pointed instead to middle managers for an over-zealous attempt to clear a backlog of applications. The story rumbled on but lacked a killer punch, until the last week of March, when a further leak showed that Hughes had approved just such a policy in 2002. The Home Office dismissed the allegations as a non-story; this was simply standard practice for clearing a backlog. As an observer at the heart of the events puts it: "The central allegation was that new guidance had been issued by ministers to fast-track people in before the date of accession so the numbers afterwards wouldn't look too bad. It was completely untrue." The real problem, according to the observer, was "an unholy alliance of civil servants with an axe to grind who went to the press, and the failure of senior management to know what was going on".

Hughes had made one fundamental mistake: she had blamed her civil servants, in public, for the chaos at the IND. In so doing, she was laying the foundations for future trouble. She was, however, caught in no man's land. To reform the IND she needed the civil service. But the incompetence of the civil servants was the source of the very problems that they had to sort out. Hughes had repeatedly warned Blunkett and the Permanent Secretary that, as a minister puts it, the attempt at reforming the IND was "being built on foundations of sand", but she had been unable to wield sufficient clout on her own to begin the thoroughgoing reforms necessary. "There was no proper management structure. Nobody 'owned' anything. There was no proper communication strategy with the staff. There were no robust procedures: everything was done by e-mail and nobody knew what was going on with the e-mails . . . That's how this little team sitting in Sheffield could escape attention for so long. There wasn't the management scrutiny of day-to-day practices and procedures that there needs to be in an organisation like that."

The shit really did hit the fan. Blunkett had to leave on the day of Hughes's resignation for his cousin's wedding in Madrid. He returned the next day, to discover that the sewage system in his private bathroom had gone into reverse. And in his bathroom alone. "There was mire coming up the pan, up the washbasin and up the bath. Having had it delivered over Beverley's head and swilling around my feet, it then decided to deliver it in person."

In contrast to immigration and asylum, where Blunkett was battling with the public, over another controversial issue, ID cards, he had broad public support. Polls indicated that four out of five electors supported the idea. The arguments were within Cabinet.

For Blunkett, ID cards are essentially about controlling illegal immigration and the consequences, such as health tourism and benefit fraud. As one of the officials most closely involved in the plans puts it: "You can't open your borders and then not have any mechanisms of internal control to the rest of Europe." In a broader context, ID cards "appear to offer you solutions to some things which are very difficult otherwise. As Home Secretary you're so buffeted by events that anything that promises to bring greater order and rationality to some of the chaos is necessarily attractive". Bitingly, the official continues: "When you stop being Home Secretary, however, then you develop your principled opposition to them, because you don't need them any more."

Jack Straw, Blunkett's predecessor, is a case in point. As Home Secretary, he had toyed with the idea, only to conclude that it was not worth the fight. And yet between leaving Queen Anne's Gate and becoming Foreign Secretary he appeared to develop previously unformed principled objections to the idea. But Straw is, in his quiet way, the canniest of operators, and he could sense a possible alliance with Gordon Brown over the issue. By 2003, when Blunkett finally secured Blair's full backing for ID cards, the Prime Minister's political stock was waning, and Straw could see that Brown's was in the ascendant. ID cards provided a perfect vehicle through which to curry favour.

All roads pointed, in reality, to Brown. Blunkett's relationship with the Chancellor is complicated. In part, Brown resents Blunkett's self-confidence and his refusal to be cowed. Where other ministers moan about him but concede, Blunkett moans and fights – and has the ear of Blair. There was a typical row in the public spending round in the spring of 2004 over Blunkett's wish to match the Conservatives' pledge to increase the number of police by 40,000. Blunkett was keen to avoid being outflanked by the Conservatives on law and order; Brown claimed, however, that there was no evidence that increasing police numbers would reduce crime.

For Blair, too, it is useful to have an ally against the Chancellor's otherwise overwhelming influence. At the beginning of 2002 there was a flood of stories about street crime in the papers and on the television every other night. The Treasury, according to Blunkett, "believed that we'd engineered this in order to bring pressure to bear on the spending round. I'd love to have been able to do that! I would be the world's greatest spin doctor if I could have been able to do any of that!"

At times, Brown and Blunkett can be quite civil to each other. But there is a pattern: even when they appear to have reached an accord, something will emerge to destroy their relationship. For the first two or three years in government Blunkett was not a serious rival. He resented Brown's interference in his department but posed little threat to the Chancellor. As time went on, however, he grew in stature and started to be talked up by Number 10 as a possible successor to Blair, a move guaranteed to raise Brown's hackles. As Home Secretary he had an office to fit that role. Treasury briefings against Blunkett took on a new intensity. He was described as lacking control of his department, unable to grasp economics, impossible with figures and a megalomaniac.

In a straight fight with Brown for the leadership, Blunkett would certainly lose. "The position I'm in, both as Home Secretary and with my lack of time to do the schmoozing, would mean that I would be wiped clean if I stood against Gordon. So you just have to face that and get on with it. You could do the job less and do the internal stuff instead, but what's the point? I'm not here for the next job. I'm here to deliver in the job I've got. It's the only way you can stay content inside your head; that's why Gordon isn't."

In January 2002, however, Brown's prematurely born baby, Jennifer, died. Political rivalries seemed trivial in comparison. Blunkett wrote to Brown and Brown's wife Sarah, expressing his genuinely felt sadness. Immediately it was obvious that something had changed in the relationship between the Chancellor and the Home Secretary. From then on, the briefings stopped and the two seemed to enjoy a rapprochement. Such was its success that, a few months later, Blunkett travelled to the Browns' house in Kirkcaldy for the weekend and to visit Jennifer's grave. He also wrote again to the Browns on the first anniversary of Jennifer's death.

The rapprochement did not last long – no longer, in fact, than the return of ID cards to the top of the agenda. When Blunkett first raised the idea after the events of 11 September 2001, he faced not merely a sceptical Brown but a sceptical Blair, too. Straw had dropped the idea because he did not think it workable, either politically or practically. Blunkett, however, had plugged away, having been persuaded that the biometric technology had moved on by leaps and bounds. Blair had told him that he could run with the idea, but had been careful to stress that he would not give him his backing should he hit difficulties. His persistence over ID cards was the archetypal Blunkett strategy. As a minister summarises it: "He went through a careful process of over two years and he knew exactly what he was doing – changing the terrain through dogged persistence. One White Paper after another, keeping the thing moving, taking the setbacks and the delays, coming back, getting rebuffed in Cabinet committee but still going on. Other people would have said, 'I'm using up too much political capital here, I've got to back off.' He didn't. He kept at it."

The more Blunkett kept at it, the more he could see Blair

coming round, culminating in Blair confirming in his speech to the 2003 Labour conference that "in a world of mass migration, with cheaper air travel, and all the problems of fraud, it makes sense to ask whether now in the early twenty-first century identity cards are no longer an affront to civil liberties but may be the way of protecting them".

"I had to win," said Blunkett to a colleague. "For the Prime Minister as well as me, because I didn't ask him to put his head on the block. I didn't ask him to say what he said at conference. So I've got to do it. But it's not comfortable. It's very much like a rerun of 1968 with 'In Place of Strife', when Wilson initially supported a heavyweight secretary of state who then got turned over by two other colleagues at that level."

But a party conference speech is one thing, action another. A few days before Blair spoke, on 24 September, Straw had written to Blunkett and the PM condemning the idea. Straw argued in his letter that the plans were not good enough:

I believe the proposed plan is flawed and no tinkering with particular issues will be able to resolve what is a fundamental political matter. We remain as far apart as ever on the acceptability of charging. How will we get people to accept a fee system when asylum seekers get the card free? What about the practicality of ensuring every citizen provides a biometric (such as an iris photograph or fingerprint) sample while no effective procedures are in place for those who refuse? The potential for a large-scale debacle which harms the government is great, and any further decisions on the next steps must be made collectively. I will continue to urge strongly that this issue be shelved.[22]

A letter from Paul Boateng, the Chief Secretary to the Treasury, then warned of a political backlash because the cost of the card would be treated as a tax rise, adding that objections "raised by cabinet are substantial".[23]

The politics were fraught. Blunkett needed Brown to stay neutral, and then to neutralise Patricia Hewitt, Secretary of State for Trade and Industry, who was ideologically opposed. He saw

Brown's opposition as a personal battle, rather than one based on the merits of the case. One of his closest aides thinks that the Home Secretary was inclined to make too much of this: "David read more into Gordon than he should have done. He read into Gordon's opposition a kind of plot. He saw a Treasury hand behind other people's positions – Alistair Darling, Patricia Hewitt and others – which I don't think was true. Gordon was simply not in favour of ID cards and was genuinely just interested in public expenditure concerns." (Blunkett's anxieties over a Brown 'plot' seem even less credible in the light of the Chancellor's strong backing for Blunkett after news of his affair with Kimberly Fortier emerged in August 2004. Brown rang Blunkett immediately on hearing the news to offer his support, (as did John Prescott.) To deal with Hewitt, Blunkett arranged lunch and pointed out that, whatever she wanted, ID cards were happening and the best she could hope for was cooperation over her specific concerns. He was contemptuous of her objections which, like those of other ministers, he considered to be based on ignorance. As he puts it: "I've found that Cabinet colleagues don't always read stuff that other people have produced. Again and again they're asking the same questions that have already been dealt with" – will it be incremental, will it involve passports and suchlike.

As for Straw: "You can take two points of view. One is that he discovered after all this time that on civil liberties grounds ID cards are an outrage. Or you can take the view that he's wanted to distance himself a little from Tony and to address a domestic agenda item that would give him some kudos. You pays your money and you takes your choice."

Blunkett's behaviour in plugging away on the issue was seen by other ministers as being deliberately provocative – as a personal battle to prove his ability to win. "Prescott can't understand. He thinks I'm driven on it. I am, but only because I know that the next big thing in my area won't be asylum, because we'll have dealt with it, substantially anyway. It will be clandestine entry, clandestine working and above all – and this is why John Reid [the Health Secretary] is with me on this – the massive rip-off of the health service." Blunkett saw ID cards as having an importance beyond their practical utility. If clandestine entry, and its consequences, was not controlled, the far right would have a potent weapon. "But nobody's been prepared to talk about it, so we've got to do it – now. Because in ten years' time we'll be completely behind; other countries will have introduced biometrics. And the economic gain from doing it first is very great. We will be able to export our know-how across the world."

Blunkett faced a particular problem with Prescott, who would make clear to anyone he could his contempt for Blunkett. In March 2004 the Deputy Prime Minister wrote to the Home Secretary, accusing him of failing to consult properly over anti-terror measures and not acting like a team player, after Blunkett had outlined in a speech in India a series of measures designed to tackle suspected al-Qaeda terrorists. At the next Cabinet meeting, Prescott let rip. He was, he said, fed up with Blunkett's "cavalier" attitude to policy. As a fellow Cabinet member recalls, Prescott argued that Blunkett "never seems to tell anybody what he is doing and we end up hearing about it first when we turn on the TV and see a speech he is making halfway around the world". Prescott did not mention what lay behind his anger – that Blunkett's speech had been made on the day when Prescott had expected a clear media run for his proposals for northern regional government. As chairman of a number of key Cabinet committees, Prescott is, in any case, particularly sensitive to perceived snubs from fellow ministers. Blair, however, weighed in on Blunkett's behalf: "You have all to understand that David has the hardest job to do" (a theme he had already developed in his speech to the 2002 Labour party conference).[24]

For most of 2003 and 2004, the papers were full of leaks from Cabinet committees and inter-governmental papers on ID cards. Barely had a decision been taken than it would appear in the papers. Prescott believed that Blunkett himself was behind the leaks. "He seriously believed that I'd been leaking this stuff. I said, 'Excuse me, John, but has it not occurred to you that this has been deeply damaging to me and to what I'm trying to do?' He said, 'It's a double bluff.' I said it would have to be a triple bluff! It's bizarre. I would hardly have leaked that it was going to cost £40 a head, as it isn't." (As a junior MP, however, he had been suspected of leaking by his colleagues. An account of one private meeting of Labour MPs which appeared in a newspaper left out of the list of attendees the name of a Shadow Cabinet member who had arrived late and then sat silent throughout the meeting. Suspicion fell upon Blunkett, who would not have been able to see the supposedly absent frontbencher in his silence.)

There had been no Brown plot, but the leaks over ID cards led Blunkett to believe that: "Somebody at adviser or minister level in other departments has got it in for me. There's nobody been leaked against as much as I have: two White Papers, the ID stuff three times – including a letter that actually said 'please do not distribute this letter', with the *Independent on Sunday* actually printing the words 'please do not distribute this letter'. None of it's been done with a helpful eye. It's been done with malice."

Blunkett's persistence over ID cards needs to be seen in the context of a more general lesson he learned in his time as Education Secretary. His organisational changes had a more profound impact than the merely managerial. "When I came into the Home Office, the reluctance to change was palpable. People resisted it. Getting them to address that issue required a degree of patience which I normally don't display. So I learnt persistence but also patience in terms of seeing it through. It has reinforced in my mind as well that if you believe you're right, you've got to go for it rather than be dissuaded. On a whole range of fronts we've just had to go for things." This meant not just ID cards but also the reclassification of cannabis. And also the reform of the sex laws, which Blunkett took as the perfect illustration of his political strategy:

The whole revision of the sex offences laws [was possible] precisely because I was willing to take on the business of securing confidence. I was on the side of the people, and I knew what I was doing, that I was putting to rest some of the greater fears that people have, and I do believe that that will be the legacy of the time that I have here. [Asked to choose what I was most proud of] I could easily have said reductions in crime or the balance on asylum and legal economic migration, but I chose the sex offences legislation to demonstrate that sometimes it takes a very robust and very tough Home Secretary to be able to do things that others have not done.[25]

12

A *normal family?*

In the summer of 2004, news emerged of an affair which Blunkett had been conducting with a glamorous American: Kimberly Fortier, the forty-three-year-old publisher of the *Spectator* ('the socialist meets the socialite', as he put it to the tiny number of friends in whom he confided). Blunkett had wanted to make the relationship public for some time, in a manner of the couple's choosing. Fortier's reluctance, despite Blunkett's urgings to be open about it, meant that he had been forced to keep the affair clandestine. The eventual manner of release - an exclusive splash in the *News of the World* – was hardly his preferred method. Blunkett may easily have assumed that this was yet another example of how 'someone has got it in for me', as he believed the leaked Cabinet papers showed. At the time the story broke, newspapers reported that he thought that it had come from a political rival. In fact, Blunkett harboured no such notions; rather, he had long been astonished that the affair, which had lasted two and a half years and had necessarily involved the couple sometimes meeting in public, had not been revealed long ago.

Blunkett had been unaware of Fortier's existence until, shortly after the 2001 election, he was at home listening to Radio 4 and he heard her take part in a discussion about literature. He was struck by both her voice and her interesting take on the subject. By coincidence, he was contacted a few days later by the editor of the *Spectator*, Boris Johnson, who asked whether he would be prepared to grant the magazine an interview – his first as Home Secretary. In normal circumstances he would have refused. Not only was there no political benefit in giving such an interview to a Conservative publication like the *Spectator*, he had decided in any case to wait until the autumn, when he had settled into the job, for his first interview. But he was intrigued by the possibility of meeting the interesting-sounding woman he had heard on the radio, and so he consented to it – provided he could have dinner afterwards with Johnson, Petronella Wyatt (the columnist who had interviewed him) and Fortier.

The two hit it off immediately. At the end of the evening, Blunkett gave Fortier his private phone number and asked her to ring him. Over the next few months, the two became firm friends. They would meet for dinner and enjoy each other's company. (Their friendship was far from a secret; when I began writing this book, at the end of 2001, I was told by a number of his friends and colleagues to talk to Fortier because she and Blunkett were such good friends.)

Their relationship changed in January 2002. They moved from friendship to being lovers. Blunkett was besotted and keen to spend as much time as possible with her, casting the political dangers of discovery aside. In February 2002, for example, both Fortier and Blunkett had been invited to the leaving party thrown by Sue MacGregor, the *Today* programme presenter. They decided to arrive together, stay together and leave together – and if their joint presence raised questions, so be it. But questions were not raised. Nor were they during the next two and a half years when they attended functions together. As far as the rest of the world was concerned, they were simply friends. It says much about Blunkett's dour image that he could be seen out on the town with a glamorous (albeit married) woman and it appears not to have crossed anyone's mind that there was more to their relationship than friendship. It is inconceivable that the same could be said for most other politicians.

For all Blunkett's apparent concern with secrecy – he initially told only his two closest friends of the new relationship – he seemed not to care whether they were spotted; as if, somehow, he wanted the decision taken out of his hands. They holidayed abroad together, indicating that they were lovers rather than friends. In the first half of 2002 alone, at the beginning of the affair, they visited Spain and Venice. And in June 2004, two months before the affair was revealed, Blunkett and Fortier rented a secluded hilltop villa in Corfu and carried on as any normal couple on holiday, wandering arm in arm to the nearest village, St Stefano. They were hardly discreet. A chef at one restaurant at which they ate, Galini, later recalled their presence:

We didn't realise who he was at first but a holiday rep told us he was the Home Secretary of Great Britain and where he was staying up at Villa Katerina. He and his girlfriend were quite often in the town. They had a little boy with them and seemed really happy together. It was the beginning of the summer season so they stood out because it wasn't very busy. But they just seemed like a normal family enjoying their annual holiday.[1]

As a shop assistant at the San Stefano Market general store put it, when the story broke: 'Mr Blunkett came in with the lady and child to do some shopping. They seemed to be having a good time.' A British tourist who had spotted them in the coastal town of Kouloura remarked later that

I couldn't believe my eyes ... He was with a young woman and a child. At first I assumed she was Blunkett's daughter and the child was his grandson. The woman was in a Laura Ashley dress and looked really happy and carefree, playing with the kid a lot and mucking around. I don't really know why I should notice this, but there was a real look of happiness in her eyes. It was a look that spelt sheer joy. This probably sounds strange but I really think it was the look of love. Obviously I didn't know the real relationship at the time, but I couldn't help catching that look.[2]

The newspapers that referred to the holiday when covering the story of their affair did not report that the holiday was far from a complete success; it rained for five successive days.

Fortier fell pregnant. Alive to the political consequences of the news of his relationship with a pregnant married woman emerging, Blunkett immediately told the Prime Minister of his affair and said that he wanted Fortier to move in with him and for them to live as a family. Blair was grateful to be informed and was personally supportive. He upheld Blunkett's view that a politician's private life should be just that – private.

Blunkett had already told his sons and his former wife, Ruth, as well as two close friends and his three closest political aides.

Over the next two years, Blunkett repeatedly asked Fortier to move in with him but she would not leave her husband, Stephen Quinn, an executive at the magazine company Condé Nast. Although Blunkett was growing ever more depressed that Fortier would not cement their relationship, the affair continued, and they saw as much of each other as before. In May 2004, Fortier again fell pregnant. Blunkett was even more determined that he and Fortier should be together. Again, Fortier refused to leave her husband.

The issue was brought to head by the revelation of the relationship in the *News of the World* on 15 August 2004. Earlier in the year, Fortier had booked a villa in Italy for the summer. The plan was that she would join Blunkett for a week; he would then stay on after she had returned home to be joined by his sons, his friend, Paul Potts, and some other friends. In July, however, Fortier decided that her pregnancy meant that she should stay in London over the summer. Had she stuck to the original plan, she would have been with Blunkett in Italy when the story broke. As it was, she was able to flee London to stay with her mother in California.

The first Blunkett knew that the story was about to break was when his press adviser, Huw Evans, took a call on the Thursday afternoon from the *News of the World*'s editor, Andy Coulson. He told Evans that his paper had details of a relationship between Blunkett and Fortier, and offered him the chance to cooperate in telling his side of the story. Evans replied with the line that he and Blunkett were to follow throughout: that the Home Secretary never talked about his personal life, whatever the circumstances, and would not be changing tack.

Blunkett had carefully observed this rule since writing about his divorce in *On a Clear Day*. Naively, he had thought then that in doing so he would somehow clear the air about what had been a traumatic time for him and his sons. Far from it; when the story of the break-up of his marriage was told in his own words, it was repeatedly recycled, to the chagrin – and pain – of his children. So Blunkett resolved never to talk again about personal matters.

The following day, Friday, he and Coulson spoke briefly. Blunkett stuck to his line. He would not discuss his personal life at all, and so he would neither confirm nor deny the story, even though he was fully aware that his role in the affair was big news. Coulson tried to persuade Blunkett to do a deal: if he would talk the paper would cover the story in the most sensitive and positive way possible. Blunkett refused. In arguing that his private life was his private life he was not grasping at a self-serving principle, merely upholding one to which he had stuck for nearly a decade.

Over the next twenty-four hours, Huw Evans had a further two conversations with Coulson, sticking to the line that they would not confirm or deny anything; they would simply not talk about it. If the paper wanted to run such a story, they would have to obtain confirmation from another source – they would get none from Blunkett or his associates. Evans nonetheless managed to persuade Coulson that, in the interests of security, pictures that the paper had taken of Fortier entering and leaving Blunkett's house should be cropped. There was a long-standing agreement with the press that his residence should not be identifiable – the same applied to all ministers requiring security measures. Critically, however, in the light of future developments, neither Blunkett nor Evans sought to protect Fortier's anonymity. To do so would have been to confirm the relationship.

Blunkett braced himself for a classic *News of the World* splash.

When the first edition of the paper arrived on Saturday night, however, he and his advisers were stunned. The story was covered so sympathetically that not only had Fortier's identity been concealed but the intention could almost have been to cause as little damage as possible to Blunkett. It read more like a Mills and Boon romance than a tabloid sex scandal. The tone was set by the editorial that the paper published alongside its revelation, which said that, while

the Home Secretary's love affair with a married woman cannot be condoned ... neither is it a matter for resignation ... [T]his politician who holds one of the great offices of state (and is even spoken of as a future Prime Minister) emerges as a very human and vulnerable figure. In these tense times of terrorist threats, there is no reason to think Mr Blunkett has let his grip slip ... Inevitably Mr Blunkett may find our revelations bruising. Nevertheless, we have no doubt he still had much to offer the nation.

Over the next few days, the received wisdom was that Blunkett had agreed to some kind of deal in order to protect Fortier and to ensure the supportive tone. Why else would Fortier's name have been left out? The paper knew who she was – Coulson had named her in his conversations with Blunkett and Evans – and those who knew her could identify her even from the picture that the paper did publish, in which she was seen from behind outside Blunkett's front door. In it, she was wearing a unique and distinctive designer dress, which many people with whom she had done business would have recognised. Few could believe that Blunkett had done no deal, and that he and his advisers were astonished by the coverage. It had not crossed their minds that her name would be left out.

Her anonymity lasted, however, barely twenty-four hours. The following day she was named by the *Sun*.

Other newspapers reacted very differently in the forthcoming days. Initially, the *Guardian* ignored the story altogether; only two newspapers, the *Mail on Sunday* and the *Sunday Mirror*, went for Blunkett and, especially, Fortier. The *Mail on Sunday* published a vicious attack on her character and sent reporters to put her under surveillance in California (taking a picture of her walking her son, William, in his stroller); and a *Sunday Mirror* columnist asked, 'One wonders what kind of sexual misdemeanour would be deemed serious enough by this Government to warrant the sacking of a politician. What kind of sleazy, immoral behaviour has to occur before our supposedly Christian PM says: "This is not acceptable. You're fired."'[3] Both the *Mail on Sunday* and the *Observer* ignored the informal security protocol and published easily identifiable pictures of Blunkett's house, the *Observer* even giving details of his Derbyshire cottage.

Other newspapers responded to the lack of any real news with spurious facts. Since neither Fortier nor Blunkett would speak, the story could not really develop – although Blunkett became increasingly concerned that some of Fortier's supposed friends were taking it upon themselves to talk to journalists. It was reported, for instance, that Blunkett had requested a DNA test on Fortier's unborn child. He did not. The *Mail on Sunday* reported the following week that Blunkett had had a crisis meeting with Blair in Italy immediately after the story had broken.[4] And according to some reports, the Prime Minister was considering his Home Secretary's position. There was, however, no such crisis meeting. The two men met twice during their stays in Italy, meetings for dinner with friends and family. At one of their two dinners, the Italian tenor Andrea Bocelli (who is also blind) was scheduled to sing, but a chest infection prevented him from doing more than join Blair and Blunkett for dinner. The subject of the affair was raised once, when the Prime Minister and the Home Secretary spoke for ten minutes alone, before the first dinner. It was, however, hardly a crisis meeting; Blair had known and been relaxed about the relationship since it began.

One newspaper implied that Blunkett had abused public funds in bringing a protection officer with him for his holiday with

Fortier in Corfu. There was no protection officer. The beefy young man accompanying them was Blunkett's eldest son (who had joined them on holiday with his girlfriend). Another tried to turn a private relationship into a public scandal by alleging impropriety in help Blunkett offered to Fortier over a passport application. All he did was to pass on to her the name of the relevant official at the American embassy, information that was available to anyone.

The fact that Blunkett was away as the story was unfolding in the press made it easier to control. The *Mirror*, for instance, claimed in its coverage to have been talking to a source 'close to David Blunkett', which other newspapers angrily assumed was Huw Evans. But Evans had simply parroted the line that he would neither confirm nor deny the story. Blunkett knew precisely to whom he had spoken that week. He was in Italy, and thus could speak to people only on the phone, and then only to a limited number of close friends and colleagues. Had he been back in London, he would have been surrounded in his office and in the Commons by civil servants, lobby journalists, MPs and others, any of whom could in theory have overheard conversations in which he spoke about his mood and his reaction to the coverage. Away, that was not possible, and he was able to say with certainty that the flames of the story were not being fanned by his camp. Meanwhile, Fortier's intentions became clear when, in October, she changed her name on the masthead of the *Spectator* to Kimberly Quinn.

There was wild speculation as to the source of the story, with Blunkett reportedly believing that it had come from a political opponent seeking to do him down. But he was more surprised that it had not leaked in the past than that it had finally emerged; since they had been so public in many of their assignations, it was eventually bound to come out. In fact, Blunkett had been keen from the start to make the relationship public; it was Fortier who had insisted on secrecy. And although the fallout from such an uncontrolled and unplanned revelation as eventually occurred would be unpredictable, Blunkett was thus not as mortified as might have been expected when the story did break.

Blunkett's political opponents behaved exemplarily. David Davis, the Shadow Home Secretary, rang Blunkett's office unbidden to say that he would not be making any capital out of the story. Blunkett's private life was beyond the boundaries of acceptable political combat. He kept his word throughout.

Blunkett loved Fortier. Like any rejected lover, he found the thought of her no longer being part of his life unbearable. That emotion was made worse by the context of their relationship. When I first met Blunkett properly, in 1997, he remarked then how difficult it was for a man in his position to date. Not only were his working hours severely restricting, but his place in the public eye would put unyielding pressure on any attempt at normality. Those words were to be prescient. His attempt to build a normal relationship with Fortier, and to allow it to evolve at something resembling a normal pace, was perhaps doomed from the start. They could see each other no more than one or two evenings a week and one weekend a month. But for all his private angst when Fortier made clear to him that they could no longer see each other, he had to get through the autumn of 2004 – and, crucially, the party conference – without giving ammunition to his opponents. He could not allow his inner turmoil to interfere in the slightest with his public position. His first public appearance after the story broke, in Manchester on 2 September, passed off without any problem. One TV reporter asked whether he was distracted, to which Blunkett replied that he would not talk about his private life. No one else raised the subject.

Blunkett has spent most of his life balancing two seemingly contradictory impulses. On the one hand, he has made the plain-speaking, 'what you see is what you get' Yorkshireman his stock-in-trade. On the other, the consciously adopted blunt public image masks his private subtlety and romanticism. That contradiction was never starker than in the closing months of 2004, when for public consumption it was business as usual. Privately, however, he was a broken man, wrestling not just with the collapse of the relationship but with a still bleaker realisation: that he had lost the love of his life and might never again know true happiness.

Just as he had done when his relationship with Ruth had fallen apart, so he turned once again to politics for solace. After weeks of depression, when he had found it difficult to sleep and to concentrate, he threw himself into his work. His civil servants were amazed that, despite his personal heartbreak and the inevitable impact on his demeanour, he seemed to be unaffected professionally.

Blunkett might project the image of a shoot-from-the-hip politician, but his time at the Home Office shows how good a long-term strategist he really is – not merely over policy (such as the shrewd tactics he employed to ensure that he won the battle within the Cabinet over ID cards) but with his own career. He knew full well that, for all the mentions he received in the media as a possible successor to Blair, he could not hope realistically to win the party leadership from the Home Office. If Blair departed before the expected 2005 election, as some were predicting in the spring and summer of 2004, Blunkett would have no chance in any leadership election. If, however, Blair remained until deep into a third term, Blunkett would almost certainly be in a new portfolio and might well be in a position to mount a realistic campaign. Thus when, in the early summer of 2004, Blair's future became a live issue with coded and more explicit hints about a possible change of leader rampant throughout the media, fuelled by jockeying for position by some would-be contenders, Blunkett knew not only not to get involved but also to do his best to strengthen Blair's resolve.

In an interview with *The Times* on 15 May 2004, John Prescott had spoken of 'plates shifting', firing the starting pistol for feverish leadership speculation. Over the next few days, Cabinet ministers took to the airwaves to back Blair, as sure a sign of panic as there could be. Only two had actively engaged in destabilising

Blair: Prescott and Straw. Most either kept their counsel or were genuinely behind the Prime Minister. On 17 May, Blair had flown to Turkey for talks with the Turkish Prime Minister and his return flight had been delayed, meaning that he did not arrive back at Downing Street until the small hours. Sensing that Blair's position was in peril, Blunkett arranged to see Blair the following day to point out that his leadership was in genuine crisis. Blunkett realised that Blair had, at last, begun to understand the danger when he was called by Number 10 early on 18 May to be told that, since Blair had arrived home so late, his diary was being rescheduled to give him time to get some sleep – the first time in his seven years in office that he had changed his schedule in order to have time to rest. 'The last thing we need at the moment is a dog-tired Blair', Blunkett told one of his advisers. 'He is in a fight for his political life.' The delayed meeting went well. Blair told Blunkett that he had been surprised by some of the support he had received from unexpected quarters and that nothing would force him from office until he had achieved his agenda. He was determined to stay for – at least – three more years. (Blair later went public with his timetable with a typically bold announcement on the day after the 2004 Labour Party conference to the effect that he would resign after seeing through his third term.)

Blunkett knew then that his long-term tactics were right. As Home Secretary, with all the battles he was fighting and the constant drip of hostile coverage, he could not hope to win the leadership. Prescott and Straw had broken cover far too soon and their behaviour would be noted by Blair. Blunkett's loyalty was both the result of natural instinct and the politically sensible course to follow. With an election expected in May 2005, Blunkett could expect to be moved to a less controversial portfolio, from where he could begin to establish his credentials as a possible successor to Blair. He told friends that he thought Blair might ask him to stay in post after the election to see through the introduction of ID cards and the rest of the agenda he had set in train. His successor, he thought, might well be Alan Milburn. Given a choice of jobs, he would most like to be Chancellor of the Exchequer. Foreign Secretary did not appeal – the constant travelling would be too much. The most likely option was that he would be asked to take over John Prescott's responsibilities as Environment Secretary. Whatever job he ended up with, his achievement in being one of the few ministers to have been in the Cabinet since 1997 marked him as one of Labour's big beasts. Like any senior politician, he wanted the biggest of all jobs. He knew that the chances of that were slim (he would deflect questions from colleagues by remarking that 'you have to be insane to want to be Prime Minister'); but that was no reason to avoid doing his best to be in a position to mount a serious challenge. The rest would be up to time and chance.

13
Postscript

Time and chance, it turns out, appear to have put paid to whatever prime ministerial ambitions Blunkett may have had. As this book was going to press, Blunkett was engulfed in a crisis brought on by a series of allegations made by Fortier through the pages of the *Sunday Telegraph* on 28 November 2004. According to Fortier, Blunkett had pushed through a visa application for her thirty-six-year-old Filipina nanny, Leoncia 'Luz' Casalme. The newspaper also reported a series of other claims. Fortier alleged that Blunkett shared confidential security information as 'pillow talk' with her; ordered a policeman to stand outside her Mayfair home during May Day anti-capitalist demonstrations; gave her first-class rail tickets intended for spouses, which he obtained as an MP; put pressure on the American embassy to issue a temporary passport for her son, so that they could join Blunkett on holiday in France; used his government chauffeur to drive her to his holiday home for weekend trysts; and took her with him to Spain for a wedding, along with four security men and a driver, with much of the cost being met by the taxpayer.

Although most of the allegations could be either proven as false or explained by Blunkett, one – the supposed fast-tracking of the nanny's visa – was a different matter altogether. If true, it would necessitate Blunkett's immediate resignation. Blunkett was faced with a dilemma. On the one hand, he had stuck rigidly to his decade-long policy of not commenting about his private life. The concerted vilification attempts of his former lover were, of course, deeply upsetting, not least because she was the mother of his son, and he believed that her unborn child was also his. But why should he be forced into breaking that policy? Once it was breached, he would never again be able to claim full privacy. On the other hand, although some of the allegations were trivial, some were so damning as to make a response politically essential.

Thus he made an immediate statement: 'I am very saddened that someone I cared so deeply for should seek, quite erroneously, to damage my public position. This cannot be in the interests of any of us. I shall continue to keep my private life private and separate from my public duties.' His spokesman then gave a detailed response. Blunkett had not, for instance, authorised the placing of a policeman outside Fortier's house during May Day riots. He had told her nothing that was 'not already in the public domain', as his spokesman put it. And although he had given her a spouse's rail ticket, he had – albeit mistakenly been under the impression that, since the two were a couple, this was permissible under the rules. As for the trips to Derbyshire in his official car: the journeys were made by the driver on government business, collecting and dropping off ministerial boxes. They were not arranged specially, and involved no cost to the taxpayer.

The visa allegation was not, however, so susceptible to instant dismissal. Blunkett responded that his driver, whom Fortier had alleged had been sent by Blunkett to pick up the nanny's passport for processing, had had no involvement in the application process, and that his own had amounted to nothing more than checking that the form was 'in good order' which it was. Yes, officials had been involved in the process, but only by virtue of reading out the contents of the form to the Home Secretary. He could not, after all, see them for himself.

But he recognised only too well the toxic nature of the allegation, and that a clear denial was not enough. He thus immediately requested his permanent secretary, Sir John Gieve, to appoint an independent investigator. The following day, Sir Alan Budd was handed the task. Then, on the Wednesday of that week (1 December), the *Daily Mail* published an apparently damaging pair of letters from the Home Office to the nanny: a pro forma response to her application indicating that its processing would

entail a long wait, and then, nineteen days later, a letter informing her that she had been granted her visa. Blunkett himself
responded (when door-stepped on an official visit to, of all places,
the Passport Office) by confirming that the letters were genuine but arguing that they proved nothing other than that the
processing of the form had been efficient.

Allegations over Blunkett's public behaviour threatened his
career, but misstatements that centred on his private life were far
more hurtful, since his long-held refusal to talk about his private
life meant that he could not respond, however ill informed the
comments. It was reported, for instance, when news of the
relationship broke in August 2004, that Blunkett had requested
a DNA test on Fortier's unborn child to prove paternity. He had
not then, nor has he since.

As for her oldest son, Blunkett had known from the beginning
that the child was his, as a result of two previous DNA tests.
Fortier herself had been keen to have the tests, the first – a matter
of weeks after his birth to establish paternity, given that Fortier
and her husband had undergone fertility treatment, and the
second, over a year later, because Fortier, not Blunkett, wanted
further confirmation. Both tests showed that Blunkett was indeed
the father.

There had also been a further allegation in the *Sunday Telegraph* of 28 November to the effect that Blunkett had forced two
civil servants, Jonathan Sedgwick and John Toker, to take a
statement to a meeting at Fortier's solicitors, the Simkins Partnership. Fortier had hired Simkins to attempt to close down coverage
of the affair by sending letters to newspaper editors, citing recent
European privacy rulings. On 4 October 2004, Simkins wrote to
my publishers on behalf of Fortier and her son, 'to place you on
notice of our client's rights to (inter alia) privacy . . . there can
be no justification for the publication of any detail concerning
[the son's name] in the forthcoming book'. The letter concluded
that 'in the event the book does infringe our client's rights,
then you may anticipate that she will commence proceedings to

prevent any sales or distribution of the book'. The book, Simkins demanded, was not even to make any reference to her relationship with Blunkett that was not already in the public domain. I could understand her wish to protect her son's privacy and, although I was aware of his paternity, I had not intended to write about it. Fortier herself had apparently not made any intervention on the matter in public, and there seemed no reason not to abide by her request for her son's privacy. The first twelve chapters of this book reflect this.

But Mrs Quinn, as she now wishes to be known (in her solicitor's October letter, she was still referred to as Kimberly Fortier), clearly has an unusual concept of privacy. At no stage had Blunkett made any comment about the affair until being forced to respond to her claims made in the *Sunday Telegraph* on 28 November. He has otherwise kept his own counsel. Mrs Quinn, however, appears to expect others to follow rules by which she herself does not abide. The allegations she made about Blunkett's behaviour can have had no intention but to move what was a private dispute into the public domain.

From the outset, Fortier has been portrayed as the victim, a naive American at sea in the high-stakes world of politics and at the mercy of the dark arts of a political master. Yet newspaper coverage has constantly cited Fortier's 'friends' who have prolonged the story at every stage, smothering the truth with misleading impressions of events. Typical of this is the idea that surfaced in newspapers at the time of her *Sunday Telegraph* allegations. 'Friends' reported that Blunkett was calling Fortier incessantly and was causing her enormous stress. Yet when she fled to California in August, it was Fortier who was calling Blunkett in Italy – five, six, seven times a day, and in the middle of the night, constantly seeking reassurance from him about the press coverage and the future. Indeed, Blunkett's family and colleagues worried that he was not able to sleep because she was ringing at such bizarre hours.

With or without her agreement, it was the Fortier camp which was fanning the flames. Her media connections, after all, were second to none. Her own position is publisher of the *Spectator*, at the heart of the Telegraph Group. Her husband is a senior executive at Condé Nast. A close friend is a leading figure in the public relations world. On the day after her allegations were first published (in itself an incendiary tactic), her husband gave an interview to the *Daily Telegraph*. Along with a statement that he had made to *The Sunday Times* two days earlier, this was the first comment on the subject by any directly involved party, and shows how keen they were to win public sympathy – as well as destroying any claim to having the boy's privacy uppermost in their minds. As Stephen Quinn put it in the interview: '. . . I love my wife and I adore [the boy's name] and I'm very much looking forward to the birth of our baby in February. And our future as a family is going to be wonderful. I have NO interest in commenting on all the issues that have been raised except to say one should be capable of forgiveness in a marriage. It's undignified to discuss it in public.'

So undignified, that this is precisely what he then goes on to do:

I'm focusing on my obligations as a father to [the boy's name] and to our baby who is due in February. They are my children and I love them and I am not interested in biological details . . . But when he was born I fell completely in love with him . . . I have done everything for him since he was born, staying up at nights, nappy-changing I'm considered the exemplary father at home, I can tell you rather more, I have to say, than I was with my grown-up sons.

Had both parties remained quiet when the story broke in August, the matter would almost certainly have remained private. But one side chose not to. Blunkett had already grown increasingly concerned that some of Fortier's 'friends' (*sic*) were taking it upon themselves to talk to journalists. He regarded one 'friend' in particular, drawn from Fortier's media circle, as poisonous, feeding the story to make Blunkett appear domineering and uncaring and casting Fortier as an innocent victim. The fact is that only one camp has talked to the media, and only one camp has raised the subject of paternity in public.

To judge from most of the press coverage – even that which was essentially favourable to Blunkett – the story was that of an outsider, who just happened to be the boy's biological father, seeking to establish paternity in order to wrench the boy from his real family. The truth is rather different. For two years, Blunkett had had regular access to his son, had bonded with him like the father he was, and had grown to love him. Fortier was seeking to sever that bond and to deny Blunkett access to his own child – and the boy access to his own father. The further DNA test on the boy which Blunkett consented to in 2004 needs to be seen in this context. It was not to establish paternity. He had more than enough proof that he was his father from the two previous DNA tests that had been carried out. Rather, the test was part of the legal process of seeking access to his son. The previous tests were not legally binding. Blunkett agreed to a third test merely because it was needed for formal legal recognition of what he and Fortier already knew.

Blunkett had not wished to resort to legal action, but Fortier had effectively refused to acknowledge his existence, let alone to reach an accommodation with him as father of her child. The picture emerging from the Fortier camp was one of Blunkett as a man still obsessed with his former lover and unwilling to accept that she no longer wished to be with him. Nothing could be farther from the truth. Blunkett was a grown-up, and well understood that his relationship with Fortier was over. But his relationship with his son was rather different, and could not be switched off at Fortier's whim. He was not the type of man to walk off into the sunset, forgetting all about his flesh and blood.

Blunkett had been quite open about his relationship with Fortier when the need arose. Fortier had fallen pregnant in January 2002, immediately after her relationship with Blunkett had become sexual. Blunkett knew that he had to tell the Prime

Minister, informing Blair that he wanted Fortier to move in with him, and for them to live as a family.

Fortier's son was born in September 2002. The birth was difficult and Blunkett – along with his son, Alastair – spent five successive nights in the hospital with Fortier, comforting her. It may seem astonishing that their frequent holidays and public dinners together did not lead to gossip; it is still more so that news of the Home Secretary's appearance for five nights running at the side of a married woman giving birth did not leak out.

The boy was given an unusual middle name. A quick look at Blunkett's family tree would have provided a clue to the boy's paternity. He shared his name with one of Blunkett's close relatives.

In May 2004, Fortier again fell pregnant, although she kept news of her pregnancy from Blunkett until August. Blunkett knew by this time that the relationship was on the rocks, but he could not simply walk away from his duties as a father. As in his political life, he took his responsibilities seriously. There were four choices open to Fortier: to live with Blunkett, the two of them bringing up their son and her unborn child together; to leave her husband but not move in with Blunkett, but allow him access to his son; to remain with Quinn and tell him the truth about her relationship with Blunkett, and grant the father appropriate access; or to stay with Quinn without making clear the full story, and deny Blunkett any access, working on the assumption that, as a typical politician, he would care more for his job and status than for his child and would walk away from his son.

It says much about how little she knew of Blunkett's character that Fortier should choose the latter course and assume that he would put his job above his child.

At the time of writing, Blunkett's future remains unclear. The ultimate impact of the central allegation hangs on the report from Sir Alan Budd. But whatever the result, Blunkett is now a different man. In the public mind, he is no longer the dour figure of old, but either a decent man striving to do best by his children, or a party to adultery. And whether or not he remains in office his political standing has been severely damaged, perhaps irreparably.

Notes

Preface

1. Peter Hitchens, 'Blunkett Past and Present', *Spectator*, 18 April 1998.

1 An extraordinary ordinary man

1. Hansard, 29 June 2004, col. 137.
2. *The Times*, 23 June 2004.
3. *Observer*, 7 March 2004.
4. ibid.
5. BBC, *The World Tonight*, 31 May 2002.
6. *Daily Telegraph*, 29 May 2004.
7. *Reclaiming Britishness*, Foreign Policy Centre.
8. *Guardian*, 26 April 2002.
9. Hansard, 12 June 1991.
10. <http://media.guardian.co.uk/presspublishing/story/ 0,7495,908604,00.html>.
11. *The Times*, 21 October 2003.
12. BBC, *The World This Weekend*.
13. Tim Adams, *Observer*, 16 July 2000.

2 "My your God go with you, whoever he or she might be"

1. *On the Record*, 26 November 2000.
2. *On a Clear Day*, Michael O'Mara, 2002, pp. 43–4.
3. Matt Wells, 'Blunkett accuses media over reports from "behind enemy lines"', *Guardian*, 4 April 2003.
4. *Observer*.

5. Simon Hoggart's Diary, *Guardian*, 8 August 2001.
6. *Tribune*, 5 December 1986.
7. *Daily Mail*, 29 May 1995.
8. Hansard, 20 June 1990, col. 1023.
9. ibid., 8 December 2000, col. 250.
10. *The Times*, 9 March 2004.
11. *Democracy in Crisis*, Hogarth Press, 1987, p. 109.
12. *Politics and Progress*, Politico's, 2001, p. 81.
13. *Independent*, 7 July 1987.
14. *Guardian*, 18 January 1993.
15. *Democracy in Crisis*, p. 82.
16. Press release, 3 September 1993.
17. Hansard, 8 December 2000, col. 250.
18. *Democracy in Crisis*, p. 89.
19. ibid.
20. Hansard, 1 December 1993, col. 1127.
21. Hattersley, *Choose Freedom*, Penguin, 1987, p. 44.
22. Hattersley, *Guardian*, 26 July 1997.
23. *Guardian*, 29 July 1997.
24. *Observer*, 7 March 2004.

3 "A strong, well-built boy"

1. *On a Clear Day*, p. 17.
2. *Observer*, 16 July 2000.
3. ibid.
4. *On a Clear Day*, p. 15.
5. ibid., p. 21.
6. ibid., pp. 24–5.
7. ibid., p. 30.
8. ibid., pp. 42–3.
9. ibid., p. 54.
10. ibid., p. 55.
11. ibid., p. 56.

4 The fight to be educated

1. *On a Clear Day*, p. 67.
2. ibid., p. 60.
3. *Daily Telegraph*, 29 May 2005.
4. *On a Clear Day*, pp. 66–7.
5. ibid., pp. 63–4.
6. *Daily Mail*, 13 July 2002.
7. *On a Clear Day*, p. 68.
8. *Daily Mail*, 13 July 2002.
9. Blunkett records a well-intended but insensitive attempt to boost his mood: "In an effort to raise my spirits, a well-meaning woman at the youth club said there was a girl in a wheelchair whom I ought to meet – she could act as my eyes and I could be her legs, she said. How insensitive people can be!" *On a Clear Day*, p. 70.
10. ibid., p. 70
11. ibid., pp. 72–3.
12. ibid., p. 76.

5 A leap into the unknown: college and the real world

1. *On a Clear Day*, p. 71.
2. ibid., p. 81.
3. ibid.
4. ibid., p. 82.
5. ibid., p. 86.
6. The Guide Dogs for the Blind Association breeds from 300 Labradors, golden retrievers and Alsatians; some 1,200 puppies a year are born, of which 80 per cent will become guide dogs. The dogs begin training at six weeks, when they are sent to a 'puppy walker', who spends a year ensuring that the dogs learn to live in a family, to meet new people and to obey commands such as 'sit', 'down', 'stay', and 'come', and also to respond to random situations which they will encounter when working as guide dogs – 'fight or flight', in the jargon. They are then transferred to the care of an instructor

in the dog supply unit, where they are taught strict obedience, how to ignore irrelevant sounds and smells, how to distinguish between useful features such as kerbs and lamp-posts, bollards and gates, and how to walk straight and bend where appropriate. Crucially, they are taught that when their harness is on they must work, but when it is off they may relax. Finally, a 'mobility instructor' teaches how to judge whether, for example, a gap in a crowd is sufficiently wide for her and her owner to pass through and when to speed up and slow down.

7. *On a Clear Day*, p. 131.
8. ibid., pp. 116–17.
9. ibid., p. 98.
10. ibid., pp. 113–14.
11. ibid., p. 108.
12. ibid.
13. ibid., p. 116.
14. ibid., p. 121.
15. ibid., pp. 123–4.
16. ibid., p. 125.
17. ibid.

6 Not the typical student: The Socialist Republic of South Yorkshire

1. *On a Clear Day*, p. 104.
2. ibid., p. 105.
3. ibid., p. 106.
4. ibid., pp. 114–15.
5. Seyd, *History of the City of Sheffield*, Sheffield Academic Press, 1993, p. 139.
6. ibid, p. 144.
7. *On a Clear Day*, pp. 118–19.
8. ibid., p. 119.
9. ibid., pp. 119–20.
10. ibid., p. 120.

11. *Democracy in Crisis*, p. 71.
12. *On a Clear Day*, p. 128.
13. *Democracy in Crisis*, p. 72.
14. *On a Clear Day*, p. 129.
15. *Democracy in Crisis*, p. 72.
16. South Yorkshire Passenger Transport Executive, *Facts and Figures*, 1984.
17. *On a Clear Day*, pp. 141–2.
18. *Democracy in Crisis*, pp. 100–1.
19. *On a Clear Day*, p. 137.
20. ibid., p. 143.
21. Wainwright, *Labour: A Tale of Two Parties*, Hogarth Press, 1987, p. 108.
22. ibid., pp. 108–9.
23. Seyd, p. 164.
24. *Daily Mail*, 29 May 1995.
25. *On a Clear Day*, p. 150.
26. Wainwright, p. 110.
27. Benn, *The End of an Era, Diaries 1980–90*, Hutchinson, 1992, p. 175
28. *On a Clear Day*, p. 146.
29. ibid., p. 144.
30. See Chapter 7 on the NEC for a more detailed exposition of Blunkett's political position.
31. *On a Clear Day*, p. 146.
32. ibid., p. 147.
33. ibid., pp. 147–8.
34. Cited in Hitchens, "Blunkett Past and Present", *Spectator*, 18 April 1998.
35. ibid.
36. *On a Clear Day*, p. 148.
37. Seyd, p. 151.
38. ibid.
39. Andy McSmith, *Faces of Labour*, Verso, 1977, p. 155.
40. *On a Clear Day*, p. 149.

41. McSmith, p. 156.
42. Seyd, p. 177.
43. Hansard, 21 February 2000, col. 1265.

7 A national figure: Labour in the 1980s

1. *On a Clear Day*, p. 151.
2. Benn, p. 325.
3. *London Labour Briefing*, November 1981.
4. Lansley, Goss and Wolmas, *Councils in Conflict*, Macmillan, 1989, p. 31.
5. ibid., p. 97.
6. ibid.
7. Report of the Annual Conference of the Labour Party, 1984.
8. ibid., pp. 140–1.
9. Hughes and Wintour, *Labour Rebuilt*, Fourth Estate, 1990, p. 9.
10. *On a Clear Day*, p. 156.
11. Benn, p. 347.
12. ibid., p. 422.
13. ibid.
14. Report of the Annual Conference of the Labour Party, 1985.
15. Benn, p. 425.
16. Westlake, *Kinnock*, Little, Brown, 2001, p. 327.
17. McSmith, p. 170.
18. ibid.
19. ibid., p. 171.
20. Hansard, 24 June 1991, col. 718.
21. Hughes and Wintour, p. 11.
22. Kilfoyle, *Left Behind: Lessons from Labour's Heartlands*, Politico's, 2000, p. 173.
23. Benn, p. 456.
24. ibid.
25. ibid., p. 457.
26. ibid.
27. ibid., pp. 458–9.

28. *Guardian*, 19 December 1985.
29. Hughes and Wintour, p. 57.
30. *Financial Times*, 23 April 1986.
31. MacIntyre, *Mandelson*, HarperCollins 1999, p. 109
32. Benn, p. 452.
33. Hughes and Wintour, p. 27.
34. ibid., p. 155.
35. ibid.
36. ibid., p. 132.
37. McSmith, p. 179.
38. Blunkett press release, 10 June 1988.
39. Hughes and Wintour, pp. 119–20.
40. Anderson and Mann, *Safety First: The Making of New Labour*, Granta, 1997, p. 416.
41. Hughes and Wintour, p. 122.
42. Anderson and Mann, p. 343.
43. *On a Clear Day*, p. 177.
44. McSmith, p. 180.
45. ibid.
46. Hughes and Wintour, p. 71.
47. ibid.
48. Blunkett and Crick, Spokesman Pamphlet No. 87, February 1988.

8 Westminster: "a good fight with a worthy opponent"

1. *On a Clear Day*, pp. 166–7.
2. Hansard, 25 June 1987, col. 71.
3. *On a Clear Day*, p. 187.
4. Offa was originally Uffa; all his siblings had names beginning with U. Blunkett did not like the name and asked whether it could be changed. Although a different-sounding name would not have been possible since it would have ruined his training, the minor swap of an O for a U was consented to.
5. Report of the Eighty-seventh Annual Conference of the Labour Party, 1988, p. 46.

6. Hansard, 14 December 1988, col. 892.
7. ibid., 6 November 1989, col. 747.
8. Gould, *Goodbye to All That*, Macmillan, 1995, p. 224.
9. ibid.
10. ibid., p. 229.
11. ibid.
12. ibid., p. 230.
13. ibid.
14. Hansard, 22 May 1990, col. 199.
15. Gould, p. 254.

9 The Shadow Cabinet: the making of a player

1. Hansard, 22 October 1992, col. 660.
2. ibid., 21 October 1993, col. 401.
3. Nick Raynsford, *Fabian Review,* 1993.
4. Kampfner, *Robin Cook*, Phoenix, 1998, p. 98.
5. Private correspondence.
6. *On a Clear Day,* p. 231.
7. Hansard, 11 November 1996, col. 53.
8. *Guardian*, 7 July 1992.
9. BBC1, *On the Record*, 28 June 1994.
10. 'Tables are here to stay', *The Times*, 21 November 1994.
11. BBC1, *Good Morning with Anne and Nick*, 1 December 1994.
12. 1 January 1995.
13. Hansard, 21 November 1994, col. 429.
14. McSmith, p. 186.
15. ibid.
16. *Diversity and Excellence: A New Partnership for Schools*, 1995.
17. *Guardian*, 9 August 1995.
18. McSmith, p. 187.
19. *Guardian*, 12 April 1995.
20. Other advisers included the chief executive of Islington council, Leisha Fullick (formerly director of education in Lewisham); Kathryn Riley of the Roehampton Institute in London; David

Reynolds of Newcastle University, who was appointed chair of the Numeracy Task Force in 1997; David Miliband, Tony Blair's head of policy; and Josh Hillman, who worked with Miliband at the Institute for Public Policy Research. See Anderson and Mann, p. 417.

21. *On a Clear Day*, p. 221.
22. ibid., pp. 216–17.
23. *Sunday Times*, 16 April 1995.
24. So great was the rivalry between the NAS/UWT and the NUT that Nigel de Gruchy, the NAS/UWT's general secretary, arranged for a standing ovation when Blunkett spoke at his union's conference the following Thursday, simply to be different.
25. *Guardian*, 15 April 1995.
26. Melanie Phillips, *All Must Have Prizes*, Little, Brown, 1997.
27. <http://www.nao.org.uk/pn/01-02/01021235.htm>.
28. MacIntyre, p. 311.
29. Rentoul, *Tony Blair: Prime Minister*, Little, Brown, 2001, p. 283.

10 Shaking the trees: Education Secretary

1. *On a Clear Day*, pp. 227–8.
2. Woodhead, *Class War: The State of British Education*, Little, Brown, 2002, p. 118.
3. ibid., p. 72.
4. <http://www.parliament.the-stationery-office.co.uk/pa/ld199798/ldhansrd/vo970514/text/70514-01.htm>.
5. ibid.
6. <http://www.newsrelease-archive.net/coi/depts/GDE/coi9156c.ok>.
7. Woodhead, p. 132.
8. ibid., p. 107.
9. Rachel Sylvester, 'Blunkett loses out in a clash of personalities', *Daily Telegraph*, 16 July 2002.
10. Toynbee, Walker, *Did Things Get Better?*, Penguin, 2001, p. 63.
11. ibid., p. 99.
12. 'Time's up for schools that fail', *The Times*, 20 May 1997.

13. George Varnava, 'Named and shamed in passion for punishment', *TES*, 30 May 1997.
14. Rawnsley, *Servants of the People*, Hamish Hamilton, 2000, p. 158.
15. <http://www.tc.columbia.edu/ceoi/about.html>.
16. Toynbee, p. 63.
17. Hansard, 6 July 2000, col. 419.
18. Toynbee, p. 51.
19. ibid., p. 60.
20. ibid., p. 61.
21. Woodhead, p. 69.
22. Rentoul, p. 438.
23. <http://news.bbc.co.uk/1/hi/education/426088.stm>.
24. ibid.
25. Private conversation.
26. ibid.
27. ibid.

11 Criminals, terrorists and louts

1. Rachel Sylvester, 'Party man Blunkett celebrates his 'promotion' to Home Secretary', *Daily Telegraph*, 5 April 2001.
2. <http://www.homeoffice.gov.uk/docs/halliday.html>.
3. *Sunday Times*, 10 June 2001.
4. Hansard, 27 June 2001, col. 653.
5. <http://www.homeoffice.gov.uk/inside/org/manage/index.html>.
6. Hansard, 13 December 2001, col. 1113.
7. ibid.
8. ibid., col. 1114.
9. ibid.
10. <http://www.newsoftheworld.co.uk/story_pages/news/news2.shtml>.
11. *Sunday Telegraph*, 28 March 2004.
12. *The Times*, 21 April 2003.
13. ibid.
14. Hansard, 4 December 2002, col. 922.

15. *The Times*, 21 September 2003.

16. ibid., 4 March 2003.

17. *Observer*, 7 March 2004.

18. *The Times*, 4 March 2003.

19. Trevor Kavanagh, 'David v Rebekah: It'll Be The Sun Wot Wins It', *The Times*, 29 January 2003.

20. Hansard, 2 December 2002, col. 611.

21. ibid.

22. *Sunday Times*, 12 October 2003.

23. ibid.

24. Partial account in *Mail on Sunday*, 7 March 2004.

25. *Observer*, 7 March 2004.

12 A normal family?

1. *News of the World*, 22 August.

2. Ibid.

3. Carole Malone, *Sunday Mirror*, 22 August 2004.

4. *Mail on Sunday*, 22 August 2004.

Picture Acknowledgements

© Evening Standard/Solo Syndication/Nigel Howard: 7 top. © Mirrorpix: 1 top. PA Photos: 1 bottom, 4 top and bottom/ Fiona Hanson, 5 top and bottom/Sean Dempsey, 6 top left and middle/Kirsty Wigglesworth, 8 Toby Melville. © Judith Potts: 7 bottom. © Reuters: 6 bottom/John Pryke. © Rex Features: 3. Courtesy Sheffield Newspapers Ltd: 2.

Index

9/11 attacks (2001) xi, xv–xxiv,
    275, 278
Ackner, Lord 4, 288
Adonis, Andrew 234, 239, 240,
    243
Age Concern 50
Ainsworth, Bob 297, 298
al-Qaeda xx, xxi, 282, 305
Albrighton Hall, Shrewsbury
    (Royal Normal College
    for the Blind Training
    Department) 70, 74–9,
    81–3, 84, 88
Allaun, Frank 140
Allen, Dave 39
Amalgamated Union of
    Engineering Workers 120
anti-terror legislation 34
Anti-terrorism, Crime and
    Security Bill 276
APEX union 113
Archers, The (radio programme)
    72
Association of Grant Maintained
    Schools 209
Association of Metropolitan
    Authorities 161
    Social Services Committee 122,
    126

Association of Teachers and
    Lecturers 218, 258
    conference (Bournemouth) 244
    conference (Harrogate) 216,
    218–19
Aston, Birmingham 285, 289
Asylum Bill 295
asylum seekers see immigration/
    asylum
Attercliffe constituency, Sheffield
    107
Audit Commission 136, 144, 168

Badat, Sajid 5
Baker, Kenneth, Baron Baker of
    Dorking 262, 268
Banham, John 144
Bank of England 248
Banks, Tony 36
Barber, Michael 210, 215,
    216–17, 222–3, 225, 228,
    229–30, 234, 239, 242,
    248, 251, 263, 272
Barker, Howard: A Passion in Six
    Days 37–8
Barnsley Education Authority
    126
Barnsley Technical College 91,
    114, 117

Barschak, Aaron 281
Barton, Joan 129
Barton, Roger 125
BBC 15, 202, 284, 289
  BBC1 138
  BBC2 297
  Home Service 72
  Radio 2 23
  Radio 4 208
Beckett, Margaret 27, 171, 173,
    199–200
Benn, Hilary 26, 232
Benn, Tony 125, 140, 141, 150,
    157, 158–9, 163–6, 173,
    274
Betts, Clive 119, 123–4, 126, 135
Beveridge principle 53
Bichard, Sir Michael 223, 228,
    230, 231, 237, 270, 271
Bichard Inquiry 43
Billings, Reverend Alan 124
bin Laden, Osama xviii, 284
Birmingham LEA 242
Bish, Geoff 175
Blackstone, Baroness Tessa 230
Blair, Euan 207, 223
Blair, Tony xv, 168, 197, 230,
    231, 246
  appoints DB Education
    Secretary 227–8
  and asylum seekers 293–4,
    296
  bond with DB 13, 54, 202–3
  Brown as potential successor
    29
  in Cabinet with DB 9–10
  and change 42

  and DB as Home Secretary
    283
  education of 204
  education reform 234
  first act as leader 203–4
  GM schools 214
  and ID cards 300, 302–3
  and Irvine 286, 287
  and the judiciary 289
  leadership contestant 200, 202
  London Oratory issue 207,
    208
  and people who stand up to
    him 28
  and pre-Blair policy
    statements 196
  relationship with Brown 203
  understanding of ordinary
    voters 34
Blunkett, Alastair (DB's son) 30,
    114, 116, 117, 178
Blunkett, Andrew Keir (DB's
    son) 30, 123, 178
Blunkett, Arthur (DB's father)
  born in Egham 56
  DB's birth 56
  and DB's education 58, 59, 64,
    66
  early life 56
  first marriage 57
  marries Doris 57
  personality 56, 59
  death 60, 67–8, 69, 71, 73
  compensation issue 68, 69, 287
Blunkett, David
  assiduous constituency MP 13
  attitudes to xi-xii, 17, 18

becomes a member of the
     NEC (1983) 140
birth (6 June 1947) 56, 57–8
blindness
     DB on his blindness 7, 11
     DB's dogs xii, 12, 18, 21,
          30–31, 90–91, 93–4,
          103–4, 108, 109, 117–18,
          126, 138, 172, 180–83,
          192–3, 200–202, 220, 227,
          228, 237–8
     origin of 58
     others' reactions to 17–18,
          77–8
     and political achievement xi
     practical difficulties 18
     and preference for the
          countryside 31–2
     TV appearances 22
     used to his advantage
          18–19, 161
bond with Blair 13, 54, 202–3
at Buckingham Palace 266
a centraliser 43
chairs Association of
     Metropolitan Authorities
     Social Services Committee
     122, 126
childhood 64–5
and Crick 92–3
daily routine 2
education 58, 59, 60–63, 65–7,
     74–83, 85, 87, 89–100,
     204
Education Secretary x, 17, 25,
     40, 128–9, 227–63, 280
elected to Shadow Cabinet for

the first time (1992)
     194–5
excels at team meetings 8–9
father's death 67–8, 69, 73
first girlfriend 79–80
first job 85, 86
first marriage 95–6
first TV appearance 37
his affair with Kimberly
     Fortier 8, 16, 23–4, 33,
     304
Home Secretary x, 264–307
     aim as 40–41
     anti-terror and law and
          order legislation 34
     high workload xi, 2–3, 29
     manifesto 267–8
     objective 268–9
influences 73, 92–5
joins the Labour Party (1963)
     74
Labour Party chairman 197,
     199
leads Sheffield Council *see
     under* Sheffield City
     Council
loveless marriage and divorce 8
maiden speech in the
     Commons 179
oesophagus surgery 292–3
racism accusation 14
relations with the media 21–4
relationship with Brown 36,
     42, 300–302, 304
religious beliefs 11–12, 39–40,
     46, 88, 101
separation from Ruth 178

Blunkett, David – *cont.*
  Shadow Education Secretary
    ix, 34, 196, 197, 203–226
  Shadow Health Secretary 47,
    195–7, 199
  spectrum of political attitudes
    x
  support network 8
  supports community self-
    improvement and active
    citizenship 46
  understanding of ordinary
    voters 34–5
  personality
    attitude to disability 55
    bluntness 23, 26
    confidence 12, 22, 179, 186,
      300
    courteousness 29–30
    credibility 13
    dourness 8
    emotional 13–14
    frugality 30
    hardworking 1–2
    humour 21
    interest in poetry 7–8, 77,
      181–2, 198–9
    loyalty 19–20
    memory 1, 180
    need to prove himself to
      doubters 16–17, 77
    outspokenness 4–6
    passionate 8
    perfectionism 25
    sensitive to press criticism
      3–4
    social skills 19

  temper 12–13
  thrives on stress 15–16
  writings
    *Building from the Bottom:
      The Sheffield Experience*
      (with Green) 51–3, 130,
      135
    *Defence of Local
      Democracy, Services and
      Jobs* 145
    Democracy in Crisis (with
      Jackson) 3, 43–4, 47
    Health 200 policy statement
      196
    *The Labour Party's Aims
      and Values, An Unofficial
      Statement* (with Crick)
      176
    On a Clear Day xii, 35, 93,
      132, 138
    Policy and Progress 44, 51
Blunkett, David (DB's cousin)
    279–80
Blunkett, Doris Matilda
    Elizabeth (née Williams;
    DB's mother)
  compensation issue 68, 69, 73,
    287
  DB's birth 56
  and DB's education 58, 66,
    89–90, 97
  and death of Arthur 67–8, 69
  encourages DB 69
  and family chores 64
  first marriage 56
  health 71
  heart condition 56, 58

marries Arthur 57
personality 57
relationship with DB 69
Blunkett, Emma 279
Blunkett, 'Grandma' (DB's
     paternal grandmother) 60
Blunkett, Hugh Sanders (DB's
     son) xvi, 30, 122, 126, 178
Blunkett, Ruth (née Mitchell;
     DB's first wife) 87–8, 92,
     95–6, 98, 117, 178
Blunkett, Sanders (DB's paternal
     grandfather) 60, 122
Blyton, Enid 58
Boateng, Paul 26, 232, 303
Bobbitt, Phillip: *The Shield of
     Achilles* 42
Bolton guide dog training centre
     90, 118, 200
Bootle by-election 20
Bordeaux 118
Boswell Heath 14–15
Bottomley, Virginia 196–7
Boyce, David 81–2
Boyce, Jimmy 119
Bradford 49
Breakfast with Frost (television
     programme) 207
Bream, Julian 70
Brighouse, Tim 215, 216–17,
     241–2, 251
Brightside Mafia 120
British Council 37
British Medical Association 196
British National Party 289
British Students Sports
     Federation 136

Bromley Borough Council 113
Brown, Gordon xvii, 23, 197
     body language 9
     death of his first child 301
     extension of the
          Chancellorship 42
     and ID cards 300, 302, 303–4
     Laura Spence issue 246–7
     and people who stand up to
          him 28
     as potential successor to Blair
          29, 301
     relationship with Blair 203
     relationship with DB 36, 42,
          300–302, 304
     and sterling crisis 44
     and unemployment benefits
          35–6
     VAT on private school fees
          issue 208–9
Brown, Jennifer 302
Brown, Lynn 116
Brown, Sarah 302
Bulgaria 297, 298
Bulger, Jamie 275
Burngreave Cemetery, Sheffield 68
Butler, R.A. 97
Butler, Sir Robin 229
Byers, Stephen 7, 20, 25–6, 28,
     231, 232, 234, 236, 242–3,
     248

Cabinet 9–10, 26
Cabinet Office
     DA (Domestic Affairs)
          committee 295
     Strategy Unit 272

Caborn, Richard 125
Callaghan, James, Lord
      Callaghan of Cardiff 153
Cambridge Educational
      Associates 233
Campaign Group 150, 157
Campbell, Alastair xv, 215, 265
Capita 233
Castle, Barbara 274
Center for Educational Outreach
      and Innovation, Columbia
      University: *Re-*
      Centralization or Strategic
      Management 251–2
Chesterfield 140
Child Poverty Action Group 50
citizenship 46, 47, 262–3, 275
City of London 44
City Technology Colleges 205
Clarke, Charles 26, 27, 175, 232,
      241
Clarke, Kenneth 138, 257
Collins, Sir Andrew 289
community 46, 47, 49, 50, 51, 54,
      110, 128, 267
community sentences 6, 284–5
Competition Commission 27
Comprehensive Spending Review
      247, 253
Conservative Party
   police increase pledge 301
   re-election (1987) 167
   wins 1979 election 128
Constitutional Affairs,
      Department for 287
'Consumer and the Community'
      review group 166, 175

Cook, Gaynor 5
Cook, Robin 5, 36, 44, 151, 171,
      172, 196, 200, 276
Corston, Jean 238
Coulson, Andy 24
council tax 190
council tenants 129
Crick, Professor Bernard 89,
      92–3, 95, 175, 176, 262–3
Criminal Justice Bill 288
Cumberland Lodge, Windsor 95
Cunningham, Dr Jack 142, 161,
      183–4, 186–7, 190

Dacre, Paul 23
Daily Express ix, 24, 207
Daily Herald 59
Daily Mail 23–4, 38, 123, 217,
      221
Daily Mirror 94, 202
Daily Telegraph, The 4, 35, 244,
      245
Darling, Alistair 304
Davies, Liz 213
Davis, David 297
Day, Sir Robin 138
de Gruchy, Nigel 330n
Dearing Report 259
Derbyshire 32, 63–4
Desmond, Richard 24
Dobson, Frank 36
Doggett, Eileen and Neil 81
Donaldson, Lord 288
Donetsk 122
Dopit I (Cabinet committee) 282
Doreen (DB's half-sister) 56, 59
Downing Street Policy Unit 234

drugs issue 81, 99–100, 306
Dunvegan, Isle of Skye 82
Dunwoody, Gwyneth 150, 160
Durham University 89
Dyson, Alderman Sidney 107,
    108

East Midlands Airport 108–9
East Midlands Gas Board 56, 57,
    67, 68, 73, 85
Ecclesfield, Sheffield 104
education
    assisted places scheme 260–61
    City Academies 239–40
    class size 250–51
    Columbia University paper
        251–2
    Dearing Report 259
    Excellence in Schools White
        Paper 238–9
    failing schools 248–50
    Foundation Schools proposal
        210, 212, 213, 226, 238,
        260
    Fresh Start 250
    grant-maintained (GM)
        schools 206–212, 214,
        216, 260
    higher 238, 259
    left-liberal education
        establishment x
    literacy 204, 205, 225, 226,
        234, 242, 255–6
    national curriculum 204, 222,
        234, 262–3, 275
    numeracy 205, 222, 225, 226,
        234, 242, 256

Oxbridge admissions 246–7
'Standards Fund' 253–4
teachers 258–9
*Teachers:: meeting the
    challenge for change*
    Green Paper 258
VAT on private school fees
    208–9, 216
Education Action Zones (EAZs)
    232–3, 234
Education and Employment,
    Department for (DfEE)
    17, 21, 42–3, 223
    Blunkett Note 239
    DB moves to the Home Office
        264
    'delivery' concept 228–9
    Employment Service 271
    preparations for DB's arrival
        228
    relationship with Number 10
        239–40
    Social Exclusion Unit 255
    Standards and Effectiveness
        Unit 228, 229, 241, 243,
        245, 272
Edwards, Pamela 79–80, 82, 87
Egham, Surrey 56
Elizabeth II, Queen 266
euro, the 44–5
European Monetary System 44
European Parliament elections
    (June 2004) 22
European Union (EU) 43, 295,
    296, 298
Evans, Paul 229
Evening Standard 244

Fabian Society
  *Building from the Bottom: The
    Sheffield Experience* (DB
    and Green) 51–3, 130,
    135
  seminar on education policy
    (January 1995) ix
Falconer, Charles, Lord 232, 286,
  287
Fares Fair scheme 113
Federation of Law Centres 51
Federation of Women's Aid 51
Financial Times 164–5
Fir Vale, Sheffield 115
Foot, Michael 141, 154, 211
forced marriages 6
Foreign and Commonwealth
  Office 263, 296
Fortier, Kimberly 8, 16, 23, 33,
  308–317
Fortuyn, Pim 6
Fraser, John 36
Friends of the Earth 50
Fullick, Leisha 210, 215, 329n

gang masters 267–8, 295
Garforth, Leeds 49
Gash, Norman xii
General Medical Council 234
General, Municipal, and
  Boilermakers Union 68
General Teaching Council (GTC)
  234–5
George Orwell School, Islington
  250
geriatric care 71–2, 114–15
Giddens, Anthony 134

Gieve, John xvii, 270
Glendenning, Bob 117
Gloucester 5
Golding, Winifred 102, 109
Goldsmith, Peter 286
Gorbachev, Mikhail 173
Gould, Bryan 44, 169, 174,
  187–92, 194, 195
Gould, Philip 165
Greater London Council (GLC)
  113, 119, 124, 125
Green, Geoff 51, 131
Green, Paul 155, 164
Grenoside, Sheffield 118
Griffiths, Eddie 119
Grimsby, Lincolnshire 56
Grisham, John 29
Guardian, The 15, 54, 94, 212
Guide Dogs for the Blind
  Association (GDBA) 94,
  181, 182, 193, 200,
  324–5n
Gulf Wars 36–7
Gummer, John Selwyn 185

Hackney Council 146
Hackney Downs school,
  Clapton, London 216
Hadfield steel works, Sheffield 124
Haigh, William 173
Hain, Peter 169
Halliday Report on sentencing 265
Hamilton, John 161
Hansard Society 262
Hardie, Keir 123
Harman, Harriet 223, 224–5
Harrison, Royden 94, 139–40

Hastings, Stewart 101–2

Hattersley, Enid 109–110, 155, 184

Hattersley, Roy 54, 109–110, 135, 149, 150, 169–70, 174, 176, 184, 211–14, 249–50
  Choose Freedom 54

Hatton, Derek 146, 155–6, 158–9, 163

Haven sexual assault referral centre, Camberwell 19

Healey, Denis 116–17

Health, Department for 43

Heathrow Airport, London 282

Heffer, Eric 143, 150, 155, 156, 157

Heseltine, Michael 168

Heslop, David x

Hewitt, Patricia 27, 168, 303, 304

Highgrove House, near Tetbury, Gloucestershire 10

Hillman, Josh 330n

Hillsborough stadium, Sheffield 64

Hinton, Les 24, 44

Hobbes, Thomas 105

Hodge, Margaret 145, 146, 151

Hodgson, Geoffrey 175

Hoggart, Richard 175

Hollybank College, Huddersfield 98–9

Home Office 228, 263
  accommodation centres 15
  changing its *raison d'être* 269
  civil servants 272–4, 295
  DB's initial view 274
  DB's work pattern 21
  delivery 272
  Group Executive Board 271

Immigration and Nationality Directorate 271, 297–9
  public arguments 3–4
  reforms 43
  responsibility for criminal justice 287
  restructuring 269–70
  role of 42
  standards unit 267
homosexuality issue 38, 39
House of Commons xxiii
  guide dog policy 93–4
  Members' Lobby 31
  Prime Minister's Questions 201, 298
House of Lords 288
How to be Home Secretary (BBC programme) 268
Howard, Anthony 41
Howard, Michael 21, 269
Howells, Kim 230
Hudson, Hugh 166, 178
Hughes, Beverley 19–20, 272, 295, 297–300
Hughes, Colin 150, 166, 171–2, 176
Human Fertilisation and Embryology Bill 39
Humberside Police Authority 43, 251
Hussein, Saddam 36

ID cards xx, 14, 25, 300, 302–6
immigration/asylum 13, 15, 34, 289–300, 307
  gang masters 267–8
  speaking English issue 14

Independent, The 46
Independent on Sunday, The 306
Industrial Relations Act 105
Inland Revenue 188, 189, 190
Inner London Education
 Authority (ILEA) 209
Iraq 36–7, 224
Ironmonger, Sir Ron 106–7, 112,
 120
Irvine, Derry, Lord 284–7, 289
Islington, London 13, 211, 233
 councillors 38–9, 167
Islington Arts and Media School,
 London 250
ITN 220

Jackson, Ben 118
Jackson, Helen 116, 118, 119,
 126
Jackson, Keith 3, 125, 126
 Democracy in Crisis (with
 Blunkett) 3
Jamieson, David 238
Jenkin, Patrick 135, 143, 145, 147
Jenkins, Sir Simon 4, 49
Jessop Hospital, Sheffield 123
Jeuda, Diana 171
Jones, Superintendent 104–5
Jospin, Lionel 290
Jowell, Tessa 27, 232
Joynson-Hicks, Sir William 41
judiciary
 attitudes to DB 34
 DB's attitude to 42, 69, 287–9

Kaufman, Gerald 166, 171, 172,
 174, 195

Kavanagh, Trevor 10, 265
Kay, Mr Justice 261
Keele University 215, 216
Kemp, Martin 21
Kennedy, Dame Helena: *Just
 Law* 41
Kilfoyle, Peter 162–3, 220
King, Wilf 66, 76–7
Kinnock, Neil 140–42, 145–6,
 148–66, 170–76, 178, 179,
 183, 184, 186, 190, 194–5,
 203, 211, 221
 *Statement of Democratic
 Socialist Aims and Values*
 (with Hattersley) 174
Kitson, Michael 164
Knight, Ted 144

Labour Councils in the Cold
 (Labour Party
 Coordinating Committee
 pamphlet) 167
Labour Party
 Aiming Higher policy
 document 221
 Brighton conference (1996)
 212–15
 calamitous defeat (1983) 141
 Campaign Strategy Committee
 165
 Clause IV of the constitution
 203, 221
 conference of 1996 206
 conference of 2002 305
 Coordinating Committee 150,
 167
 DB joins 74

DB as Shadow Education
Secretary 34
DB's first encounter with
Southey Green Ward
branch 88–9
Diversity and Excellence
policy document 209, 211
drubbing in European
Parliament elections (June
2004) 22
elections (1997) 227, 264
elections (2001) 264, 266, 284
electoral defeat (1992) 193, 194
Excellence for Everyone policy
document 215, 217
expulsion of Militant 141, 142
Freedom and Fairness
campaign 164–5
'Kinnock – The Movie' party
political broadcast (1987)
166, 178
Learn as You Earn 221
Lifelong Learning 221
manifesto launch
(Birmingham, 2001) 265
*Meet the Challenge, Make the
Change* 167
Millbank HQ 227
modernisation 141
NEC 38, 46, 113, 135, 139–42,
145, 148–53, 155–64, 169,
171, 173–5, 177, 183, 184,
186, 194, 195, 197
Local Government
Committee 142, 143
Organisation Committee
143

*New Labour, New Life for
Britain* 222, 225
Policy Review 141
Shadow Communications
Agency 165
Target 2000 221
and trade unions in Sheffield
130
unilateralism 170–74
Walworth Road HQ 194
Lambeth council 147, 154, 156
Langdon, Dr 75–8
Larkin, Philip 7
Laski, Harold 139
Layden, Sir John 161
Lee, Mike 185, 194
Leeds General Infirmary 293
Leeds LEA 233–4
Leicester 56
Lestor, Joan 36, 171
Letwin, Oliver 4
Lewis, Isidore 107, 108
Lewis, Leigh 271
Licensing Bill 27
Literacy Task Force 222
Liverpool Council 146, 148,
154–5, 158–9, 161
Livingstone, Ken 119, 123, 124,
144, 158, 179
Local Education Authorities
(LEAs) 209, 210, 212, 217,
229, 232–4, 243, 252, 253,
280
Local Government Campaign
Unit (later Local
Government Information
Unit) 142, 186

Local Government Finance Bill
180
London Labour Briefing 144
London Olympic bid (for 2012)
185
London Oratory School 207,
208, 216, 223–4
Lord Chancellor's department
263, 287
Lowe, Stuart 103
Lowes, Ian 163
Lucy (guide dog) 21, 31, 201–2,
220, 227, 228, 237–8

Maastricht summit 44
McAvoy, Doug 220–21
McCluskie, Sam 149, 164
McCreath, Graeme 90
MacIntosh, Andrew 119
McMahon, Professor Michael
293
Madrid bombings 283
Magdalen College, Oxford 246
Mail on Sunday 223
Major, John 201
Majorca 31
Malta 80–81
Manchester 286
Manchester Road School for the
Blind, Sheffield (now
Tapton Mount) 60–63,
65–7, 110
Manchester University 89
Mandela, Nelson 123
Mandelson, Peter 165, 173, 189,
190, 224
March, Paddy 202

Marlow, Tony 201
Marx, Karl 93, 105
Marx Memorial Lecture 93
Mawhinney, Sir Brian 196, 278
Maynard, Joan 119, 152, 177
Meacher, Michael 36, 44, 149,
151, 152, 153, 163, 164,
183
Mendelson, John 116
Methodism 11–12, 39, 46, 80,
101
metropolitan county councils 113
Metropolitan Police anti-
terrorism branch 282
Michie, Bill 119, 121, 125
Milburn, Alan 27, 28, 43, 287
Miliband, David 210, 215, 239,
330n
Militant Tendency 125, 127, 141,
142, 146, 147, 153–6,
158–64, 177, 213, 220
Mill, John Stuart 105
Milton, John: *Samson Agonistes*
7
Monks, John 219
Morecambe Bay cockle-picker
deaths 295
Morris, Estelle 7, 25, 26, 220,
232, 233, 235, 243, 255,
263
Mowlam, Dr Mo 194, 230
Moxon, Steve 298
Mulgan, Geoff 272
Mulhearn, Tony 163
Mullin, Chris 116
Murdoch, Rupert 44, 45
Murphy, Paul 27

Muslim Council of Great Britain
277

NALGO (National Association
of Local Government
Officers) 133, 134, 144,
184–5
Narey, Martin 271
NAS-UWT (National
Association of
Schoolmasters and Union
of Women Teachers) 218,
257, 330n
National Association of Head
Teachers conference
(Torquay, 1996) 222
National Enterprise Board 113
National Health Service (NHS)
214, 250, 251, 293
hypothecated NHS tax 48
National Offender Management
Service 271
National Schools Standards Task
Force 217
National Union of Mineworkers
(NUM) 116, 132, 150, 230
National Union of Public
Employees (NUPE) 149,
162, 166, 191
National Union of Teachers
(NUT) 25, 204, 205, 215,
218–21, 257, 259, 330n
Blackpool conference (1997)
219–21
nationalisation 51
Nationwide (current affairs
programme) 22

Nestlé 122
New Deal 28, 246, 255
New Hope for Britain (Bennite
manifesto, 1983) 51
New Labour 34, 46, 54, 103, 134,
230
befriends the tabloids 24
education 208, 215, 218, 233,
243
fixation on targets 250
Labour's selling point 49
and taxation 47
New Law Journal 288
News International 24
News of the World 8, 24
Newsnight (television
programme) 293, 297
Newsound (BBC children's news)
202
Norfolk Arms, Sheffield 109
North Sea oil compensation
issue 125
North Tyneside education
committee 231
Northern General Hospital,
Sheffield 71–2

Oake, Stephen 286, 289
Observer, The 5, 55, 175, 221,
249
Offa (guide dog) 182–3, 192–3,
200, 201
Ofsted (Office for Standards in
Education) 205, 217, 229,
233, 234, 241, 242, 245,
248, 250
Old Trafford, Manchester 105

Oldham 48
Orgreave coking plant, Sheffield
    124, 148
Orwell, George 93
O'Shaughnessy, Michael 101,
    102–3
Owen, Ed 265
Oxford University 246–7

Palmerston, Viscount 186
Paris 78
Parkinson (TV programme) 21–2
Parliament Act 277
Parson Cross estate, Sheffield 63
Patten, Chris 185, 186
Patten, John 204, 216
Peak District 32
Peel, Sir Robert xii
Pensioners' Action Groups 51
Pentagon, Washington 275
Phillips, Melanie 221
Pimlico, London 21, 30
Pitsmoor News 110
Pitsmoor, Sheffield 110
Poetry Please (Radio Four
    programme) 7
Polaris 170, 171
police 278–83, 301
Police Federation 16, 25
    conference (May 2002) 278–80
Police Reform Bill 280
poll tax issue 183–9, 213
Pontesbury Congregational
    Church 79
Portillo, Michael 186
Potts, Paul 30, 32–3, 109
poverty 35, 68–9

Powell, Jonathan xvi, 227, 236
Prescott, John xvii, 151, 224
    attitude to DB 26
    at Buckingham Palace 266
    and ID cards 304
    leadership contestant 200
    suspects DB of leaking
        information 305–6
    'Two Jags' nickname 26–7
Press Association 24
Prime Minister's Delivery Unit
    272
Prime Minister's Policy Unit 239,
    252
Prison Officers Association 25,
    280
    conference (Southport, May
        2003) 16
prisons 6, 16
probation units 16
Productive and Competitive
    Economy review group
    169
Puttnam, David, Lord 235, 236,
    244

Quality Commission 168
Queen Anne's Gate office,
    London 32
Question Time (television
    programme) 138, 182

'rainbow coalition' 38, 124
Randall, Tony 75, 85
rate capping 135, 142–3, 144,
    146, 147–8, 156, 183
Rates Act (1984) 154

Ravenhill, Mark: *Shopping and Fucking* 37
Reid, John 9, 27, 304
religious hatred incitement clause (abandoned) 276–8
Rentoul, John 225
Reynolds, David 329–30n
Richardson, Jo 153, 171, 173
Ridge, Tom 283
Riley, Kathryn 329n
Ripon Grammar School 261
Roberts, Alan, MP 17
Rodgers, Bill 112
Roma (gypsies) 297
Romania 297, 298
Rossetti, Christina 7
Rotherham College of Technology 88
Rowton Castle, Shrewsbury, Shropshire (Royal Normal College for the Blind School Department) 66, 67, 69–71, 74
Royal Festival Hall, London 153, 228
Royal National Institute for the Blind 84–5
Royal Normal College for the Blind (later Royal National College) *see* Albrughton Hall, Shrewsbury; Rowton Castle, Shrewsbury
Ruby (DB's first guide dog) 31, 90–91, 93–4, 97, 99–100, 103–4, 108, 109, 117
Ruddock, Joan 36, 171

Ryan, Conor ix, 209, 210, 215, 235, 239, 245, 253

Sadie (DB's current guide dog) 31, 32
St Olave's grammar school, Bromley, Kent 223, 224
Salerno, Maria 79–80
Salerno family 80–81
Sangatte refugee camp, France 12, 25, 285, 290–92
Sarkozy, Nicolas 290, 291
Sawyer, Tom 149, 152, 153, 161, 166, 173, 203
Sayle, Alexei 21
Scargill, Arthur 132, 148, 230
Scotland, Baroness 4
self-reliance 35, 40, 46, 47
Sell, Hanah 173
sex offences 6, 285, 306–7
Seyd, Pat 94–5, 105
Shakespeare, William 37
Sharrow Lane Junior School, Sheffield 98
Sheffield
    DB 'a Sheffield lad to his boot straps' 32
    DB brought up in 31
    DB's constituency 13
    Labour Party and trade unions 130
    Southey Green Ward 88–9, 101, 103
    transport issue 111–14
    unemployment rate 134
    unique closeness to the countryside 32

Sheffield – *cont.*
  World Student Games debacle
    (1991) 135–6
Sheffield Brightside 119, 120,
  151, 152
Sheffield City Council
  Central Policy Unit 51
  DB becomes a Labour
    councillor 101–6
  DB chairs Family and
    Community Services
    Committee (Social
    Services) 114–16, 133
  DB as councillor 106–121
  DB as leader x, xi, 10, 11,
    34, 35, 37–8, 40, 46,
    72, 93, 114, 122–37,
    138, 160, 162, 167,
    175, 269, 274
  described 105–6
  Employment Department 124,
    130, 131, 132, 134
  Housing Department 133
  Labour returns to power
    (1970) 106
  local elections (1968) 106
  'Socialist Republic of South
    Yorkshire' nickname x,
    123
  statistics 144
  Strategy Unit 131
Sheffield Hallam 116
Sheffield Labour Party manifesto
    (1983) 131
Sheffield Morning Telegraph
    84
Sheffield Royal Infirmary 67

Sheffield Star 109, 129
Sheffield Town Hall 97, 114, 116,
    127, 227
Sheffield University 89–97, 290
Sheffield Wednesday football
    club 64
Shephard, Gillian 216
Shipman, Harold 5
Short, Clare 36, 171, 172
Shrewsbury Methodist Church
    78
Shrewsbury School 74
Shrewsbury technical college 76,
    77
Simpson, Lorraine 92
Skegness, Lincolnshire 60
Skinner, Dennis 170, 173
Skye, Isle of 81–2
Smith, Andrew 27, 232
Smith, Chris 36, 171, 235
Smith, Elizabeth 198, 199
Smith, Councillor Harry 163–4
Smith, Harry (ITN reporter)
    220
Smith, John 44, 169, 187, 188,
    189, 191, 192, 195,
    197–200, 202
  Social Ownership 51
Smith, Mrs (puppy walker) 201
Smith, Peter (ATL general
    secretary) 219, 257–8
Smith, Peter (guide dog trainer)
    201
Social Justice Commission 47
Social Market Foundation 218
Socialist Workers Party 219,
    220

Soham murders 43
Songs of Praise (television
    programme) 49
South Yorkshire County Council
    132
South Yorkshire Metropolitan
    County Council
    (SYMCC) 111, 112, 113
    Executive and Policy
    Committee 114
Southampton University 39
Southey Methodist church,
    Sheffield 96
Spectator 8
Spence, Laura 246–7
Springboks rugby team 105
Stamford Bridge football ground,
    Chelsea 85
Standards Task Force 241
Stanley Tools 56
sterling crisis (1992) 44
Stevens, Sir John xvii, 281–4
Stonefrost, Maurice 160
Stonefrost committee (NEX)
    inquiry 161, 162
Straw, Jack xvii, xviii, 13, 21,
    166, 169, 205, 265, 266,
    269, 270–71, 279, 296,
    300, 303
Stubbs, William 262
student loans 30, 238
Sun, The 10, 24, 265, 289
Sunday Mirror 178
Sunday Telegraph 14
Sunday Times xv, 99, 208,
    219–20, 267, 284, 298
Sussex Police Authority 281

Tambo, Oliver 123
Tapton Mount School *see*
    Manchester Road School
    for the Blind, Sheffield
taxation 47–9
Taylor, Ann 28, 205, 209
    *Opening Doors to a Learning
    Society* 204
Teacher, The newspaper 220
Teddy (guide dog) 91, 117–18,
    126, 138, 180–82
Terrorism Act xx, xxi, 5
Thatcher, Margaret, Baroness
    128, 139, 154, 166, 168,
    178, 182, 184, 188, 233
Thatcherism 175
Thatcherite Conservatism 46
Thompson, Edward 93
Thomson, Robert 29
Thornhill, Mr (lecturer) 105
Times, The 29, 44, 49, 94, 187,
    249, 289
Times Educational Supplement
    207, 216, 249
tobacco issue 196
Today programme 13, 15, 279,
    284, 285, 286, 297
Tooze, Mr (headmaster) 66–7
Toynbee, Polly 15
Trade and Industry, Department
    of 295
trade unions
    and Labour Party in Sheffield
    130
    and the NEC 149–50
Trades Union Congress (TUC)
    219

Transport and General Workers
  Union (TGWU) 173
Treasury 2, 245, 246, 255, 263,
  273, 301, 304
Tredinnick, David 257
Tribune 38, 173
  'Disarmament Appeal' 171
Tribune Group 150, 159, 164
Trident 171, 172, 174
Turnbull, Sir Andrew 270

UEFA (Union of European
  Football Associations)
  185
Underwood, John 190
unemployment benefits 35–6
unilateralism 170–74
Union of Shop, Distributive and
  Allied Workers (USDAW)
  171
United Nations (UN) 36, 123
  Charter 36
  High Commissioner for
  Refugees 291

Vine, Jeremy 23
voluntary movement 50–51

Waddington, Margaret 77
Wade, Rebekah 24, 289
Wainfleet All Saints, Lincolnshire
  56, 60
Wainwright, Hilary 120, 125
Walker, Peter 94
Walkland, Stuart 94, 95, 105
Warwick University 94
Waterfield, Valda 126, 134

Watkins, Ken 94
Whitehouse, Paul, Chief
  Constable of Sussex
  281
Whitty, Larry 158
Willetts, David 238
Williams, Eric (DB's uncle) 60
Williams, James Henry (DB's
  maternal grandfather) 56,
  59–60, 67, 71–4
Williams, Joe (DB's uncle) 60
Williams, Mary (DB's aunt) 60
Williams, Shirley 113
Wilson, George 120–21
Wilson, Harold, Lord Wilson of
  Rievaulx 73, 153, 275
Wilson, Richard 270–71
Wimbledon tennis
  championships 7–8
Windsor Castle 281
Wintour, Patrick 150, 166,
  171–2, 176
Women Against Pit Closures
  movement 50
women in politics 20
Woodhead, Chris x, 217, 234,
  235, 237, 240–45, 255,
  259, 262
  Class War 242
Woodward, David, Chief
  Constable of Humberside
  43, 251, 279
Wooldridge, Val 31
Woolf, Lord 284, 288
Worcester College 66
Work and Pensions, Department
  of (DWP) 295, 296

workfare 35, 36
World Student Games debacle
    (1991) 135–6
World This Weekend, The (radio
    programme) 208

World Trade Centre, New York
    275

Yelland, David 10
York University 89